CORPORATE SOCIAL RESPONSIBILITY IN CHINA

A Vision, an Assessment and a Blueprint

CORPORATE SOCIAL RESPONSIBILITY IN CHINA

A Vision, an Assessment and a Blueprint

Benoit Vermander
Fudan University, China

World Scientific

NEW JERSEY · LONDON · SINGAPORE · BEIJING · SHANGHAI · HONG KONG · TAIPEI · CHENNAI

Published by

World Scientific Publishing Co. Pte. Ltd.

5 Toh Tuck Link, Singapore 596224

USA office: 27 Warren Street, Suite 401-402, Hackensack, NJ 07601

UK office: 57 Shelton Street, Covent Garden, London WC2H 9HE

Library of Congress Cataloging-in-Publication Data
Vermander, Benoît, 1960–
　　Corporate social responsibility in China : a vision, an assessment and a blueprint / by Benoit
Vermander (Fudan University, China).
　　　　pages cm
　　Includes bibliographical references and index.
　　ISBN 978-9814520775 (hardcover : alk. paper)
　　1. Social responsibility of business--China.　2. Business enterprises--Law and legislation--China.
I. Title.
　　HD60.5.C6V47 2014
　　658.4'080951--dc23

　　　　　　　　　　　　　　　　　　　　　　　　　　2013040320

British Library Cataloguing-in-Publication Data
A catalogue record for this book is available from the British Library.

Copyright © 2014 by World Scientific Publishing Co. Pte. Ltd.

In-house Editor: Lee Xin Ying

Typeset by Stallion Press
Email: enquiries@stallionpress.com

Printed in Singapore.

Contents

Foreword   ix

Acknowledgments   xi

Introduction   xv

PART ONE: CSR IN THE CHINESE CONTEXT: A VISION   1

Chapter One   What is CSR?   3

1.1. A Pragmatic Approach to CSR   3
1.2. The Company as an Interdependent Self   10
1.3. Specific Dimensions of CSR   18
1.4. Related Concepts   21

Chapter Two   The Legal, Professional and Social Framework   29

2.1. Laws and Regulations   29
2.2. From the Letter to the Spirit   35
2.3. Development of CSR among Chinese Entrepreneurs   39
2.4. CSR and Civil Society   41

Chapter Three   Chinese Cultural Resources Relevant to CSR   47

3.1. CSR and Chinese Thought   48
3.2. CSR as Practical Wisdom   56
3.3. Contemporary Chinese Culture and CSR   58

Chapter Four   CSR and Corporate Strategy   67

4.1. Benefits of Implementing CSR   67
4.2. "Social License" and Stakeholders in the Chinese Context   72
4.3. From Research to Action   73

Chapter Five   Corruption and Business Activities   77

5.1. Nature and Extent   78
5.2. Causes and Effects   83
5.3. The Struggle Against Corruption   88
5.4. Business and the Corruption Trap   94

**PART TWO: THEMATIC ANALYSIS AND LINES
OF ACTION: AN ASSESSMENT**   99

Chapter Six   Environmental Standards and Concerns   101

6.1. Pressing Concerns, New Priorities   101
6.2. Scarcity of Resources and the Sustainability Imperative   104
6.3. CSR and Environmental Impacts   117

Chapter Seven   Safety Issues   121

7.1. Safety at the Workplace   123
7.2. Safety and Engineering   128
7.3. Case I: Road Safety   134
7.4. Case II: Food Safety   137

Chapter Eight   Social Standards and the Working Force   143

8.1. China's Labor Contract Law and Corporate Policies   143
8.2. Migrant Workers and the Evolution of the Labor Force   153
8.3. Child Labor, Mistreatments and the Supply Chain   161
8.4. Schooling and CSR   164
8.5. Social Coverage   168

Chapter Nine   Gender Equality/Training/Well-Being at Work   179

9.1. Gender Equality   179
9.2. Training and Learning Opportunities   186
9.3. Suffering at Work   186

Chapter Ten   Conflict Management and Prevention   195

10.1. New Labor Challenges   195
10.2. Trade Unions, Bargaining and the Social Scene   199
10.3. Collective Contracts and Other Issues   204

PART THREE: TRANSVERSAL ISSUES: A BLUEPRINT   209

Chapter Eleven   Making Ethical Assessments: Finances,
                  Engineering and Conflicts of Interests   211

11.1. Practicing Discernment   211
11.2. Financial Ethics   216
11.3. Engineering Ethics   229
11.4. Conflicts of Interests   231

Chapter Twelve   CSR and Corporate Governance   235

12.1. Codes and Their Implementation   235
12.2. Integrating CSR within Governance Mechanisms   242
12.3. Governance, Transparency and the Media   246

Chapter Thirteen   Reports, Foundations, Projects and Networks   253

13.1. Reporting   253
13.2. Foundations and Charities   254
13.3. Pilot Projects   259
13.4. Knowledge Networks, a Path for Reflection and Action   264

Chapter Fourteen   Social Entrepreneurship   271

14.1. A Sector in the Making   271
14.2. Fair Trade and Related Movements   275
14.3. From Social Entrepreneurship to Community Investment   278

Chapter Fifteen   The Role of the Corporation
                   in Tomorrow's China   283

15.1. The Corporation and Global Public Goods   283
15.2. China 2030   287

Chapter Sixteen   Conclusion and Prospects   291

16.1. Global Challenges and the Art of Interpretation   293
16.2. Ethical Empowerment, Cultural Diversity
      and Sustainable Development   296
16.3. Corporate Cultural Resources and China's New
      Developmental Model   297

Chapter Seventeen   Recommendations   301

17.1. Structures and Processes   301
17.2. Policy Areas   303
17.3. Ethical Issues   307
17.4. Channels of Action   310
17.5 Long-Term Vision   311

Bibliography   313
Index   329

Foreword

The corporate social responsibility movement emerged in developed countries in Europe and America in the 1980s and has soon extended to all around the world along with economic globalization. With the help of many prominent multinationals, this movement was introduced to China where it has thrived and has cast far-reaching influences on the philosophy and conduct of the Chinese enterprises and the Chinese society.

As a product of the modern society transformation, the corporate social responsibility movement has, to some degree, broken (blurred, to be more precise) the traditional boundary between the government and society, and the modern enterprise now fulfills its responsibilities and contributions to its employees, consumers, communities and society while pursuing profits. The shift from a single and narrow-minded pursuit for profit to the sense of social responsibility is indeed motivated by consideration for practical benefits, for example, to attain a better enterprise image and wider acceptance of consumers for products and service; but it is more important because the self-reflection and active efforts of the enterprise has provided new possibilities of all-rounded, coordinated and harmonious social development. Therefore, it is safe to say that the corporate social responsibility movement caters to the development of modern society.

The importance of corporate social responsibility and the leading role long played by multinationals in this regard has led to high expectations of the Chinese society for such companies. As a matter of fact, however, strong response is often provoked in China when multinationals' imperfect fulfillment of their social responsibility fails to meet these high expectations. Such a response should not be interpreted as differentiated or discriminatory treatment for multinationals. To be honest, multinationals are generally advanced both in terms of rich experiences and the practical implementations in fulfilling social responsibilities, such as the protection of the labor rights and environment.

Against such a background of economic and social transformation in China, the publication of *Corporate Social Responsibility in China: A Vision, an Assessment and a Blueprint* is timely and important. The book collects representative cases and practices of many multinationals in social responsibility fulfillment, with innovative ideas and general principles as well. It will be a helpful reference for other multinationals and domestic enterprises in their efforts to fulfill their social responsibilities.

Moreover, to be socially responsible is a major issue increasingly confronting Chinese enterprises (including state-owned and private ones) which will go global and invest in other parts of the world. This book discusses domestic enterprises' practices in fulfilling their social responsibilities, but it may be inspiring and helpful for those going global and operating under different systems and cultural backgrounds.

To stress corporate social responsibility does not mean that social responsibilities should be shouldered exclusively by enterprises; instead, corporate social responsibility is only a part of the general social responsibility which should be fulfilled through joint efforts and contributions by the government, enterprises, society and individuals. I believe China's governmental departments and the public can read this book to gain a more profound and systematic understanding of the concept, framework and practices concerning corporate social responsibility, which is necessary to fertilize the corporate social responsibility soil in China.

I would like to recommend this book to you.

Lu Mai (卢迈)
Secretary General, China Development Research Foundation
(中国发展研究基金会)
October 8, 2013

Acknowledgments

This book is the result of a long collaborative process, triggered by a number of conferences held in Shanghai and Beijing in partnership with several institutions (notably the Chinese People's Institute of Foreign Affairs, Fudan University, the Taipei Ricci Institute, BNP Paribas and the Chirac Foundation) during the years 2005–2010. These events had benefited from the contribution and participation of Michel Camdessus, former Director General of the International Monetary Fund, who helped us to link into one the two series of questions, the first having to do with the synergy existing between sustainable development and cultural diversity, the other concerning the mode and degree of the participation of China on the tackling of global challenges. The contribution and the strength of conviction displayed by Michel Camdessus have been for me an inspiration throughout these years.

As my research and contacts on the field developed, I became more and more interested in the question of how these issues were shaping the vision and the practices of the corporations — both multinational and national — operating in China. As questions surrounding the implementation of CSR in China became more and more pressing during the last years, the writing of this book has been influenced by this unfolding debate. Henri-Claude de Bettignies, who was then holding the Chair of Responsible Leadership at the China Europe International Business School in Shanghai, invited me to participate in several events related to the topic, giving me opportunities to express and share my insights on the subject.

It is on this basis that the project entered its decisive stage. Here, I wish to thank in a special way Bureau Veritas, Michelin and Saint-Gobain for having sponsored the research, networking, editing and publication of the English version of this work, and for having done so with unrestricted openness. Not only did they contribute financial resources, they also shared with me their experience on the field, providing me with very valuable insights. It goes without saying that they are not responsible for the statements and opinions expressed in this book, and that I assume entire responsibility for them.

Maverlinn Consulting Firm has been instrumental in gathering the coalition of sponsors and experts that has made this publication possible. It has provided me with invaluable assistance in the whole process of researching, writing, editing and publication. I wish to express my gratitude to Chia-lin Coispeau who believed in this project from the start and helped me unwaveringly to bring it to completion. Soline Bich, Huang Yiling, Andy Ding, and other members of the staff of Maverlinn, assisted me in the collection of a good part of the material I have been using.

Amandine Monteil has provided me with a draft of the sections concerned with social standards and labor conflicts and has contributed many valuable suggestions throughout the writing of this book. I want to thank her warmly for sharing her knowledge and expertise with such generosity. Philip J. Chmielewski at the Seaver College of Science and Engineering, Loyola Marymount University, initiated me to the topic of engineering ethics, especially during the months he spent in Shanghai in 2011 and 2012. The sections of this book dealing with these questions owe much to his inspiration and research. Olivier Coispeau proceeded to a careful re-reading of the whole manuscript and brought much needed improvements to the sections concerned with economic theory and financial ethics. Christine Swanson gathered materials on the CSR theory and also on environmental challenges in China. Previously, Cerise Phiv and Alice Lin had already helped me with various drafts of this section. At a later stage, Stephan Rothlin forwarded generously to me additional materials, sharing his teaching and consulting experience in Beijing and Hong Kong. Yves Chapot, Philippe Lanternier, Emmanuel Normant and Bertrand Cristau have also contributed comments and suggestions. Over the last years, exchanges happening at Fudan School of Philosophy, especially with my friend and colleague Li Tiangang, have encouraged me to develop and specify my ideas on the practical impact of Chinese cultural resources in today's context. The expertise on training programs developed at the Taipei Ricci Institute, notably by Matilde Hong, and the support of the Institute's whole team, have constituted a precious adjuvant. Other friends have come up with suggestions, criticisms and advices, friends whom I am unable to thank publicly due to the nature of the responsibilities that are theirs.

Loyola Marymount University (LMU), in Los Angeles, welcomed me as a Malatesta Scholar from September 2012 till the end of January 2013, which allowed me to work on key parts of this book in much better conditions than would have been the case otherwise. My thanks go to the LMU Jesuit community for its generous and friendly support, and also to Fudan University for having discharged me of my teaching duties during the same period.

A final word of explanation on the scope of this book: at the start of the project, it was conceived as a guide intended for foreign companies operating in China. In the course of the discussion and preparation, it clearly appeared that its lessons could be enlarged, and that material on CSR was still needed for Chinese companies as well, hence the decision of establishing also a Chinese version. The editorial shift and additional research that followed this decision have actually contributed to enrich the content of the English version. As it stands today, this publication hopes to be of help for all companies, whatever their size, nationality and modes of ownership, operating in and from China. Though primarily targeted at executives and corporate decision-makers, this book is also meant for analysts, academics, students and people engaged in not for profit organizations. The range of issues, references and case studies developed throughout this book tries to honor the diversity of those interested in the subject.

Benoît Vermander
September 2013
Shanghai

Introduction

Over the years, many corporations have been trying to determine what they can and should do to contribute to the sustainability of the economic, social and ecological environment within which they operate. This book aims at helping companies to review and better exercise their corporate social responsibility (CSR) in the Chinese context. Throughout these pages, we will be developing a vision, an assessment, and a blueprint, so as to offer decision-makers a framework in which they can locate the strategic and ethical decisions they need to make. The *vision* will try to answer two questions: (a) How to define CSR and make the notion fully relevant in Chinese context? (b) What are the resources and obstacles provided by China's socio-economic, cultural, and legal contexts that define the modus operandi of corporations being conscious of their social responsibilities? On this basis, the *assessment* will analyze the most pressing challenges to be answered, and will focus on specifics, such as processes and product safety, financial transparency, training, and personnel participation. Finally, a *blueprint* will be offered, helping corporations and other groups to make such insights and concerns, as part of the toolbox they are using when weighing the social, cultural and ecological impact of their strategies and practices. This introduction briefly maps the course that we will follow in the process.

As a starting point, we will argue that CSR is to be understood and implemented not only as a specific dimension of the corporate strategy but also, and more importantly, as an internal driving force nurtured by the contribution of the team members of the corporation. CSR goes beyond the realm of legal obligations; it has to do with a sense of excellence and of responsibility grown from within the company. At the same time, in China as in other countries, the exercise of CSR is framed by a set of laws and norms that defines more and more precisely the basic obligations of the company vis-à-vis society. These norms spell out a set of minimal requirements that companies need to respect, and on which they can build up further initiatives. In China, it is the law itself that is increasingly pressing companies to foster in their midst a CSR culture. Even if both the legal framework and its implementation are obviously in need of improvements, the overall direction is clear and cannot but inspire the management strategies followed by companies, both Chinese and international.

CSR is also anchored into cultural values and traditions, which are reflected in specific corporate cultures that are sometimes hard to translate from one national environment into another. Dialogue and mutual understanding of one another's cultural background and values help the protagonists to forge a new language and modes of communication through which they can elaborate codes of cooperation and conduct. Furthermore, as we will argue at length, Chinese cultural resources, in their flexibility and diversity, are conducive of creative and responsible corporate behaviors. And Chinese traditions are now part of a global wisdom heritage; entrepreneurs can mobilize their lessons and the attitudes they foster for adapting and enriching corporate cultures and strategies that are both effective and socially responsible — in China and elsewhere.

Practically, the CSR agenda takes shape on a triangle-shaped borderland: one determined by the company's domain of operation, the needs resulting from national constraints and social expectations; and the way these constraints and expectations are translated into laws, norms, standards and codes of various types. Taken together, several topics and lines of action spell out the dominant CSR agenda in today's China.

The importance recently taken by *environmental concerns* in China makes this area the keystone of CSR practices in the view of the public and the state alike.

In China, *safety* is probably the most debated of all CSR-related topics: stories linked to (a) food or product safety; (b) industrial or environmental hazards; or (c) work-related deaths and injuries are exposed on the internet and other forms of media daily. Accidents and malfunctions have generated an atmosphere of suspicion now deeply anchored within the consumers' mentality. On the other hand, companies having asserted an excellent record on safety issues enjoy a strong comparative advantage over their competitors.

The building-up of *engineering ethics* has been identified as the key factor for ensuring safety at every step of the production process, and its acculturation into China's engineering curriculum and culture would certainly contribute very much to reduce the industrial hazards that periodically capture the imagination of the public opinion. The CSR-based corporate culture and engineering ethics are mutually reinforcing.

A CSR-based management of *labor issues* must start from the recognition of a few hard facts: the aggregate labor force will start to shrink from around 2015, initially slowly but faster from the late 2020s, and is projected to be more than 15 percent smaller than its peak by 2050. The smaller labor force will support a growing elderly population. The rapid wage growth in recent years among migrants and low-skilled workers is accompanied both by rising expectations and evidence of compression in productivity growth. As migrant workers shift from being a "floating" to a more permanent urban population, they will increasingly expect better non-wage benefits as well, including social security coverage and other urban social entitlements such as free education and social housing.

The 2008 enactment of the Labor Contract Law was a major step forward for regulating labor issues in China. It reflected the willingness of the government to *upgrade labor relations and better protect workers in all forms of employing organizations*, whether public or private. The continuous improvement of employees' morale, training and living standards should be approached as both an ethical and a managerial imperative. Otherwise said, the social dimension of CSR-related strategies accompanies a shift in China's global economic model and prospects, a shift that modifies the way the comparative advantages of conducting production and business in China must be evaluated.

The issues linked to labor contract law often connect with practical problems associated with a significant proportion of *migrant workers* in the working population. This specificity of the Chinese labor market raises questions for the companies operating in the country. It allows for a greater flexibility of the workforce. At the same time, questions of employees' level of retention and training as well as of social fairness weigh heavily on the executives in charge of human resources, especially when the entirety of the supply chain is taken into consideration. This last point holds special importance in Chinese context: *labor standards need to be audited and implemented throughout the entire supply chain.* The recurrence of issues such as underage labor, grueling working conditions and bonded labor at some factories calls for the building up of a coalition among the stakeholders bearing shared responsibility for the social standards effectively applied.

When it comes to CSR-related issues within the corporation's internal working and management, *social coverage* also must be identified as a field of discussion and discernment. Assessing how social protection issues determine the prospects and worries of its workforce helps the company to better appreciate how to deal with its workers so as to ensure a win-win model of cooperation.

Compared to many other societies, China promotes *women's rights and opportunities.* This also applies to the workplace. However, observations in the field show that there still exists a gap between principles and realities. Pervasive discrimination practices are often difficult to point out and remedy: they are rooted into the climate and culture of the workplace more than in any existing regulation.

Especially in China, companies' *CSR training programs* often need to compensate for the deficiencies in training and reflexive capacities that affect the curriculum offered by many educational institutions, be it at the managers' level or below.

The nature and organization of work —including mechanisms of evaluation, communication and work sharing —have a lasting impact on *employees' mental health.* Excessive focus on individual, short-term performances rather than on team performances and long-term goals is certainly the main reason for workers' frustration and mistakes in judgment.

The *way to manage tensions and conflicts within the organization,* the type of measures taken to prevent such conflicts from surfacing, the style of dialogue and communication fostered in a given corporate culture — all of this is part of the CSR agenda. The communication and bargaining style developed within the corporation is an integral part of the CSR-based values that the said corporation intends to foster and implement.

Still an emerging concept in China, *social entrepreneurship* may be defined as business ventures organized around a social or collective purpose. Such a trend needs to be closely watched by corporations, as it has already helped some of them to redirect their CSR and philanthropic efforts throughout inventive channels, initiating partnerships with employees, young entrepreneurs or advocacy groups so as to ensure the sustainability and professional management of specific social initiatives centered around *community investment*.

We will further this analysis by reflecting on how to foster sound ethical assessments. *Lived ethics* is about recognizing and qualifying the problem met by operatives (bribery, conflicts of interests, neglect of procedures, insider trading) — especially when veiled interests blur the issues at hand. A transversal approach to CSR will lead us to evaluate the role fulfilled by codes and other internal documents; to specify the relationship between CSR concerns and corporate governance; to use creatively instruments such as foundations, pilot projects and networks, and to enter whole heartedly into a broader vision of the role that corporations can play in tomorrow's China.

The interconnectedness of the issues that China and the international community are dealing with makes it necessary for all actors to engage in a global assessment of their priorities and means of action. In 2006, an international taskforce has submitted a report called *International Cooperations in National Interest, Meeting Global Challenges*. Some of the goals that the international community taken as a whole strives to achieve can be understood with reference to the concept of "global public goods". Private companies are not direct channels for the distribution of public goods, as the growth of these goods and the access to them are driven by international cooperations and governed by the principle of gratuity. However, corporations are among the actors that create the potential for increasing and sharing these goods, through innovation, business practices, cooperation among themselves and sometimes philanthropy. Once a company identifies the relationship between its line of business and the public goods that a society strives to nurture and share among its citizens, it becomes able to reformulate its vision and social contribution in ways that resonate with a large coalition of actors.

The process through which public goods are perceived and pursued can be illustrated, in the Chinese context, by the work conducted together by the World Bank and the Development Research Center of China's State Council — the report *China 2030: Building a Modern, Harmonious, and Creative High-Income Society* has received widespread attention — resulting as it was from a joint effort by the World Bank and China's State Council. The report intends to be a blueprint for the course of development to be followed over the next two decades, and to provide an inspiration not only to policy-makers but also to all social actors aiming to make China a greener, fairer and more affluent society. It enables a company to integrate these challenges and directions into its new corporate vision for China.

Ultimately, a corporate strategy that focuses from the start on CSR values and practices sees its creative potential greatly enhanced. The change in focus, the enlargement of one's field of vision and the connection with a whole new field of ideas and partners, all of this suggests to executives hitherto unsuspected possibilities. This is even truer in China: the scope of the country, the intricate character of the challenges met by companies, and the richness of the cultural and social fabric provide entrepreneurs with an abundance of new resources and viewpoints through which to rethink their ways of proceeding and social relevance. It is our hope that this book will help all actors involved to cross-breed entrepreneurial and social resources in the process through which China is tackling the challenges generated by its current developmental model.

PART ONE

CSR IN THE CHINESE CONTEXT:

A VISION

Though the definition and implementation of CSR practices raise similar questions in China as in other parts of the world, it remains true that practical issues and priorities differ from one national or cultural context to another. Besides, the very size of China and its impact on the global economy make a number of issues more acute. This first part of the book will sketch and progressively enrich an approach to CSR that balances a global vision with an appreciation of the Chinese context in its legal, social and cultural dimensions. Through recapping how CSR and related concepts developed in the last decades, it will examine how these developments may help us to reinterpret Chinese cultural and social resources relevant for entrepreneurial activities. It will also investigate how corruption and misbehaviors adversely affect the understanding and implementation of a company's social responsibility. Finally, it will try to integrate a China-based understanding of the CSR imperative into corporate strategies.

CHAPTER ONE

What is CSR?

1.1. A Pragmatic Approach to CSR

"Corporate Social Responsibility" (CSR) is a term that refers less to any rigidly defined legal, ethical or technical code than to an evolving set of principles, attitudes and practices having both global and local dimensions. There is no rigorous definition of what the expression refers to: "Notwithstanding the plethora of studies and debates that have taken place over the course of the last quarter century, there still exists no commonly accepted definition of CSR," states Stefano Zamagni.[1] And other authors write: "One of the challenges of examining the concept of CSR is simply identifying a consistent and sensible definition from a bewildering range of concepts and definitions that have been proposed in the literature."[2] Acknowledging the plasticity of the term does not amount to rejecting it as meaningless or useless — far from it: "CSR" is an expression that crystallizes concerns and debates, the frontiers of which are mobile but are shaped by convergent forces. Let us first approach the realities "CSR" encompasses through an array of propositions that will showcase both its fluidity and its richness.[3] In this chapter, we will focus on a global approach to

---

[1] Zamagni, S. (2012), The Ethical Anchoring of Corporate Social Responsibility and the Critique of CSR, in M. Schlag & J.A. Mercado (eds.), *Free Markets and the Culture of Common Good*, Dordrecht: Springer, p. 191.

[2] Reinhardt, F.L., R.N. Stavins & R.H.K. Vietor (2008), Corporate Social Responsibility Through an Economic Lens, *Review of Environmental Economics and Policy*, 2(2), pp. 219–239.

[3] The World Business Council for Sustainable Development (WBCSD) defines CSR as "the commitment of business to contribute to sustainable economic development, working with employees, their families, the local community and society at large to improve their quality of life" (WBCSD, http://www.wbcsd.org/work-program/business-role/previous-work/corporate-social-responsibility.aspx,

CSR, highlighting documents, dimensions and concepts that have progressively shaped the field. The Chinese understanding of corporate responsibility has developed within this general framework. However, CSR with Chinese characteristics is also the product of official declaration and policies, specific legal dispositions, and Chinese cultural heritage, which will be the focus of Chapters 2 and 3.

One of the initiatives epitomizing the globalization of the values and issues that underlies a CSR-based corporate strategy has been the United National (UN) Global Compact, which formulates ten principles having to do with human rights, labor standards, the environment and anti-corruption.[4] However, note that the Global Compact does not make explicit use of the term CSR; second, that it is not a regulatory instrument, but rather a forum and a network associating governments, companies, labor organizations, and various civil society coalitions. Still, the formulation of the Global Compact was testifying to the generalization of a set of concerns and policy directions that had been gaining ground throughout the 1990s. Nowadays, virtually every global corporation has a CSR policy or department, fostering a variety of projects that may have to do with education, food safety or the environment.[5] The shifts in opinions and strategies

---

accessed July 31, 2013). Business for Social Responsibility (BSR) defines global CSR as "business decision-making linked to ethical values and respect for people, communities and the environment" (BSR, http://www.bcn.ufl.edu/ckibert/Poland/MiscMaterials/CSR-Overview-bsr.htm, accessed July 31, 2013). I will not attempt here to draw a list of definitions of CSR. The reader interested in a comprehensive approach may refer to: Mullerat, R. (2010), *International Corporate Social Responsibility: The Role of Corporations in the Economic Order of the 21st Century*, Alphen: Kluwer Law International. See also Idowu, S.O. & C. Lelouche (eds.) (2011), *Theory and Practice of Corporate Social Responsibility*, Berlin: Springer. Rather, I will try to outline how various definitions of CSR concur to map a dynamic field of evolving focuses, approaches and strategies.

[4] An introduction to the UN Global Compact, detailed presentations and additional documents can be found on http://www.unglobalcompact.org/AboutTheGC/index.html (accessed May 24, 2013).

[5] The year 2008 may have witnessed the crest of the "first CSR wave", with, for instance, several articles and surveys in *The Economist* on CSR and global corporations. During the same year, the beginning of the financial crisis signaled a shift

occurring throughout the 1990s had been prepared by theoretical and social debates happening in the 1930s and 1970s on whether a firm should or should not sacrifice profits in the social interest.[6] The abruptness of the debate was considerably mitigated from the 1980s on by a number of factors: concerns linked to the environment and to natural resources made the *time factor* in profit-seeking a critical element for rethinking the terms of the questions; social and cultural evolutions broadened the understanding of the finality of a company; the globalization process raised a new series of practical and ethical issues. Among other approaches, the concept of *corporate citizenship* was popularized in the 1980s and 1990s, encouraging a shift in business organizations' social involvement from a passive response to social pressure, and finally to a proactive engagement in social and environmental issues, and a belief that such engagement is part of corporate duty: companies need to develop in a way that preserves resources for long-term growth and fosters economic and social sustainability.[7] In other words, the understanding of the responsibilities of a firm both toward its shareholders and its stakeholders has been and is still evolving according to an array of cultural, social, economic and international factors. This may already explain why CSR cannot be defined in a way that would delimitate its meaning and implications once and for all.

The pragmatic approach that nowadays characterizes the quest for defining and implementing CSR is illustrated by a number of recent publications and programs. The *ISO 26000 Guidance on Social Responsibility* provides companies of all sizes with more recent and detailed criteria and insights than the Global Compact might have

---

(but not a decline) in the approach of the topic, with comparatively less attention paid to philanthropy-like projects and more discussion on the ethical and strategic dimensions of CSR.

[6] An excellent summary of these debates can be found in: Reinhardt, F.L., R.N. Stavins & R.H.K. Vietor (2008), Corporate Social Responsibility Through an Economic Lens, *Review of Environmental Economics and Policy*, 2(2), pp. 219–239.

[7] See Melé, D. (2008). Corporate Social Responsibility Theories, in A. Crane, A. McWilliams, D. Matten, J. Moon & D.S. Siegel (eds.), *The Oxford Handbook of Corporate Social Responsibility*, Oxford: Oxford University Press, pp. 46–82.

done. The *ISO 26000 Guidance on Social Responsibility* and the *User Guide on ISO 26000 Guidance on Social Responsibility* (the latter is published by the European organization NORMAPME, see Box 1.1), among other companion publications, provide their readers with a flexible but still precise and up-to-date definition of CSR.[8] The *ISO 26000 Guidance on Social Responsibility* was launched by the International Organization for Standardization (ISO) on November 1, 2010 as a guidance paper (and not as a standard to be used for certification purposes or in contracts).

Box 1.1 The User Guide on ISO 26000 Guidance on Social Responsibility

"CSR addresses the voluntarily responsible behavior of enterprises toward society and presupposes legal compliance. Societies differ: by nation, history, culture, language, religion, level of education, way of thinking, density of regulation and other factors. In European nations, many CSR-related activities are regulated, a significant distinction from other regions. Different societies want to develop but also to maintain their special character. So, behaving in a socially responsible manner is something full of dynamics because societies' needs and demands are locally specific and subject to continuous change."

Source: NORMAPME User Guide for European SMEs on ISO 26000 Guidance on Social Responsibility, 2011, p. 5, http://www.normapme.eu/public/uploads/files/csr%20user%20guide/User%20guide%20ISO26000_version%20EN_final_18072011.pdf, accessed July 31, 2013.

While the *ISO 26000* tries to encompass different national and professional contexts, the cultural dimension of CSR is stressed from the start (Box 1.2). Cultural particularities should not be seen as an excuse for escaping from the responsibilities attached to CSR, but rather as a reason for deepening and refining the analysis that leads to its actual implementation.

---

[8] ISO 26000: NORMAPME User Guide for European SMEs Available, July 25, 2011, http://www.normapme.eu/en/page/527/iso-26000-normapme-user-guide-for-european-smes-available, accessed May 24, 2013.

Box 1.2 CSR as a Cultural Construct

"CSR refers to an organization's moral obligation toward others who are affected by the organization's actions. An organization's social responsibilities are always shaped by the culture and the historical period in which the organization operates. Just as a society's values, norms and mores change over time, so does the definition of what is socially responsible behavior."

Source: Sims, R.R. (2003), *Ethics and Corporate Social Responsibility: Why Giants Fail*, London: Praeger, p. 44.

The *ISO 26000* has been preceded by *SA8000*, an auditable certification standard encouraging organizations to develop, maintain and apply socially acceptable practices in the workplace. The standard, developed in 1997, measures the performance of companies in eight areas: child labor, forced labor, health and safety, free association and collective bargaining, discrimination, disciplinary practices, working hours and compensation. Its practical character makes it particularly useful for assessing social standards within factories. The direct impact of the standard remains very modest in scope: in September 2012, China was the third country out of 66 for the number of facilities certified, with a total of 485 factories representing less than 340,000 workers.[9] However, the standard has certainly inspired national regulations and helped to normalize conceptions of what a socially responsible workplace is meant to be.

Note that the role played by the standards' adoption has proven to be essential in the process through which countries and industry sectors develop an understanding of a CSR-based integrated approach. Quality management cannot be easily separated from a set of values that foster social responsibility. China's apparel and textile industry provides one with a most interesting example of the process that leads from management concerns inspired by the progressive

---

[9]SA8000 Certified Facilities: As of September 30, 2012, *Social Accountability Accreditation Services*, September 30, 2012, http://www.saasaccreditation.org/certfaclists/2012_Q3/Q3%20SA8000%20Certs%20List,%20Public%20List.pdf, accessed May 24, 2013.

globalization of an industrial sector to a set of explicitly ethical and social stipulations (see Box 1.3).

Box 1.3 China's Textile Industry: From ISO 9000 to CSC9000T

Though technically not CSR-related, the *ISO 9000* family of standards focuses on quality management systems. Over a million organizations worldwide are independently certified, making *ISO 9001* (the first and leading standard of the family of standards) one of the most widely used management tools in the world today. China now accounts for a quarter of all certifications. Additionally, China's apparel and textile industry has built up its own standards, with explicit reference to CSR values and the establishment of a responsible global supply chain. The *CSC9000T* is based upon the Chinese laws and regulations and relevant international conventions; it is also a management system for improving social responsibility management, while the *ISO 9000* is a quality management system. Although the purposes of the two management systems are different, they apply the same management model, enabling local enterprises familiar with the *ISO 9000* management to implement the *CSC9000T* more easily.

Sources: ISO 9000 — Quality Management, *International Organization for Standardization*, http://www.iso.org/iso/home/standards/management-standards/iso_9000.htm, accessed May 24, 2013. See also: CSC9000T Document, *Responsible Supply Chain Association*, http://www.csc9000.org.cn/en/CSC9000T_Document.asp, accessed May 24, 2013.

In October 2011, the European Commission endorsed a similarly pragmatic approach when it approved a new *European Strategy on CSR for 2011 to 2014*. It defined CSR as the "responsibility of enterprises for their impacts on society" and as compulsory in respecting core standards, in particular, the recently updated OECD Guidelines for Multinational Enterprises, the ten principles of the UN Global Compact, the *ISO 26000 Guidance on Social Responsibility*, the International Labor Organization (ILO) Tripartite Declaration of Principles Concerning Multinational Enterprises and Social Policy, and the UN Guiding Principles on Business and Human Rights. This core set of internationally recognized principles and guidelines represents an evolving and recently strengthened global framework for CSR.[10] What is worth noting is the recognition of the evolving nature of CSR's definition and obligations.[11]

The fact should also be stressed that, according to the publications just quoted, CSR has to do with the "voluntarily responsible behavior" of enterprises. As we shall see, the reality is slightly more complex:

— CSR indeed goes beyond the realm of legal obligations; it has to do with a sense of excellence and of responsibility grown from within the company. And some *legal* behaviors can still be *socially* irresponsible (operating casinos may be an example of legal but socially irresponsible business operations).

— At the same time, in China as in other countries, the implementation of CSR is framed by a set of laws and norms that define more and more precisely the basic obligations of the company *vis-à-vis* society. These norms spell out a set of minimal requirements that companies need to respect, on which they can build up further initiatives.

— Even if its scope goes beyond legally binding obligations, implementing CSR goes along with a set of sanctions and rewards that companies need to carefully scrutinize. Besides legal sanctions, this might have to do with company morale, public reputation, the positioning *vis-à-vis* competitors, trust gained or lost with public authorities, etc. One of the goals of this book is to help the reader to better assess gains and losses linked to the implementation of CSR in the Chinese context.

---

[10] A Renewed EU Strategy 2011–2014 for Corporate Social Responsibility, *European Commission*, October 25, 2011, ec.europa.eu/enterprise/policies/sustainable-business/files/csr/new-csr/act_en.pdf, accessed May 24, 2013.

[11] Other frameworks that could be quoted include the OECD Guidelines for Multinational Enterprises, adopted for the first time in 1976 and renewed in 2011. The OECD Guidelines consist of recommendations for responsible business practice that are adopted by governments, which then in turn encourage their domestic enterprises to adhere to these recommendations. They cover topics such as disclosure, human rights, employment and industrial relations, environment, combating bribery, consumer interests, science and technology, competition and taxation.

Summarizing these different definitions and approaches, we can say that corporate social responsibility is a mechanism of self-regulation through which a company: (a) monitors its compliance with law, ethical standards and international norms; and (b) determines for itself and puts into application standards, objectives and ways of proceeding that go beyond the minimum legal requirements, so as to optimize its impact on its direct stakeholders, on the environment and on the society at large.

1.2. The Company as an Interdependent Self

CSR is understood and implemented on the basis of a set of principles. Principles are not only ethical in nature. They also have to do with management, strategy and common sense. A great deal of the literature dedicated to CSR tries to determine the most important principles that companies should keep in mind when understanding the nature of their social responsibility, the rewards attached to it, and the dangers linked to its neglect. The attitudes, analyses and values that lead a company to understand in such a way its interaction with its social environment cannot be captured by a single catchword. It is rather by paying attention to an array of expressions that we start to sense what the present-day understanding of CSR amounts to, and the expectations attached to it.

ISO 26000 and the *NORMAPME User Guide* stress four basic attitudes needed for devising and implementing a CSR-based management policy, attitudes which are ultimately anchored in a sense of personal responsibility:

— *Accountability:* the fact that a company and its executives are able to take responsibility for the impact it may have on its specific environment, explaining and justifying the decisions they are taking.
— *Transparency:* making information available about the enterprise's decisions and activities regarding the relevant social, economic and environmental aspects of its operations.

— *Ethical behavior:* all decisions should be taken and carried out in an honest, fair and reliable way, clearly stating and solving conflicts of interests, and not accepting illegal benefits.
— *Networking with social organizations*: identifying who has an interest in the company's decisions and activities so as to better understand their possible impact and how to address it.

Note that the term "accountability" has no immediate equivalent in Chinese. Its "acculturation" in China is recent and is a result of the capacity-building programs conducted for Chinese non-governmental organizations (NGOs) by their foreign counterparts: Anthony Spires gives an account of the debates that took place when the expression was still new: "One translation common in Hong Kong has been *wenzezhi* (问责制, literally, "ask", "responsibility", "system"), and the verb *wenze* (问责) has been used in mainland Chinese media to mean "to be held accountable" when referring to the actions of government officials. Yet this expression was not adopted. During the ensuing debates and discussion… one of the Chinese participants proposed the term *gongxinli* (公信力, literally, "public", "trust", "strength"). After more discussion, it was decided that *gongxinli* would be the term used in all of their Chinese-language training materials as the best equivalent of the English "accountability". In the training sessions that I attended, the term *gongxinli* was new to many people's ears. Although the written characters helped to clarify the meaning, the training materials devote much space to explaining, with examples, what accountability is and why it matters… While its definition may be elusive, the importance of accountability — and its concomitant transparency — is easily understood by people in China, where corruption is rampant."[12]

An article by Mostovicz *et al.* (2011) offers an alternative formulation of similar principles and attitudes in Box 1.4.

---

[12] Spires, A.J. (2012), Lessons from Abroad: Foreign Influences on China's Emerging Civil Society, *The China Journal*, 68, pp. 133–134.

Box 1.4 Personal Attributes Needed for CSR

"Corporate responsibility cannot be practiced if various personal attributes do not exist in the individuals within the company. These consist of the four pillars of leadership, ethics, personal responsibility and trust, all of which are dynamic in nature. Incorporating these personal qualities can help improve the planning and practice of CSR programs as well."

Source: Mostovicz, E.I., A.K. Kakabadse & N.K. Kakabadse (2011), The Four Pillars of Corporate Responsibility: Ethics, Leadership, Personal Responsibility and Trust, *Corporate Governance*, 11(4), p. 491.

The authors of the above quoted article are conscious that the qualities they identify as central to CSR are always to be nurtured, and are never fully acquired. As they note in Box 1.5, *leadership* has to do with the capacity to recognize one's own limitations in terms of choice and objectivity.

Box 1.5 Leadership and Inner Freedom

"Leadership is the ability to choose freely without being influenced by external social forces, whilst simultaneously maintaining full awareness of one's inherent subconscious motivations."

Source: Mostovicz, E.I., A.K. Kakabadse & N.K. Kakabadse (2011), The Four Pillars of Corporate Responsibility: Ethics, Leadership, Personal Responsibility and Trust, *Corporate Governance*, 11(4), p. 492.

The same sense of limitation and the capacity of recognizing potential or actual failures are inscribed into the other qualities linked to a CSR-based corporate culture (Box 1.6).

It is worth noticing that, in today's China, *trust* is indeed enjoyed by business leaders, and represents both a virtue and an asset. At the global level, the Edelman Trust Barometer 2012 finds on average less than 50 percent of the population trust that business is "doing what is right" — that is, that corporations are working in the best interests of society — but it registers a strikingly different situation in China: 71 percent of

Box 1.6 Taking Responsibility

"Trust is the ability not only to seek shared benefit but also to face failure and to put the blame squarely on one's shoulders if a problem arises. Only when assuming full responsibility for a failure can a person commit to devising a solution."

Source: Mostovicz, E.I., A.K. Kakabadse & N.K. Kakabadse (2011), The Four Pillars of Corporate Responsibility: Ethics, Leadership, Personal Responsibility and Trust, Corporate Governance, 11(4), p. 493.

people polled trust business leaders, compared to 61 percent the year before.[13] Trust put in NGOs was even higher, and still rising, while trust in the government has been dropping. This gives business leaders in China both capital to build upon and the duty to respond to the trust society bestows on them.

Other authors try to encapsulate the personal and collective qualities needed for exercising CSR into one word, loaded with specific meaning. Such is the case with *stewardship* (Box 1.7).

Box 1.7 Finding a New Purpose in Business

"Addressing issues of well-being in emerging and developing markets where multinational corporations often have as much power as governments requires commitment to a new, more humanistic paradigm for business that includes a positive duty to pursue the common good in a responsible manner… In stewardship, the purpose and role of business is to serve by contributing to the flourishing of humankind. Business serves by providing the goods and services that enable people as consumers to flourish; opportunities for meaningful and creative work that enable people as workers along the value chain to flourish; and support that enables communities to flourish. Stewardship aligns with the sustainability movement's emphasis on people and planet issues."

Source: Karns, G.L. (2011), Stewardship: A New Vision for the Purpose of Business, Corporate Governance, 11(4), p. 342.

---

[13] 2012 Edelman Trust Barometer Executive Summary, http://www.scribd.com/doc/79026497/2012-Edelman-Trust-Barometer-Executive-Summary, accessed May 24, 2013.

Accountability, leadership, trust, stewardship... Taken as a whole, these words — and others — suggest the corporate culture embodied by the attention to and implementation of CSR. Still, however we name and describe the values and attitudes conducive to CSR, the real issue is to examine how these values can be embedded into the company's culture and day-to-day operations.

The main point here is that no company can develop a CSR culture without identifying the variety of players who collectively create the environment in which it operates — CSR is a multi-dimensional construct, composed of concern for: (a) shareholder/owners; (b) stakeholders; and (c) the community as represented by the state. Specifically, the concept of CSR would probably not have been developed if not for the recognition of the importance of the *stakeholders* (Box 1.8).

Box 1.8. Identifying Stakeholders

"A firm consists of a variety of different constituencies, such as employees, suppliers, customers, shareholders, and the broader community. All of these constituencies have a strategic and/or moral stake in the firm, and each is guided by its own interests and values. Senior management often faces problems, such as enhancing the viability of the firm while simultaneously balancing the needs of the various stakeholders."

Source: Waldman, D.A. *et al.* (2012), Cultural and Leadership Predictors of Corporate Social Responsibility Values of Top Management: A GLOBE Study of 15 Countries, *Journal of International Business Studies*, 37(6), p. 824.

In other words, the notion of CSR takes on a new significance when a company culture sees itself as being embedded into a network of constituencies and relationships, as an ***interdependent self***. In contrast, when the company culture stresses pride and loyalty without balancing these values with an emphasis on duties and obligations toward the greater social context to which the company belongs, CSR as a concept and a practical attitude cannot be easily grasped and implemented.[14]

---

[14] Waldman, D.A. *et al.* (2012), Cultural and Leadership Predictors of Corporate Social Responsibility Values of Top Management: A GLOBE Study of 15 Countries, *Journal of International Business Studies*, 37(6), p. 826.

Conceiving the corporation to which one belongs as an interdependent self helps the actors to better identify its core business in relationship to an array of local and global issues (see Box 1.9 for a case study on global issues).

Focusing on the stakeholder dimension of CSR notably allows a corporation to define the scope and extent of *shared responsibility along the supply chain* — a responsibility involving not only industrial partners but also legislators, standards organizations, customers and scientists. *A company is held responsible for practices upstream in the supply chain, and the problem, as we will see throughout this book, is especially acute in China.* However, as there are issues that the corporation cannot solve by itself, it is led to foster coalitions and debates among its various stakeholders: (a) organizational stakeholders (e.g. employees, customers, shareholders, suppliers), (b) community stakeholders (e.g. local residents, special interest groups), (c) regulatory stakeholders (e.g. municipalities, regulatory systems) and (d) media stakeholders.[15]

In such an approach, companies also understand that their strategies both shape the ones of the stakeholders and are shaped by them in a way that engineers the overall social dynamics. The conclusion of a study focusing on the information and communications technology sector in China bears larger lessons: "Companies recognize that the challenges in the global supply chain are not ones that can be remedied by the private sector alone. The most successful scenarios are those in which the government, suppliers, NGOs, customers, multilateral organizations and others have collaborated and committed to their respective responsibilities in order to improve labor and environmental conditions and build a foundation for sustainable growth."[16]

---

[15] A good summary of the issues raised by an enlarged vision of stakeholder responsibility in the Chinese context is found in Tsoi, J. (2010), Stakeholders' Perceptions and Future Scenarios to Improve Corporate Social Responsibility in Hong Kong and Mainland China, *Journal of Business Ethics*, 91(3), pp. 391–404.

[16] BSR (2007), Corporate Social Responsibility in China's Information and Communications Technology (ICT) Sector, July 12, 2007, http://www-wds. worldbank.org/external/default/WDSContentServer/WDSP/IB/2007/09/07/0 00310607_20070907130905/Rendered/PDF/407790ENGLISH010social0ICT01PU BLIC1.pdf, accessed May 24, 2013.

Box 1.9. Case Study: Identifying the Global Dimension of a Corporation's Core Business

Sustainable Mobility

"The development of mobility for people and goods, essential to worldwide social and economic development, must go hand in hand with measures to reduce its negative impact, on a social and an environmental level. Reducing pollution, improving safety and traffic flow, transitioning gradually toward renewable energy sources, using intermodal transportation systems where appropriate, these are just a few of the challenges for the future of mobility. It is the Michelin Group's responsibility to contribute to finding long-term solutions to these questions, but these solutions can only result from concerted research efforts. For this reason, we take part in research programs regarding concepts and technologies for the transportation of the future, aimed at establishing sustainable mobility."

Source: Excerpt from the Michelin Performance and Responsibility Charter.

Sustainable Habitat

"An internal sustainable habitat mission was set up in late 2010 to support the Group's strategy. Led by members of senior management and comprising representatives from R&D, Environment, Health and Safety (EHS) and Marketing, this multidisciplinary team is working on three key areas based on life cycle assessment. These include:

— proposing a policy for managing and recycling jobsite waste in each business;
— developing an eco-innovation policy; and
— defining the priorities of the Group regarding building an assessment scheme and eco labels and drawing up recommendations so that our customers can be fully informed and make fact-based decisions.

For each area, the mission has identified member company practices in all host countries and drafted recommendations to help teams improve by promoting a shared vision and the use of common resources."

Source: Excerpt from Saint Gobain's 2011 Sustainability Report.

UESTIONS

— How do we identify the relationship that exists between our core business activities and the sustainability issues that are debated at the local and global level?

— How does the perception of the sustainability issues linked to our business operations change the understanding and formulation of our corporate vision?

— Do we foster coalitions among actors implied in the sustainability issues that are linked to our business operations?

— Do these coalitions include actors from Chinese corporations, state organizations and university or research centers?

— Are we able to fully articulate the specific contribution our corporation is able to make when tackling the issues thus determined?

— Are the standards that govern the consultation and auditing of our partners, especially along our entire supply chain, consistent with the mission and obligations we assign to ourselves?

The fact remains that the concept of stakeholders has been sometimes criticized for being over-extended and confused. Stakeholders are variously defined as the ones "affecting or being affected" by the operations of the corporation, the actors "without whose support the organization would cease to exist", the groups and individuals engaging in transactions with the business — or else approached in an highly pragmatic fashion, the list of potential stakeholders then includes governmental bodies, political parties, lobbies, trade unions, local communities, financial partners, suppliers, customers, employees, and even competitors. This has made the very concept of stakeholders criticized as an "an essentially contested concept", undermining its operational value.[17] We do not need to enter deeper into this debate here. Suffice it to say that envisioning the corporation as an "interdependent self", as

---

[17]See especially: Miles, S. (2012) Stakeholders: Essentially Contested or Just Confused, *Journal of Business Ethics*, 108(3), pp. 285–298.

we suggest doing here, allows decision-makers to rank "actual or potential stakeholders" (and subsequently to deal with them) according to the situations and issues one is facing, justifying an essentially mobile categorization of stakeholders. Dealing with supply chain issues, with environmental responsibility, with training within the corporation proper and with financial accountability — all these questions come with a different ranking of core stakeholders and with different patterns of interaction, while the interrelatedness of the issues at stake makes decision-makers aware that new stakeholders may surge into the landscape at any time, modifying the terms of the situation faced.

1.3. Specific Dimensions of CSR

The approach we have sketched envisions CSR in a dynamic and integrative way: that a company holds specific responsibilities toward its social environment is a reality that is gradually recognized once the said company becomes conscious of the interdependence that links its shareholders, its stakeholders and the community represented by the state together. Already framed by laws, rules and norms, its sense of responsibility will thus be awakened, nurtured and implemented through its search for excellence and the values and attitudes that go along with it.

This global approach to CSR translates into different concerns and management areas. We will detail these dimensions with reference to the Chinese context in the second part of this book. Still, we can already identify some of the dimensions that we will analyze and illustrate later on.[18]

---

[18] A list of CSR dimensions is provided by the European Commission (2011): "According to these principles and guidelines, CSR at least covers human rights, labor and employment practices (such as training, diversity, gender equality and employee health and well-being), environmental issues (such as biodiversity, climate change, resource efficiency, life-cycle assessment and pollution prevention), and combating bribery and corruption. Community involvement and development, the integration of disabled persons, and consumer interests, including privacy, are also part of the CSR agenda."

— CSR has to do with the *management and empowerment of personnel*: There is no way of awakening corporate responsibility if a sense of responsibility toward oneself, the organization and the social context is not nurtured in each individual. Only men and women who have experienced empowerment and responsibility in the tasks they have to fulfill can create and maintain a company that collectively proves to be responsible in its choices and behaviors.

— This also goes with an overall commitment to *ensuring well-being in the workplace* (Box 1.10), from the respect of legal obligations to proactive policies targeting areas of special concerns that may differ from business to business.

Box 1.10. CSR in the Workplace: Areas of Concentration

— Presence and effectiveness of programs to ensure a fair working wage (minimum wage), reasonable working conditions and hours.

— Employee development and training programs which develop the skills of all workers.

— Training for managers and supervisors to improve workers' communication capacities.

— Leadership and achievement in protecting the health and safety of employees.

— Employee involvement in the health and safety management of the organization.

— Voluntary or self-applied standards which go beyond minimum regulations.

Source: Excerpt from AmCham Shanghai CSR Awards Best Practices.

— Today, CSR finds an urgent expression in *caring for the environment*: the public expects companies to minimize the use of natural resources, to dispose waste properly, and to avoid natural disasters, at the very least. The long-term future of companies' activities — and even sometimes their short-term outlook — is also based on the collective management of such resources. Therefore, and even if this was not the case in other times, environmental responsibility is seen as the touchstone of CSR.

— *Safety* is also a keyword now associated with CSR, and even more so in the Chinese context. Besides the avoidance of natural disasters, safety translates into two major areas of concerns: *safety at work* (avoiding injuries and accidents, both inside and outside the factory); and *product safety*, in terms of usage and quality.

— CSR is also seen as the rationale behind **business and financial ethics**. Non-ethical behaviors in terms of business and finance are detrimental not only to the normal functioning of the markets but to society as a whole, and to social ethos in particular: it destroys relationships of trust among all social actors, erodes behavioral standards, and nurtures discouragement and cynicism. Not only should companies adhere to the strictest legal standards, they also should develop a culture of transparency and responsibility that prevents both the occurence of unethical practices and the loss of confidence in economic and social institutions that most countries are experiencing nowadays.

— Besides financial and business ethics, specialized areas of professional ethics have also been emerging. Of particular interest is the rise of **engineering ethics**, understood as a set of case studies and standards that help engineers to assess how they should behave along the entire production process. The pervasive role of technology in our lives explains the importance of concerns linked to engineering ethics and to other branches of applied ethics such as bioethics.

— Finally, the stress on CSR helps it shareholders to reflect on **the ultimate goals of a company**. Social trends — sometimes reflected in the reframing of mission statements — have made the perception of a company's objectives much broader than was the case in the past: contribution to social well-being, empowerment and self-realization of the employees, a passion for innovation, a commitment to fair trade, the sharing of benefits (social enterprises) have all found a place in the way specific companies have started to assess their goals and mission. Such a development illustrates the fact that CSR is not to be seen as a rigid set of norms and practices but rather as an evolving complex of concerns and attitudes that can be translated into various innovative initiatives and policies according to the nature of the company's business and the way it formulates its ultimate objectives.

1.4. Related Concepts

It would be difficult to appreciate the full impact of a notion such as CSR without referring to an array of concepts and concerns that have taken shape since the middle of the 1980s. As these concerns are now acquiring full force in China, it is useful to recall some basic notions and relate them to the development of CSR.

1.4.1. *Sustainable development*

Sustainable development refers to development that "meets the needs of the present without compromising the ability of future generations to meet their own needs", as it was famously defined by the Brundtland Report released by the UN in 1987. This implies striking a delicate balance between the human need to improve lifestyles and feelings of well-being on one hand, and the preservation of natural resources and ecosystems, on which we and future generations depend, on the other. It is generally understood that the stress on sustainability links a sense of fairness with the resolution to drastically reduce our present waste of resources. As is the case everywhere in the world, and probably more acutely than elsewhere, sustainable development is now a key issue in China, as environmental concerns, long-term economic and political models, as well as a threatening social gap, are becoming hotly debated topics. Companies are expected to contribute to sustainability through law-abidance, technological innovation, better management practices and creating a sense of fairness that contributes to social harmony. They are also asked to balance short-term and long-term interests in a way that does justice to the generations to come. The stress on sustainable development can be seen as the general background on which different areas which collectively form CSR are assessed and prioritized.

To state the obvious, since 1979 the Chinese developmental dynamics and the impressive poverty reduction it engineered have been created by private sector investments, both national and multinational. The very inscription of the privately owned firm into the legal and economic landscape has changed the conditions under which development could take its course: "The emergence of the firm as an independent economic agent and the development of the incorporated form of business organization have profound implications for the shape and dynamics of the society, polity and economy of China. In a country where the state had owned and operated work units that encompassed nearly every aspect of the life of an individual, this transformation changes the rules and incentives governing the actions and interactions among all economic agents including the state and its instrumentalities at various levels. These changes have produced the expected growth benefits and improvements in the living standard for the majority of the population."[19] In this respect, the Chinese development has been indeed sustainable, as it has created the institutional and conditions for its continuation, reinforced by continuous improvements in national regulations, global integration, education, expertise and infrastructures. At the same time, some factors make the present course unsustainable: corruption (see Chapter 5), environmental degradation (Chapter 6), and overall factors of growth and consumption, which the Chinese government is actively trying to transform so as to foster a new economic paradigm (Chapter 15). In all these fields, the contribution coming from private firms plays a decisive role, hopefully enabling China to make its developmental model sustainable as well as to equalize the social field and to foster much needed improvements in terms of the quality of life.

1.4.2. *Cultural resources/cultural diversity*

We have seen that the approach to CSR is shaped by cultural values and attitudes. Besides, management practices can reduce or enhance the cultural resources of the actors interacting with the company: business practices nurture or diminish cultural resources exactly as it does with natural resources. And there is a link between sustainable development and cultural diversity that makes the former an integral dimension of CSR.

"Culture" can be defined as a set of resources that helps to stabilize or to change, according to circumstances, the model of human

---

[19] Tam, O.K. (2002), Ethical Issues in the Evolution of Corporate Governance in China, *Journal of Business Ethics*, 37(3), p. 303.

development specific to a community. The value system, the technical know-how developed by preceding generations, the sense of identity and solidarity developed within a nation can all be used for fostering debate and reflection on how to live together in such a way as to enhance our sense of evolving as a meaningful and ethical community. Culture allows us to confront various situations as they arise, from very simple to more complex ones, by choosing from a list of practices and knowledge that cannot be applied automatically but requires reinterpretation and invention each time. By definition, cultural resources are diverse, varying with time and space. And yet, they are meant to help us to confront challenges shared by the human species as a whole. Otherwise said, culture is at the same time what gathers and what divides us, as it represents the sum of diverse, and sometimes contradictory, answers to universal questions and challenges. Culture is plural in essence: a given cultural model exists and asserts itself by coming across other cultural expressions.

"Cultural resources" are ways of life, practical knowledge, belief systems, or landscapes and cultural relics that belong to a community as a whole. The community takes its sense of identity from them, using them as tool for preserving and adapting its existence. It is ultimately the stuff from which people are able to create and enrich new resources that will help their descendants to go on with the task of living a meaningful existence. In this respect, nurturing cultural resources and cultural diversity belongs to the goals and duties that a company assigns to itself.

The term culture applies also to corporations. Organizations and corporations are sometimes characterized as having strong or weak cultures, rigid or adaptive cultures, functional or dysfunctional cultures, and so forth.[20] They develop their own symbols, stories, references and models of behaviors. A given corporate culture may be more or less conducive to CSR-based values and practices. DeJoy (2005) sums up how corporate culture evolves over time: "Organizations may share certain cultural traits, but the culture of each organization is thought to be unique and must be understood in its own context.

---

[20] Kotter, J. & T. Heskett (1992), *Corporate Culture and Performance*, New York: Free Press.

Organizational cultures are thought to be self-perpetuating, in that, culture is passed along, and new members are indoctrinated into the prevailing cultural practices and beliefs. This self-sustaining feature also means that cultures are often resistant to change and that producing culture change can be an unpredictable and slow process."[21]

1.4.3. *Circular economy and green development*

A concept progressively developed since the late 1970s, "circular economy" has gained a new prominence in China, notably thanks to its promotion by the World Bank (Box 1.11).

Box 1.11. Circular Economy

"Circular Economy (CE) is a general term covering activities that reduce, reuse and recycle materials (referred to as the 3R approach) in production, distribution and consumption processes. Basically, this 3R approach strives to reduce harmful impacts of economic activities on the environment by minimizing impacts throughout the production life cycle. The ultimate objective of the CE approach is to achieve the decoupling of economic growth from natural resource depletion and environmental degradation... Aiming to decouple economic growth from increasing resource use and environmental degradation, the CE approach is an economic growth model designed to enhance the efficiency of raw material use through the adoption of the 3R approach that translates into sharply reduced resource inputs and pollution discharges per unit of production. The circular economy approach focuses on the life-cycle of economy-environment interactions. It builds on the industrial ecology tradition which promotes the restructuring of industrial processes along the lines of ecosystems, whereby the waste of one manufacturer becomes the input of another."

Source: The World Bank (2009), *Developing a Circular Economy in China: Highlights and Recommendations*, pp. 3, 9 and 10, http://www-wds.worldbank.org/external/default/WDSContentServer/WDSP/IB/2009/07/15/000333037_20090715021249/Rendered/PDF/489170REPLACEM10BOX338934B01PUBLIC1.pdf, accessed July 31, 2013.

---

[21] DeJoy, D.M. (2005), Behavior Change Versus Culture Change: Divergent Approaches to Managing Workplace Safety, *Safety Science*, 43(2), p. 107.

In other words, the environmental dimension of the CSR imperative goes beyond the mere reduction of resource waste to become a strategic appraisal and build-up of the company's capacity to contribute to the circular economy model. In close association with the Chinese government, the World Bank clearly links such an approach to the concept of "green development" (Box 1.12).

Box 1.12. Green Development

"Green development is a pattern of development that decouples growth from heavy dependence on resource use, carbon emissions and environmental damage, and that promotes growth through the creation of new green product markets, technologies, investments, and changes in consumption and conservation behavior... Concerned that past and current economic growth patterns are environmentally unsustainable and that the environmental base needed to sustain economic prosperity may be irreversibly altered, the Chinese authorities proposed a new approach toward green development in the 12th Five Year Plan. The plan emphasizes continued rapid growth together with ambitious targets for energy efficiency, natural resource management, and environmental sustainability."

Source: The World Bank and the Development Research Center of the State Council of PRC (2012, p.39), China 2030: Building a Modern, Harmonious, and Creative High-Income Society, http://www.worldbank.org/en/news/2012/02/27/china-2030-executive-summary, accessed May 24, 2013.

1.4.4. Externalities and CSR

Another concept sometimes used when trying to understand and justify the rooting of CSR into corporate culture is one of *externalities* — defined as costs or benefits resulting from an activity or transaction that affect an non-involved third party, that is, factors having an impact on the consumption and production opportunities of others, while the price of the product does not take those externalities into account. As a result of externalities, there are differences between private returns or costs and the returns or costs to society as a whole. Water or air pollution resulting from industrial activity generates negative externalities. Conversely, a classical example of positive externality is provided by the pollination of crops operated by the bees kept by a beekeeper.

Usually, market decisions based on a series of short-term equilibria will not pay much attention to externalities, merely considered as "systemic noise" in the fast-moving economic environment, unless strong social anxiety (manifested by social unrest on environmental issues, for instance) or heavy economic penalties (health and environment costs related to nuclear accidents) create a sudden awareness of the consequences of such a situation. As a result, one of the biggest risks of so-called rational market decisions on such issues will be routinely based on a wrong assessment of the long-term payout (benefits less costs) for a whole community, and not only for a single economic agent.[22]

Economists have recognized that the negative payout associated with negative externalities constitute a form of market "blind spot". Mere market-based decision-making fails to yield efficient outcomes from a general welfare perspective. Positive externalities as well as negative ones are among the main reasons governments intervene in the economic sphere. The proposition that technical externalities require either government regulation or contractual bargaining was fiercely debated. Contractual bargaining would only work if property rights are well defined, if bargaining transaction costs are low, and provided no party knows more than the other about the transaction. Economic agents can solve the problems through mutually beneficial transactions: a landlord and a polluter could enter into a contract in which the landlord agrees to pay the polluter a certain amount of money in exchange for a specific reduction in the amount of pollution. Such contractual bargaining can be mutually beneficial. In all cases, the implementation of CSR by corporations is seen as a way of alleviating the effects of negative externalities with the heaviest social cost.

Though technically accurate, this approach does not fully do justice to the dynamics of CSR as sketched in the preceding paragraphs. One

---

[22] See for instance: Sen, A.K. (1977), Rational Fools: A Critique of the Behavioral Foundations of Economic Theory, *Philosophy & Public Affairs*, 6(4), pp. 317–344.

way of remedying its limits might be to stress the fact that CSR also encompasses a number of socially positive externalities. Increased levels of training and social awareness, with the associated effects in terms of productivity and societal cohesiveness, might constitute a good example of the positive externalities that the practice of CSR spontaneously generates. CSR is not motivated only by the necessity to remedy negative externalities; it aims at fostering and optimizing the positive externalities that business activity can and should generate.

CHAPTER TWO

The Legal, Professional and Social Framework

As we have already seen, the exercise of CSR presupposes compliance to the legal framework of a country. A legal framework applies to a range of issues: environmental protection, employers' rights, or safety norms. This framework, which may be open to juridical and prudential interpretation, also provides the company with references on the priorities and general principles devised by state authorities when it comes to the role of companies and businesses in the overall social development. Taken globally, laws and norms provide companies with an interpretative outlook through which they can assess how their social responsibility is conceived and monitored in a given national context. It is in this light that we recall here some legal provisions that influence the implementation of CSR in China. We will detail specific dispositions later in this study.

2.1. Laws and Regulations

The year 2007 can be seen as a watershed in the building of a consistent body of CSR regulations understood as entrusting specific duties and objectives to all companies operating in China. On that year, at the 17th Party Congress, the Chinese Communist Party stressed the importance of environmental conservation and the necessity to "put people first" in order to achieve a "balanced and sustainable development."[1] Later in the same year, China passed its first Labor Contract Law and started to promote CSR by passing local legislations

---

[1]Refer to Hu Jintao's Report at the 17th Party Congress, http://www.china.org. cn/english/congress/229611.htm, accessed July 31, 2013.

on environment protection and laborers' rights, following the directions of the central government. Nowadays, a large number of laws and guidelines determine the spirit and content of CSR-related policies in China. They comprise:

1. **The People's Republic of China's (PRC) Company Law (2005).**[2]
   "This Law is enacted in order to standardize the organization and behavior of companies, to protect the legitimate rights and interests of companies, shareholders and creditors, to maintain the socio-economic order and to promote the development of the socialist market economy." (Article 1)

2. **The PRC's Circular Economy Promotion Law (2008).**[3]
   "This Law is formulated for the purpose of facilitating a circular economy, raising resources utilization efficiency, protecting and improving the environment and realizing sustainable development." (Article 1)

3. **The PRC's Law on Work Safety (2002).**[4]
   "This Law is enacted for enhancing supervision and control over work safety, preventing accidents due to lack of work safety and keeping their occurrence at a lower level, ensuring the safety of people's lives and property and promoting the development of the economy." (Article 1)

---

[2] For the English translation, see: http://www.china.org.cn/china/Legislations Form2001-2010/2011-02/11/content_21898292.htm, accessed July 17, 2013. The Chinese version (中华人民共和国公司法) is available at: http://www.gov.cn/ziliao/flfg/2005-10/28/content_85478.htm, accessed July 17, 2013.

[3] For the English translation, see: http://www.bjreview.com.cn/document/txt/2008-12/04/content_168428.htm, accessed July 17, 2013. The Chinese version (中华人民共和国循环经济促进法) is available at: http://www.gov.cn/flfg/2008-08/29/content_1084355.htm, accessed July 17, 2013.

[4] For the English translation, see: http://english.gov.cn/laws/2005-10/08/content_75054.htm, accessed July 17, 2013. The Chinese version (中华人民共和国安全生产法) is available at: http://www.gov.cn/banshi/2005-08/05/content_20700.htm, accessed July 17, 2013.

4. **Guidelines for the State-Owned Enterprises Directly under the Central Government on Fulfilling Corporate Social Responsibilities (2007).**[5]

   "These Guidelines are proposed to comprehensively implement the spirit of the 17th Chinese Communist Party National Congress and the scientific outlook on development, and give the impetus to state-owned enterprises (SOEs) directly under the central government to earnestly fulfill CSR, so as to realize coordinated and sustainable development of enterprises, society and environment in all respects."

5. **Implementation Outline of the Harmonious Development Strategy for the 12th Five-Year Plan to the State-Owned Enterprises Directly under the Central Government (2011).**[6]

   "The implementation outline is proposed to comprehensively implement the spirit of the Communiqué of the 5th Plenum of the 17th Central Committee of the Chinese Communist Party and the session of the 5th Plenary Session of the 12th Five-Year Development Plan, and put into practice the 12th Five-Year Development Plan for SOEs directly under the central government, and to achieve the objective of helping SOEs become strong and excellent to accelerate the construction of world-class enterprises with international competitiveness."

6. **The Twelfth Five-Year Plan for National Economic and Social Development of the PRC (2011–2015).**[7]

   "We will confront increasing resource and environmental restrictions, thus crisis awareness should be enhanced. We will establish

---

[5] For the English translation, see: http://www.sasac.gov.cn/n2963340/n2964712/4891623.html, accessed July 17, 2013. The Chinese version (关于中央企业履行社会责任的指导意见) is available at: http://www.sasac.gov.cn/n1180/n1566/n259760/n264851/3621925.html, accessed July 17, 2013.

[6] The Chinese version is available at: http://www.sasac.gov.cn/n1180/n1566/n259760/n264836/14197866.html, accessed July 17, 2013.

[7] For the English translation, see: http://cbi.typepad.com/china_direct/2011/05/chinas-twelfth-five-new-plan-the-full-english-version.html, accessed July 17, 2013. The Chinese version (中华人民共和国国民经济和社会发展第十二个五年规划纲要) is available at: http://www.gov.cn/2011lh/content_1825838.htm, accessed July 17, 2013.

green and low-carbon development ideas and focus on energy conservation and emission reduction, improve incentives and constraint mechanisms, and stimulate the establishment of resource-saving and environmentally friendly production and consumption to strengthen sustainable development and improve ecological standards." (Part VI: Green development — Construct Energy Conservation and an Environmentally Friendly Society).

7. **Employment Promotion Law of the PRC (2007).**[8]

This law is intended to fight unemployment and prohibit job discrimination. Rather than providing specific rules, it sets out guidelines for governmental institutions at the local and national levels, regarding the support to individual businesses and small enterprises, the role of enterprises in financing vocational skills training and continuing education for their staff, the prohibition of discrimination against migrant workers, and the right of discriminated employees to lodge a lawsuit in a people's court.

8. **Labor Contract Laws of the PRC (2007).**[9]

"This Law is formulated to improve the labor contract system, to specify the rights and obligations of the parties to labor contracts, to protect the legitimate rights and interests of workers, and to build and develop harmonious and stable employment relationships." (Article 1)

9. **Social Insurance Law of the PRC (2010).**[10]

This law aims at improving the social security safety net for the whole population in China, mainly by making companies con-

---

[8]For the English translation, see: http://www.baliprocess.net/files/China/China_employment%20promotion%20law_2008-eng.pdf, accessed July 17, 2013. The Chinese version (中华人民共和国就业促进法) is available at: http://w1.mohrss.gov.cn/gb/zt/2007-08/30/content_197492.htm, accessed July 17, 2013.

[9]For the English translation, see: http://www.lehmanlaw.com/resource-centre/laws-and-regulations/labor/labor-contract-law-of-the-peoples-republic-of-china.html, accessed July 17, 2013. The Chinese version (中华人民共和国劳动合同法) is available at: http://www.gov.cn/flfg/2007-06/29/content_669394.htm, accessed July 17, 2013.

[10]For the English translation, see: http://www.grandwaylaw.com/en/newsdetail.asp?ProductID=351&CategoryID=25, accessed July 17, 2013. The Chinese version (中华人民共和国社会保险法) is available at: http://www.gov.cn/flfg/2010-10/28/content_1732964.htm, accessed July 17, 2013.

tribute to the social insurance system for their staff, and by reinforcing controls over social security funds management.

10. **The 12th Five-Year Plan for the Environmental Health Work of National Environmental Protection (2011).**[11]

"(1) Survey on environmental health issues; (2) Environmental health risk management; (3) Environmental health scientific research; (4) Capacity building on environmental health; and (5) Environmental health publicity and education." (Part IV Key Areas and Major Tasks).

11. **2011 Main Points of Pollution Prevention and Control Issued by Ministry of Environment Protection of PRC.**[12]

"The main points are proposed to comprehensively implement the scientific outlook on development and the spirit of the 4th Session of the 11th National People's Congress and the 4th Session of the 11th Chinese People's Political Consultative Conference National Committee, and to fulfill the tasks determined by the national environmental protection work conference."

12. **Guidance to Business Credit Building on the 12th Five-Year Period (2011).**[13]

"Social credit system is the cornerstone of the modern market economy system. Business credit building is an important part of the construction of social credit system, a fundamental project to establish a unified, open, competitive and orderly market system, and also the frontal strategy of regulating the market order. In order to enhance the guidance of business credit building during the 12th Five-Year period, establish a good business credit

---

[11] For the English translation, see: http://english.mep.gov.cn/Plans_Reports/12plan/201201/P020120110355818985016.pdf, accessed July 17, 2013. The Chinese version (国家环境保护"十二五"环境与健康工作规划) is available at: http://www.mep.gov.cn/gkml/hbb/bwj/201109/W020110926592540126412.pdf, accessed July 17, 2013.

[12] The Chinese version (2011年全国污染防治工作要点) is available at: http://www.mep.gov.cn/gkml/hbb/bgt/201104/t20110420_209460.htm, accessed July 17, 2013.

[13] The Chinese version (关于"十二五"期间加强商务领域信用建设的指导意见) is available at: http://finance.sina.com.cn/roll/20111114/104710811881.shtml, accessed July 17, 2013.

environment and promote the development of the business sector, we made the following guidance."

13. **Shanghai Municipal's Local Standards of CSR (2009).**[14]
    "The Standards stipulates the fundamental behaviors for the imple-
    mentation of social responsibility by the enterprise as well as the
    Corporate Social Responsibility Evaluation System. The Standards
    are applicable for the implementation and the evaluation of social
    responsibility for the enterprises carrying out production and oper-
    ation activities in Shanghai."

14. **Miscellaneous — CSR Guide to Chinese Industrial Enterprises
    and Industry Association (second version) (2011).**[15]
    This guide was released in association with 10 industrial federa-
    tions, including coal, machinery, iron and steel, petro-chemical,
    light industry, textile, construction materials, non-ferrous metals,
    power and minerals. It constitutes the basis under which the draft-
    ing of codes by individual federations is now engaged, with vary-
    ing degrees of interest and success.

Among other regulations worthy of attention, three are especially concerned with the environment, two of them presenting the
additional interest of having been enacted by local stock market
authorities:

— Measures on the disclosure of environmental information (for trial
  implementation) (环境信息公开办法(试行)) in May 2008.[16]

---

[14]For the English translation, see: http://csr.pudong.gov.cn/csr_bjz_csras/List/
list_0.htm, accessed July 17, 2013. The Chinese version (上海市企业社会责任地方
标准) is available at: http://csr.mofcom.gov.cn/aarticle/t/200905/20090506247049.
html, accessed July 17, 2013.

[15]This refers to 中国工业企业及工业协会社会责任指南 (第二版), which was issued
by the China Federation of Industrial Economics on April 17, 2011.

[16]The English version is available at: http://www.chinaenvironmentallaw.com/
wp-content/uploads/2008/04/environmental-information-disclosure.pdf,
accessed July 17, 2013. The Chinese version is available at: http://www.gov.cn/
flfg/2007-04/20/content_589673.htm, accessed July 17, 2013.

— Guidelines on the environmental information disclosure for the listed companies on the Shanghai stock market (上海证交所"上市公司环境信息披露指示") in May 2008.
— Guidelines on social responsibility for the listed companies on the Shenzhen stock market (深圳证交所"上市公司社会责任指引") in 2006.[17]

In Chapter 11, we will discuss the guidelines established by the Shanghai and Shenzhen stock markets. For now, suffice it to say that the specific content of the social responsibility annual report, as defined in Shanghai, must at least include the following: (a) promotion of social development, including staff health and safety protection, protection and support of the host community, product quality checks, etc.; (b) promotion of environmental and ecological development; and (c) promotion of sustainable economic development (including job opportunities and development for staff).

Note that the movement toward self-regulation by professional branches is still in its infancy. As already indicated, the *CSC9000T* of the China National Textile and Apparel Council (中国纺织工业协会) published in 2007 constitutes the first CSR standards created by a professional association in China.

2.2. From the Letter to the Spirit

A document of November 2012 authored by Jiang Xin, Deputy Secretary-General of the China Federation of Industrial Economics, illustrates the evolution of the Chinese authorities' agenda very well when it comes to CSR. Jiang Xin notes that CSR is one of the "kernel factor of the transformation of economic development", and that such a transformation in turn forces enterprises to actively seek "responsible ways of production and patterns of operation", and promotes a "Chinese CSR take" on this new feature and trend of development. He also stressed the attention paid by China to the localization of CSR sectors, standards, guidelines

---

[17]Analyses of the Shanghai and Shenzhen regulations are available at: http://www.world-exchanges.org/sustainability/m-6-7-1.php, accessed July 17, 2013.

and norms: "The China Textile Industry Federation advanced *CSC9000T*, local standards of CSR were advanced in Shanghai and Nanjing, and the National Standard Committee is probing to nationalize the standards of *ISO 26000*. Additionally, some central governmental departments have promulgated special policy documents to normalize and guide CSR. The State-Assets Supervision and Administration Commission of State Council promulgated the 'Guiding Opinion of Implementing Social Responsibility by Central Enterprises', 'Outlines for Implementing a Harmonious Development Strategy by Central Enterprises for the 12th Five-Year Period', and has started the study and drafting of the 'Direction of Management of Social Responsibility for Central Enterprises'; the Ministry of Commerce released the 'Direction of Social Responsibility for Overseas Contract Engineering Industries' to normalize overseas operation of enterprises; the National Attestation and Supervision Commission released the 'Guiding Opinions for Attestation Organizations to Implementing Social Responsibility'; and the Banking Supervision Commission released 'Opinions to Strengthen the Social Responsibility of Banks among Financial Organizations'."[18]

CSR policy-making is located mainly at the Ministry of Commerce (MOFCOM), which sees CSR as a major enabler for transforming the economic growth model. International cooperation plays a major role in the conceptual developments that prepare further regulation. The Sino–German Corporate Responsibility Project, initiated in 2007, or the Sino–Swedish project on CSR (started in 2008) both constitute examples of the global dialogue in which Chinese authorities and entrepreneurial actors have been gradually involved with.[19]

Here are some excerpts from one of the texts mentioned above. It offers principles that can be met in other CSR-related areas, and provides us with a good example of the spirit and objectives promoted by this entire body of legislation (Box 2.1).

---

[18]Jiang, X. (2012), The Development of Corporate Social Responsibility Under China's Economic Transformation, November 19, 2012, http://www.docstoc.com/docs/157186141/The-Development-Of-Corporate-Social-Responsibility-In-China, accessed July 31, 2013.

[19]See Muhle, U. (2010), *The Politics of Corporate Social Responsibility, The Rise of a Global Business Norm*, Frankfurt: Campus Verlag, pp. 204–206.

Box 2.1 CSR, Environmental Health and National Policies

— "Put prevention first and implement comprehensive prevention and control. Based on the policy and concept of prevention first, we will focus on strengthening the management of environmental health risks, deepen scientific research, keep improving relevant policies and measures, adopt multiple approaches and measures including laws, administration and economic policy in a comprehensive way to improve the health risk prevention level and achieve source control."

— "Provide a solid foundation and make a comprehensive arrangement. We should focus on basic surveys and studies, identify environmental health issues and understand the development trend. In view of how characteristics of environmental health issues in different areas differ between city and countryside, we should make appropriate arrangements with classified guidance based on the local conditions."

— "Strengthen cooperation and ensure effective implementation. Targeting key issues, we will strengthen the coordination, communication and cooperation with the relevant departments of the Ministry of Health and various departments within the Ministry of Environmental Protection, develop scientific and appropriate policy measures, make careful arrangements, ensure effective implementation of plans and strive for breakthrough in key issues."

Source: The 12th Five-Year Plan for the Environmental Health Work of National Environmental Protection, *The PRC's Ministry of Environmental Protection*, September 21, 2011, http://english.mep.gov.cn/Plans_Reports/12plan/201201/P020120110 355818985016.pdf, accessed July 17, 2013.

Later in this book, we will deal with regulations inspired by similar principles applying to minimum wage, financial transparency and work safety, among others. Taken together, they demonstrate that China's legal framework is evolving into a body of regulations that strives to: (a) ensure safety for employees, neighboring communities, consumers and the environment; (b) promote transparency in the management decision process, in financial and business transactions, and in contract allocation; (c) enhance mechanisms and business practices conducive to a circular economy; and (d) foster workers' and consumers' awareness, power-sharing and training. Even if both the legal framework and its implementation are obviously in need of improvements, the overall direction is clear (see Box 2.2) and can only inspire the adoption of management strategies followed by all companies, whether Chinese or international.

Striking a note of caution, some analysts consider that the development of a specific body of CSR-related regulations in China as one of the factor that promotes an "utilitarian" approach to CSR worldwide: "CSR has now emerged as a strategic way of managing a company by anticipating the changes in consumer taste and future social and environmental regulations, building workers' creative motivation, and preventing the company's reputation (and, by extension, its shareholder value) from being damaged. It gives responsible companies a comparative advantage ... This idea has been popular, especially in certain emerging countries. In China, the 'Guidelines to the State-Owned Enterprises Directly Under the Central Government on Fulfilling Corporate Social Responsibilities' (promulgated in 2010 by the state) have eight methodological principles, including constantly improving the ability to make sustainable profits by advocating scientific and democratic decision making, improving product quality and service to protect consumer interests (only in this way can companies establish a good image), and promoting independent innovation and technological advancement by increasing investment in research and

---

Box 2.2 The Rise of CSR in China

"China's Corporate Law was amended in 2005, including for the first time a CSR provision. In 2007 and 2008, several regulations on CSR were issued by the Chinese central and local authorities to promote voluntary CSR initiatives, especially in the state-owned sector and among publicly listed and export-oriented companies. The Wenchuan earthquake, in 2008, accelerated the Chinese corporations' move toward philanthropy and social responsibility: corporate donations in the country soared to 107 billion yuan (or 16 billion dollars), three times their level in the previous year."

Source: Yu, X. (2011), Social Enterprise in China: Driving Forces, Development Patterns and Legal Framework, *Social Enterprise Journal*, 7(1), p. 16.

development. In 2007, the China Social Compliance (CSC) 9000 for the Textile and Apparel Industry was designed to prepare for the industry's necessary shift toward production sectors that generate the highest value added. It explains to manufacturers how to stop using their archaic management methods and develop employees' initiative in the areas of responsibility and training, which are sources of productivity gains."[20]

Contrary to the conclusions above, we think that such an approach summarizes neither the whole of the letter nor the spirit of China's body of legal stipulations on CSR. However, it remains true that the modernization of China's productive sector and the adoption of internationally recognized CSR regulations are, in the mind of the legislator, two closely interrelated topics. This is actually to be considered as a positive trend, as "modernization" in this case is not only about the adoption of technical standards and ways of proceedings: it diversifies the yardstick of entrepreneurial success by enlarging the criteria through which to appreciate its extent and nature.

2.3. Development of CSR among Chinese Entrepreneurs

In the next three chapters we will come back to the question of the integration of CSR within Chinese cultural resources and contemporary Chinese entrepreneurial outlook. As a preliminary step, let us first recall a few facts about the development of CSR-related concerns and topics within the Chinese entrepreneurial world.

When the notion of CSR initially appeared in China in the course of the 1990s, it was met with skepticism, not only among entrepreneurs but also among many economists, some arguing that this was a typically Western notion that could potentially be used for reining in China's path

---

[20]Doucin, M. (2011), Corporate Social Responsibility: Private Self-Regulation is Not Enough, *Global Corporate Governance Forum*, 24, http://www-wds.worldbank. org/external/default/WDSContentServer/WDSP/IB/2011/12/22/000386194_2 0111222042002/Rendered/PDF/661030BRI0Box365730B00PUBLIC00PSO0240 CSR.pdf, accessed July 17, 2013.

to prosperity.[21,22] Things started to change when growing concerns gradually emerged about the side effects of the developmental process.[23] *Nanfang Zhoumou (Southern Weekend)*, a leading publication in China, started to rank the CSR performance of Chinese companies and the world's Top 500 international companies operating in China in 2006. According to its 2006 report, large global companies were below par in fulfilling their social responsibilities, threatening China's economic and social security, exploiting unfair advantages, and lowering their environmental, labor, and ethical standards when operating in China. State-owned Chinese companies were also criticized for their inadequate contribution to different social causes and their questionable environmental practices. The report went on to state that privately owned Chinese companies have made significantly larger donations to public philanthropy than global companies and state-owned Chinese companies.[24] This critical approach to CSR practices coincided with a number of initiatives, such as the launch of the CSR China Forum, held for the first time in Beijing in 2005. Rising inequalities, major ecological accidents, well-publicized cases of corruption, the pledge of the migrant workers and other issues were not only challenging some tenets of China's course of development, they were igniting a debate about the social impact of foreign and national companies in China and, specifically, the entrepreneur as a role model. The attention paid to philanthropy was typical of the social debate on CSR at this stage: voluntary contributions of companies were receiving more attention than a

---

[21] Background provided by: Tang, L. & H. Li (2009), Corporate Social Responsibility Communication of Chinese and Global Corporations in China, *Public Relations Review*, 35(3), pp. 199–212.

[22] Among the first works in Chinese dedicated to CSR, see Liu, J. (1999), *The Firm's Social Responsibility (Gongsi de shehui zeren)*, Beijing: Law Press. (刘俊海,《公司的社会责任》,法律出版社1999年.)

[23] See for instance Li, Y. & C. Gong (2009), Research on Developments of CSR Theory in China (*Guonei qiye shehuizeren lilun yanjiu xinjinzhan*), *Journal of Xi'andianzi kexue University* (Social Sciences Edition), 19(1). (黎友焕、龚成威,《国内企业社会责任理论研究新进展》,西安电子科学大学报（社会科学版）, 2009年1月, 第19卷第一期, http://www.gdcsr.org.cn/Article/1354.html, accessed July 31, 2013.)

[24] Based on an analysis of the report and related materials in Tang & Li (2009).

systemic approach to their impact on society and the environment. Professional forums, press events (see the "CSR Reputation Management" event held by *China Newsweek*), publications such as the *China CSR* (produced in Hong Kong), academic initiatives (Center for Responsible Leadership at CEIBS, Shanghai) and public or professional appraisal of Chinese firms' CSR performances would rapidly enlarge the terms of the discussion.[25] Nowadays, CSR concepts and practices are fairly well known and discussed among the new generation of Chinese entrepreneurs, even when their relevance to the national context and their feasibility still come under questioning.[26]

2.4. CSR and Civil Society

It certainly would be impossible to implement CSR in China without the existence of a civil society striving toward accrued personal responsibility and sense of collective empowerment. There is much soul-searching on internet forums about the way many Chinese citizens still shy away from the basic duties related to belonging to communities that go beyond the limits of one's nuclear family. These debates should not hide the fact that NGOs and other organizations have been recently flourishing in China. They follow a model different from the one pursued in the West, often based on cooperation between the local government and the group of citizens interested in helping migrant workers in their education, or in environmental protection for instance: the structuring of civil society takes shape through the participation of civil organizations in the mechanisms established by the

---

[25] Cf. Chen, J., Q. Huang, & H. Peng (2011), *Research Report on CSR in China (Zhongguo qiye shehuizeren yanjiu baogao)*, Beijing: Social Sciences Literature Press. (陈佳贵、黄群慧、彭华岗等共同主编,《中国企业社会责任研究报告（2011）》, 北京社会科学文献出版社, 2011年.)

[26] Among other titles cited in the Chinese bibliography at the end of this book, see for instance Shu, L. (2010), Empirical Research on Awareness and Practice of CSR in Chinese Private Enterprises (*Minying qiye shehuizeren renzhi yu shijian de diaocha yanjiu*), *Soft Science (Ruankexue)*, 24(10), pp. 97–102. (疏礼兵,《民营企业社会责任认知与实践的调查研究》, 软科学2010年10期, 97–102页, http://www.cqvip.com/Read/Read.aspx?id=35638359.)

state, and this participation ultimately fosters their empowerment.[27] The active collaboration of a growing number of young Chinese to associations framing a renewed civil society also constitutes the fertile ground on which CSR finds its promoters and actors.[28,29,30] However, it should also be noted that the interest expressed by many young Chinese toward philanthropic organizations is partly fostered by rising tensions on the marketplace, which make them look for alternative job opportunities.

As a matter of fact, civil and charitable associations are anchored into Chinese history. Traditionally, Confucian lineages were providing funds for public work and education. For a long time, Buddhist lay associations had been helping the poor and organizing disaster relief. Devotees' associations typical of popular religion were structured as networks of solidarity. After the introduction of Christianity in China, the new religion made itself known through hospitals, orphanages and schools. The revival of civil society happening in China from the 1980s on could not go without a new focus on charitable and social works. For sure, foundations and other non-profit organizations (NPOs) still need to go through a complex and harrowing process before approval (or rejection), and are controlled as to their goals, organization model and finances. Besides this, the lack of training and available personnel constitutes a severe limitation for associations desirous to foster collective initiatives. Still, NGOs have been better able to work with local governments now. Academics

---

[27]Cf. Yu, J., H. Jiang & J. Zhou (2008), *Chinese Civil Society Growing Through Participation: Research on the Chamber of Commerce of Wenzhou (Zai canyu zhong chengzhang de zhongguo gongmin shehui: Ji yu zhejiang wenzhou shanghui de yanjiu)*, Hangzhou: Zhejiang University Press, 2008. (郁建兴、江华、周俊,《在参与中成长的中国公民社会：基于浙江温州商会的研究》, 浙江大学出版社 2008年.)

[28]See for instance Kang, X. & H. Han (2007), Administrative Absorption of Society: A Further Probe into the State-Society Relationship in Mainland China, *Social Sciences in China*, 28(2), pp. 116–128.

[29]Yu J. & S. Wang (2011), The Applicability of the Governance Theory in China, *Fudan Journal of the Humanities and Social Sciences*, 4(1), pp. 22–36.

[30]Kang, X. & H. Han (2008), Graduated Controls: The State-Society Relationship in Contemporary China, *Modern China*, 34(1), pp. 36–55.

and entrepreneurs have been providing expertise and funding.[31] The government supports the initiatives that come with obvious social benefits. The phenomenon is quite clear in the metropolises of the East Coast. All people involved in these efforts underline the legal and practical difficulties they meet with, but they also see the development of such services as vital for social progress. Today, as it becomes more segmented, the Chinese society is calling for volunteers ready to reach out to people marginalized or isolated, and for close-knit networks working at the ground level. The core issue is not about "how much" NPOs and charities can contribute to China's society, and it is certainly not about them substituting for state organizations, as the latter functions according to a well-designed model. It is about the inventiveness and capacity to "feel" social and personal needs not yet answered — inventiveness and flair that characterize local initiatives. It is about the quality of care and creativity that local communities are ready to contribute. It is also about their capacity to think and collaborate together, thus contributing to social solidarity and cohesiveness. And, finally, the evolution of China's civil society also influences the participation of the country in world affairs.[32]

Still, the building-up of a civil society meets with difficulties that are not so different from the ones encountered when trying to foster and implement CSR:

— It is sometimes hard to isolate the institutions and instruments through which civil society expresses its true self. Many associations in China, including those calling themselves NGOs, are established by the government or have significant government backing. Many of the more than 400,000 associations registered with the Ministry of Civil Affairs (MCA) are in practice quasi-governmental bodies. MCA regulations distinguish between

---

[31]Cf. Gan, M. (2011), Traditional Religious Culture and Charitable Activities of Chinese Entrepreneurs (*Chuantong zongjiao wenhua yu zhongguo qiye cishan shiye*), *World Religious Cultures (Shijie zongjiao wenhua)*, 2, pp. 1–5. (干满堂,《传统宗教化与中国企业慈善事业》, 世界宗教文化2011年第二期, 1–5页。)

[32]Cf. Xu, G. (2011), Global Governance: The Rise of Global Civil Society and China, *Fudan Journal of the Humanities and Social Sciences*, 4(1), pp. 1–21.

three categories of NGOs: social organizations (*shetuan*); private non-enterprise units (*minban feiqiye*); and foundations (*jijinhui*). Government-backed NGOs make up a majority of *shetuan* and foundations, and a substantial, though smaller, percentage of *minfei* MCA regulations prohibit NGOs from establishing branch organizations in other areas, and also from engaging in public fundraising. Only a few government-based NGOs such as the China Red Cross Society and China Charity Federation are authorized to raise money publicly for disaster relief.[33]

— However, the administrative landscape in which NGOs operate is presently undergoing major transformations. Since 2011, 19 provinces have been encouraged to launch pilot programs for direct registration. As part of the experimental policy, Guangdong province saw 4,200 NGOs registered between July and December 2012. According to a plan sketched by the State Council in March 2013, by the end of the same year new regulations will be unveiled, establishing four categories of NGOs — industrial associations, charities, community services and organizations dedicated to promoting science and technology — and allowing for direct registration with civil affairs authorities, abandoning pre-examination and approval by other regulators. Additional rules will permit overseas NGOs to set up branches. MCA estimated that there were more than 490,000 NGOs in Mainland China at the end of 2012, and that at least one million NGOs either operated without legal identities or had to register as companies under the current registration policy.[34] 400,000 of these unregistered NGOs may be dedicated to senior residents. The direct registration policy would be primarily aimed at making these NGOs better service providers.[35] The shift is part of a general policy encouraging both associations and businesses to be the main providers of social services.

---

[33]Cf. Shieh, S. & G. Deng (2011), Emerging Civil Society: The Impact of the 2008 Sichuan Earthquake on Grass-roots Associations in China, *The China Journal*, 65 (January), pp. 183–184.

[34]A research institute at Tsinghua University even estimates that three million informal organizations remain unregistered. Cf. Tang, Y. and D. He (2013), Spring in the air for NGOs?, *China Daily*, April 17, 2013, http://www.chinadaily.com.cn/2013-04/17/content_16413466.htm, accessed July 17, 2013.

[35]New Rules for NGOs to Improve Operations, *China Daily*, April 17, 2013, http://www.chinadaily.com.cn/china/2013-04/17/content_16413055.htm, accessed July 17, 2013.

— Examining the trends emerging after the efforts that followed the Sichuan earthquake of May 2008, Jessica Teets observes: "Civil society groups and international capacity-building organizations must focus on building human resources and professional skill levels. Groups need to build capacity specifically in transparent auditing processes and in professional management skills, especially project management ... In order to increase trust levels of civil society, groups must publicize their activities and work processes. Many people in the society and government do not understand how these groups conduct projects or what their goals are in society. In addition to this ignorance, many also distrust groups that are viewed as foreign proxies. Groups need to learn how to use online platforms and media to broadcast their existence and activities in order to increase the knowledge of and trust in them, similar to the platforms maintained by environmental groups. They often do not advertise their activities for fear of the government increasing monitoring; however, this publicity is necessary to increase exposure, legitimacy and trust."[36]

These traits are parallel to the ones observed when discussing the potential for accrued transparency and accountability of companies, big or small. Presumably, individuals having nurtured the capabilities linked to such institutional improvements will be precious recruits for both the for-profit and not-for-profit sectors. Ultimately, the development of civil organizations exhibiting initiative, transparency and professionalism in their social endeavors, on the one hand, and the growth of CSR cultural and human resources within corporations, on the other, prove to be two interrelated phenomena.

---

[36] Teets, J. (2009), Post-Earthquake Relief and Reconstruction Efforts: The Emergence of Civil Society in China?, *The China Quarterly*, 198(June), p. 345.

CHAPTER THREE

Chinese Cultural Resources Relevant to CSR

As we have already noted, CSR is anchored into cultural values and traditions that inspire corporate ways of proceeding — and these ways of proceeding are sometimes hard to translate from one national environment to another. This may create distress for managers and employees alike, as misunderstandings and distrust are then prone to arise. However, striving for mutual awareness of one another's cultural background and values helps the protagonists to forge new languages and modes of communication through which they can elaborate codes of cooperation and conduct. Cultural communication is of particular importance for putting into application CSR-related issues and policies, as business in China involves actors coming from very different backgrounds. Furthermore, China's practices and regulations themselves reflect the cross-breeding and globalization process through which the Chinese economy and society have been evolving during the last three decades or so.

We aim here at interpreting Chinese cultural resources in such a way as to illustrate how they can potentially nurture CSR values and foster their implementation. It has been said and written that the Chinese culture is alien to the values often identified as the pillars of socially responsible behavior: China's cultural heritage, it has been argued, might foster profitable business, but not responsible business. We believe such a view to be based on a stultified understanding of what Chinese cultural resources are about. We will try to show that these resources are much more varied and prone to positive interpretation than it is often realized. If concepts such as trust, leadership, accountability or stewardship are interpreted and understood differently in different contexts, the tenets to which they refer can be fostered on the basis of different cultural resources. Indeed, China is rich in traditions and references conducive to the best contemporary CSR practices. They just need to be extolled and revived.

3.1. CSR and Chinese Thought

Let us note first that Chinese cultural and wisdom traditions are often accounted for and summarized in a way that does not do justice to historical evidences or even to mere intellectual probity. Chinese traditions are plural; in the course of history, acrimonious debates have opposed the various schools of spirituality, philosophy and wisdom that jointly constitute China's intellectual landscape.[1] Confucianism, Taoism and Buddhism were divided among a variety of schools. Furthermore, while several of these schools have been dealing with the practicalities of state and family government, their aims and scopes were loftier and larger: generally speaking, Chinese wisdom has considered nature, the supernatural, the human body and social communities as governed by cosmic laws that, from one realm to another, are analogically similar — though Chinese thinkers differed among themselves as to what these laws were supposed to be. Chinese thought cannot (and should not) be summarized into a set of ready-to-made advices and rules of conduct: its favorite channel of expression was storytelling and conversations, and stories are susceptible to being interpreted in diverse ways, keeping their ultimate meaning open. *Stories and conversations kept Chinese traditions sensitive to the ambiguities of concrete situations, and nurtured a sense of openness and adaptability* (see Box 3.1 for more details).

Chinese culture and wisdom are not to be reduced to a set of principles to be blindly followed. They were and are still developed throughout the *conversation* that men and women perpetually lead and renew for assessing the world they live in and how to react to the changes that affect it. Consequently, encapsulating Chinese wisdom into a fixed set of management principles that smart entrepreneurs

---

[1]See Vermander, B. (2011), Chinese Wisdom, Management Practices and the Humanities, *Journal of Management Development*, 30(7/8), pp. 697–708.

Box 3.1 The Conversational Tradition in Chinese Thought

"It is in the discussion of particular facts of human existence that Confucius, and after him the philosophers in the conversational tradition, produce their particular insights, short, incisive stabs, into the human condition. To organize his insights into a system would be to devitalize them; therefore his disciples have tried to keep them as close to their original, particular, concrete form as possible and have preserved these conversations or sayings on different particular occasions. The same can be said for all the later philosophers in the conversational tradition. And the fact that this can be said for later philosophers is important: it shows that the form of the conversations is not an archaism, the fumbling attempt of the first Chinese philosophers to put their ideas, pell-mell, into some sort of order, but is an integral part of Confucian thought, and, indeed, an important clue to the character of Chinese thought in general. "

Source: Holzman, D. (1956), The Conversational Tradition in Chinese Philosophy, *Philosophy East and West*, 6(3), p. 226.

would be well advised to follow is a most misleading intellectual endeavor — unfortunately, one that has generated a booming business, as China's ascent has translated into a frantic quest for the cultural roots that might justify and nurture such unprecedented transformation.

The *historical* character of Chinese entrepreneurial wisdom is the first element through which to qualify its aptitude at generating CSR-related values and practices. Practical inquiries on the Chinese entrepreneurial spirit might be best conducted through the study of cities and communities governed by a local ethos, as was — and somehow still is — the case in Hangzhou, Suzhou or Wenzhou, for instance.[2,3] Likewise, *geography* might be after all as relevant as culture when trying

---

[2] Skinner, G.W. (1977) (ed.), *The City in Late Imperial China*. Stanford: Stanford University Press.

[3] Cooke, J.L. (ed.) (1993), *Cities of Jiangnan in Late Imperial China*, New York: Suny Press.

to account for China's mode of development: the Yangzi watershed of eastern China has served over the past 500 hundred years as the hotbed of economic development. A third of China's waterways are located in Jiangsu, Shanghai and Zhejiang, astride the mouth of the Yangzi. Together with its navigable tributaries, the Yangzi network extends to 18,000 km. During the imperial time, transport by inland waterways was 30 to 40 percent cheaper than transport by land and significantly less subject to breakage and loss.[4] Linked together by the imposing Yangzi water system, merchants' and entrepreneurs' communities had been developing a form of capitalism that was not widely different from the one taking shape in the Rhine valley: solidarity, guild culture, philanthropic endeavors, responsibility toward the rich but fragile aquatic environment that was making the economy strive — those were values shared both on the Rhine and on the Yangtze. Stating such basic facts suggests that "entrepreneurial wisdom" might be at the same time more dependent on physical and historical factors, and more universal in scope than usually recognized, and that, consequently, the discourse on "cultural uniqueness" may suffer from fatal flaws.

Chinese wisdom can be "wisely" appreciated only if we refrain from *instrumentalizing* its inspiration and vision (i.e not to reduce it to a set of easily applicable rules), and if we give due consideration to its complexity, fluidity and internal plurality. An example can be given by looking at a basic Confucian tenet, the one of "filial piety" *(xiao 孝)*. It finds its place in the management literature: Filial piety is considered as a recipe for success (it empowers the entrepreneur, and ensures successful family businesses and harmonious employer-employee relationships); it is also seen as detrimental to corporate responsibility (it supposedly deprives employees of the faculty to analyze, decide and raise objections, it centers the company on itself rather than on its environment).

The traditional expressions of filial piety have been ranted at, and one has come to see in it a simple formalism or an impediment to personal freedom. These criticisms are not unfounded. But, taken at its

---

[4]Elvin, M. (1973), *The Pattern of the Chinese Past*, Stanford: Stanford University Press, pp. 131–145.

root, filial piety opens up a space for wisdom and responsibility, both communal and individual. The starting point of Confucius is very simple: who loves his father does not want to make him grieve, and will thus abstain from committing any crime. The root of virtuous conduct is the love and respect for one's parents that is inscribed into one's nature and that at the same time needs to be nurtured through rites and education.[5] But this leads us further: "When the dead are honored, and the memory of the ancestors is alive, the strength of a people reaches its fullness."[6] In other words, filial piety makes us return to our origins, it makes us connect with the ancestors thanks to whom we are able to experience the emergence of life, the mystery of birth and growth — and then it makes us participants in this process of growth. Filial piety requires us to become anchored into the soil of life so as to undergo and experience the fullness of growth in all things human. *True filial piety even includes the duty to disobey.* A textbook case is discussed by Mencius when speaking about Shun, one of the mythical emperors of ancient times: how to practice filial piety when you have the misfortune of having a degenerated father? Shun does not inform his father of his marriage, fearing that his father, by prohibiting it, would sin against himself by breaking the principle of continuation of generations.[7] This constitutes true obedience, which is thus to be distinguished from mere formal docility.

The theme of the father-son relationship leads one to ruminate on beginnings and origins: "A tree you can barely get your arms around grows from a tiny shoot. A nine-story tower begins as a heap of earth. A thousand-mile journey begins under your feet."[8] Chinese wisdom originates from the simple act of sitting on the edge of one of the rivers that criss-cross central China and observing the interplay between the

---

[5]See *Analects*, II, 5 to II, 8.

[6]See *Analects*, I, 9.

[7]"If Shun had told his parents, he would not have married. A man and woman living together is a great bound of humankind. If he'd told his parents, he would have forsaken that great bound, and that would have been an act of hatred toward his parents. That's why he did not tell them." (*Mencius*, V.A.2; see also IV.A.26.)

[8]*Laozi*, Chapter 64.

water and the plants that grow on the banks — these plants, like life, are soft and weak, while death goes always with the hard and the rigid. Laozi mentioned: "In the world, nothing is supple and weak in relation to water. Yet of those things which attack the firm and unyielding, nothing is able to do better."[9] It was Mencius who said: "There's an art to seeing water."[10] Therefore, "the one who is filled with virtue is comparable to a baby" Laozi says, because such a person has endorsed the sweetness, the fragility of life.[11] Her bones are weak, her sinews feeble, but with power she grabs.

In the Taoist tradition, the wise person must be as cautious as "the one crossing a lake in winter"[12] for it is sometimes wisdom that breaks down, "as ice gives way to spring".[13] Chinese wisdom locates itself just on this juncture, on this passage between the solid and the fluid, at this moment when one may lose one's footing — and yet one has to continue. The prevalence of aquatic metaphors in its stories and rhetoric suggests that it does not pretend to have a "bottom" — a core teaching — that it is fluid and bottomless. The surrounding culture has often betrayed, distorted or contradicted such original wisdom, but it still operates as a paradoxical teaching that finds in the text the spirit what overflows its letter on all sides — and it is after all wisdom itself that declares: "Renounce your sageness and discard your wisdom."[14]

More generally, even interpretations of the Confucian ethics that are more conservative than the one sketched here emphasize the fact that Confucianism promotes openness to the wider community, rather than encouraging people to restrict oneself to a narrowly defined set of loyalties (see Box 3.2).

3.1.1. *Buddhist resources for CSR*

Buddhism provides China with another set of cultural resources that possesses much significance for the development of an endogenous

---

[9] *Laozi*, Chapter 78.
[10] *Mencius*, 7A, 24.
[11] *Laozi*, Chapter 55.
[12] *Laozi*, Chapter 15.
[13] *Ibid.*
[14] *Laozi*, Chapter 19.

Box 3.2 Confucian Ethics

"Traditional Confucianism focuses on self-cultivation through the exercise of the five virtues: benevolence (*Ren*) within the wider society; respecting those for whom respect is required by the relationship of righteousness (*Yi*); appreciating ritual forms (*Li*) of a particular place and time, and knowing how to express oneself properly in interactions with others; obtaining wisdom of knowing what is right and wrong (*Zhi*); and being faithful (*Xin*). The importance of Confucian principles for organizations extends beyond employees to relationships with the wider community that should be based upon benevolence, honor and structure with others in society."

Source: Zhao, L. & J. Roper (2011), A Confucian Approach to Well-being and Social Capital Development, *Journal of Management Development*, 30(7/8), p. 743.

CSR approach. Present in China for the two last millennia, the Buddha's teachings have been an inspiration for the philanthropic efforts deployed by generations of Chinese officials and entrepreneurs. The poet and statesman Su Dongpo (1036–1101) invokes Buddhist principles when he asks a local magistrate to work relentlessly against the state of misery that is leading to widespread infanticide in the area, adding: "When I was serving at Mizhou, there was a famine year and many parents were forced to abandon their children. I was able to collect funds and obtain several thousand bushels of rice for the purpose of feeding orphans. Every family that took care of one child was given six bushels of rice per month."[15] At the same time, Buddhism in its Chinese garb has been often criticized for putting an excessive emphasis on the acquisition of "merits" (*gongde*) through donations to temples or charities, without leading powerful or wealthy individuals to look at the roots of their decisions and behaviors. Till today, many Chinese entrepreneurs conceive of the donations they make as a way to ensure that their karmas are favorable, without examining their personal or professional practices. It remains true that

---

[15]Su, D. (2008), *Selected Poems and Prose*, Lin Yutang Chinese-English Bilingual Edition, Taipei: Cheng Chung, pp. 68–69.

their (important) financial contributions do shape the complex and ever-evolving relationship between the state, corporations and non-governmental organizations (NGOs), even if their motives seem to be more inspired by social and religious conservatism than by a proactive approach to their entrepreneurial responsibilities.[16,17]

At the same time, the globalization of Buddhism and the increased sophistication of the doctrine preached to well-educated individuals in urban settings give renewed relevance to Buddhism's influence on CSR practices. The following passage may sound rather theoretical, but the stress it puts on the overcoming of the self constitutes indeed a *leitmotiv*[18] among educated Chinese Buddhists. Similar approaches have received more and more attention among Buddhist followers of social standing: "Avoiding harm and doing good are necessary for CSR, yet insufficient to end suffering... A more meaningful model of CSR lies in a critical condition to make it work — detachment from self. The Noble Truths suggest that suffering can be eliminated at the cause. Dependent origination then contributes a greater depth to the root cause of suffering — starting at the self of an individual. According to the law of conditionality, the voiding of 'me and mine' then eliminates attachment to the self and cravings for sensual pleasure from possession. Without attachment and cravings, there is no ambition for status, nor the need for over-consumption of materials. Once ambition and consumption excess are eliminated, there is no reason to maximize profitability or productivity. When material wealth and production is no longer a motivation, there is no cause for excessive exploitation of resources. No excessive resource consumption by some means no grounds for lack of access to essential consumption and adverse impacts, including waste and pollution, to others. When extremism created by the self and attachment is ceased by moderation from no attachment to

---

[16]See Laliberte, A., K. Wu & D. Palmer (2011), Social Services, Philanthropy and Religion in Chinese Society, in D. Palmer, G. Shive & P. Wickeri (eds.), *Chinese Religious Life*, Oxford University Press, 2011, pp. 139–154.
[17]Laliberte, A. (2009), *Entre désécularisation et resacralisation: Bouddhistes laïcs, temples et organisations philanthropiques en Chine*, Social Compass, 56(3), pp. 345–361.
[18]From the german word meaning "guiding motive".

obsession of 'me and mine', suffering can be eliminated... Collectively, the smaller the 'self' of an individual, the more beautiful the future of the whole world."[19]

Additionally, Buddhism constitutes a cultural and spiritual common ground for East Asian nations and cultures. The mobilization of its resources for nurturing CSR values and practices further anchors China and Chinese entrepreneurs into their regional environment.

What does such a line of interpretation imply when trying to approach and nurture corporate responsibility in Chinese context?

— First, there are ways to read and appreciate Chinese cultural resources, in their flexibility and diversity, which are conducive of creative and responsible corporate behaviors. Traditions should not be summarized by a few stock sentences supposedly encapsulating their nutshells. They are evolving, and are to be understood as historical products always subject to reinterpretation.

— Chinese traditions are now part of a global wisdom heritage; entrepreneurs can mobilize their lessons and the attitudes they foster for adapting and enriching corporate cultures with strategies that are both effective and socially responsible — in China and elsewhere.

— Chinese thinkers have seen traditional values, such as respect for the elders or filial piety, as nourishing a sense of discernment and personal responsibility; these values foster chains of solidarity, the meaningful maintenance of which each individual was responsible for.

— Wisdom was linked to a deep respect for the natural environment and for the sometimes paradoxical lessons it offers to the observer, among them a sense of caution and fluidity that discards reckless behaviors while predisposing people to perpetually adapt to change. These are certainly attitudes precious for the nurturing of a corporate culture focused on sustainability and sense of responsibility.

---

[19]Kraisornsuthasinee, S. (2012), CSR Through the Heart of the Bodhi Tree, *Social Responsibility Journal*, 8(2), pp. 186–198.

3.2. CSR as Practical Wisdom

The study of Chinese cultural resources has implications for our over-all understanding of CSR: it may help us to consider CSR as anchored into forms of *practical wisdom* that have flourished within different cultures and contexts. Social actors make use of practical wisdom for patterning their behaviors, reaching appropriate decisions and following the optimal course of action. We may consider the "wisdom systems" that govern the practical knowledge mastered by these actors as *looms*, allowing one to develop ever-evolving weaving patterns. Wisdom cannot just be *stored*: only through the action of the weaver can it be *shaped* and brought into life.

The Greek term generally in use for speaking of "practical wisdom" is *phrônesis*: "Two key elements figure in the acquisition and exercise of *phrônesis*: knowledge of the 'first principles' of praxis, the final ends or causes of human action; and knowledge about means to attaining these ends, which rests on excellence in deliberating."[20] The concept has been applied to Japanese companies' ways of proceeding, and then generalized to collaborative managerial strategies: "A company has to know what is 'good' (ideal), and make judgments in particular situations (practice) to realize such goodness. Such phronetic capability has to be shared collectively with organizational members, not just by one phronetic leader, in order for strategies to be implemented. Building such organizational phronesis helps a firm become a resilient organization which can proactively deal with any environmental changes to realize its idealistic vision."[21]

The reference to Japanese companies' ways of proceeding already shows that the concept of *phrônesis* has equivalents in Asian thought: in Classical Chinese, the character *zhi* (智) points toward, a kind of knowledge rooted in the heart's natural light on the one hand, and an innate talent to elaborate "stratagems" on the other. It is interesting to

---

[20]Johnstone, C.L. (2009), *Listening to the Logos: Speech and the Coming of Wisdom in Ancient Greece*, Columbia: University of South Carolina Press, p. 207.

[21]Nonaka, I. & R. Toyama (2007), Strategic Management as Distributed Practical Wisdom, *Industrial and Corporate Change*, 16(3), p. 391.

note that one of the most famous sentences in the *Analects*[22] of Confucius says that "the wise man" (*zhizhe* 智者) takes pleasure in contemplating the water, while the "good man" (*renzhe* 仁者) enjoys watching the mountain. There is no clear-cut opposition between the two attitudes; rather "wisdom" and "goodness" (or "humaneness") seem to complement each other, as the water and the mountain collectively compose a landscape that contents the eye and the heart. However, water provides one with a metaphor for wisdom because of its ability to adapt, through its twists and turns, to concrete situations, while the mountains reveal the immutable goodness of a constant heart. One may note in passing that, in the same sentence of the *Analects*, wisdom is associated with joy, while goodness is associated with longevity. Later on, the expression *zhihui* (智慧) was popularized by the Chinese translations of the Buddhist Sanskrit term *Prajna*, meaning perfect wisdom and knowledge. Other expressions, especially the one of *shengren* (圣人, Sage or Saint), may enrich the understanding of our theme: it refers in particular to the ancient kings of legendary times, whose listening capacities made them merge into the very nature of the cosmos. The Taoist *zhenren* (真人, authentic man), refers to the one able to dwell within himself in such a way as to abolish the boundary between Heavens and Man.

As the examples quoted above already suggest, Chinese wisdom works preferentially through stories, sayings and fables. The advantage of a story is indeed that it can be continually reinterpreted. And this is part of wisdom: the story that is told inspires the listener without trapping her into a definite meaning, a sequence of action to be automatically reduplicated. It allows the listener to pursue his/her own adventure — to continue the story. Chinese wisdom is made less of lessons than of parables.

Following this track, the wise leader, thus, is not wise merely by the fact of having access to a given amount of stock sentences and principles. For sure, she anchors herself in a given cultural heritage. However, at the same time, she is engaged in a constant work of *reinterpretation and reformulation* that changing circumstances and contacts

---

[22] *Analects*, VI, 23.

with other wisdom traditions encourage her to undergo. It is her capacity to engage in dialogue that actually makes her wise. Wisdom evolves through practices fostered by expanded contacts and social inventiveness. Wisdoms are mediums for expressing and transforming experience, knowledge and action. The wise leader understands and applies rules of wisdom insofar as she is interpreting, transforming and sharing them at the same time. If wisdom is *capital*, a wise leader will make its composition change and grow (as a weaver will transform a set of threads into a piece of cloth created through the use of its loom) — and only the risks a leader undertakes toward this end will be ultimately translated into lived wisdom. Such an approach may help us to link CSR practices with the different belief and wisdom systems through which we give meaning to our lives.

3.3. Contemporary Chinese Culture and CSR

It might seem that these considerations, even if they do justice to the wisdom of ancient times, are a far cry away from contemporary realities. Both Chinese and foreign entrepreneurs regularly lament the difficulties they meet with when trying to instill a sense of personal and corporate responsibility within the organization. The Chinese media, forums on the internet or everyday conversations are filled with expression of doubts on the capacity of Chinese society, and specifically of its companies, to foster the common good, a long-term vision and responsible behaviors. For sure, there is a dose of rhetoric in all this, and in every national context cultural impediments exist that make CSR a work forever in progress. Still, academic studies also seem to find fault with the dominant Chinese ethos when it comes to a sense of responsibility and accountability.

For instance, a global study finds cultural traits such as in-group collective ethos and stress on power distance (which are both pervasive in China) detrimental to CSR-based corporate values (Box 3.3).

In a more pragmatic way, another author tries to encapsulate the peculiarities of present-day CSR culture as lived and expressed by Chinese entrepreneurs (Box 3.4).

Box 3.3 High Power Distance — Impact on CSR

"When there is a strong belief in society that there should be distance among people in terms of power, relatively high-level managers who have the power may be more self-centered or lacking in concern for shareholders/ owners, broader stakeholder groups, and the community/society as a whole when they make decisions. Thus, in such societies, there may be more tendencies toward the manipulative use of power on the part of managers without concern for constituencies. These findings may raise concerns for proponents of CSR in a global context, pointing toward power distance values as a strong cultural variable relevant to managerial decision-making, particularly for stakeholder CSR. Our findings are especially suggestive that cultures with stronger power distance values may induce managers to show little concern for such identifiable stakeholders as employees, environmentalists, and customers."

Source: Waldman, D.A. et al., (2012), Cultural and Leadership Predictors of Corporate Social Responsibility Values of Top Management: A GLOBE Study of 15 Countries, *Journal of International Business Studies*, 37(6), p. 834.

These findings, and other similar ones, indeed reveal some cultural and societal traits that influence the acceptance, understanding, and implementation of CSR in present-day China: (a) continued importance of the role of the state; (b) profit and growth seen not only as a priority but also as being in potential conflict with other imperatives; and (c) short-term concerns taking precedence over sustainability issues. At the same time, some policy areas have been progressively shaping the development of a pragmatic CSR culture by the stress put on safety, energy consumption or social harmony. Though such policies have been devised precisely because of the underlying problems they target, they have been promoting a kind of *"capitalism under state sovereignty"* conducive to the building up of a specific CSR culture.[23]

---

[23]A thesis suggested by the book by Aglietta, M. & G. Bai (2013), *China's Development: Capitalism and Empire*, New York: Routledge.

Box 3.4 Characteristics of CSR in China

"CSR in China shows two important characteristics. First, most socially responsible behaviors of firms are government-oriented due to the overwhelming impact of the government on the economy in China. Second, economic responsibility should be regarded as the first social responsibility by firms because 'economic construction' is the central aim of government and the state... For economic issues, Chinese top 100 companies pay much attention to 'turnover or profit' and 'profit and tax submitted to government', while less attention is paid to 'employment'. For legal issues, much attention is paid to 'safety of products or services'. For ethical issues, those companies pay much attention to 'energy saving', while little attention is paid to 'advocate self-discipline' and 'volunteer policy'. For philanthropic issues, 'donation to disaster victims' is the most emphasized, while 'donation to the disabled' is the least addressed... The most addressed interests of stakeholders are 'turnover or profit' (stockholder), 'profit and tax submitted to government' (government), 'improvement of products and services' (consumer), 'valued relationship with suppliers and co-partners' (supplier or co-partner), and 'salary and welfare' (employee)."

Source: Gao, Y. (2009), Corporate Social Performance in China: Evidence from Large Companies, *Journal of Business Ethics*, 89(1), pp. 26, 30, 31.

It should also be stressed that, if the history of China indeed presented some traits detrimental to the implementation of CSR, other Chinese characteristics, still very much present today, are to be seen as the assets on which to nurture a culture of corporate responsibility, both global in scope and shaped by resources specific to China:

— The first of these characteristics would be the stress on *local territories* that Taoism and other Chinese traditions have developed, and which remains very much alive today: the territory to which one belongs (village, neighborhood, work unit) was seen as a living body, and the "body" metaphor is central in China's perception of the world. Every territory is a living body, and, in Chinese medicine, every "body" is a living territory. Forces (or "energies") that are to be understood and tamed shape physical and spatial bodies. All space in China is conceived of as being inhabited by energies, which — because they sustain us — must receive our recognition in return.[24] China is thus a collage of innumerable micro-universes. Within the space of a lane, around a chessboard, in all protected enclosures, people reconstruct the space where life is nurtured and tasted. The cosmos becomes a lived reality by the mere fact of harboring men, women and children, who share and manage it in their own space and their own fashion. Such a way of apprehending the space in which we live allows us to *inhabit the Earth*. This attachment to a given territory and the perception of the forces that shape it are still visible in the behavior of many Chinese entrepreneurs working and living in their native surroundings, where they have assumed a decisive role. It can also sometimes be glimpsed in the way employees behave within the company compounds, even if this territorial consciousness stops at the fences that define the space of reference. In that respect, the problem that Chinese entrepreneurs, decision-makers and social leaders face nowadays is to mobilize resources that would help society to reach a new awareness of the regulations that govern the relationship between small communities, larger communities, and nature. The challenge they face is to pragmatically assess and interpret parts of their tradition that might be helpful in this task.

— In that respect, one knows the importance of the concept of *harmony*, as a balancing tool among different interests and voices. Harmony has always been and still remains a central concept in Chinese thought. In this line, the emphasis put since the 1990s on *hehe wenhua* (culture of harmony and cooperation) is an attempt at conciliation between traditional social thought and today's realities. Such conciliation is not an easy task. Anyone who wants to make use of the traditional harmony concept meets immediately with a problem: the concept suited a homogeneous society with clear-cut levels of authority and firm control over external influences well. However, contemporary societies (be it in China or

---

[24]Among other resources available on this topic, see Lagerwey, J. (2010), *China: A Religious State*, Hong Kong: Hong Kong University Press.

elsewhere) are characterized by their fluidity, their internationalization, a constant diversification in thinking and norms of conduct, and an ever-increasing degree of human, economic and cultural interactions. In this context, if harmony is still a value worth referring to, it certainly has to refer less to a former state of things to which one returns (a sheer impossibility) than to a new ideal to be defined and worked out through embracing social and cultural diversity and the many debates this entails. The ambiguities surrounding the concept of harmony may have complicated the task of former President Hu Jintao who had consistently stressed the building of a "harmonious society" (*hexie shehui*), which has had an undeniable influence over China's understanding of the CSR imperative (Box 3.5).

At the same time, it is helpful to reinterpret Chinese traditional thinking not only through the category of harmony but through the category of *justice* as well. At this point, we meet with a problem: for many Chinese, intellectuals and ordinary people alike, implementing *justice* appears as a task almost contradictory with the one of realizing harmony, at least when one understands "justice" in its "social" meaning: "Justice" (*yi* 义) conceived of as "personal righteousness" has always been enhanced by the Chinese philosophical tradition, especially by Confucianism. There is however a related concept — *equality* (*pingdeng* 平等), that is central to part of the Taoist and even the

Box 3.5 Hu Jintao on a Harmonious Society

"President Hu Jintao, on September 15, 2006, defined a harmonious society as a society 'which gives full play to modern ideas like democracy, rule of the law, fairness, justice, vitality, stability, orderliness and harmonious co-existence between the humankind and nature'. This policy is understood to mean a renewed focus on addressing social and environmental challenges, with reduced priority for economic growth where it conflicts with these aims."

Source: See, G.K.H. (2009), Harmonious Society and Chinese CSR: Is There Really a Link?, *Journal of Business Ethics*, 89, p. 2.

Confucian and Legalist traditions. This is first an ontological concept, referring to the equality of nature of all sentient beings, a concept that Buddhist thought further developed and reinforced. Equality is also an existential concept, strongly linked to "simplicity", "rusticity", or "frugality" (*pu* 朴). Some early Confucians argued that all human beings had equal potential, and promoted education that was not based upon class distinctions. The Legalist thinker Han Fei Zi also introduced the idea of equality before the law, with the exception of the ruler.[25] Community values include a call to more simplicity and equality — a call still reverberated today in various sectors of the Chinese society.

— Another regulatory concept to be taken into account is the one of **diversity**. The state and society gradually corroded China's diversity, simplifying ecosystems in the interest of maximizing the human crop. Over the centuries, China lost many of its ecological buffers, forests, wetlands and wildlands.[26] What is noteworthy here is that biodiversity and diversity of thought might well partially go together. When a single model of development is promoted, the landscape itself becomes uni-dimensional. As long as peculiar cultures and models of developments are respected, cultural diversity in China concurs with biodiversity as it entails various ways of relating to nature. This call toward the enhancement of cultural diversity is now echoed throughout many sectors of Chinese society, especially when debating the developmental models that could enhance the specific resources of West China.

— **Community values** constitute another basic dimension for defining sustainable models of development, and it is indeed a dimension akin to the spirit of the Chinese tradition. What is at stake nowadays is to assess community values as tools for devising *incremental* models of development. Linking "community" and "development", i.e. thinking in terms of "community development", helps

---

[25] Bai, T. (2012), *China: The Political Philosophy of the Middle Kingdom*, London/New York: Zed Books, p. 24. See also pp. 60–64.

[26] McNeill, J.R. (1998), China's Environmental History in World Perspective, in M. Elvin & T.J. Liu (eds.), *Sediments of Time*, Cambridge: Cambridge University Press, p. 35.

one to assess the cost of a given project from various standpoints: it channels the wisdom proper to the inhabitants of a locality where projects for irrigation, transportation or industrial development are planned. It makes ecological concerns arise through a communication and bargaining process.

To express its CSR and sustainability priorities, the Shanghai-based Shanghai Pudong Development Bank (SPD Bank, 浦发银行) has chosen the words of "Green (绿色)", "Happiness (幸福)" and "Responsibility (责任)" to express the company's mission, referring explicitly both to the 12th National Plan and to Chinese traditional values. Though such an exercise has obvious limitations, the SPD report conveys the company's willingness to focus more on human values, care for common people, the weak and the marginalized, and it asserts the fact that a rethinking of one's values, ways of proceeding and priorities, according to an ethics of care and sharing, may be the only way to help a corporation become a global and sustainable player.[27] This testifies to a shift that may ultimately reconcile traditional and modern China on the basis of the sustainability imperative (see also Chapter 4 on CSR and Corporate Strategy).

Recent research based on interviews of Chinese CEOs has also identified three specific topics which Chinese entrepreneurs insist upon, when asked to articulate their own understanding of CSR: the importance of good faith; providing employment opportunities; and contributing to social stability. These concerns do not contradict Western approach to CSR but rather express a specific ranking of priorities.[28] Differences still exist: Compared to their counterparts in the US, PRC managers generally subscribed more strongly to a traditional stockholder view, as they feel that efficiency and business survival take priority over ethical and socially responsible behavior, and that the interests of stockholders should be privileged over all other considerations. On the other hand, they also agreed more strongly with the assertion that

---

[27]SPD Bank (2010), *Corporate Social Responsibility Report*.
[28]Xu, S. & X. Yang (2010), Indigenous Characteristics of Chinese Corporate Social Responsibility Conceptual Paradigm, *Journal of Business Ethics*, 93(2), pp. 321–333.

businesses have a social responsibility beyond making a profit. PRC managers endorsed more strongly the propositions that ethics and social responsibility are essential to the long-term profitability and survival of a business ... However, they were also less likely to feel that social responsibility and profitability can be compatible.[29]

At another level, a question often discussed among business executives has to do with behavioral features present in the current Chinese society and generally frowned upon by Westerners, and whether or not these features can be considered as consistent with CSR. A few examples may help one to discern the fault lines running throughout everyday cultural practices:

— At least theoretically, the Western culture embraces free discussion irrespective of seniority, while the Chinese culture privileges the respect to be shown to elders. The dilemma is less acute than it appears: if norms and priorities are clearly conceived and ranked by all participants, etiquette rules can be managed in such a way as to ensure that decisions that are both rational and ethical be taken without infringing on decorum and traditions. As long as ethical discernment has been nurtured among the members of a group, the style governing reciprocal relations is not an obstacle *per se* to sound decision-making.

— Gift making is a frequent issue in business. Every company has its own set of conducts as to the giving and receiving of presents, rules that take into consideration value, context and agents. The nature of the business also governs the suitability of gift making. Till today, it remains true that gifts in China help to build up relationships, and that the gift making tradition may contribute to nurturing trust, a sense of person-to-person relationship and appreciation. While corporate rules need to emphasize the "don'ts" related to the practice, so as to avoid not only venality but also the mere suspicion of it, sensible provisions can make room for

---

[29]Shafer, W.E., K. Fukukawa & G.M. Lee (2007), Values and the Perceived Importance of Ethics and Social Responsibility: The US versus China, *Journal of Business Ethics*, 70(3), pp. 278–279.

cultural sensitivity on this issue and other similar ones. Clarity in the formulation of the rule and its purpose is central. The study of this issue will be furthered in Chapter 5.

— The same thing cannot be said about banquets and toasting: if their role in Chinese corporate culture is well documented, contemporary society now passes harsh judgment on the excesses that go with them. As we will see, in government circles, more and more regulations severely restrict or forbid such conducts. Cultural sensitivity does not apply to excessive and/or compulsory drinking.

— The same principle is to be stressed even more firmly when it comes to the risks of sexual harassment associated with feasting and drinking habits. Also, sexual discrimination occurs when female employees are excluded from activities organized by the company because of the drinking and sexual overtones of the "recreation" offered. In such matters, a zero tolerance policy strictly applies.

In conclusion, traditions and cultural sensitivities can be integrated into the style and practices of CSR, provided that the rules and rationale be clearly formulated and that they respect principles and norms determined by laws, social consent and ethical principles. Such discernment is generally easier to conduct than is generally assumed, provided the issues at stake are clearly exposed and openly debated.

CHAPTER FOUR

CSR and Corporate Strategy

This chapter intends to frame into a whole the rationale for actively implementing CSR in the present Chinese context. At such, it serves as a transition between the approach defined in the course of our first three chapters and the study of the various CSR-related fields of action that we will be dealing with in Part Two. However, before examining these fields of action, the present chapter will first analyze how CSR can be incorporated into the corporate strategy, by examining its benefits, its links with philanthropy and how research in the area of CSR can help in its implementation. Chapter 5 will further illustrate this with a focus on combating corruption. Taken together, Chapters 4 and 5 will sketch the tenets that determine a corporation's day-to-day exercise of CSR in the Chinese context.

4.1. Benefits of Implementing CSR

Entrepreneurs have sometimes perceived CSR — its concept as well as its implementation — as an impediment to the development of business operations: it was presumed to divert resources, renounce to the maximizing of comparative advantages a firm may possess, and ignore the tough realities of the market. However, the corporate benefits linked to socially responsible behaviors and initiatives have been receiving more and more attention, and can be spelled out in several ways, as in Box 4.1. Benefits linked to good corporate citizenship can also be identified in a slightly different way (Box 4.2).

Other potential benefits can be identified. A major (and yet often overlooked) benefit is that CSR, as a self-regulation mechanism, helps a company to assess the relevancy and potential pitfalls of its business model, alerting it to risks that may be linked to hazardous behaviors, a failure to understand and meet the public's expectations, and a lack of

Box 4.1 Corporate Benefits of CSR

— Higher motivation and productivity among employees;
— An increased reputation and trust that leads to higher appreciation from customers and suppliers and therefore greater economic success;
— Enhanced recognition as operating publicly in society involves consideration for the intentions of customers, representatives of local communities, banks and other important contacts;
— An acknowledgement of commitment: CSR is not a short-cut to business success but an investment that may pay off in the longer term; and
— A higher acceptance within the community.

Source: NORMAPME User Guide for European SMEs on ISO 26000 Guidance on Social Responsibility, 2011, pp. 5–6, http://www.normapme.eu/public/uploads/files/csr%20user%20guide/User%20guide%20ISO26000_version%20EN_final_18072011.pdf, accessed July 31, 2013.

Box 4.2 Other Corporate Benefits of CSR

— Improved relations with employees (e.g. improves employee recruitment, retention, morale, loyalty, motivation and productivity);
— Improved customer relationships (e.g. increased customer loyalty, acts as a tiebreaker for consumer purchasing, enhances brand image);
— Improved business performance (e.g. positively impacts bottom-line returns, increases competitive advantage, encourages cross-functional integration); and
— Enhanced company marketing efforts (e.g. helps create a positive company image, helps a company manage its reputation, supports higher prestige pricing, and enhances government affairs activities).

Source: Sims, R.R. (2003), *Ethics and Corporate Social Responsibility, Why Giants Fail*, London: Praeger, p. 58 (partly based on Carroll, A.B., K. Davenport & D. Grisaffe (2000), Appraising the Business Value of Corporate Citizenship: What Does the Literature Say?, *Proceedings of the International Association for Business and Society*, Essex Junction, Vt.).

transparency and accountability. To illustrate with a metaphor, the attention given by a company to CSR standards and imperatives works a bit like a thermostat, maintaining a system at its desired set-point.

Furthermore, *Creating Shared Value* (CSV) is now being seen as a major adjuvant to CSR theory.[1] Recognizing the link between the competitiveness of a company and the sustainability of the communities with and in which the company operates is key for making the devising of business strategies and CSR awareness one and the same endeavor. Reconceiving products and markets, redefining productivity in the value chain, and building supportive industry clusters at the company's locations: these tasks define three ways through which to create shared value. The support provided by large agro-business companies to farmers trapped in a cycle of low productivity, poor quality, and environmental degradation provides managers with an example of such strategies. Otherwise said, if there indeed exists trade-offs between short-term profitability and CSR-based objectives, overall, the total sum of benefits proposed by a company to its stakeholders makes its CSR corporate strategy a competitive advantage.

Also, more and more corporations list as privileged partners companies that can show a good track record on CSR-based behaviors, including concerns for sustainable development. Such a trend has a cumulative effect conducive to the spreading of corporate responsibility across a culture or a nation. (See Box 4.3 for a case study.)

In the Chinese context, there are additional reasons for making CSR part of any company's business model and strategy:[2]

— The state places great emphasis on the social role of companies, both national and transnational, now expected to show environmental responsibility, to contribute to social harmony (avoidance of risks, contribution to social causes in times of natural disasters

---

[1]Porter, M.E. & M.R. Kramer (2011), Creating Shared Value. *Harvard Business Review*, 89 (1/2), pp. 62–77.

[2]On the Chinese approach to the integration of CSR within the corporate strategy, see for instance Jiang, Q. & Q. Gu (2008), *CSR and Corporate Strategy* (*Qiye shehuizeren he qiye zhanlue xuanze*), Shanghai: Shanghai People's Press. (姜启军、 顾庆良，《企业社会责任和企业战略选择》，上海人民出版社，2008年。)

Box 4.3 Case Study: Choosing Business Partners

"In the initial choice of all our partners and when evaluating our continued relationships with them, we wish to include in our selection criteria their attitude toward the principles of sustainable development and to contribute to the widespread adoption of such practices."
Source: Excerpt from the Michelin Performance and Responsibility Charter.

"We expect from our suppliers and their subcontractors:
— Compliance with the standards and regulations in place in their country, and the possible application of more stringent Michelin standards for certain projects at our request;
— Provisions, where applicable, for the elimination of their products at the end of their service life;
— Introduction, progressively if necessary but in accordance with a predefined plan, of an environmental management system, designed in particular to:
  • measure any possible adverse effects their operations have on the environment; and
  • identify and reduce industrial risks.
— Implementation of measures to reduce the negative effects of their activities on the environment; and
— Proposals and actions aimed at reducing waste and packaging."

Source: Excerpt from the Michelin Purchasing Code.

QUESTIONS

— Are the criteria under which we chose our business partners and suppliers clearly articulated? How do we balance cost considerations, technical and legal requirements, and ethical standards?
— Are these criteria expressed and made known in such a way as to make them a reminder and an incentive to our potential partners? Are CSR issues explicitly raised during a binding process or a negotiation?
— Do these criteria come with concrete specifications related to our core business that help our partners to articulate their CSR commitments, enhance them if needed, and report to us on their implementation?

or at the local level), and to insert their action into a framework of sustainable development. A company's record on all these fronts contributes to the definition of its credit with local and national authorities.

— The general public and internet users are strongly moved by stories detrimental to the reputation of a company, and are also sensitive to success stories and creative initiatives.[3] Though it is true everywhere that corporate reputation can be made and unmade by waves escaping the control of all protagonists, the volatility of the Chinese public opinion is particularly striking. Mobbing, rumors or heated debates make companies vulnerable. Conversely, a well-advertised long-term strategy of responsibility and social initiatives can build up a capital of sympathy and public trust, especially if illustrated by inspiring stories on pilot projects for instance.

— At least, in East China, and among Chinese entrepreneurs, CSR-related issues have been identified at an earlier time and in a clearer fashion than generally assumed. A pioneering large-scale survey made in East China in 1995 (700 persons working at responsibility level) showed: (a) the presence of business ethics concerns among business executives and their identification as issues of peculiar importance; (b) diverging responses and opinions when practical cases were discussed; (c) a strong dissatisfaction with the leadership's response to these issues: only 19 percent of the respondents were satisfied with the ethical standards of their superiors.[4] Progressively, CSR and business ethics have become topics of concern among the Chinese entrepreneurs and in society at large (Box 4.4).

---

[3]See for instance Yang, G. (2009), *The Power of the Internet in China: Citizen Activism Online*, New York: Columbia University Press.

[4]Wu, X. (1999), Business Ethical Perceptions of Business People in East China: An Empirical Study, in G. Enderle (ed.), *International Business Ethics, Challenges and Approaches*, Notre Dame, London: University of Notre Dame Press, p. 327.

Box 4.4 Business Ethics — A Growing Influence

"Business ethics has become a new and popular topic in East China. Most business people are sensitive to business ethical issues, and they have various ethical perceptions ... Quite a lot of business people are dissatisfied with both the ethical standards of their superiors and their coworkers and the ethical climate of their enterprises. Third, more and more business leaders begin to believe that high business ethical standards are advantageous both to the enterprise and to the individuals in it, while some business leaders have not properly understood the relationship between business ethics and business law as well as the right, duty and responsibility in business activity ... The current state of business ethics in East China is complex and flexible, and it will remain so in the not too distant future."

Source: Wu, X. (1999), Business Ethical Perceptions of Business People in East China: An Empirical Study, in G. Enderle (ed.), *International Business Ethics, Challenges and Approaches*, Notre Dame, London: University of Notre Dame Press, pp. 341.

Two decades after CSR-related concerns started to be identified by clusters of Chinese entrepreneurs, the reality remains fluid and complex, and disagreements on specific issues are still strong, but the general acceptance of the relevance of CSR, as well as knowledge of its principles and applications, has steadily increased.

4.2. "Social License" and Stakeholders in the Chinese Context

Another dimension shapes the way CSR is integrated into corporate strategies at large: in the Chinese context, the understanding of CSR is colored by the fact that contributions to the community in which a firm exercises its activity amounts to a kind of "social license" to operate. Philanthropic initiatives anchor a company into its social environment. This is true of Chinese family businesses that traditionally cement alliances with different constituencies in a local setting that is often the one of their lineage or their upbringing. In a similar vein, foreign companies are expected to contribute to the environment in which they operate through various philanthropic actions. Chapters

13 and 14 of this book will examine models and examples of philanthropic projects and community investment. Clearly, philanthropy is an important dimension of CSR.[5] However, two dangers need to be highlighted:

— Philanthropy is not a substitute for responsible behavior. The prime social responsibility of companies is to comply to laws that determine their social, environmental, business and financial obligations, and to go beyond the letter of the law so as to create shared value. Philanthropic action, including community investment, must work within this requisite of compliance, and never compensate for its dereliction.

— Accountability also applies to philanthropy and community investment. It is part of the social responsibility of a corporation to make sure that its community actions are efficient, measurable as to their effects, transparent and, if possible, innovative — as its for-profit operations are supposed to be. Chapter 14 will examine these requisites in light of the current development of social enterprises. We will then suggest that fostering alliances between corporations, local communities and socially innovative actors sets up the framework in which to think or rethink community investment.

4.3. From Research to Action

The growing acceptance of CSR and business ethics in China as well as its integration into the realities of the market can also be highlighted by looking at the amount of the research devoted to the question.

---

[5]For an understanding of CSR by Chinese companies in the context of Shanghai and its implementation, see: *Qiye juanzeng shehuigongyi yanjiu ketizu* (Research team on companies' donations for social benefit) (2001), Report on Companies' Donation for Social Benefit — Research and Comments on Shanghai Companies' Donations for Social Benefit (*Gongsi juanzeng shehuigongyi yanjiu baogao — shanghai qiye juanzeng shehuigongyi qingkuang de diaocha pinlun*), Sociology (*Shehuixue*), 1, pp. 1–12. (企业捐赠社会公益研究课题组，《公司捐赠社会公益研究报告—上海企业捐赠社会公益情况的调查评论》，社会学2001 年第1 期，1–12 页, http://2010.cqvip.com/onlineread/onlineread.asp?id=10512241, accessed July 17, 2013.)

Based on a survey of university courses and research publications, an article offers interesting information on teaching and research in the field of business ethics and CSR in China (see Box 4.5):

Box 4.5 The State of CSR Research in China

"There were 3,477 academic articles with titles containing *qiye shehui zeren* (CSR). Although the first article and book were published as early as in 1989 and 1990 respectively, it is only after 2003 that this theme began to draw a great deal of scholarly attention. Since 2000, over 300 articles have been published every year on average. Altogether there were 53 books, 51 of which were published in the last ten years. Regarding the specific research themes in Economic and Business Ethics, *chengxin* (integrity) and *jingji yu lunli/daode* (economy and ethics/morality), were among the most heavily addressed issues. A total of 7,534 articles were found with *chengxin* in their titles and *qiye* (business) or *jingji* (economy) as their themes. Approximately 99 percent of them were published after 2000. In total, 4,830 articles were published with both *jingji* and *lunli/daode* in their titles (excluding those with *jingji lunli*), with 150 articles in the 1980s, 2,107 in the 1990s, and 2,573 in the 2000s. In addition, environmental ethics, ethics management and justice also received much attention ... The portion of Chinese experts who participated in training was higher than that of their Japanese counterparts. In addition, Chinese experts focused more on general themes, while Japanese experts concentrated more on specific topics. It may be because the field itself was still in its early stages of development in China, and that Chinese experts tended to think of things from a more holistic perspective, thus it is imperative for them to answer the general questions of a field first... In China, 81 experts responded to the question regarding the major ethical issues in the field of Economic and Business Ethics in East Asia that are foreseen to emerge over the next five years. The top ten ethical issues identified by the expert respondents were: CSR (34), environmental ethics (34), international ethics (25), business ethics (20), human resource management ethics (15), economic ethics (12), consumption ethics (10), ethics and economic/business performance (10), financial ethics (10), and ethics management (10)."

Source: Zhou, Z., C. Nakano & B.N. Luo (2011), Business Ethics as Field of Training, Teaching, and Research in East Asia, *Journal of Business Ethics*, 104(1), pp. 24–26.

Such results should not be interpreted in too optimistic a fashion: the education that most managers and engineers receive in China does not prepare them to effectively confront the ethical and CSR challenges that they are going to meet in the field. However, CSR becomes progressively integrated into discussions on global corporate strategies. The authors of the article quoted above even consider that Economic and Business Ethics would be a promising field in East Asia. They believed that the developments of the society and economy in each country further provided a fertile ground for the developments of the field. Moreover, Economic and Business Ethics is increasingly attracting attention at the international level, and the East Asian countries, especially China, Japan, and Korea, are also actively participating in the international arena. As they put it, Economic and Business Ethics in East Asia will "benefit from the international communications", and "grow along with developments of the field globally".[6] Research and teaching should indeed benefit from the regionalization of the issues at stake: China, Japan, Korea and, progressively, Vietnam will need to share and compare their traditions and experiences, and regional training and research programs will greatly enrich the amount of analyses and tools available to both the researcher and the practitioner.

*   *   *

A corporation's exercise of its social responsibility will thus rely on a firm conviction that such commitment is beneficial to its long-term growth and sustainability, provided it is carried on with consistency and not on a *à la carte* basis. It furthers and expands its respect of legal prescriptions, both national and international, by engaging in pilot initiatives that connect to specific communities, defined on a geographical or transversal basis. In the Chinese context, the corporation understands that these initiatives somehow concur to assert its "social license to operate" in the view of the government and the general public alike. However, it makes sure that, when it participates in

---

[6]Zhou, Z., C. Nakano & B.N. Luo (2011), Business Ethics as Field of Training, Teaching, and Research in East Asia, *Journal of Business Ethics*, 104(1), p. 27.

initiatives going beyond its legal obligations, it does so with rigor and a sense of purpose, applying the same basic rules of management and monitoring that apply to its for-profit operations. To better define and implement CSR obligations and initiatives, the corporation relies on sound research and makes sure that such research is shared and developed within the national and professional context to which it belongs. The firm also makes a realistic assessment of the factors that, in this given context, are detrimental to the sound exercise of CSR, so as to minimize their effects and not to fall into ethical and practical traps that would devoid its social commitment of any meaning. This last point is the one that will guide our analysis throughout the course of the next chapter.

CHAPTER FIVE

Corruption and Business Activities

Assessing the conditions under which CSR-values and practices can be implemented in China requires at some point an evaluation of the extent to which corruption may weigh on business activities. For sure, corruption is a phenomenon that affects, at various degrees, all countries in the world, taking different shapes according to social, political and cultural prevailing conditions.[1] The Chinese government has made the struggle against corruption one of its top priorities, while recognizing the pervasive character of the phenomenon and how difficult it would be to eradicate it.[2] President Xi Jinping has exhorted fellow leaders to learn from the experience of other countries where corruption has played a "big role in conflicts that grew over lengthy periods", and led to "popular discontent, social unrest and the overthrow of the political power".[3] The new leadership describes the challenge created by corruption practices with striking expressions: "Combating corruption and promoting political integrity, which is a major political issue of great concern to the people, is a clear-cut and long-term political commitment of the Party. If we fail to handle this issue well, it could prove fatal to the Party, and even cause the collapse of the Party and the fall of the state ... We must maintain a tough position in cracking down on corruption at all times, conduct thorough

---

[1] A work of reference remains: Rose-Ackerman, S. (1999), *Corruption and Government: Causes, Consequences, and Reform*, Cambridge: Cambridge University Press.
[2] *China Daily* (2012), CPC Outlines Anti-Corruption Plan for New Year, December 31, 2013, http://usa.chinadaily.com.cn/china/2012-12/31/content_16073433.htm, accessed July 17, 2013.
[3] *CNN* (2013), Opinion: Corruption as China's Top Priority, January 6, 2013, http://blog.huanqiu.com/likuntang/2013-01-26/2680309/, accessed July 17, 2013.

investigations into major corruption cases and work hard to resolve problems of corruption that directly affect the people. All those who violate Party discipline and state laws, whoever they are and whatever power or official positions they have, must be brought to justice without mercy."[4] And indeed, corruption generates much public discontent. According to an online survey jointly conducted in February 2011 by Xinhuanet.com and Sina.com, the top five concerns expressed by the public were: (a) housing prices; (b) income distribution; (c) inflation and commodity prices; (d) combating corruption; as well as (e) employment promotion and equal employment opportunities.[5,6] The importance that the topic conveys for public opinion is evidenced by other surveys[7] as well as by the traffic and comments that corruption cases trigger on the Chinese internet.

5.1. Nature and Extent

The World Bank simply defines corruption as "the abuse of public office for private gain".[8] Behind this straightforward definition lie behaviours and practices that by nature are insidious, changeable, and opaque. Public office is abused for private gain when an official accepts, solicits, or extorts a bribe. It is also abused when private agents actively offer bribes to circumvent public policies and

[4] Hu Jintao, *Keynote Report on the 18th CPC National Congress*, Chapter 12, paragraph 7, http://www.china.org.cn/china/18th_cpc_congress/2012-11/16/content_27137540_12.htm, accessed July 31, 2013.

[5] *Xinhua* (English Edition) (2011), Graft Remains Top Public Concern Prior to Annual Parliamentary Session: Survey, February 24, 2011, http://news.xinhuanet.com/english2010/china/2011-02/24/c_13748537.htm, accessed July 17, 2013.

[6] Sun, X. (2011), Commodity, Housing Prices to be Focus of "Two Sessions", *Xinhua*, March 3, 2011, http://english.cri.cn/6826/2011/03/03/1821s623844.htm, accessed July 17, 2013.

[7] The most notable reference is *The Blue Book on Chinese Society* (*shehui lanpishu*), published each year by the Chinese Academy of Social Sciences.

[8] World Bank (1997), *Helping Countries Combat Corruption*, September, http://www1.worldbank.org/publicsector/anticorrupt/corruptn/cor02.htm, accessed July 17, 2013.

processes for competitive advantage and profit. Public office can also be abused for personal benefit even if no bribery occurs, through patronage and nepotism, the theft of state assets, or the diversion of state revenues. Corruption is thus linked to administrative and political malfunctioning that reverberates on different social levels, including business activities. Corruption takes an existence of one's own, and creates ways of proceeding that permeate all aspects of social and economic life, beyond the circles or structures that initiated its dynamic. This is why the definition coined by the World Bank is sometimes enlarged, when, for instance, one speaks of "corruption" for sport-fixing or match-fixing — a phenomenon endemic in China's soccer competitions, for instance.

In 2012, China ranked 80 out of 176 countries surveyed in Transparency International's Corruption Perception Index.[9] This placed it above India (94th) and Russia (133th), but below Brazil (69th). The US ranked 19th, and South Korea 45th. China's ranking has stayed about the same on this index since 2002, although it ranked 75th in 2011, and saw its ranking noticeably lowered in 2006–2007 — a period during which there were some 100,000 corruption scandals investigated by Chinese authorities, with probably 60 percent or more of those investigations involving foreign companies.[10]

Especially after 1992, the policy of reforms and opening up allowed for the sale of land-use rights and the privatization of state-owned enterprises or their assets — opaque processes that were rife with opportunities for looting.[11] In today's China, sales of land by local governments and privatization of public services are still venues for the enrichment of officials, though practices have diversified, some sophisticated, and some remaining plain and obvious. Cases of bribery are routinely reported or suspected. For instance, in January 2013

---

[9] The survey is available at www.transparency.org, accessed July 17, 2013.

[10] Cf. Lu, J. (2007), Commercial Bribery: What Are the Boundaries?, *China Law & Practice*, March, http://www.chinalawandpractice.com/Article/1690356/Channel/7576/Commercial-Bribery-What-are-the-Boundaries.html, accessed July 17, 2013.

[11] See for instance: Wedeman, A. (2012), *Double Paradox: Rapid Growth and Rising Corruption in China*, Ithaca: Cornell University Press.

the *Caixin* magazine has raised the issue of possible briberies linked to the process of initial public offerings (IPO). According to their sources, the buying of votes needed to gain an IPO approval could be supplemented or substituted by accrued business offered to the law or accounting firms from which the members of the Public Offering Review Committee (PORC) were chosen. Still, the magazine took care to note: "Since taking office in October 2011, China Securities Regulatory Commission (CSRC) head Guo Shuqing has reshuffled personnel on a large scale in an attempt to end the corruption. Many officials from the CSRC's public offering department and the PORC have traded positions with people in other departments."[12]

Experts have identified several types of corruption, often divided into "black corruption" (graft, bribe, fraud, embezzlement, extortion, smuggling and tax evasion), "grey corruption" (public institutions engaging in business activities who impose fines, collect administrative fees or charge service fees and put the income into their own coffers), and "white corruption" (nepotism in personnel recruitment and promotion, bending the law or preferential treatment in favor of relatives and friends).[13,14,15] Fixed bidding, illegal expropriation of properties, bribes, gratuities, corruption linked to the power of examining and approving projects and kickback of public projects are among the practices that enter into conflict with the normal pursuit of business activities. A number of administrative bodies have been set up for investigating and preventing these practices (including an improved reporting system), and their powers have been gradually extended, while corruption practices have become increasingly sophisticated.

---

[12] Lu, Y. (2013), How 300,000 Yuan, Shark Fin Soup Buy IPO Approval, *Caixin Online*, January 31, 2013, http://articles.marketwatch.com/2013-01-31/investing/36658628_1_review-process-ipo-yuan, accessed July 17, 2013.

[13] Cf. Heidenheimer, A.J. & M. Johnston (2002), *Political Corruption: Concepts and Contexts* (3rd ed.), New Brunswick, N.J.: Transaction Publishers.

[14] Dai, C. (2010), Corruption and Anti-Corruption in China: Challenges and Countermeasures, *Journal of International Business Ethics*, 3(2), pp. 58–70.

[15] He, Z. (2000), Corruption and Anti-corruption in Reform China, *Communist and Post-Communist Studies*, 33(2), pp. 244–245.

Periodic anti-corruption campaigns testify to both the deep concerns of the central leadership and the pervasive nature of the problem.

Bribery sometimes originates from criminal groups and black societies that keep on their payroll a large number of local officials. Gangs use violence to monopolize a local commercial activity and, through bribery, subsequently operate large-scale business. The growing scale of the operations has certainly weakened the traditional territorial cultures and loyalties characteristic of the secret societies of the past: so as to maximize profits and expand power and territorial bases, members from different triads have come together to run both legitimate and illicit business.[16] In general, although cases of briberies are numerous, the commitment of the authorities to maintain law and order is unequivocal. Still, some authors argue that, in the context of the retrocession of Hong Kong, Mainland Chinese authorities have somehow deployed a "United Front" tactic to include triad leaders as their allies. A "patriotic triad" label served such a function and allowed triad leaders to bridge with state-owned enterprises in China. Triad leaders were thus co-opted but also had to comply with demands for law and order by officials in exchange for business opportunities.[17] However, the "Strike Hard" campaigns periodically launched against organized crime testify to the extent to which Chinese authorities are anxious to rein in black societies — and this nowadays certainly applies to Hong Kong and Macao as well. The pervasiveness of local official connections remains a prominent concern for the central authorities. For this reason, laws and interpretative acts have progressively included into the definition of "black societies" the fact of taking advantage of protection and connivance by state functionaries for playing the bully over an area or trade. The existence of a "protective umbrella" is thus as an optional aspect for labeling a group as a "black

---

[16] Broadhurst, R. (2012), Chinese 'Black Societies' and Triad-like Organised Crime in China, in F. Allum and S. Gilmour (eds.), *Handbook of Transnational Organised Crime*, London: Routledge, pp. 157–171.

[17] Lo, T.W. (2010), Beyond Social Capital: Triad Organized Crime in Hong Kong and China, *British Journal of Criminology*, 50(5), pp. 851–872.

society" and, subsequently, for determining the targets of the successive campaigns of "Strike at the Black" and "Eradicate the Evil".[18]

To what extent do gangs victimize business operations? Conducted in 2004–2005 (and thus not fully reflecting present trends), a UN survey of the prevalence of crime victimization among businesses in four cities (Hong Kong, Shanghai, Shenzhen and Xi'an) showed that the prevalence of most crime against business was highest in Shenzhen: bribery and corruption were 2.5 times more likely in Shenzhen than Hong Kong. The prevalence of extortion was similar in Shenzhen and Hong Kong (3.1 percent) but the prevalence of corruption was much lower in Hong Kong (2.7 percent) than in Shenzhen (8.5 percent). Extortion in Hong Kong was reported almost exclusively by small retail businesses, but in Shenzhen it was reported by a diverse range of businesses including medium-sized enterprises. Shanghai reported relatively low levels of extortion and bribery, but corruption by party officials was significant in Xi'an. Taken as a whole, these figures suggest that the victimization of business by criminal groups is common but not prevalent, and strongly varies according to local factors.[19]

It is not easy to select indicators that help one to track and evaluate the extent of corruption and its costs for a firm. Cai *et al.* (2011) argue that entertainment and travel costs (ETC) can be an efficient measure of corruption since Chinese managers commonly use the ETC accounting category to "reimburse expenditures used to bribe government officials, to entertain clients and suppliers, or to accommodate managerial excess". And they provide strong evidence that the firm's ETC consists of "a mix that includes expenditures on government officials both as 'grease money' and 'protection money', implicit CEO pay, and managerial excesses".[20] Wang and You (2012) also find this indicator very

---

[18]Cf. Broadhurst (2012).

[19]Broadhurst, R., B. Bouhours, J. Bacon-Shone, L.Y. Zhong & K.W. Lee (2010), *Hong Kong, The United Nations International Crime Victim Survey: Final Report of the 2006 Hong Kong UNICVS*, Hong Kong and Canberra: The University of Hong Kong and The Australian National University.

[20]Cai, H., H. Fang & L. Xu (2011). Eat, Drink, Firms And Governments: An Investigation of Corruption from Entertainment Expenditures in Chinese Firms, *Journal of Law and Economics*, 54(1), pp. 55–78.

helpful, and its results positively correlated with the ones they obtain through their own evaluation criterion: "Our corruption is measured as the proportion of days within a year that a firm interacts with four government departments, taxation, public security, environment, labor and social security ... Corrupt practices may also be involved in firms' day-to-day operations, which can take many forms. For example, illegal payment to persuade tax inspectors, bribery to obtain and/or speed up the compulsory licenses (or permits) during production or for future production, and entertainment spending to smooth relationships or build networks."[21] The two studies mentioned above find a lower level of corruption in the southeast and central areas, and the highest corruption in the northwest. However, these results need to be interpreted cautiously, as the indicators they select may better detect one particular form of corruption rather than the whole spectrum of patterns and practices. In addition, some industries, especially the construction sector, are supposed to be especially prone to corrupt practices, especially when contracts are signed outside the realms of the Tangible Construction Markets (TCMs), a mechanism set up by the government for curbing corruption in the construction tender process.

5.2. Causes and Effects

If corruption in China is unanimously considered as serious, its overall effect on development remains debated. Some researchers see its effects as manageable, and express optimistic views on its progressive weakening. Comparing the level of corruption in the US between 1870 and 1930 with the one found in China from 1996 on, Ramirez (2012) concludes: "The 'life-cycle' theory of corruption operated in the US and may well be operating in China. Corruption seems to be a negative by-product of modernization and development, as many researchers in the literature have suggested. As China modernizes and continues to develop, its government may be in a better position to implement

---

[21] Wang, Y. & J. You (2012), Corruption and Firm Growth: Evidence from China, *China Economic Review*, 23(2), p. 424.

corruption-control reforms."[22] Still, such results should be taken with caution, for they are based on a quantitative analysis of newspaper reports, which may reflect corruption levels and practices in a way much less reliable than is assumed by the above-mentioned study.

Economists tend to disagree on the impact of corruption based on the lack of accessible metrics to model it. However, research suggests that a one-unit increase in the corruption index reduces the growth rate by 0.545 percentage points.[23] The cost of corruption is multifaceted and not easy to assess using conventional economic metrics. Evidence based on the observation of emerging countries suggests that each component adds up at various speeds according to prevalent economic conditions in the form of three key negative externalities: political and economic instability, slower social progress and environment degradation.

(a) Macroeconomic stability may be undermined by loss of government revenue and excessive spending on "white elephant" projects. If the costs of bribery become too high or unpredictable, foreign firms will disengage unless marketing or sourcing considerations require them to maintain a presence in that country. High levels of corruption add to the risk of a country being marginalized in the international economy.

(b) The less wealthy part of the population suffers most. When access to public goods and services requires a bribe in remote areas, the lower income population may be excluded. And when corruption results in shoddy public services, the poor lack the resources to access poverty alleviation public services such as private schooling, micro-banking or healthcare. Evidence from the private sector suggests that corruption increases the cost of doing business, curb private investment and that small and micro firms bear a disproportionately large share of these costs, and that bribes can prevent firms from growing.

---

[22] Ramirez, C.D. (2012), Is Corruption in China 'Out of Control'? A Comparison with the US in Historical Perspective, Georges Madison University, Department of Economics, *Working Paper* 12–60, p. 27.
[23] Mo, P.H. (2001), Corruption and Economic Growth, *Journal of Comparative Economics*, 29(1), pp. 66–79.

(c) Allocation of natural resources and the environment are also adversely affected. For some firms, complying with environmental regulations generates costs that can be avoided by bribery. The environmental costs of corruption may take the form of ground water and air pollution, soil erosion, or climate change, and can be global and intergenerational in their reach, creating an immense liability for future generations. The same reasoning applies to food and drug quality and production safety.

(d) As for economic planning implementations in the market and public trust, corruption distorts both market competition and the implementation of developmental policies. At the same time, it negatively influences individuals' economic behavior, diminishing the level of public trust, without which no sound social and economic development can take place. Corruption partly originates from weak social trust in the institution, and further erodes it. One of its indicators in the present-day economy is the overall extent of cash transactions and the way they are handled. Adjusting for the size of its economy, China has about five times as much cash in circulation as the US. The finding of huge amounts of cash has become a dramatic fixture of all publicized corruption cases: Wen Qiang, the former police chief of Chongqing, was caught in 2009 with nearly a million dollars in renminbi, hidden in a water tank at a relative's home. In another case, the brother of China's former railway minister was caught hiding about five million worth of renminbi at his home.[24]

The empirical evidence suggests that despite China's unique GDP sustained growth pattern, corruption has had the same sorts of negative consequences in China that it has everywhere else. And there is also every reason to believe that if corruption is not better controlled or even reduced in China, over the longer term it could create serious

---

[24]Chinese Way of Doing Business: In Cash We Trust, *New York Times*, April 30, 2013, http://www.nytimes.com/2013/05/01/business/global/chinese-way-of-doing-business-in-cash-we-trust.html?pagewanted=1&_r=0&ref=global-home, accessed July 17, 2013.

damage to the entire economy and subsequently impact the GDP growth rate. Nevertheless, 30 years of steady growth sets China apart from the usual development models where rising corruption has wrought crippling damage and stifled economic growth.[25]

The paradox remains that the developmental process *per se* is replete with opportunities for corruption. According to the World Bank, the simultaneous processes of developing a market economy, designing new political and social institutions and redistributing social assets have created "fertile ground for corruption in transitional countries".[26] China, during the formative period of the 1990s, is indeed a case in point. He (2000) has described the process that occurred throughout the following steps:[27]

1. The co-existence of dual economic systems during the whole transition period provides incentives and opportunities for corrupt practices.
2. The breakdown of the prior distribution of national income among different social strata, (translating into the relative reduction of officials' income) drives government officials and public institutions to seek extra income to supplement their own or their staff's relatively low and fixed official salaries.
3. The loopholes in, and weakness of, regulatory policies and institutions contributed to the growth of corruption.
4. The incompleteness of political reform undermines anti-corruption efforts.
5. The decline in the moral costs of corruption stimulates its further spread.

Present-day China is significantly different from the one that He Zengke was describing in 2000. Corruption patterns have changed

---

[25] Cf. Wedeman (2012), *op. cit.*
[26] World Bank (2000), *Anticorruption in Transition: A Contribution to the Policy Debate*, Washington D.C.: World Bank, p. vii.
[27] He, Z. (2000), Corruption and Anti-corruption in Reform China, *Communist and Post-Communist Studies*, 33, pp. 243–270.

accordingly. On the positive side, anti-corruption agencies have been considerably reinforced and now exhibit a much higher level of technical know-how; laws and regulations have been strengthened; media and public opinion are much more assertive than was the case 10 or 15 years ago. On the negative side, corruption mechanisms have become more and more sophisticated, especially with regard to financial activities; higher and higher land prices provide local officials and entrepreneurs with accrued opportunities for high profits; and — though the exact mechanism is hard to assess — higher income inequality as measured by Gini coefficients "significantly raises the incidence of corruption in China".[28]

Dong and Torgler (2010) further detail their findings as follows: "As a robust result we observe that anti-corruption efforts significantly depress corruption, while we similarly find strong evidence that North China seemed to be more corrupt than South China, probably due to the fact that people in North China are more collectivistic than the people in South China. As a novel result, we also find relatively strong evidence that even the media that is under specific control of the government does indeed act as a control instrument for corruption in China ... Moreover, our findings support the hypothesis that various social heterogeneities breed corrupt practices. Our results also support the theory that relatively high relative wages within the public sector prevent officials from corruption ... Fiscal decentralization tends to discourage local corruption ... while administrative decentralization seems to encourage local corruption. Finally, clear evidence has been given that openness substantially suppresses the incidence of corruption while an abundance of resources and state-owned enterprises are shown to be the breeding ground for corruption."[29] The assertion on North China being more "collectivistic" than South China needs to be seriously qualified. It is true that the economy of North China continues to rely on state-owned enterprises more than is the case in the southern part of the country. It is also true

---

[28] Dong, B. & B. Torgler (2010), The Causes of Corruption: Evidences from China, BASEL, CREMA, *Working Paper No.* 2010–07, p. 19.
[29] *Ibid.*, pp. 31–32.

that cultural differences exist from one region to another. But it would be better to state that the forms that corruption takes and that the relationship existing between civil society, the private sector and the state take different shapes according to local factors, without drawing too quickly general conclusions on the overall level of corruption or on its cultural roots. And, in any case, the cultural geography of China cannot be summarized through an opposition abruptly drawn between the north and the south of the country.

5.3. The Struggle Against Corruption

That authorities show much determination in their struggle against corruption is a fact periodically reasserted through media campaigns and much-publicized trials of corrupt officials. As an example among many others, in November 2011, the former president of the state-owned Shanghai Pharmaceutical Group was sentenced to death, with a two-year reprieve, for taking more than USD 1.8 million in bribes and embezzling another USD 5 million.[30] The fall of Cheng Liangyu — the former first secretary of Shanghai — in 2006, under accusation of misallocation of social pension fund and involvement in real estate corruption, is well remembered (his case had precedents in the cases of the former Beijing party secretary and mayor, Chen Xitong and Wang Baosen in 1995). As to the fall of Bo Xilai in 2012, the story goes well beyond the scope of this study. But the most spectacular cases are not the ones that give the best insights on everyday reality: from 2007 to 2012, more than 15,000 civil servants were allegedly involved in 13,000 of the 81,000 commercial bribery cases investigated by authorities.[31] Additionally, *Xinhua* reported that in 2012, a total of 4,698 officials at the county level or higher were punished by the Chinese Communist Party (CCP)'s disciplinary body, while 961 officials were

---

[30] Shoesmith, T. (2011), Commercial Bribery in China, October 11, 2011, http://www.pillsburylaw.com/publications/commercial-bribery-in-china, accessed July 31, 2013.

[31] Transparency International (2013), China: New Leaders, New Opportunities to Tackle Corruption, March 5, 2013, http://www.transparency.org/news/feature/china_new_leaders_new_opportunities_to_tackle_corruption, accessed July 17, 2013.

transferred to judicial organs, according to the figures from the CCP's Central Commission for Discipline Inspection.[32] Nearly 73,000 people were punished for corruption or dereliction of duty in 2012.[33] According to the report it delivered during the CCP's 18th Congress, over the past five years, the Central Commission of Disciplinary Inspection (CCDI) opened investigations into 643,759 cases and settled 639,068 of them, and 24,584 people were handed over to prosecutors for breaking the law.[34]

The struggle intensified further at the beginning of the year 2013: new regulations from the Political Bureau of the CCP Central Committee and from the Central Military Commission have restricted practices such as ostentatious floral displays and luxury banquets for officials; not only were expensive official banquets traditionally held for the Chinese New Year prohibited, but in advance of the Spring Festival, holiday radio and television stations were to ban advertisements for expensive gifts such as watches and gold coins. Valentine's Day came with renewed reminders, as it may also have become an opportunity for fraud and corruption among some officials. China's prosecutors handled 3,657 corruption cases, and 1,481 cases involving dereliction of duty and rights violations during the first quarter of 2013.[35]

One will notice that the abundance of figures and new regulations may be interpreted in several ways: it reveals the scope of the problem; it speaks of the determination of the authorities and of the pressure that some officials may now experience; but it also speaks of a certain disarray, as these figures are somehow difficult to reconcile and interpret, the nature and level of both offences and punishments remaining at times mysterious. A clearer indicator may be provided by Wang Haixiao, who estimates that on average, the number of cases

---

[32] Xi's Anticorruption Corruption Move Arouse Expectations, *Xinhua*, January 24, 2013.

[33] *Ibid.*

[34] Report of *The CPC Central Commission for Discipline Inspection (CCDI) submitted to the 18th CPC National Congress*.

[35] China's prosecutors handled 3,657 corruption cases, and 1,481 cases involving dereliction of duty and rights violations, during the first quarter of 2013.

investigated in each province per year is 1,228 out of a mean of 377,000 officials per province, i.e. 32.58 cases per 10,000 officials.[36]

The party-state nesting that characterizes China's governance model explains the following: the struggle against corruption is led first and foremost by the relevant instances of the CCP (a principle asserted anew by the 16th Congress in 1992). Besides inner-party supervision, controls and initiatives also emanate from the National People's Congress and the local people's congresses, governmental bodies, judicial supervision, and — now implicitly recognized by the power as legitimate and sometimes even beneficial — the general public and the media. The Party takes the unified leadership of the work of combating corruption. The Party and government both administer this, while the Discipline Inspection Commissions of the Party organize and coordinate it (their personnel amounts to 350,000 persons, the size of China's judiciary and procuracy combined[37]), and different governmental departments take their due responsibilities (with the Ministry of Supervision and the National Audit Office being most prominent among them). In most cases, from the local to the central level, it is the committee of discipline inspection (PCDI at the provincial level, for instance) that first launches investigation of a Party official and, if proceedings are conclusive, will dismiss him/her. After completion within the agency, the PCDI transfers the case to the procurators who will sue the official and others involved in the crime. Sometimes (in less than 20 percent of the cases being raised[38]), procurators take the lead, especially when it is possible to investigate a decision-maker in his/her capacity as a government official, not as a party cadre *per se*.

---

[36] Wang, H. (2013), Do Informal Institutions Tie the Autocrats' Hands? A Mixed-Method Study of Factional Politics and Anticorruption in China, University of Notre Dame, Department of Political Science, *Working Paper Series*, p. 18, available at SSRN: http://ssrn.com/abstract=2206321, accessed July 17, 2013.

[37] See Fu, H. (2011), *The Upward and Downward Spirals in China's Anti-Corruption Enforcement*, University of Hong Kong Faculty of Law Research Paper No. 2011/014, p. 8, available at SSRN: http://ssrn.com/abstract=1883348 or http://dx.doi.org/10.2139/ssrn.1883348, accessed July 17, 2013.

[38] *Ibid.*, p. 6.

This makes for a rich but rather intricate system of control, which is not without its flaws. Factional politics often both triggers and complicates the struggle against corruption.[39] Corruption within the judiciary proper is also a complicating factor: "The superior judges rely on their subordinates to carry out their instructions at the ground level, as it were, while the subordinates rely on the superiors for favored treatment in task assignment, promotion, political protection, which fall in the superiors' competence. Such mutual dependence leads to mutual tolerance of corruption on either side as long as their corrupt interests do not collide. Hence, the opportunities for corruption are structurally extended to judges of all ranks along the hierarchy. Judicial corruption proliferates further."[40] And yet, the increasing sophistication of the legal instruments now available as well as the urgency of the challenge at hand should allow the authorities to enter into a new stage of the anti-corruption struggle. China has ratified the UN Convention Against Corruption (UNCAC) and has signed over 100 judicial assistance treaties with over 70 countries and regions. Still, according to Transparency International, the country's penal code is "not yet in line with this international initiative". Amendments aligned with the UNCAC are therefore needed to curb domestic bribery. Regulation and punitive measures are especially necessary to make new laws effective.[41] This appreciation may not do full justice to the legal and judicial instruments already available.

The characterization and punishment of corrupt practices are mainly regulated by the relevant dispositions of the Criminal Law. The PRC Criminal Law makes it illegal to: make a bribe, whether the target of the bribe is a state official (Art. 389), a non-state official (Art. 164) or an entity or working group (*danwei*) (Art. 391); it is illegal also, for these putative targets, to accept a bribe (Art. 385, 163 and 387). It also prohibits individuals or work units to serve as an intermediary in the commission of an illegal bribe (Art. 392). Article 389 of the Criminal

---

[39] See Wang (2013).

[40] Li, L. (2011), The 'Production' of Corruption in China's Courts, *USALI Working Papers Series*, p. 43.

[41] Transparency International (2013).

Law defines "paying bribes" as giving money or property to any government official for the purpose of seeking an improper benefit. These dispositions and others have been further clarified by an December 26, 2012 interpretation issued by the Supreme People's Court and the Supreme People's Procuratorate. Illegitimate or improper benefit is defined as referring to any benefit obtained through a violation of any law, administrative regulation, rule or policy, or demanding that a government official provide assistance or facilitation in a way that violates any law, administrative regulation, rule, policy or industrial norms — including seeking competitive advantage in a way that violates the principle of equity and fairness. It reiterates the principle that only bribes that are greater than 10,000 yuan are illegal (paying an official or civil servant anything below that figure is not a punishable offence). In calculating the amount of bribes paid, multiple bribes must be aggregated by the tribunals. Various circumstances (amount of bribes having being paid, number of people having been bribed, origins of the funds being used) characterize the criminal offence as "severe" or "extraordinarily severe". The latter category includes bribes being paid to government officials who are responsible for supervising and administering matters in relation to food, pharmaceuticals, manufacturing safety or the environment, etc., that endanger public health or the security of public property.

Other legal dispositions addressing corrupt practices can be found in: the Administrative License Law; the Civil Servant Law; Regulations on Disclosure of Government Information; the Government Procurement Law; the Anti-monopoly Law; the Bidding Law, the Anti-unfair Competition Law and the Whistle-blowing Act. Other sources comprise dispositions applicable to specific industries, such as the rules enacted by the Ministry of Health when it comes to the pharmaceutical industry. These various dispositions target practices such as transferring property at a discounted or commercially unreasonable price; issuing or transferring equity of a company at a less than fair value; granting an interest in an enterprise where the target did not make the corresponding investment or did not provide the corresponding service; transferring money under the cover of gambling, inscription on a payroll, loan, guaranteeing marketing fees, sponsorships, club memberships, charitable contributions, consulting fees, and other service fees (but in most cases gifts are not considered as bribes, though the campaign of the Spring Festival 2013 shows that tolerance in this regard is rapidly diminishing). Taken together, the examination of the legal dispositions having been enacted during the last two or three decades provide the analyst with a good summary of the variety and inventiveness of corrupt business practices in China.

For sure, anti-corruption policies do not stop at repression. They also include prevention. The easiest method for eliminating corruption remains to suppress unreasonable administrative approvals, which were ubiquitous before the era of reforms and opening up. Between 2000 and 2010, 2,183 items requiring administrative examination and approval has been canceled or adjusted, accounting for 60.6 percent of the total.[42] Identifying policy-related sources of corruption is obviously helpful in bringing it under control. Trade restrictions; government subsidies; price control; multiple forex regimes; low wages in civil service; natural resource endowments; and sociological factors have been well known for being sources of corruption.[43] Corruption tends to flourish when institutions are not strong enough and government policies generate economic rents.

Studies about the success of anti-corruption policies reveal a paradox: on the one hand, the CCP's determination to win the fight against corruption manifests itself in many ways. On the other hand, prosecution cases are not rising — they may actually be decreasing — and the CCDI appears often as a lone fighter in the struggle against corruption, as local and provincial officials seem reluctant to join in. This can be partly explained by the fact that official corruption sometimes becomes syndicated over the years (famous cases have implicated hundreds of officials in Xiamen and Shenyang for instance). Central authorities will need to enroll more forcefully local levels in their struggle against corruption, as well as empower the media, civil society and international bodies.[44]

---

[42] Cai, X. (2011), Ministry of Supervision Presentation in Bogota, December 6, 2011: *On China's Anti-Corruption Strategy.*
[43] Mauro, P. (1997), *Why Worry about Corruption?*, Washington DC, MF, Economic Series 6, http://www.imf.org/EXTERNAL/PUBS/FT/ISSUES6/, accessed July 31, 2013.
[44] See Fu (2011).

5.4. Business and the Corruption Trap

The demand for corrupt service — i.e. the supply of bribes or favours, both key tools for corruption — originates from the wish on the one hand to reduce cost and on the other to enhance the value of certain assets. A widespread economic fallacy is to consider that, after all, corruption can be one of the ways to grease the wheels, support growth and remedy possible inefficiencies in public governance. Unfortunately, payoffs are more likely to be invested in illegal business or diverted to foreign bank accounts, as they need to be kept secret. Small-scale facilitating bribes should be fought as strongly as large ones as they feed on themselves and virally infect the whole economy in search of all the possible payoffs.

In many instances, corruption is not seen only as a way to smooth around the rough spots so as to obtain quicker results, but also as a way to load the dices for the benefit of some privileged ones. Corruption has genuinely been interpreted as a symptom of excessively restrictive government policies, with corporate entities attempting to find a shelter from government-induced distortions such as excessive taxes, regulation, and graft. However, widespread corrupt practices attack simultaneously the most promising macroeconomic flows and the most valuable assets of an economy, leading ultimately to one of its key constituents becoming severely damaged: trust in institutions and authorities. But while costs may vary and systemic corruption may co-exist with strong economic performance, experience suggests that corruption is bad for development, as most corrupt behaviours seem to be consistent with a rent-seeking model.

Corruption, a bit like drugs and similar substances, creates long-term damageable and addictive secondary destructing effects to any economy, even if for some time the resulting benefits seem good and possibly stable. Ultimately, corruption creates a shadow economy. This parallel economy weakens the rule of law to a point where any meaningful market transactions can hardly get concluded in a free market environment. This has an impact down to the smallest markets and the way the more modest transactions are concluded. The rule of law, as a way to peacefully regulate transactions, can then quickly be overwhelmed by the rule of white-collar criminality and also by violence as a way to enforce the law of the strongest on the weakest.

Furthermore, corruption introduces inefficiencies in the government contracting process, and finally impacts directly the quality of common goods. Undue benefits are captured by the few managing the gateway to such "free goods" and hijacking higher illegal payoffs, until the very growth determinants of the economy are undermined. The process spreads in the whole economy and finally the underground competition to gain control of both the shadow economy and the gateway to common goods can undermine the political stability of a whole country. A high level of corruption is a sign that something has gone wrong in the relationship between the state and the people.

Corporations are often caught in a "prisoner's dilemma" when dealing with corrupt administrations. A socially responsible firm should in any case strengthen rules of conduct on the weakest spots and educate its executives on why and how to react when a situation happens. No senior manager should assume that a simple "house rules playbook" suffices to do the job. Management example, reward of good professional behaviour, accessible channels to discuss difficult cases and regular training are necessary to infuse a clear conscience on the matter and forge a sound and robust corporate culture on corruption. In many instances, corruption tends to proliferate on illiquid markets and soils where limited options are available. Therefore, one of the effective ways to protect oneself is to open competition and seek out multiple options (e.g. location of a new factory).

There are some international classic cases on "soft spots", and China is no exception to that, where paying bribes can be found "useful" for a firm to access revenues:

— Launching of "white elephant" projects with doubtful social impact;
— Being included in the list of qualified bidders;
— Accessing some confidential information that would provide an unfair competitive advantage;
— Being selected as the sole contractor for or sole buyer of public assets; and
— Inflating prices or reducing quality, a different way to achieve the same goal.

Symmetrically, there are well known cases where paying bribes can be "useful" for a firm to curb expenditures:

— Pay to lighten the regulatory burden, when it needs to be interpreted (e.g. taxes, customs duties);
— Enforcement of criminal laws (e.g. employment, commercial dispute, illegal business etc.);
— Reduce delays to obtain key administrative documentation (e.g. business licence, import-export licence) or service (e.g. access to service); and
— Manipulate debt guarantees and other off-budget contingent liabilities agreed upon without scrutiny.

The development of corruption increases the market value of common good gatekeepers, leading frequently to bargaining for accessing certain "wealthy" positions in the public sector. The value of these positions would be defined by the size of such illegal additional income, the sustainability of the situation, the balance of power between briber and bribee, and finally the acceptable risk related to bribes. The resulting erosion of the legal framework induces less possible recourse and less protection for the weakest, who will see no chance to receive fair and equitable treatment. The bottom line is the steady enhancement of mistrust and social tensions.

The new Chinese leadership is now signalling that the price for both "Tigers" and "Flies" associated with corruption has significantly raised, with social media adding pressure from the civil society on activist capability to microblog hot cases (Weibo) on a nationwide basis. This is a healthy way to reduce the payoff for corruption, provided the presumed innocence of the suspected ones remains guaranteed till the due process is completed. The adequate response from the private sector includes improving the fundamental governance structures of companies operating in China. In this respect, industry leaders and policy-makers should jointly continue to be at the forefront of this effort. Part Three of the present book will come back to the ethical and practical challenges associated with such efforts. However, some basic principles and common sense observations may be already in order:

— If a firm needs to engage in dubious practices in order to develop on a given market segment, it has to strictly avoid such lines of development.

— Corruption practices are more and more subject to international regulations and agreements, and executives may be judged and condemned in a certain country for corruption practices that transpired in another country.

— Anti-corruption regulations originating from within the company proper should generally be stricter than the ones enacted by the national legal framework, especially when it comes to gift practices. In China, an international corporation should be aware of the fact that, should an official be investigated for corruption, his contacts with foreign-owned companies will be under particular scrutiny. It also happens that competing companies accuse each other of illegal practices, and strict internal regulations will help a firm to protect itself against such allegations if they are unfounded.

* * *

To some extent, even our analysis of the concerns raised by corruption practices somehow documents the conclusion drawn from the first chapters of this book: in the last decade, CSR has become a prominent topic for Chinese decision-makers — national and local officials, regulators, Chinese and foreign entrepreneurs, management-level employees, social leaders and netizens. Even if CSR remains an evolving and sometimes vaguely defined domain, the pressing and general character of the demands attached to it requires corporations to define and implement policies that need to be both specific and clearly interrelated. CSR policies must be understood as forming together an "engine" that brings out the best of the corporation's resources and inventiveness, opening up its sense of mission, fostering cooperation among its members and with all stakeholders, and facilitating technical, commercial and social innovation. Part Two will now detail the most important fields that are generally included within CSR, and will specify the constraints, resources and challenges that define these fields in China. Part Three will take again a transversal perspective, looking at the overall dynamics through which corporations can successfully implement CSR as a global imperative rooted into a specific context.

PART TWO

THEMATIC ANALYSIS AND LINES OF ACTION:

AN ASSESSMENT

Corporate social responsibility, we have seen, is embedded into ever-evolving social and cultural practices and concerns. Its priorities and modes of implementation reflect both the consciousness that the company has of itself and of its mission, and the expectations expressed by its stakeholders and notably, those by the state. CSR-related norms and practices vary according to the cultural contexts in which the company operates. This being said, it should be stressed that: (a) every cultural context — and China in particular — provides the company, its employees and the public with specific resources for implementing CSR as long as cultural resources are dynamically and positively used and interpreted; (b) furthermore, this work of creative reinterpretation takes place in a context where values and attitudes are cross-fertilized, creating new corporate cultures that reflect the diversity of the companies' operational settings.

Practically, the CSR agenda takes shape on a triangle-shaped borderland: the domain determined by the company's field of operation; the needs resulting from national constraints and social expectations; and the way these constraints and expectations are translated into laws, norms and codes of various types. Part Two will examine the various topics and lines of action which, taken together, spell out the dominant CSR agenda in today's China.

CHAPTER SIX

Environmental Standards and Concerns

The importance taken by environmental concerns in China makes this area the keystone of CSR practices in the view of the public and the state alike. It is thus necessary to examine in some detail what makes such preoccupations so crucial both for companies and society at large. Reasons specific to China lend environmental concerns a prominence that goes even beyond the one they have reached in Western countries — for very good reasons.

6.1. Pressing Concerns, New Priorities

We have already mentioned the 12th Five-Year Plan for the Environmental Health Work of the National Environmental Protection. Other laws and regulations are similarly inspired by official concerns over a situation that has not improved over the years: the 2012 Human Development Index Ranking ranks China at 101 out of 187 nations.[1] The 2012 Yale Environment Index ranks the country 116 out of 132.[2] Figures, detailed below (often compiled through collaboration between domestic agencies and international organizations such as the World Health Organization (WHO) and the World Bank) confirm this worrying outlook, making environmental protection a recognized national priority that must be translated into vigorous actions. Companies,

---

[1]UN Development Programme, Human Development Report Office (2012), *Human Development Report*, http://www.undp.org/content/undp/en/home/librarypage/hdr.html, accessed July 17, 2013.

[2]Yale University (2012), EPI Rankings, http://epi.yale.edu/epi2012/rankings; Country Profile: China, http://epi.yale.edu/dataexplorer/countryprofiles?iso=CHN; accessed July 17, 2013.

both international and local, have become much sought-after partners for contributing to the clean-up efforts and structural solutions. The level of social responsibility shown by a company is primarily evaluated by the way it tackles its environmental impact. This trend has been exemplified by the progressive development of China's Green Watch program (Box 6.1).

Some historical background information is in order here: China's astounding economic development, already pursued for over three decades, does not need to be documented. However, the overall environmental effects of such growth and its social implications have been of rapidly growing concern, in China and abroad. In that respect, the

Box 6.1 China's Green Watch Program

"Despite long-standing efforts to control pollution with traditional regulatory instruments, China continues to have severe pollution problems. This has led China's State Environmental Protection Administration (SEPA) to test the effectiveness of environmental performance rating and disclosure in a program supported by the World Bank. In 1999, SEPA launched its Green Watch program in Zhenjiang City, Jiangsu Province and Hohhot City, Inner Mongolia Autonomous District.... The first Green Watch ratings were disclosed through the media in 1999. The program was extended from Zhenjiang to the entire Jiangsu Province in 2001, and to eight other provinces during 2003–2005. Nationwide implementation of Green Watch has been promoted since 2005... Evidence for the Green Watch program throughout Jiangsu Province indicates both increasing participation by firms and improvement in their compliance rates... Green Watch has significantly increased market and stakeholder pressure on managers to improve their firms' environmental performance. More specifically, controlling for the characteristics of locations, firms, and individual managers, we find that firms with better ratings perceive positive impacts on market competitiveness, overall market value, and relationships with different stakeholders, while the firms with bad ratings are more likely to perceive deterioration."

Source: Jin, Y., H. Wang & D. Wheeler (2010), Environmental Performance Rating and Disclosure: An Empirical Investigation of China's Green Watch Program, *The World Bank Policy Research Working Paper Series*, 5420.

ratification by the National People's Congress of the 11th Five-Year Plan, in March 2006, constituted a turning point, a shift that has been confirmed and furthered by the ratification of the 12th Five-Year Plan in 2011: China intends to take the path of sustainable development. The Chinese government was still fostering and foreseeing a high growth rate, while focusing on the nature and quality of the projected growth. Obviously, financial and economic ups and downs registered from 2008 on have altered the hierarchy of priorities. Unemployment has become a primary social concern, and the engine growth had to be re-launched at several occasions. This did not mean that environmental tensions and their social implications became secondary concerns. As a matter of fact, they constitute structural challenges that weaken China's competitiveness and social fabric, whatever the economic conjuncture looks like. In that respect, corporations and civil society share a common interest: to make environmental protection a cornerstone of the developmental model (Box 6.2).

Box 6.2 The Parable of the Elevator: Accelerated Growth... and its Risks

China Becomes the World's Largest Elevator Provider

China has become the world's largest manufacturer and seller of elevators, with an average annual growth of 20 percent over the past ten years, the organizers of the upcoming 2012 World Elevator Summit said on Tuesday. By the end of 2011, China had installed more than two million elevators nationwide, while its elevator sales and production volume both topped 450,000 units, accounting for more than 60 percent of the global total, the organizers said. China's elevator export volume exceeded 47,000 units in the same period. The huge demand has helped boost the development of domestic elevator producers, who now occupy almost 40 percent of the domestic market, up from 20 percent ten years ago, it said. There is still a great deal of room for future development, as the country's per capita ownership of in-service elevators is only one-third of the global average, it added.

Source: China Becomes the World's Largest Elevator Provider, *Xinhua*, September 5, 2012.

(Continued)

Box 6.2 (*Continued*)

Workers Killed as Elevators Plummets 34 Floors to the Ground
Nineteen workers at a construction site in Wuhan, Hubei province, died on Thursday after the elevator they were using fell 100 m to the ground. The tragedy happened around 1 pm when 19 painters at the construction site of Donghujingyuan, a residential real estate project, were taking an elevator, according to the local fire department. A malfunction occurred as the elevator was going up and it began to accelerate, local media reported. As soon as it reached the top 34th floor, the steel cables broke, leaving the car to fall free. Residents living near the construction site said the maximum capacity of the elevator used by the workers is 12 passengers, reported cnhan.com, a major news website in Wuhan. More than 347,000 work-related accidents happened in 2011, and more than 75,500 people died in such accidents, according to the State Administration of Work Safety.

Source: Workers Killed as Elevators Plummets 34 Floors to the Ground, *China Daily*, September 14, 2012, http://www.chinadaily.com.cn/china/2012-09/14/content_15756953.htm, accessed July 31, 2013.

12 Injured in 18-floor Elevator Plunge
Twelve elderly people were injured when an elevator malfunctioned and plunged 18 floors to the ground… One of the injured, who was not identified, was quoted by Sohu as saying there were about 14 to 15 people in the elevator… The elevator's load is limited to 13 people or 1,000 kilograms in weight. Its next safety inspection date was due on July 29, 2012.

Source: 12 Injured in 18-floor Elevator Plunge, *China Daily*, May 10, 2012, http://www.chinadaily.com.cn/china/2012-05/10/content_15261500.htm, accessed July 31, 2013.

6.2. Scarcity of Resources and the Sustainability Imperative

The nature and degree of environmental responsibility to be exercised by companies depend to some extent on the amount and quality of natural resources (land, forests, water, minerals, etc.) possessed by the country where it operates. What makes corporate responsibility more stringent in China is the paucity of resources that the country has had to rely on, now and during the course of its history, both in absolute and relative terms. China's per capita fresh water, arable land and forest resources account for 28 percent, 40 percent and 25 percent of the world average, respectively.[3] This scarcity of resources partially explains the environmental challenge it must confront.[4]

Furthermore, the use and management of these natural resources has been at times erratic, both in the past and since the beginning of China's economic success story. Pan Yue, the then-deputy director of the State Environmental Protection Administration (now Ministry of Environmental Protection[5], of which Pan Yue is Vice Minister), was sounding the alarm in March 2005 — at a decisive moment in the process through which China has decided to shift toward a more sustainable model of development: "Five of the ten most polluted cities worldwide are in China; acid rain is falling on one third of our territory; half of the water in China's seven largest rivers is completely useless; a quarter of our citizens lack access to clean drinking water; a third of the urban population is breathing polluted air; less than a fifth of the rubbish in cities is treated and processed in an environmentally sustainable manner. Because air and water are polluted, we are losing 8–15 percent of our gross domestic product. This does not include the costs for health and human suffering: in Beijing alone, 70–80 percent of all deadly cancer cases are related to the environment. Lung cancer has emerged as the number one cause of death."[6] Pan Yue had also described the year 2006 as "the grimmest for China's environmental situation", with 161 serious environmental accidents and failure to

---

[3]China's National Report on Sustainable Development (2012), http://www.china-un.org/eng/zt/sdreng/, p. 6, accessed July 31, 2013.

[4] Among several surveys and analyses of China's overall environmental situation, see Hofman, I. & P. Ho (2012), China's 'Developmental Outsourcing: A Critical Examination of Chinese Global 'Land Grabs' Discourse, *Journal of Peasant Studies*, 39(1), pp. 1–48, http://dx.doi.org/10.1080/03066150.2011.653109, accessed July 17, 2013.

[5] http://english.mep.ch.

[6]*Der Spiegel* (English Edition), SPIEGELInterview with China's Deputy Minister of the Environment: "The Chinese Miracle Will End Soon", March 2005, http://www.spiegel.de/international/spiegel/spiegel-interview-with-china-s-deputy-minister-of-the-environment-the-chinese-miracle-will-end-soon-a-345694.html, accessed July 17, 2013.

meet the target of reducing pollution emission by 2 percent (see also Box 6.3).[7] Several of these figures are not accurate anymore, but these statements still sketch out the environmental challenges met by China as well as the crucial role to be played by companies, small and big, national and local, in their resolution. As a matter of fact, through the Green Watch program, the Ministry of Environmental Protection has made the exposure and punishment of polluters operating against the law one of its main missions. Other ministries have been engaged in positive interaction for promoting clean technologies.

"Green GDP Accounting" refers to an accounting system deducting natural resources depletion costs and environmental degradation

---

Box 6.3 The 2005 Songhua River Incident: A Turning Point in Environmental Awareness

The Songhua River runs through the old industrial region of northeast China with many industries located along its banks, including many chemical plants, before joining the Amur River and flowing into Russia. It is the main water source for many cities, including Harbin, the capital of Heilongjiang Province. On November 13, 2005, an explosion took place at the Jilin Chemical Industrial Co. plant (a PetroChina subsidiary) in the Jilin city, about 380 km upstream from Harbin. Five persons were killed and nearly 70 injured. More than 10,000 residents were evacuated as a precaution against further explosions and severe pollution from the plant. The explosion, and the fire fighting efforts, led to the spillage of about 100 tons of chemicals, mainly benzene, into the Songhua River. Ten days after the explosion, a contaminated stretch of water 80 km long reached Harbin and took 40 hours to pass through it. As a result, the Harbin municipal government had to temporarily shut down its water supply, leaving around 3.5 million people without access to tap water. The incident caused a serious water crisis in the region along the river.

Source: World Bank (2008), Addressing China's Water Scarcity: A Synthesis of Recommendations for Selected Water Resource Management Issues, Washington D.C.: World Bank Publications, p. 128.

---

[7]Articles from *WSJA*, January 12–14, 2007. Air and water pollutants were supposed to be reduced by 2 percent in 2006 but they instead rose by 1.8 percent and 1.2 percent.

costs, so as to assess the quality of economic development in a real sense. According to the evaluation published in September 2006 by the SEPA and the National Bureau of Statistics, economic loss caused by environmental pollution was 511.8 billion yuan, accounting for 3.05 percent of national GDP in 2004. Environmental costs by water pollution, by air pollution and by solid wastes and pollution accidents accounted for 55.9 percent, 42.9 percent and 1.2 percent of the total costs, respectively.[8] Since then, the project taken as a whole has been discontinued, but statistics released on specific topics confirm the overall accuracy of these figures, which constitute a low-range estimate.

Scarcity of resources is stringent in the case of water, making water conservation a major social responsibility for corporations operating within China. Every Chinese citizen has, on average, a water reserve of 2,200 m^3, merely 28 percent of the world's average level, yet the nation is setting an ambitious goal to exceed the global average living standard in this century.[9] Nearly 42 percent of the population lives in China's northern provinces (which include 60 percent of its cultivated land), where they have access to only 14 percent of the country's water supply. Moreover, 90 percent of the cities' water tables, and 75 percent of the rivers and lakes are polluted. Overuse of water resources has caused the ground to sink in around 50 cities.[10] Also, China emits as much organic pollution into the aquatic environment as the US, Japan and India combined. In 2006, some 80 percent of China's 7,555 most polluting factories were situated near rivers and lakes, as well as in densely populated areas. 60,000 died from diarrhea, bladder and stomach cancer and other diseases that can be caused by water-borne pollution. According to Tortajada and Biswas (2013),"In 1972, the country drew about 20 km^3 of groundwater. By 2010, it was drawing 112 km^3 a

---

[8] The environmental pollution costs should include costs of over 20 items while the Chinese Green GDP accounting had only covered costs of 10 items (health, agricultural and materials losses caused by air pollution; health, industrial and agricultural production losses, and water shortage caused by water pollution; economic loss caused by land occupation of solid wastes, etc.).

[9] Water Will Define China's Future, *Global Times,* February 11, 2011.

[10] *Ibid.*

year, an increase of 560 percent in less than 40 years. Today, almost 70 percent of North China's irrigated areas depend on groundwater — Nearly the entire rural population and half of the urban population depend on groundwater. A report issued by the Geological Survey of China in February 2013 confirmed the fact that 90 percent of the country's groundwater is polluted, much of it seriously so (see also Box 6.4). The report also said that a survey of 11 cities across China indicated that 64 percent of water sources were "severely" polluted and 33 percent "'lightly'" polluted. Only three of the sources could be considered clean.[11]

Box 6.5 presents a case study of possible corporate responses to the water challenge, by taking a look at Saint-Gobain.

Together with water management, air pollution is a prominent concern for corporations and the public alike. China is now the world's leading emitter of sulphur and of greenhouse gases. According to various forecasts, China's CO_2 emissions will account for about 20 percent of the world's total by 2025. The World Bank estimated in 2007 that, of the 20 most polluted cities in the world, 12 were Chinese. Moreover,

---

Box 6.4 China's Water Scarcity — The Thirst for Clean Water

"Over 300 million people living in rural China have no access to safe drinking water... Per capita water availability in northern China is less than one-fourth that in southern China, one-eleventh of the world average, and less than the threshold level that defines *water scarcity*... Of the 27 major monitored lakes and reservoirs, only 29 percent met standards safe for human consumption after treatment... The population is expected to continue to grow, reaching 1.5 billion sometime around 2030. These three trends pose serious challenges for improving China's water resources management."

Source: World Bank (2009), *Addressing China's Water Scarcity*. Rep. no. 48725, The World Bank: The Water Sector Board Practitioner Notes, May 2009, www.worldbank.org/water, accessed July 17, 2013.

---

[11]Tortajada C. & A.K. Biswas (2013), The Problem of Water Management, *China Daily*, March 5, 2013, http://www.chinadaily.com.cn/opinion/2013-03/05/content_16276592.htm, accessed July 17, 2013.

Box 6.5 Case Study: Saint-Gobain Water Policy

"Our long-term goal is to withdraw the minimal amount of water required and aim for zero industrial liquid discharge while preventing new impacts on other ecosystems or stakeholders. To support the deployment of this policy across the industrial base, we defined an EHS (Environment — Health — Safety) standard for water that sets out the minimum requirements to be fulfilled in the long term. We have also introduced an assessment grid for risk exposure and site vulnerability. This group-wide assessment grid examines three interdependent quantitative and qualitative risks:

1. The risk of water constraint: factors that can affect or compromise water supply, and therefore business, at any given site.
2. The risk of pollution: factors relating to site discharges and their impact on the receiving environment.
3. The risk of flooding: vulnerability factors relating to the frequency and intensity of adverse weather phenomena, particularly natural disasters.

Priority will be given to sites identified in 2012 as having the highest levels of risk... In 2011, based on 2010's output, the group's concerned sites withdrew 73.6 million m^3 of water, down 3.3 percent from 76.1 million m^3 in 2010... In 2011, the group's liquid water discharges totaled 48.1 million m^3. The water standard, which will be applied for the first time in 2012, requires sites to limit the number of discharge points and ensure discharge quality before channeling effluent into the municipal sewage system, natural environment, or other outlets. A risk assessment for accidental chemical pollution will also be included in the water standard... Due to the complex nature of many of the group's processes, it is difficult to calculate the rate of water recycling and reuse. In applying the water standard, we intend to make improvements in this area and ultimately produce a reliable metric for the entire scope of reporting."

Source: Saint-Gobain Sustainable Development Report, 2011.

the number of vehicles on the roads rose from 5.5 millions in 1990 to 70 million in 2010, with a forecast of 200 millions for 2020.[12]

---

[12]China Auto Web, How Many Cars Are There in China?, September 5, 2010, http://chinaautoweb.com/2010/09/how-many-cars-are-there-in-china/, accessed August 6, 2013.

UESTIONS

— How precise and reliable is our assessment grid as to our actual consumption of water and other natural resources?

— Are sources of waste and environmental risks both clearly and periodically identified?

— Do we have a proactive program of waste reduction that first tackles the most obvious causes and locations?

— How are our environmental targets defined and evaluated? Are they ambitious enough in terms of commitment, innovation and investment?

— Is our practical experience in tackling these issues clearly formulated, and do the lessons learned translate into advice and procedures shared in the corporation and beyond?

— Does our waste and risk reduction policy engage our subsidiaries and providers, the local communities and other stakeholders?

China's energy dependence on coal poses a particular problem, considering that the country has abundant supplies of coal and already burns more of it than the US, Europe and Japan combined. The gradual closing down of small-scale mines should improve the situation; besides, the International Energy Agency projected in its 2012 World Energy Outlook that by 2035, about 55 percent of China's overall electricity generation would come from coal, based on government policy commitments, down from roughly 80 percent in 2010. Nuclear power, by comparison, could make up 10 percent of overall electricity generation from around 2 percent in 2010, according to the report's projections. Still, when it comes to the environmental impact of the energy sector, most experts exhibit little optimism.[13]

---

[13]Burkitt, L. & B. Spegele (2013), Beijing Fog Prompts State Media to Shift Tone, *WSJ*, January 14, 2013, http://online.wsj.com/article/SB100014241278873245957045782416405202226304.html?mod=WSJAsia_hpp_MIDDLETopStories, accessed July 17, 2013.

A WHO estimate resulting from a study conducted together with the Chinese authorities holds that 470,000 Chinese died prematurely in 2008 due to air pollution, and specific studies, one of them led conjointly by Peking University's School of Public Health and Greenpeace, came up with more alarming specific indicators concerning four major Chinese cities, putting the cost of healthcare to treat pollution-related ailments in Beijing, Shanghai, Guangzhou and Xi'an at more than USD 1 billion.[14,15,16] According to a Health Ministry survey of 30 cities and 78 counties, increasing air and water pollution, as well as the use of pesticides and food additives, are the main causes behind the quickly rising cancer rates. Cancer is the number one cause of death in China.[17]

In January 2013, stringent air pollution problems generated accrued public debate. An air monitor at the US Embassy in Beijing showed on January 12, 2013 that the PM2.5 level — the measure of tiny particulates that are especially hazardous because they penetrate tissue and can lead to diseases such as cancer — reached 886 mg/m^3, a level 35 times the WHO's recommended standard. China's Central Television made poisonous air the lead item in its prime-time news broadcast on the evening of January 13, and again in its midday news program the following day. On January 14, the *People's Daily* ran a front-page editorial under the headline "A Beautiful China Starts with Healthy Breathing". Also on January 14, the government announced it was closing some factories and 700 construction sites in the northeastern industrial city of Shijiazhuang, at that time the most heavily polluted city in China according to official figures.[18] In the first three months of 2013, two major air pollutants — nitrous dioxide and particulate matter called

[14] PM2.5 Kills Thousands, Researchers Say, *China Daily*, September 12, 2012.

[15] Kahn, J. & J. Yardley (2007), As China Roars, Pollution Reaches Deadly Extremes, *New York Times*, August 26, 2007, http://www.nytimes.com/2007/08/26/world/asia/26china.html?_r=1&oref=slogin, accessed July 17, 2013.

[16] Pierson, D. (2013), China's Smog Taints Economy, Health, *Los Angeles Times*, January 26, 2013, http://www.latimes.com/business/la-fi-china-smog-20130126,0,885158.story, accessed July 17, 2013.

[17] Larsen, J. (2011), Cancer Now Leading Cause of Death in China, May 25, 2011, http://www.earth-policy.org/plan_b_updates/2011/update96, accessed August 6, 2013.

[18] Burkitt & Spegele (2013).

PM10 — increased by almost 30 percent in Beijing over the same period in 2012. During the winter of 2012–2013, cities in northern China grappled with record levels of air pollution, which have stirred fear and anger among many Chinese. To prevent cost increases, large state-owned enterprises in the oil and power industries have been suspected to consistently block proposed environmental policies that would cut down the levels of pollutants. In March 2013, researchers released new data that showed that outdoor air pollution had contributed to 1.2 million premature deaths in China in 2010 (a figure much higher than the WHO figure for the year 2008 quoted above). Outdoor air pollution was the fourth leading risk factor for death, the researchers said.[19,20]

As is the case with water scarcity and pollution, these figures have been triggering concern throughout the Chinese society, prompting greater vigilance to the effects of corporate activity on health. Observers agree that an increasing number of local protests taking place target industrial concerns detrimental to water and air quality and thus endangering the health of the neighboring communities. In 2007, Chen Xiwen, Director of the Central Rural Work Leadership Group Office, had already stated that peasants' petitions to the government stemmed from land expropriation (around 50 percent); embezzlement and corruption in village committees (around 30 percent); and environmental pollution (around 20 percent).[21] The environmental pollution figure has probably been steadily rising since.

The seriousness of the situation is hastening the setting up of more proactive and encompassing policies. In September 2013, the government unveiled a plan aimed at tackling the country's air pollution. It envisions cutting China's total coal consumption to below 65 percent

---

[19] Wong, E. (2013a), Air Pollution Linked to 1.2 Million Premature Deaths in China, *New York Times*, April 1, 2013, http://www.nytimes.com/2013/04/02/world/asia/air-pollution-linked-to-1-2-million-deaths-in-china.html?src=rechp, accessed July 17, 2013.

[20] Wong, E. (2013b), 2 Major Air Pollutants Increase in Beijing, *New York Times*, April 3, 2013, http://www.nytimes.com/2013/04/04/world/asia/two-major-air-pollutants-increase-in-china.html?ref=global-home&_r=0, accessed July 17, 2013.

[21] Yu, W. (2007), *Huanjing wuran yinfa shangfang you shenggao qushi* (Environmental Pollution Has an Increasing Trend), *Southern Metropolis Daily*, January 31, 2007. (虞伟，环境污染引发上访有升高趋势，南方都市报 2007年 1月31日).

of its total primary energy use by 2017, while the share of non-fossil fuel energy will be raised to 13 percent. A number of new industrial projects located in areas with already high pollution levels will be banned from setting up their own coal-fired power plants. The overall cut in energy consumption per unit of industrial value added would be around 20 percent by 2017 compared to 2012. Technical improvements in coal-fired plants, steel mills and cement plants will be considerably hastened, and more radical transformations will apply to chemical engineering, papermaking, dyeing and tanning industries. Upgrades at refinery enterprises should improve the quality of fuel oil. Other measures (elimination of outdated plants and vehicles, heavier penalties for environmental violations, stricter implementation of protection standards) are also detailed, measures which will affect all industrial sectors.[22]

Soil conservation is another issue that needs to trigger the exercise of corporate responsibility in China. In the last decade, China has lost around 8 million hectares of cultivable land. Some studies are forecasting the loss of 10 million additional hectares of arable land by 2030. Local governments often sell their land to cities or urban developers, even using land as "loan insurance". Often, the land sits unused or inefficiently rushed through the process of urbanization. One survey conducted by the government showed that about 43 percent of requisitioned land remains idle; the resulting loss of farmland is seen as a serious threat to food self-sufficiency.[23] Among 200 large land expropriation projects of 11 counties of a certain province, only 42 projects are used for public utilities, while 148 projects are used to pursuit profits, among which 35 are real estate projects. The development of the western part of China could further exacerbate the trend if the land requisition initially implemented in the east were to be imposed on an even more fragile natural environment. The ecosystem of 60 percent of

---

[22]Mu, X. (2013), China Reveals Multi-Pronged Air Pollution Battle Plan, *Xinhua*, September 12, 2013, http://news.xinhuanet.com/english/china/2013-09/12/c_132715799.htm, accessed September 27, 2013.

[23] Guo, L., J. Lindsay & P. Minro-Faure (2008), *China: Integrated Land Policy Reform in a Context of Rapid Urbanization*, Agricultural and Rural Development Notes, Issue 36, February, Washington DC: World Bank.

the country's territory is already considered vulnerable. Deserts occupy more than 20 percent of the territory and are extending at a rate of around 2,500 km² per year. Acid rainfall is affecting 30 percent of the country. With 38 percent of its territory concerned, China is confronting the most important land erosion problem in the world. It is worth noting that the sensitivity of the soil conservation problem is so great that, till today, surveys on soil pollution are still treated as a "state secret".[24]

In their industrial practice as in their social and philanthropic initiatives, corporations should pay attention to the maintenance and nurturing of biodiversity. With only 22 percent *of forested land* in 2010, compared to the world's average of 34 percent, China is poor in forest resources.[25] Virgin forests account for 1 percent of its total territory. Its wood stock per inhabitant is around one sixth of the world average. The proportion of young and middle-aged forests is of 70 percent of all secondary growth forests, and the growth stock per forest unit is low.[26,27] Besides, simple conifer forests comprise two-thirds of China's planted forests, with four great conifers accounting for 80 percent of the total. China's biodiversity ranks eighth in the world and first in the northern hemisphere.[28] The country has 15–20 percent

---

[24] *Shanghai Daily* (2013), Soil Pollution Survey: A 'State Secret', February 26, 2013, http://www.china.org.cn/environment/2013-02/26/content_28059593.htm, accessed August 6, 2013.

[25] In 2004, the per capita forest area ranked the 134th and per capita forest reserves the 122nd in the world (the forest area per capita is only 0.12 ha in China, 12 percent of the world average, forest stock per capita is less than 13 percent of the world average). The geographical distribution of China's forest resources was rather uneven, with only 5.86 percent of forest coverage in the five northwest provinces (autonomous regions) that accounted for 32.19 percent of the national territory.

[26] Mongabay (2013), China, http://rainforests.mongabay.com/20china.htm, accessed July 17, 2013.

[27] See also Shen, X. (2005), China's Forests: Their Quality and Sustainable Management, *Chinese Cross Currents*, 2(4), pp. 100–129.

[28] More than 32,800 species of higher plants and about 104,500 species of animals have been identified.

Box 6.6 China's Biodiversity Under Threat

"China has some 2,487 known species of amphibians, birds, mammals and reptiles according to figures from the World Conservation Monitoring Center. Of these, 19.7 percent are endemic, meaning they exist in no other country, and 11.2 percent are threatened. China is home to at least 32,200 species of vascular plants, of which 55.9 percent are endemic. 11.3 percent of China is protected under the International Union for Conservation of Nature's categories I-V."

Source: Mongabay.com (2000), China Forest Information and Data, http://rainforests. mongabay.com/deforestation/2000/China.htm, accessed July 17, 2013.

of the world's endangered species, higher than the world average of 10–15 percent (see Box 6.6 for figures in 2000).[29]

Boxes 6.7 and 6.8 details some conservation efforts made, with Box 6.8 focusing on the case study of Guerlain's orchid preservation.

As can be expected, *China's environment is also affected, or potentially affected, by global warming.*[30] A 2006 official report said that temperatures would keep rising through this century as a result of increased energy consumption and greenhouse gas emissions. The report predicted that the average annual temperature would rise 1.3–2.1°C by 2020, and 2.3–3.3°C by 2050. Another report released by the State Oceanic Administration beginning of 2007 also warned of a rapid rise in sea levels. It said that the country had witnessed an average annual sea-level rise of 2.5 mm in recent years, and predicted that in the next years, the sea level would continue to rise by 9–31 mm over the 2006 level.[31] Tibet's 46,000 glaciers

---

[29] China probably contains around 10 percent of all species living on earth. It has an especially high number of plant species (about 30,000), including 3,116 genera, of which 243 are endemic. China is also one of the eight original centers of crop diversity in the world. It is the original source of approximately 200 of the world's 1,200 species of cultivated crops. It contains nearly 600 varieties of domesticated animals and poultry.

[30] See the GAIN Index at: http://index.gain.org/country/china (China ranks 96 out of 161 countries on the Global Adaptation Index). This index measures a country's ability to adapt to global climate change.

[31] National Program Targets Climate Change, *China Daily*, February 16, 2007, http://www.china.org.cn/english/environment/200366.htm, accessed August 6, 2013.

Box 6.7 China's Forest Conservation

"China's forest coverage rate rose from 8.6 percent in the early 1950s to 18.21 percent in 2008. Forested area increased from 115.28 million ha in the early 1950s to 174.91 million ha in 2008. In the five years ending in 2005, China's forests grew 4.06 million ha annually.... China plans to raise its forest coverage rate from 18.21 percent in 2008 to 26 percent by 2050. A minimum of 4.65 billion *mu* (310 million ha) of forests will be retained and maintained."

Source: Developments in China's Forestry Sector, *Xinhua News Agency*, March 20, 2009, http://www.china.org.cn/environment/report_review/2009–03/20/content_17473108.htm, accessed May 11, 2012.

Box 6.8 Guerlain and Orchids Preservation

Guerlain, a French luxury brand created in 1828, and part of the LVMH group since 1994, operates in the field of fragrances, cosmetics and skin care products. Guerlain created an international R&D and biodiversity center across the world, through the creation of its Orchidarium platform, with a presence in Switzerland, France, China and Thailand. In Yunnan, Guerlain partnered with Joseph Margraffor a decade, a renowned German scientist, to protect and develop the "Vanda coerulea orchid", then amongst the endangered species, while researching and applying "Vanda coerulea orchid's exceptional longevity properties" in its cosmetics line. In the south of Yunnan, Guerlain endeavored to protect and plant this rare orchid, to help it grow in a natural environment and, from 2012 on, has extended this biodiversity preservation effort to Thailand.

Sources: Simmler, C., C. Antheaume & A. Lobstein (2010), Antioxidant Biomarkers from Vanda coerulea Stems Reduce Irradiated HaCaT PGE-2 Production as a Result of COX-2 Inhibition, *PLoS One*, 5(10), http://www.ncbi.nlm.nih.gov/pmc/articles/PMC2965657/, accessed July 17, 2013.

See also: Arguelles, A. (2010), Growing Orchids with Guerlain, *Vanity Fair*, http://www.vanityfair.com/online/beauty/2010/02/guerlain, accessed July 17, 2013.

are shrinking fast. In some areas, average loss has been well in excess of 10 percent since measurements began in the 1960s and 70s. The UN Development Program has published even more dramatic figures, saying the plateau's glaciers could have almost entirely disappeared by the end of the century. As average temperatures continue to rise, 50 square miles are lost each year.[32] China's emissions, which grew 10 percent in 2010 according to BP, are likely to start falling only after 2030, the report says. It says China's emissions reduction efforts up to 2020 will cost 10 trillion yuan ($1.5 trillion), including 5 trillion yuan for energy-saving technology and new and renewable energy. "Assuming no measures to counter global warming, grain output in the world's most populous nation could fall from 5 to 20 percent by 2050, depending on whether a 'fertilization effect' from more carbon dioxide in the air offsets losses", says the report.[33]

Additionally, during the last two decades, logging and mining operations led by Chinese companies in Southeast Asia and Africa have been targeted as particularly detrimental for the global environment. Responding to the challenge, China is to improve efforts to guide and help domestic investors in shouldering CSR and protecting the environment, according to a statement released by the Ministry of Commerce in March 2013. As part of the commitment, the ministry, together with the Ministry of Environmental Protection, has launched the "Guidelines on Environmental Protection for China's Outbound Investment and Cooperation".[34]

6.3. CSR and Environmental Impacts

A March 2006 survey by the Chinese Academy of Sciences ranked China 56th out of 59 countries surveyed in terms of resource-use

---

[32]Spencer, R. (2007), Tibetan Shepherds Welcome Climate Change, *The Telegraph*, February 15, 2007, http://www.telegraph.co.uk/news/worldnews/1542788/Tibetan-shepherds-welcome-climate-change.html, accessed August 6, 2013.
[33]Global Warming Threatens China's Advance, *The Sydney Morning Herald*, January 18, 2012, http://www.smh.com.au/business/world-business/global-warming-threatens-chinas-advance-20120118-1q5x1.html, accessed May 11, 2012.
[34]Green Guidance on the Way for Chinese Companies Operating Abroad, *China Daily*, March 1, 2013, http://www.chinadailyapac.com/article/green-guidance-way-chinese-companies-operating-abroad, accessed August 6, 2013.

efficiency. Though remarkable efforts have been consented around 2007–2009, the trend has not been reversed yet: in 2011, energy consumption climbed 7 percent, the fastest rate since 2007, according to a publication by the National Bureau of Statistics of China.[35] China's consumption of resources is still higher than its growth rate. Besides, China is now importing vast quantities of grain, soybeans, iron ore, aluminum, copper, platinum, potash, oil and natural gas, forest products for lumber and paper, and the cotton needed for its world-dominating textile industry. China's consumption of steel has soared and is more than twice that of the US. There was a 69 percent increase in steel use worldwide between 2000 and 2010, with China experiencing an increase of over 400 percent for the same period.[36] China is now the number one producer and number one consumer of steel in the world. In addition to steel, China also leads in the use of other metals, such as aluminum and copper. As just noted, the overall direction has not been altered yet: "Demand for coal, which China relies on for about 70 percent of its energy needs, rose 9.7 percent in 2011 from a year earlier… That's the highest growth since 2005."[37]

Corporations need to evaluate and tackle their environmental responsibility in the global context that we just sketched: China's authorities have been increasingly straightforward in their assessment of the systemic environmental imbalance presently experienced by the country. This gives special weight to the environmental impact of all decisions taken by corporations — be they related to the location of their plants, factors of production, waste treatment or technological choices. The firm is now perceived, both by the public and the state, as the key player — the one that can lead the national efforts deployed toward environmental rehabilitation. This gives extra sensitivity to the

---

[35]Statistics taken from: http://www.stats.gov.cn/tjgb/ndtjgb/qgndtjgb/t20120222_402786440.htm, accessed July 17, 2013.

[36]World Coal Association (2010), Coal & Steel Statistics, http://www.worldcoal.org/resources/coal-statistics/coal-steel-statistics/, accessed May 9, 2012.

[37]Chua, B. & W. Zhu (2012), China Energy Consumption Rises at Fastest Pace in Four Years, *Bloomberg News*, February 22, 2012, http://www.bloomberg.com/news/2012-02-22/china-energy-consumption-rises-at-fastest-pace-in-four-years.html, accessed May 9, 2012.

decisions that managers need to take, but also opens up a field of opportunities for image building, employees' mobilization and corporate innovation as well as for redrafting a corporation's model of cooperation with its supply chain (see Box 6.9 for an illustration by China Mobile, and Box 6.10 for an example from Suning).

Box 6.9 China Mobile: Environmental International Standards and the Supply Chain

"We have introduced the Social Accountability 8000 International Standard (*SA8000*), *ISO14000* and other CSR standards into our supplier rating criteria in the process of bidding, which has subsequently led our suppliers to evaluate their employees' health, safety, and environmental protection... We required our suppliers to strictly adhere to state standards for environmental protection and to take on social responsibilities. For example, during our centralized procurement of lead-acid batteries in 2012, suppliers unable to fulfill the environmental requirements were disqualified from the bidding process. Likewise, we terminated the collaboration with suppliers who were selected in the 2011 bidding process but were unable to fulfill the environmental requirements. In Henan, we used *SA8000*, as well as *ISO14000* environmental certification, to assess and confirm our suppliers' employee working hours, salaries and disbursements, and safety and health conditions. In 2012, we assessed 174 suppliers, of which 167 passed our assessment. In Jilin, we refined and optimized our suppliers' product quality, product warranty, and environment standards, and strictly controlled suppliers' raw materials, production techniques, construction management procedures, product labeling, and user guides, thus improving our product quality. We have also incorporated product environment indexes as a criterion in our procurement process, and do not purchase products from suppliers who do not meet our environment protection requirements."

Source: China Mobile Limited (2012), China Mobile Limited Sustainability Report, p.15, http://www.chinamobileltd.com/en/ir/reports/ar2012/sd2012.pdf?year= 2012, accessed July 17, 2013.

Box 6.10 Suning: Strategic Supply Chain Management and the Environmental Protection Project 2012

Suning is the leading retailer in household electric appliance in China. In 2011, Suning established the first environmental responsibility model applicable to Chinese retail enterprises, aiming at the formation of a green value chain and of a measurable environmental management system. Suning cooperated with China National Hardware Association and over 20 kitchen ware and sanitary ware brands to carry on green kitchen plans and speed up the popularization of energy-efficient products. Also, Suning participates in the "Earth Hour" initiative of World Wide Fund for Nature (WWF). Its chain stores in Nanjing, Shanghai and Wuhan are all rated as "low-carbon demonstration stores" by Chinese authorities.

Source: Suning (2011), Suning's 2011 Corporate Social Responsibility Report (苏宁电器2011企业社会责任报告), http://www.cnsuning.com/snsite/index/gysn/qyshzr/csrbg/attachment/353/_attachment1335682563729.pdf, accessed July 17, 2013. Suning's official website can be found at: http://www.cnsuning.com/snsite/index/index.html.

CHAPTER SEVEN

Safety Issues

In China, safety is probably the most volatile of all CSR-related topics. Issues and stories linked to food or product safety, environmental hazards, or work-related deaths and injuries are exposed daily on the internet and in the media. Public complaints frequently point to a low level of implementation of the existing regulations, to the difficulties met when trying to assert a chain of responsibility in the production process, and to the disregard of standards, which may be caused by greed or by a mere "devil-may-care" attitude. Scandals and major accidents have gravely tarnished the reputation of companies (see Box 7.1 for an example) or even full sectors of production. Accidents and malfunctions have also generated an atmosphere of suspicion now deeply ingrained within the consumers' mentality. Conversely, companies

Box 7.1 Wenzhou High-Speed Train Crash

On 23 July 2011, two high-speed trains traveling on the Yongtaiwen railway line collided on a viaduct in the suburbs of Wenzhou, Zhejiang Province. The two trains crashed into each other, and four cars fell off the viaduct. 40 people were killed and 122 were injured. A total of 55 people were found responsible for this bullet train crash. Liu Zhijun, former Minister of Railways of the PRC, Zhang Shuguang, former deputy chief engineer of Railways of the PRC and Ma Cheng, former Chairman of Board and General Manager at China Railway Signal and Communication Corp, producer of the railway signaling system, were held chiefly responsible for the crash. According to the investigation, design flaws, sloppy management and the mishandling of a lightning strike that crippled the equipment were behind the train crash. There were serious design flaws in the control equipment, which was designed by the Beijing National Railway Research

(Continued)

Box 7.1 (*Continued*)

and Design Institute of Signals and Communication, a subsidiary of China Railway Signal and Communication Corp. And investigators believe the design defects occurred because of the institute's sloppy management. In addition, workers at Shanghai Railway Bureau did not respond properly when vital controls and the train-tracking facility were put out of action by lightning.

Source: State Administration of Work Safety and Press Reports (2011), *7.23 Yongwenxian tebie zhongda tielu jiaotong shigu diaocha baogao* (Report of Major Road Accidents on the Yongwen line), http://www.chinasafety.gov.cn/newpage/Contents/Channel_5498 /2011/1228/160577/content_160577.htm#_Toc312855798, accessed July 17, 2013.

establishing an excellent record on safety issues enjoy a strong comparative advantage over their competitors.

For a company operating in China, the special attention to be given to safety goes beyond technical issues and respect of regulations. It is a privileged channel through which to: (a) assert one's corporate culture of transparency and responsibility; and (b) ensure that internal regulations are fully understood and respected, establishing mechanisms of report, evaluation and compliance that can be used not only for dealing with core safety issues but also for enhancing a sense of mission and excellence. In other words, the issues discussed in the following sub-sections are meant to be taken as a whole, so as to help each corporation to nurture a systemic "safety" culture operating at all levels of the production and distribution process, instilled into all employees, mangers, contractors and partners, and generating a sense of corporate excellence and responsibility manifested both within and outside the corporation. We will first discuss two transversal issues: safety at the workplace; and safety and the engineering process. Afterwards we will focus on two specific cases, namely road safety and food safety. These two cases have been chosen, first, because they have shown to be of crucial importance in China, and second, because the lessons drawn from them can be extended to other issues.

7.1. Safety at the Workplace

A law enacted in June 2002 provides companies with a clear legal framework when it comes to safety on the workplace (Box 7.2).

Box 7.2 Law of the PRC on Work Safety

Article 17

The principal leading members of production and business units are charged with the following responsibilities for work safety in their own units:

(a) Setting up and improving the responsibility system for work safety in their own units;
(b) Making arrangements for formulating rules and operating regulations for work safety in their own units;
(c) Guaranteeing an effective input into work safety in their own units;
(d) Supervising and inspecting work safety in their own units and, in a timely manner, eliminating hidden dangers threatening work safety;
(e) Making arrangements for the formulation and implementation of their own units' rescue plans in the event of accidents; and
(f) Submitting to higher authorities timely and truthful reports on accidents due to lack of work safety.

Article 21

- Production and business units shall give their employees education and training in work safety to ensure that the employees acquire the necessary knowledge about work safety and are familiar with the relevant rules for work safety and safe operating regulations. No employee who fail to pass the qualification tests after receiving education and training in work safety may be assigned to posts.

Article 22

- Before using new techniques, technologies, materials or equipment, production and business units shall get to know and master their technical properties for safety and adopt effective protective measures for safety, and they shall provide their employees with special education and training in work safety.

(Continued)

Box 7.2 (*Continued*)

Article 34

- Workshops, stores or warehouses where dangerous articles are manufactured, marketed, stored or used may not share the same building with the employees' living quarters; a distance shall be kept between the two for the sake of safety.
- At manufacturing and marketing places and in the living quarters of employees, there shall be exits that meet the requirements for emergency evacuation and are indicated clearly and kept unobstructed. The said exits may not be sealed or blocked.

Article 35

- When carrying out dangerous operations such as blasting and hoisting, production and business units shall send special persons to the sites to ensure safety and to see that operation rules are abided by and safety measures are adopted.

Article 56

Departments in charge of supervision and control over work safety conducted in accordance with the law, and those performing supervision over and inspection of production and business units to see how the latter implement the laws and regulations related to work safety, national standards or industrial specifications, shall exercise the following functions and powers:

(a) Entering production and business units for inspection, acquiring relevant materials and data for investigation, and getting information from the departments and persons concerned;

(b) Enforcing rights on the spot or demanding rectification of, within a time limit, violations of law related to work safety, which are discovered in the course of inspection; and with regard to practices deserving administrative penalties according to law, making decisions to impose such penalties in accordance with the provisions in this law, other laws and administrative regulations;

(c) When, in the course of inspection, hidden dangers that may lead to accidents are discovered, they must be eliminated immediately; when it is impossible to ensure safety before major ones are eliminated, in

(Continued)

Box 7.2 (*Continued*)

the course of their elimination, give orders to evacuate workers from the danger areas and to suspend production, business operation or application, and when major dangers are eliminated, allowing resumption of production, business operation or application upon examination and approval;

(d) Sealing up or seizing facilities, equipment and devices that are deemed, on firm grounds, not up to the national standards or industrial specifications to ensure work safety, and, in accordance with law, making a decision within 15 days to deal with the case.

• No supervision or inspection may hinder the normal production and business activities of the units undergoing inspection.

Source: PRC Government (2002), Law of the PRC on Work Safety (Order of the President No. 70), http://english.gov.cn/laws/2005–10/08/content_75054.htm, accessed July 17, 2013.

A few points deserve observation: the law contains some practical dispositions reflecting situations observable on the field ("Workshops, stores or warehouses where dangerous articles are manufactured, marketed, stored or used may not share the same building with the employees' living quarters.") At the same time, it aims at encouraging a culture of safety that goes through training, awareness, and the building of a sense of responsibility, both personal and collective. Once more, let us observe that the recent legal effort concerned with CSR-related issues cannot be equated with the mere building up of a body of regulations; it rather strives at fostering principles to be interpreted and applied in context. We thus cannot separate too strictly between the legal obligations of corporations on the one hand and the way they foster their CSR culture on the other. Rather, what is increasingly asked from companies is to build, inculcate and implement their corporate culture in such a way as to make it *fulfill not only the letter but also the spirit of the law*. Or, to put it differently, in the Chinese context, the law itself is asking for the progressive fostering of a CSR culture more and more.

The fostering and implementation of a corporate safety culture still requires tremendous efforts: China's workplace death rate is still much higher than those of other developed countries. In the UK, there were 171 worker fatalities between April 2010 and March 2011. When population size is taken into account, China's workplace death rate is more than 21 times higher than the UK's. In 2010, 79,552 people died in work-related accidents in China, an official figure that probably does not account for a large number of unreported fatalities.[1] In 2011, workplace accidents claimed a total of 75,572 lives.[2] The objective is to make death rates drop 10 percent a year, and such a goal seems to be consistent with the trend observed during the last years. The State Administration of Work Safety (SAWS) now speaks of "people-oriented occupational safety and health" and of developing and implementing a "workplace safety preventive culture".[3] Safety issues and solutions are linked to the nature of the corporation's activities, and, as such, will vary from one sector or one firm to another. China's mining sector, especially its coal extracting industry, has long been notorious for disregard of standards (according to the administration's figures, 2,433 miners were killed in coal mine accidents in China in 2010, compared with 2,631 in 2009).[4]

Small-scale factories working on sub-standards are beyond the scope of this report, as progress can only come from strict official policies and controls for ensuring compliance. Township and village enterprises (TVE) are especially at risk, this being due to a low level of education of managers and workers, as well as to the often outdated technology used. Generally speaking, large-scale companies enforce standards much more strictly. They still meet with important safety problems, which are people-related in most cases. Creating a "culture of safety", closely

---

[1] Bardsley, D. (2011), China's Workplace Safety Scrutinised in New Report Showing Over 200 Deaths a Day, *The National*, December 5, 2011, http://www.thenational. ae/news/world/asia-pacific/chinas-workplace-safety-scrutinised-in-new-report-showing-over-200-deaths-a-day#ixzz2HVRfUUh2, accessed July 17, 2013.
[2] China Stresses Workplace Safety, *China Daily*, February 4, 2012, http://www. chinadaily.com.cn/china/2012–02/04/content_14538223.htm, accessed July 17, 2013.
[3] Cf. The 6th China International Occupational Safety & Health Exhibition and China International Forum on Work Safety held in September 2012, Beijing, http:// www.sino-safework.org.cn/en/page_index3.php?m=2&b=&id=2, accessed July 17, 2013.
[4] *China Daily* (2012).

linked to a sense of personal and collective responsibility, has become a manager's motto. However, there are two different approaches concerning workplace safety here. Though the debate largely transcends China's frontiers, it has deep implications for this country: "The first of these approaches, behavior-based safety, focuses on the identification and modification of critical safety behaviors, and emphasizes how such behaviors are linked to workplace injuries and losses. The second approach, in contrast, emphasizes the fundamental importance of the organization's safety culture and how it shapes and influences safety behaviors and safety program effectiveness."[5] Behavior-Based Safety (BBS) process has become a major focus for training. Contrary to what could be expected, research indicates that mandatory BBS training programs produce better results than voluntary ones: "Employees in a mandatory BBS process demonstrated significantly greater levels of trust in management (both abilities and intentions), trust in coworkers (both abilities and intentions), and overall satisfaction with the overall BBS training received."[6] The reasons for this state of affairs, as formulated by the authors of the study just quoted, have to do with the greater degree of overall involvement and the fact that compulsory participation eliminated the possibility of negative consequences for the ones participating (being ratted-out by a co-worker or reprimanded by a supervisor). In contrast to behavior change, culture change approaches to safety are more "top-down". The focus is on understanding and often changing the fundamental values and beliefs of the organization, and this almost always involves working with the leadership of the enterprise.[7]

Whatever the scope of their differences, behavioral and culture change approaches to workplace safety should not be seen as contradictory. Both approaches plead for a strategic approach to safety management, seeing the process as ongoing and continuous. Most safety incidents are the product of person-environment interactions, which

---

[5] DeJoy, D.M. (2005), Behavior Change Versus Culture Change: Divergent Approaches to Managing Workplace Safety, *Safety Science*, 43(2), p. 106.

[6] DePasquale, J.P. & S.E. Geller (1999), Critical Success Factors for Behavior-based Safety: A Study of Twenty Industry-wide Applications, *Journal of Safety Research*, 30(4), p. 242.

[7] DeJoy (2005, p. 108).

means that changes apply to personal behaviors *and* to the corporate environment. Particularly in China, behaviors indeed need to be studied and regulated, and incentives of all kinds need to be devised so as to ensure better safety practices. At the same time, measures that target individual behaviors need to be inscribed into a corporate climate and mode of interaction that provides for continuous feedbacks on the structural factors causing accident-prone behaviors or generating other risks.

7.2. Safety and Engineering

Safety, as an area of corporate responsibility, is linked first and foremost to the way the production process operates. A complex chain of causation is actually involved in any safety assessment. It starts with the way both the product and equipment have been conceived and tested from the start. It mobilizes the engineers' ethics and sense of responsibility, as the accuracy of the information they give and the judgment they pass determines the reliability of all subsequent operations; it

UESTIONS

— Taking into account the size and nature of our corporation, what is our self-understanding of the strategies we develop for ensuring safety in the workplace? What are the basic observations and principles that guide the formalization of our regulations, training programs and innovations?

— Are we sufficiently behavior-oriented, formatting our training programs according to tasks and stages in the production process?

— What is the nature and frequency of our policies? Are they compulsory? How frequent are our safety training programs?

— What are the incentives, either negative or positive, linked to safety-related behaviors?

— Do we make workplace safety a component of our corporate culture, and in which ways does this dimension affect the strategic thinking of our corporation's upper management level?

— How do we balance personal responsibility and changes in corporate culture when tackling safety issues, especially when assessing risks and accidents?

requires the agents intervening during the production process to communicate through a clear chain of command, to have received all relevant information, and to be able to make evaluations and decisions in full awareness, especially if a crisis occurs; finally, safety is maintained and enhanced only if evaluations and alerting procedures are strictly applied and continuously revised. As one can see, if the safety imperative indeed requires the application of strict technical standards, it is first and foremost rooted into a collective and personal sense of responsibility and transparency that we have already identified as being at the core of a culture of corporate responsibility.

The building-up of *engineering ethics* (see also Chapter 11) has been identified as the key factor for ensuring safety at every step of the production process, and its acculturation into China's engineering curriculum and culture would certainly contribute very much to reduce the industrial hazards that periodically capture the imagination of the public opinion.

Boxes 7.3–7.5 showcase three workplace accidents that illustrate patterns of behaviors that go directly against safety standards and culture. These accidents were widely reported and discussed in the media and on social networks.

Box 7.3 Dalian Oil Pipeline Explosion and Fire Accident 2010

On 16 July 2010, a pipeline explosion and fire hit the Xingang port, Dalian, one of the major ports in China, during a tanker offloading. Two oil pipelines exploded, sending flames hundreds of feet into the air and burning for over 15 hours, and spilling around 1,500 tons of crude oil into the sea to leave a slick pollution covering 100 km².[a] And the accident also resulted in a worker being lost and another injured, a firefighter killed and another injured, as well as direct economic losses of 223 million RMB.[b] According to the investigation, illegally filling up the desulfurization catalyst produced by in the oil pipeline contributed to the accident. Desulfurization catalyst contained hydrogen peroxide, a strong oxidant. When the tanker stopped offloading, workers at Dalian Subsidiary Q. Pro Inspection & Technical Services Co. continued filling the desulfurization catalyst in the pipeline, which caused the desulfurization catalyst to

(Continued)

Box 7.3 (*Continued*)

quickly gather and undergo strong oxidizing, resulting in a pipeline explosion and fire, and oil leakage. Q. Pro Inspection & Technical Services Co. and Tianjin Huishengda Petrochemical Technology Co., the illegal desulfurization catalyst producer, which concealed the dangerous property of the desulfurization catalyst, are mainly responsible for the accident.[c]

Source: [a] *Dalian shuyouguandao baozha qihuo* (Dalian's Pipeline on Fire), *Sina*, http:// news.sina.com.cn/z/dlsygxbz/index.shtml, accessed July 17, 2013.
[b] *Guowuyuan dui 7.16 shuyouguandao baozha deng siqi shiguzuochu chuli* (The State's Response to the 4 Pipeline Explosion Accidents), *Xinhua*, November 24, 2011, http:// news.xinhuanet.com/politics/2011–11/24/c_111192315.htm, accessed July 17, 2013.
[c] State Administration of Work Safety (2011), *Guowuyuan anweihui bangongshi guanyu zhongguo shiyoutianranqi jituangongsi zai dalian suoshuqiye "7.16" shuyouguandao baozha-huozhai deng siqi shigudiaocha chuli jieguo de tongbao* (State Report on the 4 Pipeline Explosion Accidents on July 16), http://www.chinasafety.gov.cn/newpage/Contents/Channel_4977/2011/1125/157932/content_157932.htm, accessed July 17, 2013.

Box 7.4 Shanghai Apartment Fire Accident 2010[d]

On 15 November 2010, an extraordinarily severe fire erupted in the 28-story apartment at the intersection of Jiaozhou Road and Yuyao Road, Jing'an District, Shanghai, with 58 killed, 71 injured, and caused direct economic loss of 158 million RMB. Work by unlicensed welders, multilayered subcontracting and poor management all contributed to the fire accident. At the time of the fire, the apartment was being renovated as part of a comprehensive improvement of energy efficiency projects. The sparks from welding work being done on the building, undertaken by unlicensed welders, ignited scaffolding around the structure, which led to the apartment's destruction. And according to the investigation, many layers of subcontractors resulted in responsibility for security not being implemented. Confusion in the construction job site management made safety measures hard to implement. The construction process was obviously rushed, and the subsequent inquiry recorded the illegal use of a large number of nylon mesh, polyurethane foam and other flammable materials, which resulted in the rapid spread of fire. Behind the scenes, an inadequate safety supervision department resulted in too many subcontractors as well as in undocumented welders.[e]

(Continued)

Box 7.4 (*Continued*)

Source: [d]State Administration of Work Safety (2011), *Shanghai gongbu "11.15" teda huozhai chuli jueding, 54 ming shigu zerenren shou chuli* (Shanghai Announces How It Deals with Those Responsible in the 15 November Major Fire Accident), http://www.chinasafety.gov.cn/newpage/Contents/Channel_6652/2011/0610/134115/content_134115.htm, accessed July 17, 2013.

[e]*Guowuyuan diaochazu rending shanghai qihuo gaolou shiyong yirancailiao* (Investigations by the State Ascertained Shanghai's Apartment Fire as Due to Usage of Easily Flammable Construction Material), Sina, November 18, 2010, http://news.sina.com.cn/c/2010-11-18/062921490569.shtml, accessed July 17, 2013. See also a related source: http://news.sina.com.cn/z/shzzqh/, accessed July 17, 2013.

Box 7.5 Heilongjiang Coal Mine Gas Explosion Accident 2009[f]

On 21 November 2009, a coal gas explosion hit Xinxing Coal Mine, in Hegang of Heilongjiang Province, leaving 108 killed, 133 injured and caused direct economic losses of 56 million RMB. The Xinxing Coal Mine is a highly gassy mine. It was the blasting operation that induced the coal gas outburst. The gas flowed over and mixed with fresh air and then reached the explosion limit. When it met the electric spark caused by the electric locomotive, the gas explosion occurred. Illegal production, sloppy management of work safety and bad supervision were the culprits behind the disaster. The Hegang subsidiary of Heilongjiang LongMay Mining Holding Group Co., the Xinxing Coal Mine operator, refused to carry out the suspension orders issued by the local authorities. Meanwhile, the Heilongjiang Administration of Coal Mine Safety and its Hebin branch did not fulfill their responsibilities to supervise and failed to urge the mine operator to complete rectifications and improvements even though they had issued many suspension orders.

Source: [f]State Administration of Work Safety (2010), *Guowuyuan anweihui bangong-shi guanyu heilongjiangsheng longmei kuangye jituangufen youxiangongsi hegangfen-gongsi xinxingmeikuang "11.21" tebie zhongda mei(yan) yu wasi tuchu he wasi baozha shigu diaozhachulijieguo de tongbao* (State Report on the November 21 Major Coal Mine Gas Explosion in Heilongjiang Province), http://www.chinasafety.gov.cn/newpage/Contents/Channel_5498/2010/1210/127193/content_127193.htm, accessed July 17, 2013.

Fostering a sense of corporate responsibility in engineers — which is akin to the development of a professional ethics congruent to their profession's nature and mission — means to spell out their obligations to their colleagues, employers, clients, the profession itself, and to the public. Such an endeavor takes place through the building up, teaching and internalization of *codes of conduct* that guide these engineers. Devising, teaching and internalizing codes of conducts goes along with the study of case analysis which makes one able to analyze, alongside other issues, conflicts of interest, proprietary information, market-external remuneration, and technology transfer. Furthermore, engineering ethics does not merely "restrain" engineers in their dealings. Rather, it guides, emboldens and empowers them in their efforts at innovation and risk assessment. In other words, engineering ethics guides engineers in crafting the world through the products they design. We will come back to these points in Chapter 11. What we need to underline at present is that corporate culture is sustained by engineering ethics and concurrently constitutes the channel through which engineers working for the corporation daily develop their sense of mission, honor and responsibility. *CSR-based corporate culture and engineering ethics are mutually reinforcing.* Fostering engineering ethics within the corporation is a cornerstone of CSR-based management. In general, engineers who have internalized the codes and values inherent to a wise exercise of their profession are the ones who prove to be instrumental in developing a commitment to safety at all levels of the production system, thus making sure that similar sets of values are lived and understood by the other actors in the chain. Conversely, when engineering ethics proves to be weak, dysfunctions are prone to occur at various stages of the production process.

It goes without saying that engineers are not the sole actors responsible for ensuring the safety of products and processes. They do play a crucial role in devising products, organizing the production processes, and teaching and supervising the other actors. However, in every production process, all actors form complex causation chains. State agencies are also part of the process, and supervision is often an issue of concern. This must lead a company to enact even stricter standards within its own orbit, making sure that all necessary checks are done internally before they are made at an external level. The example used below also shows that issues such as bribery and integrity prove to be crucial when safety concerns are at stake. It illustrates the fact that CSR attitudes and values constitute indeed a systemic whole, with no clear-cut separation between the financial, engineering, social, commercial and managerial dimensions. Rather, a corporate culture spells out and implements sets of values and procedures that apply to all levels of the corporation's activities. The example cited in Box 7.6 illustrates how large-scale accidents are often the result of complex causes of causation where dereliction of duties or loss of moral judgment happen both within the company and among its stakeholders, even when administrative procedures appear to have been applied.

Box 7.6 Hunan Under-construction Bridge Collapse Accident

On 13 August 2007, a bridge that was under construction over the Dixituo River in Fenghuang County of Hunan Province collapsed, with 64 killed and 22 injured, causing direct economic losses of 39.7 million RMB. Poor quality and safety management brought about the accident. The company responsible for the Hunan Dixituo river bridge — the No. 7 Company of Hunan Road and Bridge Construction Group — arbitrarily modified the original construction plan of the main arch ring, maltreated materials and stones in violation of the regulations, with poor bricking up, and started framework construction even before the main arch reached the designed capacity. Meanwhile, supervision institutions failed to fulfill their responsibilities, leaving serious hazards that gave rise to the accident. The supervising company for the Hunan Dixituo River Bridge Construction Project, Hunan Jinqu Communications Consulting & Supervision Company, failed to stop the construction company's arbitrary modification to the construction plan, and gave approval on various forms such as the bricking-up quality inspection form, the inspection application approval form, and construction process quality inspection form, when they had no knowledge of the arch strength. Local authorities, i.e. the Department of Transportation of Hunan Province and the government of Fenghuang County, also neglected their duty of supervision.

Source: State Administration of Work Safety (2008), The Collapse of the Bridge Under Construction over the Dixituo River in Fenghuang County of Hunan Province on August 13, 2007, January 25, 2008, http://www.chinasafety.gov.cn/newpage/Contents/Channel_5498/2008/0125/6648/content_6648.htm, accessed August 6, 2013.

7.3. Case I: Road Safety

Road safety has become a major public health concern in China. Though the scope of the problem goes beyond what corporations can and are actually asked to do, they are still major players in the field: on the negative side, their activities are risk-prone, and the road safety issues linked to industrial activities thus need to be tackled by them; on the positive side, the training that corporations dispense to their workers and sometimes to the general public — as well as the direct investments they consent to in certain cases — may become part of the solution brought to the broader Chinese road safety problem.

In 2008, The World Bank Office in Beijing produced a report — *China, Road Traffic Safety, the Achievements, the Challenges, and the Way Ahead* — that offers an assessment of the issue, of the achievements of the Chinese Government in the field, and an array of propositions on road safety initiatives. Information used in this sub-section came largely from this report. According to the Ministry of Health (MOH), China had the highest number of road traffic fatalities in the world in 2003 (220,000), accounting for 18 percent of global road traffic fatalities, despite having less than 5 percent of the global vehicle fleet. Recent statistics are also difficult to account for. However, it can be said that the overall number of deaths related to traffic accidents has increased with the number of vehicles on the roads, while the per capita rate of road traffic fatalities has started to decrease. The per capita rate of all injury related deaths is also decreasing and has dropped from 66.2 per 100,000 persons in 1992 to 61.5 per 100,000 persons in 2005. Of this, road traffic injury, which accounts for 28 percent, is the primary cause of injury-related death in China. The share of all deaths related to injury is also slightly decreasing and has been lowered from 11 percent in 1992 to 10.1 percent in 2005. Injury is the fifth leading cause of death overall and the leading cause of death for children and adults aged 1 to 44 years. However, injury-related deaths give only an indication of the severity of the problem. For every injury-related death, the MOH estimates that there are 1.5 cases involving severe permanent disability, 20 cases requiring hospital admission, 100 cases requiring emergency services, 13 requiring medical services, and a total of 300 injuries.[8] Box 7.7 describes the high social cost paid for these traffic accidents.

An awareness of the scope of the problem and of its implications for China already fosters a corporation's sense of responsibility, enabling it to share this knowledge with its employees and partners so as to create a climate conducive to sound behavior and collective initiatives, both within the corporation and outside of it. While many corporations take pain at ensuring safety on their sites of production, employees' behavior on the road may change drastically once they are outside the plant's compound. Awareness of and education on road safety thus needs to be holistic. It cannot be reduced to the inculcation of regulations and standards to be respected in certain places and times. It goes with fostering the sense of responsibility of each employee — a sense of responsibility, which, as we have seen already, situates the company within a diversified framework of stakeholders. *Some companies have chosen to educate their employees by making them become themselves educators*: in places where a new plant was constructed, generating increased road traffic, they encouraged their employees to give a few hours of their

Box 7.7 The Cost of Traffic Acidents

"Every year on Chinese roads between half a million to a million people are killed or permanently disabled, with millions more hospitalized, leaving behind shattered families and communities. Road traffic injuries are a public health and social equity issue, disproportionately affecting the vulnerable road users and the poor. 67 percent of those killed and injured in road traffic accidents in China are adults aged between 26 and 60 years — the breadwinners in a family. Road traffic injuries have an impact on development objectives, including delivery of the Millennium Development Goals (MDGs), because of their significant economic and social cost."

Source: World Bank (2008), China : Road Traffic Safety, the Achievements, the Challenges, and the Way Ahead, August 2008, https://openknowledge.worldbank.org/handle/10986/7778, accessed July 31, 2013.

---

[8]World Bank (2008), China: Road Traffic Safety, the Achievements, the Challenges, and the Way Ahead, August 2008, https://openknowledge.worldbank.org/handle/10986/7778, accessed July 31, 2013.

working time for going into schools and providing children with quizzes, safety kits and instructions so as to make them alert to the danger generated by increased traffic or other industry-related hazards. Experience shows that employees asked to teach responsible behaviors better internalize the norms and values they have to inculcate to others. Michelin is one such company who relies on making their employees educators, as detailed in Box 7.8.

Box 7.8 Case Study: About the Michelin Road Safety Program

"Besides the focus on road safety that goes with the nature of its industrial activities, Michelin works with relevant organizations, to hold road safety publicity and education activities.

— It became the strategy partner of Road Traffic Safety Association of China to co-promote the importance of road traffic safety in 2007.

— In 2007, it donated 300,000 little yellow hats to youths and children in western provinces, i.e. Guizhou, Chongqing and Guangxi, aimed at promoting traffic safety and self-protection awareness.

— Also in 2007, it co-held about 400 road traffic safety education sessions with influential media in Beijing, Shanghai and Guangzhou and co-built the "Michelin Safety Club" column with TV stations to improve people's road traffic awareness.

— It developed the "Michelin Safety Blue Book" and provided it to the public, media and partners for free.

— It co-publicized safe driving and held tires knowledge training with a driving school, from which about 70,000 students benefited.

— It carried out a "Community Tire Security Check" for free, and other activities since 2005 to help car owners avoid hidden safety problems.

— It issued its "Michelin China Road Safety Manifesto" in 2011.

— It initiated a Michelin Road Safety campus-line activities in elementary schools, themed "My First Step, Further Security" in 2011, helping students improve children's road safety awareness and develop good habits of safe travel."

Source: Michelin China's Official site, *Shehuizeren* (CSR), http://www.michelin.com.cn/Home/About-Michelin/Michelin-China/Michelin-and-Society, accessed July 17, 2013.

UESTIONS

— In which ways are our corporate activities linked to road safety issues? What is our record on these?

— In which ways can our expertise contribute to raise safety standards, by bringing in cultural or technical resources?

— What kind of training do our workers receive on that issue, and does this training or other accompanying measures make them able to disseminate this knowledge?

— Do some of our pilot projects or philanthropic activities comprise a road safety dimension or remedy the consequences suffered by the victims and the injured?

— When it comes to these issues, are there areas of cooperation with public authorities linked to our corporate activities?

— Can criteria and actions applied to the road safety issue be applied to other areas of direct concern for our company as well?

7.4. Case II: Food Safety

Food safety is a major concern for China customers. Elsewhere in this book (see Chapter 12, the section on "Governance, Transparency and the Media"), we provide the reader with examples of the disputes and communication challenges that the issue has generated. The extent of the food safety problem in China is not caused by a lack in regulation. The food certification system is China is actually very detailed. A first level applies to all kinds of manufacturing and products, with certification including *ISO9000*, *ISO14000*, HACCP and Certification on Green Market. Besides, specific certificates are issued at the State Council level: (a) Organic Food Certification (有机食品认证); (b) Green Food Certification (绿色食品认证); (c) Certification on pollution-free agricultural products (无公害农产品认证); and (d) Certification on Feed (饲料认证). There are also certification systems issued by ministerial level bodies, such as Healthcare Food Certification, Certification on Beverage Safety, Certification on safety of edible agricultural products, etc. The system is complemented by certification-like administrative approval and market entry approval, such as the Production Permit, Hygiene Permit and QS Certification on agricultural products. Additionally, certain certification systems are being studied or are on trial implementation, a category that includes Good Agricultural Practices (GAP) (良好农业规范), Good Manufacturing Practices (GMP) (良好操作规范), Good Distribution Practices (GDP) (良好分销规范), the *ISO22000* (食品安全管理体系), and GFSI (食品零售商采购审核标准).

It should be recognized that the increase in regulations has also fostered complications and ambiguities. The multiplication of standards sometimes hampers their meaning and efficacy. A circular released by the State Council on April 2013 calls for unifying existing regulations, intensifying supervision of the food industry, handing out punishment for food safety violations and improving the industry self-regulation. China has more than 5,000 standards on food quality and hygiene, made by different government units. In the future, a national center on food safety should be set up to consolidate these standards. Multiple standards as well as lack of some standards (for instance, regulating dinnerware made of foam plastic) are still raising acute challenges in terms of food safety.[9]

Regulations have been strengthened and are more strictly enforced in the aftermath of the tainted milk scandal. This does not mean that all lessons from what happened in 2008 have been already drawn: the 2008 Chinese milk scandal is the most well known of food safety scandals in China, involving milk, infant formulas and other products adulterated with melamine — resulting in the death of 6 infants, the hospitalization of at least 860 babies and around 300,000 people sickened at various degrees by the incriminated products. In 2010, researchers from Peking University have concluded that the potential for long-term complications after exposure to melamine remains a serious concern (four years before, watered-down milk had resulted in

---

[9]Wang, X. (2013), Food Standards to be Clarified, Unified, *China Daily*, April 17, 2013, http://www.chinadaily.com.cn/food/2013-04/17/content_16416057.htm, accessed July 17, 2013.

13 infant deaths from malnutrition).[10] After the initial focus on one firm, Sanlu, government inspections revealed that the problem existed to a lesser degree in products from 21 other companies. A number of criminal prosecutions occurred, with two people being executed, another given a suspended death penalty, three others receiving life imprisonment, two receiving 15-year jail terms, and seven local government officials, including the Director of the Administration of Quality Supervision, Inspection and Quarantine (AQSIQ) being fired or forced to resign. As of July 2010, Chinese authorities were still reporting seizures of melamine-contaminated dairy products in some provinces.

It is not known where in the supply chain the melamine was added to the milk. The whole production and distribution chain has been under suspicion: quality tests can be falsified with additives. For long, salespeople have been selling to farmers "protein powder" additives, which farmers were often buying in order to ensure their milk would not be rejected. As early as 2005 and 2006, complaints from an agent of Jinqiao Dairy Company in northwest China had been ignored by all parties concerned. Local government supervision was "practically nonexistent".[11] Sanlu began receiving complaints about sick infants as far back as December 2007, but did no tests until June 2008. Nothing much happened before media reports surfaced, indicating a surge in the number of babies diagnosed with kidney disease. Still, China's central government reacted quickly after learning of the milk crisis, partly through an official notification of the New Zealand government, alerted by the dairy company Fonterra, which owned a 43 percent stake in Sanlu. Officials offered free medical treatment to the young victims,

---

[10]Liu, J. *et al.* (2010), Urinary Tract Abnormalities in Chinese Rural Children Who Consumed Melamine-Contaminated Dairy Products: A Population-Based Screening and Follow-Up Study", *Canadian Medical Association Journal*, 82(5), pp. 439–443, http://www.cmaj.ca/content/182/5/439.full.pdf+html, accessed July 17, 2013.

[11]Gong, J. & J. Liu (2010), Spilling the Blame for China's Milk Crisis, *Caijing Magazine*, October 10, 2010, http://english.caijing.com.cn/2008-10-10/110019183.html, accessed July 17, 2013.

released comprehensive results of dairy product tests, and scrapped a national food inspection exemption system that was in place for the previous eight years. Some 5,000 inspectors were dispatched for the testing of dairy products. The Chinese market had grown at an average annual rate of 23 percent since 2000. Several foreign companies were involved in joint ventures with incriminated Chinese dairy producers or were getting their milk supply from them for biscuits, chocolate, tea powder, baby cereals and other products. The scandal thus had far-reaching consequences on the whole agro-business in China and elsewhere. Besides, at least 25 countries stopped importing Chinese dairy products. Related developments continued to occur in 2009–2010.

The tainted milk scandal was a stepping stone in the public discussion of business ethics and CSR as a whole, as it raised questions linked to culture of secrecy, corruption and chains of responsibility. Though the public focus was first on Sanlu, it soon appeared that all participants in the food supply chain were potentially concerned by a dilution of duties and values, and often cornered into adopting irresponsible behaviors, due to the quest for quick profit that the accelerated growth of the sector was making possible. Food safety, thus, was not perceived as a solely technical issue, nor were food scandals seen as the result of deviant behaviors. Rather, what was striking for the observers was the "normalcy" of the chain of causations, its anchorage into behaviors easily observable in daily life. "Safety" — or the lack of it — has to be considered as the end product of a culture determining the way each actor was understanding his/her insertion into a chain of responsibility and assessing a hierarchy of values determining everyday choices and behaviors.

In Chapter 12 (the section on "Governance, Transparency and the Media"), we will deal with the communication aspect of food safety concerns and crises. Here, let us say a word about the content of the allegations that struck KFC in China around November 2012–January 2013.Though minor in scope compared to the case discussed above, the debate reveals much about consumers' changing expectations. At that time, authorities in China said they were looking into whether KFC purchased raw chicken with higher-than-permitted levels of antibiotics from two poultry suppliers. Yum — the parent company — responded that its products are safe and that it was cooperating with the government. However, it did recognize that the company failed to report information to government departments. According to Burkitt (2012), the Shanghai Food and Drug Administration said on 20 December 2011 that 8 out of 19 batches of chicken samples Yum sent to labs for testing in 2010 and 2011 had higher than acceptable levels of antibiotics. It said authorities planned to investigate whether Yum responded appropriately to these test results. Yum has not responded to requests to answer what the company did with batches of chicken that had high antibiotic levels. Shanghai regulators said in a December 21 statement that it tested 32 samples from 8 batches of KFC chicken seized a week earlier, and the samples all passed tests for antibiotics and steroids.[12]

Obviously, concern for food safety can be instrumentalized both by competitors and the media. Scandals that occurred during the recent years have made consumers extremely sensitive to safety issues, and social media spread out allegations within a few hours, while public trust has been seriously eroded. At the same time, the trend also means that more transparent and accurate information is requested from companies, which can no longer avoid engaging in consumer education. As health and environmental concerns have been merged into one, companies must also deal with changing expectations from consumers and go from a technical and legalistic approach of safety issues to one that makes it an ideal setting for accrued product quality and social responsibility standards. In this respect, the sensitivity attached to food safety issues bears lessons for other industrial sectors.

---

[12]Burkitt, L. (2012), Yum Brands Apologizes Amid Chicken Probe, *WSJA*, January 10, 2013, http://online.wsj.com/article/SB10001424127887324081704578232791336513864.html?mod=WSJAsia_hpp_LEFTTopStories\, accessed July 17, 2013.

CHAPTER EIGHT

Social Standards and the Working Force

The sense of CSR developed within an organization does not only apply to agents exterior to it. In fact, the employees of the corporation should be seen as its first stakeholders. It would be impossible to implement CSR toward consumers and the general public without first taking into account the well-being and sense of fulfillment of the persons working within the corporation. Textbooks on business ethics and CSR, when identifying issues internal to the organization, generally focus on the following issues:

— Downsizing and layoffs: employees' job security;
— Working conditions and employees' rights;
— Discrimination and affirmative action; and
— Women in the workplace.

In this chapter, we will concentrate on *social standards* applicable to China, as well as on the way these norms may be furthered and enriched through a proactive CSR strategy. By following a specific issue — migrant labor, we will also see how a detailed knowledge of the evolutions of China's working force is intertwined with the determination of CSR-related policies. The following chapter will be dedicated to *well-being at work,* so as to identify areas of recent concern and creative initiatives. Box 8.1 provides an overview of the new labor challenges that China will face.

8.1. China's Labor Contract Law and Corporate Policies

The enacting in 2008 of the Labor Contract Law (LCL) was a major step forward in regulating labor issues in China. It reflected the

Box 8.1 China Meets with New Labor Challenges

- The aggregate labor force will start to shrink from around 2015, initially slowly but faster from the late 2020s, and is projected to be more than 15 percent smaller than its peak by 2050. The smaller labor force will support a growing elderly population.
- China will no longer have the limitless rural labor surplus that has shaped the country's comparative advantage for the past 30 years. Indeed, a number of researchers claim that the "Lewis turning point" was reached as early as 2003. The combination of shrinking/exhausted unskilled surplus labor and the concomitant massive increase in workers with senior secondary and higher education will fundamentally shift the dynamics of labor supply. This represents a huge opportunity for demand to adjust and move China up the value chain, but it also carries risks.
- The rapid wage growth in recent years among migrants and low-skilled workers is accompanied both by rising expectations and evidence of compression in the productivity growth premium. While this wage growth has been a positive phenomenon, it raises the question of how to balance the continued need for upward real wage adjustments with sustaining competitiveness, as productivity growth eases over the coming decades in the face of diminishing returns to capital investment.
- As migrant workers shift from being a "floating" to a more permanent urban population, they will increasingly expect better non-wage benefits as well, including social security coverage and other urban social entitlements such as free education and social housing, which have historically only been available to local *hukou* workers.

Source: Quoted from the World Bank and the Development Research Center of State Council (2012, p. 348), *China 2030. Building a Modern, Harmonious, and Creative High-Income Society*, http://www.worldbank.org/en/news/2012/02/27/china-2030-executive-summary, accessed May 24, 2013.

willingness of the government to upgrade its labor relations and better protect workers in all forms of employing organizations, whether public or private. This priority has been underlined again in the 12th five-year plan (2011–2015). At stake are the prevention of labor disputes and the mitigation of social tensions, but also a better equilibrium in the labor market and a more sustainable economic growth.

Corporations need to be thoroughly familiar with the dispositions of the law, not only for ensuring legal compliance, but also for assessing and ranking the issues that matter most both for the state and the public, thus being able to devise specific norms and initiatives in conformity to their corporate culture as well as to public expectations.

The LCL was passed on June 29, 2007, at the 28th session of the Standing Committee of the 10th National People's Congress, and took effect on January 1, 2008. It restates the main principles of various employment-related regulations and policies and supplements the 1995 Labor Law, which attempted to consolidate the early reform era's scattered workplace regulations but contained many loopholes in terms of workers' protection.[1] It also guarantees new social rights for workers and should contribute to a more effective enforcement by employers, local administrations and courts. The vote of the law took place shortly after a slave labor scandal that was largely covered by Chinese media. More generally, the new legislation attempted to address the increasing occurrence of labor-related disputes, sometimes resulting in public unrest.

Public consultation and debate took place for almost two years, and a large number of stakeholders were consulted. The LCL was enacted as a part of a more comprehensive legislative package, including the Employment Promotion Law and the Law on Mediation and Arbitration of Labor Disputes, as well as a number of local regulations. The key provisions of the LCL define the framework in which relationships between employers and employees now take place.

8.1.1. *Mandatory written contracts*

Employers have to sign a labor contract with all workers within one month after their job starts. Otherwise, they would have to pay the employee double salary for each month worked without a contract. If a

---

[1] *Laodong hetong fa* (*Labour Contract Law*), Ministry of Labour and Social Security (PRC), January 1, 2008, http://www.molss.gov.cn/gb/news/2007-06/30/content_184630. htm, accessed May 24, 2013. (English translation: http://en.cnci.gov.cn/Law/ LawDetails.aspx?ID=6079&p=1, accessed May 24, 2013).

written employment contract is not signed after one year, the parties will be deemed to have entered into a permanent employment relationship.

8.1.2. From fixed-term to open-ended employment contracts

Fixed-term contracts have become the dominant form of employment in the past ten years, not only in private companies but also in the public sector.[2] The LCL requires that any employee who has worked for an employer for more than ten years or who has already signed two successive fixed-term contracts be deemed to enter a permanent employment contract. In case of non-renewal of a fixed-term employment contract, if the employer does not offer to renew the employment contract on the same (or better) terms and conditions, he is required to pay the employee a severance equal to one month's salary for each year of employment (up to 12 months of wages).

8.1.3. Subcontracted labor

Since the 1990s, labor contracting through labor dispatching agencies has become widespread, especially among rural migrants and new graduates. Dispatch work has also been a way for companies to increase the flexibility of their workforce, by hiring workers they had previously fired through a dispatch agency. Dispatch workers are particularly vulnerable, with the legal obligations of both the dispatching agency and the actual employer being kept unclear and underspecified. The LCL contains several provisions that restrict the sectors where subcontracted work is authorized and the conditions for operating a dispatching agency. It also clarifies the responsibilities of dispatching agencies and actual employers toward workers, and affirms the principle of equal pay for equal work between permanent and dispatch employees.

---

[2] Daubler, W. & Q. Wang (2009), The New Chinese Employment Law, Comparative *Labor Law and Policy Journal*, 30 (2), 395–408, http://www.learningace.com/doc/5352020/01d800b2a31e201dc0ff96b3ee956dfa/daubler-wangarticle30-2, accessed June 10, 2013.

8.1.4. Part-time work

Part-time work is defined as a labor relationship in which the employee works, on average, no more than 4 hours per day, and a maximum of 24 hours a week. A written contract and social insurance are not mandatory for part-time workers. Wages have to be paid at least twice a month and cannot be below the local minimum wage standard.

8.1.5. Probationary period

The length of the maximum probationary period has been shortened. It is now proportional to contract length: 1 month for a 3–12 month contract, 2 months for a 1–3 year contract, 6 months for longer and non-fixed term contracts. During the probationary period, the salary should not be: (a) less than the local legal minimum wage standard; (b) less than the lowest salary applicable to employees working for the same employer in the same position; and (c) less than 80 percent of the salary stipulated in the employment contract.

8.1.6. Job termination

Dismissal without notice remains legal in the case of a serious breach of contract, but in most circumstances a 30-day notice is required. The LCL has increased the number of cases in which contractual dismissal is forbidden (e.g. during a medical treatment period or maternity leave). For instance, when an employee has been working for the employer consecutively for over 15 years and will reach the statutory retirement age within five years, the contract cannot be terminated. All dismissed workers are entitled to a severance package equal to one month's salary per year of employment (with an upper limit of 12 months of wages). In case of unlawful termination, the employee can choose reinstatement or compensation (with twice the severance due in the case of lawful dismissal).

The LCL also reaffirmed existing work injury, social insurance, and wage per hour provisions.

8.1.7. *Collective bargaining and legal awareness*

The All-China Federation of Trade Unions is officially the sole trade union, with 239 million members (74.5 percent of workers) but exhibits little presence or influence in many companies, especially in private export factories in coastal provinces.[3] The LCL may allow the labor union to play a more effective role in terms of workers' protection. Many of the LCL provisions relating to trade unions were already mentioned in the 1995 law, but they were seldom enforced. The LCL may give workers and their representatives more power to act and more access to local administrations and courts in case of non-compliance. According to the LCL, any change in enterprise regulations relating to wages, working time, holidays, welfare insurance, training, rules, as well as processes relating to management and production that directly affect workers, shall be negotiated with the trade union or at the employees' representative meeting or a general meeting of all workers. Unions are also empowered to help individual workers ensure their rights are protected and to negotiate collective employment contracts with employers on behalf of employees. In case of violation, unions may require the employer to rectify, and, if needed, may apply for labor arbitration or start lawsuits.

An employer must notify the labor union in advance of its decision to terminate the contract of an employee. If the union considers the termination to be unlawful, it may oppose this termination, and the employer has to respond to its request in writing. If an employer needs to cut down above 20 workers or above 10 percent of the total labor force, it shall disclose the lay-off plan to the labor union or all workers at least 30 days in advance, ask for their opinion, and report the plan to the local labor authority.

Beyond strengthening the labor unions' role, the LCL increased workers' legal awareness. While the law was being drafted and after its enactment, Chinese non-governmental organizations (NGOs) and

---

[3] Lan, T. & J. Pickles (2011), China's New Labour Contract Law: State Regulation and Worker Rights in Global Production Networks, *Capturing the Gains Working Paper No 5*, October, http://www.capturingthegains.org/pdf/ctg-wp-2011-05.pdf, accessed May 24, 2013.

the China Federation of Trade Unions organized training and "legal publicity" events. The media and the internet also played a role in diffusing legal information, especially among the younger workers (older and less educated workers rely more heavily on informal sources, such as friends and other workers).[4] The promotion of the new law was in itself an empowerment process, making workers perceive themselves as having new rights worth enforcing.[5] The LCL also increased the power of Chinese employees to handle their employment grievances on their own, by directly suing employers in the courts.[6] In 2007, China's labor dispute arbitration committees accepted 350,000 cases, an increase of 10.3 percent from 2006. During the first quarter of 2008, the labor courts in Dongguan, Shenzhen and Guangzhou accepted more than 10,000 cases, double the number over the same period the year before.[7]

8.1.8. Impact of the LCL on Chinese competitiveness

The preparation of the LCL triggered resistance from some sectors.[8] The main argument against strengthening labor legislation was its supposedly disastrous impact on labor costs and Chinese competitiveness, which would push companies into bankruptcy and turn foreign investments away from China. In the short term, companies that abused cheap labor indeed suffered losses. But this mainly impacted small and medium enterprises that were not very profitable in the first place.[9] For example, some Korean companies had already decided to

---

[4] *Ibid.*

[5] Harris, D. (2008), The Impact of China's Labor Contract Law, *China Law Blog*, September 15, 2008, http://www.chinalawblog.com/2008/09/the_impact_of_chinas_labor_con.html, accessed May 24, 2013.

[6] *Ibid.*

[7] *Ibid.*

[8] Undue Influence: Corporations Gain Ground in Battle over China's New Labor Law — But Human Rights and Labor Advocates Are Pushing Back, *Global Labor Strategies*, March 2007, http://laborstrategies.blogs.com/global_labor_strategies/files/undue_influence_global_labor_strategies.pdf, accessed May 24, 2013.

[9] Harris (2008), *op. cit.*

move their business from China to Vietnam. The overwhelming majority of companies that have quit China after 2008 were involved in very low-level or illegal manufacturing, even before the LCL was implemented.[10] Most enterprises did not leave China for Vietnam, Bangladesh or Cambodia, conscious as they are of the advantages of a better-equipped country, as well as of the potential opportunity to develop business in the emerging domestic market. For most companies, the new law has been a signal of the necessity to rely less on poor labor standards for profits and to increase productivity. However, as the LCL was entering into effect, some companies did try to circumvent the new legal requirement by firing employees; some even did so by making employees resign and then sign a new fixed-term labor contract, a move having a very negative impact on those companies' corporate image.[11] Still, in recent months the move away from China to other Asian countries has been accelerating, especially in the apparel industry of Southeast China — a move partly encouraged by the government desirous to implement changes in China's growth model.[12]

A few months after the LCL had become effective, interviews with managers revealed an appreciation of the stability that the new law could bring to Chinese labor relations, with a decreased staff turnover.[13] Improving labor conditions has also become a strategic decision for factories facing workforce shortage. This phenomenon, whose early signs appeared in 2004, should worsen in the next decades, as the scope of the active population will start to decrease. The number of people

---

[10] *Ibid.*

[11] *Ibid.*

[12] Chu, K. (2013), China Manufacturers Survive by Moving to Asian Neighbors, *WSJA*, May 1, 2013, http://online.wsj.com/article/SB10001424127887323798104578453073103566416.html?mod=WSJAsia_hpp_LEFTTopStories, accessed May 24, 2013.

[13] Li, X. (2011), How Does China's New Labor Contract Law Affect Chinese Workers?, *Harvard Law School*, November 15, 2011, http://www.law.harvard.edu/programs/lwp/papers/How%20Does%20China's%20New%20Labour%20Contract%20Law%20Affect%20Floating%20Workers%20in%20China%20_Xiaoying%20Li_.pdf, accessed May 24, 2013.

entering the labor market will very soon begin to diminish between 2012 and 2013, and the trend of rural to urban migration is expected to slow down after 2020 and to stop around 2026.[14] Beyond social stability concerns, China's new willingness to improve labor standards is also driven by macroeconomic rationales: a shift away from the low-cost sourcing and low-value export production model is necessary to re-equilibrate the Chinese development model, and boost domestic consumption.[15]

Although the LCL put Chinese labor legislation at a level comparable to the one reached by some European countries, the difficulties met when it comes to enforcement still limit its impact. The LCL reinforces sanctions against faulty employers and local cadres and aims at a better enforcement of labor legislation by courts. But the effectiveness of the control by local labor bureaus is impeded by their lack of human resources. Besides, the LCL sometimes raises problems of interpretation. For example, the ten-year triggering period as well as the maximum number of fixed-term contracts may be rendered inapplicable if an employee works sequentially for a different, albeit allied, company of a group of enterprises.[16]

Officially, at the end of 2011, 97 percent of workers in "sizable enterprises" (i.e. small- and medium-sized enterprises excluded) had a written contract.[17] But according to an independent survey, only 60 percent of interviewees had signed a contract at the time of their interview — a number that is still very low, considering that the law requires that *all* employees have a formal contract.[18] Likewise, if enrollment in work injury insurance has increased (from 39.5 percent to 49.5 percent after

[14] China's Economy Growth to Slow Down After 2020: Nobel Laureate, *Want China Times*, October 10, 2010, http://www.wantchinatimes.com/news-subclass-cnt.aspx?cid=1102&MainCatID=11&id=20101010000062, accessed May 24, 2013.

[15] Lan & Pickles (2011), *op. cit.*

[16] *Ibid.*

[17] More Workers Protected by Labor Contracts in China, *Xinhua*, October 25, 2011, http://english.peopledaily.com.cn/90882/7625563.html, accessed May 24, 2013.

[18] Becker, J. & M. Elfstrom (2010), The Impact of China's Labor Contract Law on Workers, *International Labor Rights Forum*, May 12, 2010, http://www.laborrights.org/sites/default/files/publications-and-resources/ChinaLaborContractLaw2010_0.pdf, accessed May 24, 2013.

the LCL went into effect), numbers are still far below the 100 percent required by law. Many respondents also complained that their contracts lacked provisions required by the LCL. The survey highlighted significant variations by industry (workers in the service sector being much more likely to enjoy a written contract and social insurance than those in the furniture or hardware sectors) and showed that the LCL had a stronger impact on younger workers: while 66 percent of workers aged 16–24 had a labor contract at the time of their interviews, this percentage dropped to 64 percent for those aged 25–32, 60 percent for those aged 33–40, and 56 percent for workers aged 41–52.

Widespread informal employment is a major obstacle to the sound enforcement of the LCL. While most organizations in the public sector and most medium- and big-sized private companies abide by the law, the enforcement rate is much lower in small-sized companies and familial enterprises. In 2009, the public and private "formal" sector only counted for about 40 percent of total urban employment (see Figure 8.1 for more details).

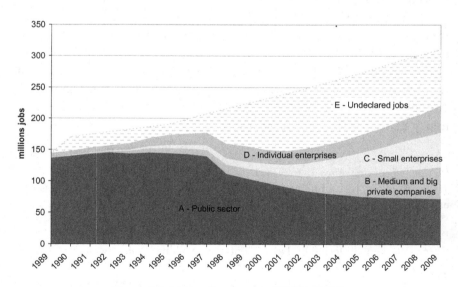

Figure 8.1. Urban Employment (1989–2009).

Source: Compiled from the *China Statistical Yearbook*, published by National Bureau of Statistics of China, for the years 1989–2009 (bilingual Chinese-English edition).

Companies that are operating in China are now expected to focus on working contracts, wages and environment as constituting an essential element of their policies and image. The continuous improvement of employees' morale, formation and living standards should be approached as both an ethical and a managerial imperative. Otherwise said, the social dimension of CSR-related strategies is not to be seen as an additional constraint put over companies' activities. Rather, it accompanies a shift in China's global economic model and prospects, a shift that modifies the way the comparative advantages of conducting production and business in China must be evaluated.

8.2. Migrant Workers and the Evolution of the Labor Force

The issues linked to labor contract law often connect with practical problems associated with the significant proportion of migrant workers in the working population. Migrants already account for 17 percent of Chinese population. They were 230 million migrants in 2011: 35 times more than in 1982 and 125 percent more than in 2000.[19,20] This specificity of the Chinese labor market raises questions for the companies operating in the country. It allows for a greater flexibility of the workforce. At the same time, questions of employees' level of retention and training, as well as of social fairness, heavily weigh on the executives in charge of human resources. Besides, the social environment is rapidly changing: the new generation of migrant workers is becoming more conscious of their rights and their bargaining power (Box 8.2). Conflicts linked to the management of this floating population have been detrimental to companies operating on large-scale working forces.

The migrant worker issue provides us with another example of the way companies need to perceive themselves as *interdependent selves* so as to determine the focus and scope of their corporate responsibilities: no personnel management can be conceived and implemented without

---

[19] School of Hard Knocks, *Global Times*, September 18, 2012.
[20] Migrant Children Have Greater Chance of Missing out on School, *China Daily*, August 8, 2012, http://www.chinadaily.com.cn/cndy/2012-08/08/content_15651090.htm, accessed June 10, 2013.

Box 8.2 Labor Market: In Search of the Point of Equilibrium?

"A migrant-worker tribe that swelled to 158 million in 2011 from 25 million in 1990 has been a key contributor to China's rapid growth. The move from the farm to the factory expanded the work force, increased productivity and supercharged China's export competitiveness. The fear is that after decades of migration, the store of rural workers is close to exhausted. Wages increased 14.8 percent in the year to June, despite a sharp slowdown in the export and construction sectors where migrants work. That certainly suggests a dearth of workers. ... Xin Meng, an expert on China's labor market at the Australian National University, calculates that most rural migrants spend only seven years away from the farm. They arrive in the city in their late teens and return to the country aged around 25 to raise children. Of the 380 million-strong rural population aged 16 to 40, just a 100 million are working in the cities. ... Ms. Xin's survey work shows that in 2011, 13 percent of migrant workers had unemployment insurance and 20 percent had health coverage — compared with 66 percent and 87 percent, respectively, of urban residents. ... When the lower supply and higher expectations of migrant workers runs up against management intransigence on pay and conditions, the results can be explosive. Riots at a Foxconn factory last month, for instance, may be symptomatic of a deeper malaise."

Source: Orlik, T. (2012), China's Workers Are Revolting, WSJA, October 1, 2012, http://online.wsj.com/article/SB10000872396390444004704578029792051820104. html?mg=id-wsj, accessed June 10, 2013.

knowledge of the global environment in which this force comes on the market. Conversely, knowledge of this environment allows the same company to come up with innovative programs concerning training, welfare, philanthropic initiatives and sustainable development. This is why we are paying special attention here to the migrant workers issue, in close relationship with the creative challenges raised in the implementation of CSR in China. The understanding of this issue opens up windows on the overall context in which a company operates, from a better knowledge of its working force base to its consumers' behaviors.

Each Chinese citizen has a *hukou* (household registration) which records the person's name, the name of its parents and spouse, as well as the date and place of birth. This latter data usually defines the residential location of a person, where he/she is entitled to specific rights and welfare benefits. Except in some localities where this distinction was recently removed, residents in a single location also have different social rights according to their "agricultural" or "non-agricultural" status.[21] The *hukou* status of parents is generally transferred to children.[22] This "internal passport" system has been put in place in the 1950s to restrict population mobility. Until the 1980s, it proved an efficient tool for the government to control the number of people who could move from a rural registration to an urban one, and from one part of the country to another.

Despite a number of national and local policies tending to gradually relax *hukou*-related restrictions, rural migrants remain "second-class" citizens in most Chinese cities, where they are still discriminated in term of social entitlements (healthcare, education, etc.) and access to job opportunities. Although concerns about the high cost of healthcare and schooling, as well as the unequal access to good quality public services, are shared by a growing number of disadvantaged urban dwellers, the *hukou* system reinforces disparities, by imposing supplementary costs for migrant households.[23] Likewise, if the informal sector employment is not restricted to migrants, their access to lucrative employment opportunities in the public sector remains limited, and they face greater challenges than local workers in accessing decent work even in the private sector. In 2010, over 60 percent of migrants would have been working in the informal sector.[24] Migrants account for the vast majority of workers in "sweatshops" and export-oriented factories of the Pearl Delta, where basic work standards tend to be frequently overlooked, even after the 2008 Labor Contract Law was passed. In December 2012, Li Keqiang — who has since become the Chinese Premier — said in a statement posted on a

---

[21] Chan, K.W. & W. Buckingham (2008), Is China Abolishing the *Hukou* System?, *The China Quarterly*, 195, 582–606.
[22] World Bank and Development Research Center of China's State Council (2012, p. 362), *op. cit.*
[23] *Ibid.*, p. 302.
[24] *Ibid.*, p. 351.

government website that: "China must take migrant rural workers and gradually change them into urban residents. This requires that we push forward household registration reform." The statement did not offer additional details.[25]

Migrants' conditions vary significantly according to their locality of residence and their status. Discriminations seem to be stronger in bigger cities than in smaller towns, and in the case of rural to urban migrations than in the case of urban to urban or rural to rural migrations. Intra-provincial migrations appear to be better accepted by local citizens and authorities than more distant migrations. Moreover, better-educated and richer migrants find ways to circumvent restrictions.

In 2010, China had officially 253 million rural residents who left the agricultural sector (*nongmingong*), thus representing about 20 percent of the country's total population. Among them, "only" 159 million had migrated outside their place of *hukou* registration, the remaining 94 million having transferred from the agricultural to the non-agricultural sector without leaving their district.[26] Over 100 million migrant workers would live in a city for at least six months in a year.[27] The massive influx of rural residents into cities has become a major phenomenon, starting from the 1980s. In 2000, 36.2 percent of the Chinese population lived in cities. This ratio increased to 51.3 percent in 2011 and may reach 67 percent in 2030 — an extra 300 million people compared to the 2012 number. In many large cities, migrants already account for a quarter to a third of the population. *It is expected that, by 2025, they will represent almost 40 percent of the Chinese urban population.*[28]

---

[25] Mozur, P. & T. Orlik (2012), China's Laborers Lingering in Cities: Laborers From Rural Areas Are Staying Longer and Gaining Better Benefits in Urban Centers, Lifting Country's Economy, *WSJA*, December 30, 2012, http://online.wsj.com/article/SB10001424127887323300404578202920521347466.html, accessed May 24, 2013.

[26] National Bureau of Statistics of China (2012), *2011 nian wo guo nongmingong diaocha jiance baogao* (2011's Report on Chinese Rural Migrants), April 27, 2012, http://www.stats.gov.cn/tjfx/fxbg/t20120427_402801903.htm, accessed May 24, 2013.

[27] Yu, H. (2012), Experts Debate Reforms for Sustainable Urbanization, *Caixin*, April 25, 2012.

[28] McKinsey Global Institute (2009), Preparing for China's Urban Billion, March 2009, pp. 19–20, http://www.mckinsey.com/insights/urbanization/preparing_for_urban_billion_in_china, accessed June 10, 2013.

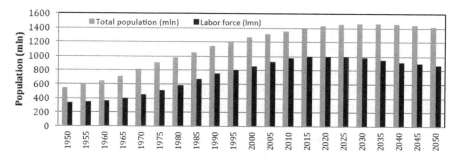

Figure 8.2. Total Population and Labor Force, 1980–2050.

Source: Taken from Figure 1.5 of World Bank (2012), China 2030: Equality of Opportunity and Basic Security for All, p. 304, http://www.worldbank.org/content/dam/Worldbank/document/SR4 – 293-390.pdf, accessed July 31, 2013.

And yet, at the same time, the shortage of migrants is becoming a concern for Chinese industries. The "Lewis turning point" (where the limitless supply of migrants from the countryside dries up and urban wages surge) may already have been reached in 2003.[29] The World Bank points out that this exhaustion of the rural unskilled surplus labor will be concomitant with rapid population ageing. *As a result, Chinese labor force will start to shrink from around 2015, initially at a slow pace, with a progressive acceleration from the late 2020s on* (Figure 8.2).

Still, the situation remains very fluid, and analysts disagree on the significance of some major trends. It is true that, over the past five years, migrant workers' wages have increased significantly. The increase in monthly and hourly earnings for wage-salary earners between 2008 and 2012 are 12 percent and 14 percent a year, respectively. Between 2010 and 2011, the real hourly earnings increased even more — 23 percent. But wage growth of these magnitudes seems to have stopped in 2012. The real hourly wage growth between 2011 and 2012 was only 3.7 percent. If one strips out the increases of those with higher experience and skill levels, wages in 2012 rose just 1.7 percent, compared to 23 percent in 2011. And there are still restrictions on migrant access to social welfare and services in cities. If the restrictions on migrant access

[29]Cai, F., Y. Du & M. Wang (2009), *Employment and Inequality Outcomes in China*, Paris, OECD Seminar on Informal Employment.

to social welfare and social services in cities were abolished, and hence the duration of migration greatly increased, observe some analysts, then any conceivable labor shortages would disappear.[30]

The real issue may lie in the social standards that will apply in the future to the migrant population: "The proportion of migrant workers with unemployment insurance increased from 11 percent in 2008 to 21 percent in 2012. Similarly, those with health, pension, and work-injury insurances increased from 13 percent, 18 percent, and 17 percent in 2008 to 27 percent, 31 percent, and 23 percent in 2012, respectively. However, the large majority of migrant workers still work in cities without any protections. In addition, in recent years, the proportion of migrant workers with some type of employment contract seems to have reduced sharply, from 66 percent in 2010 to 59 percent in 2012. In 1995, migrant workers in Shanghai earned 50 percent of the hourly earnings of the urban *hukou* workers. By 2009, migrants in the same city only earned 40 percent of the hourly earnings of their urban counterparts."[31]

These figures remain controversial, and the situation greatly varies from sector to sector and from region to region. Increasing migrants' wages and reducing inequalities between migrants and urban citizens are among the objectives of the new five-year plan. There have been recent signs of rapid convergence of the average wages of migrant and local workers: the rise in hourly wages of migrants relative to local *hukou* workers from only 35 percent in 2001 to 78 percent in 2010.[32] In 2011, migrant workers' average wage surged 21.2 percent, up to 2,049 yuan — a progression not only due to inflation and the raise of minimum wage standards in many localities, but also the employer's voluntary policies (this might indeed be less true in the service sector, hence the trend observed in Shanghai). Sporadic labor shortages in jobs

---

[30] *Cf.* Meng, X. (2013), *WSJ*, What Worker Shortage? The Real Story of China's Migrants, January 4, 2013, http://blogs.wsj.com/chinarealtime/2013/01/04/what-worker-shortage-the-real-story-of-chinas-migrants/?mod=WSJBlog&mod=chinablog, accessed May 24, 2013.

[31] *Ibid.*

[32] World Bank and Development Research Center of China's State Council (2012, p. 355), *op. cit.*

that urban dwellers refuse to take have already constrained companies to improve work conditions and significantly increase wages in order to retain their migrant workers and attract new ones. This pattern is particularly evident after the Chinese New Year, when migrants return to the countryside to celebrate this festival with their family. Year after year, it has proved more and more difficult to get migrants back into the urban workforce after the Spring Festival. In 2012, a governmental report said that this phenomenon had been longer lasting and wider in scope than ever.[33] The phenomenon was even more obvious in 2013, with a concomitant shift happening in migrant workers' preferences from the manufacturing to the service sector.[34] Better educated, less impressed by urban life, and facing a lighter economic pressure than their parents, "second generation" migrants have higher expectations regarding labor conditions and social entitlements.

This also translates into a shift in migration patterns, with a trend of the inland population to migrate closer to the original residence, often within their native province, instead of going to coastal export factories. For the first time, in 2011, more migrants chose to work in their own provinces (52.9 percent) rather than outside.[35] Most Chinese migrants keep a close relation to their village, where they endeavor to keep their land, which still plays a role of unemployment and old-age insurances. Concerns about the sustainability of the urbanization process also push the government to encourage rural dwellers to move to smaller cities within their own provinces.

Starting in 2001, 15 provinces had abolished the agricultural/non-agricultural distinction in their household registration system by 2009.[36] But this measure did not significantly change the life of most

---

[33] Dammon Loyalka, M. (2012), Chinese Labor, Cheap No More, *The New York Times*, February 17, 2012, http://www.nytimes.com/2012/02/18/opinion/chinese-labor-cheap-no-more.html, accessed May 24, 2013.

[34] Chu, K. (2013), China: A Billion Strong but Short on Workers, *WSJA*, May 1, 2013, http://online.wsj.com/article/SB10001424127887323798104578455153999658318.html?mod=WSJAsia_hpp_LEFTTopStories&mg=id-wsj, accessed May 24, 2013.

[35] National Bureau of Statistics of China (2012), *op. cit.*

[36] World Bank and the Development Research Center of China's State Council (2012, p. 364), *op. cit.*

migrants as *hukou* "unification" only applied to permanent residents within each locality. Besides, without supporting entitlement reforms, such a reform is symbolic, as people would continue to enjoy different rights depending on the place of their original *hukou*.[37] Other local experiences include a mechanism designed to protect peasants' rights on their land during a limited transitional period, so that unsuccessful migrants could get back to agriculture if they come back from urban areas. In February 2012, a new regulation issued by the State Council made *hukou* registration more flexible, but only in small- and medium-sized cities. If the distinction between rural and urban residents has been blurred, new and more complex divisions have been created, and inequalities linked to the original place of residency remain a fixture of China's social landscape.

What can companies learn from this analysis of the conditions under which the migrant worker force lives and operates? The lesson is at least threefold:

— Workers come from specific environments and live under very different conditions. A detailed understanding of their background allows entrepreneurs to modulate their expectations, training programs, incentives and social packages. For entrepreneurs willing to better analyze the challenges and provenance of their working force, the results on corporate morale, cohesiveness and flexibility can be highly beneficial.

— Second, the attention given to the social trends that have been sketched in this section helps managers to anticipate evolutions in labor cost, labor quality and workers' expectations. It thus provides companies with additional tools when making strategic decisions on their use of production factors and their corporate model of labor relations.

— Migrant workers (an evolving population, as we have seen) are a privileged target for corporate programs linked to their living conditions, training and long-term prospects. These programs can be partly inserted into traditional training or welfare projects, and can be partly philanthropic in nature.

---

[37] *Ibid.*, p. 363.

8.3. Child Labor, Mistreatments and the Supply Chain

Underage labor in China is illegal, and the country has signed the relevant international conventions. The issue first concerns the agricultural sector, as compulsory education is still not fully enforced everywhere in the country, including the informal sector. Some schools send their students to do factory work as a form of job training. In these situations, however, much of the work done is tedious and unskilled rather than career-orientated. In 2004, a headmaster was found to be employing 35 students between the ages of eight and sixteen in a toy factory that he owned. Child labor is still found most prevalently in toy production, textiles, construction, food production, and light mechanical work. The problem might have been especially acute at the beginning of the 2000s, with the changes in the social network — especially the increase in school fees — occurring at that time. Though it has not disappeared, it has most probably improved since. The Child Labour Index 2012 compiled by risk analysis firm Maplecroft ranks China as the 36th country in the world, by decreasing order, where the risk of child labor occurs. This makes China less risky than the Philippines (25th) and India (27th), but riskier than Vietnam (37th), Indonesia (46th) and Brazil (54th). This ranking still includes China in the "extreme risk" category, along with 40 percent of the world's countries.[38]

According to the International Labor Organization (ILO), there are over 215 million children working across the world and of these, 115 million are thought to be involved in hazardous work. The above-mentioned index enables companies to identify risks of children being employed within their supply chains in violation of the standards on the minimum age of employment. It also analyses the risk of the involvement of children in work, the conditions of which could have a negative impact on the health, safety and well-being of child

---

[38] Conflict and Economic Downturn Cause Global Increase in Reported Child Labour Violations — 40 percent of Countries Now Rated 'Extreme Risk' by Maplecroft, *Maplecroft News*, January 5, 2012, http://maplecroft.com/about/news/child_labour_2012.html, accessed May 24, 2013.

laborers. And indeed, the child labor issue has also to be addressed by giant corporations having to monitor an over-extended supply chain. Beginning 2013, Apple recognized the discovery of multiple cases of child labor in its supply chain, including one Chinese company that employed 74 children under the age of 16. It uncovered 106 cases of underage labor being used at Apple suppliers in 2012. Apple's annual supplier report — which monitors nearly 400 suppliers — found that children were employed at 11 factories involved in making its products. A number of them had been recruited using forged identity papers, with the complicity of labor agencies. They also found cases of juveniles being used to lift heavy goods.[39]

Other offences documented in the Apple report ranged from mandatory pregnancy tests, to bonded workers whose wages are confiscated to pay off debts imposed by recruitment agencies. Bonded labor was discovered at eight factories. And investigators found 90 facilities that deducted wages to punish workers. Mandatory pregnancy testing was found at 34 places of work, while 25 tested for medical conditions such as hepatitis B. At four facilities, payroll records were falsified to hide information from auditors, and at one, a supplier was found intentionally dumping waste oil "into the restroom receptacle".[40] This illustrates the fact that, in China, the child labor issue is to be integrated into an overall analysis of the supply chain, which includes investigating the choice of the auditors inspecting and assessing the record of the factories along the entire chain, checking on the accuracy of all information submitted, conducting random evaluations, and assessing the strictness of standards issued for ensuring full legal compliance with both national and international norms on labor conditions.

Still, the problem can be haunting: "Supply chains are often long, complex and difficult to define. In most cases, a manufacturer purchases goods and services from a number of suppliers (direct suppliers), who in turn may have their own suppliers (indirect suppliers). Even where

---

[39] Garside, J. (2013), Child Labour Uncovered in Apple's Supply Chain, *The Guardian*, January 25, 2013, http://www.guardian.co.uk/technology/2013/jan/25/apple-child-labour-supply, accessed May 24, 2013.
[40] *Ibid*.

voluntary or legal obligations apply only to direct suppliers, companies can face significant logistic and legal challenges, for example, with respect to oversight, audit and enforcement, especially in the context of international sales."[41] However, it is exactly the danger of diluted responsibility and its corrosive effect on issues as sensitive as child labor that is now driving new legislation on the supply chain's responsibility. Requirements already exist in California, stipulating that a business covered under the Supply Chains Act must disclose whether it:

— Verifies product supply chains to evaluate and address risks of human trafficking and slavery, and specify if the verification was not conducted by a third party;
— Audits suppliers to evaluate compliance with the company's standards for trafficking and slavery in supply chains, and specify if the verification was not an independent, unannounced audit;
— Requires direct suppliers to certify that materials incorporated into the product comply with laws regarding slavery and human trafficking of the country or countries in which they are doing business;
— Maintains internal accountability standards and procedures for employees or contractors failing to meet company standards regarding slavery and trafficking; and
— Provides training to company employees and management (those who direct responsibility for supply chain management) on human trafficking and slavery and mitigating risks within the supply chains of products.[42]

In the US, provisions still in discussion include the Business Transparency on Trafficking and Slavery Act (BTTSA), the federal analogue to the Supply Chains Act. As proposed, the BTTSA would require a business to disclose to what extent, if any, it maintains a policy aimed at identifying and eliminating supply chain risks concerning human

---

[41] Ostrau, M.S. & A.C. Waler (2012), Corporate Social Responsibility and the Supply Chain, p. 14, http://www.techlaw.org/wp-content/uploads/2010/07/Fenwick-Corporate-Social-Responsibility-and-the-Supply-Chain-August-2012.pdf, accessed June 10, 2013.
[42] California Civil Code (2011). § *1714.43*(c)*(1)–(5)*. See also Ostrau & Waler (2012, pp. 10–15), *op. cit.*

trafficking and slavery; assesses its suppliers' management and procurement systems to verify whether each supplier has in place appropriate systems to identify human trafficking and slavery risks within that supplier's supply chain; requires its suppliers to have recruiting practices that comply with the company's standards for eliminating exploitive labor practices; and prohibits the use of its corporate products, facilities or services to obtain or maintain persons under exploitive conditions.[43]

Companies should be alert to global trends that tend to extent CSR practices to the monitoring of the entire supply chain, and to the international implications of laws and regulations passed in one given country. Such trends will most certainly reinforce some of the changes intervening in Chinese workplaces, some of which we have already studied, while others will be analyzed in the course of the next chapter.

8.4. Schooling and CSR

It would be hypocritical for corporations to strictly prohibit child labor within their factories without reflecting on its causes and integrating the issue into their proactive CSR policies. Lack of alternatives, such as affordable schooling, is a powerful factor driving child labor. Even when schooling is available, schools may be difficult to reach or they may dispense an education that may not seem worth the effort. The issue goes far beyond child labor, and, numerically, has much to do with the surge of the migrant working force. In recent years, some corporations have been giving special attention to educational programs directed toward the children of migrant workers, at the same time as local governments, NGOs and educational institutions have been preoccupied with the question of the quality and amount of schooling provided to the children of migrant workers. As the issue is directly linked to the policies companies follow when it comes to their activities' location, social packages, training programs or work contracts, public and private institutions have been challenging corporations on the issue at stake. This might take the form of alerting them to the problems met by the children of their employees (in their hometown or in the cities), or soliciting them for participation in educational programs or

---

[43] *Ibid.*

other initiatives. The issue has become symptomatic of the intertwining occurring between management policies and global concerns. We take it here as a case study for detailing further how a thorough knowledge of their social environment may help companies to be more effective both in their internal managerial policies and in determining the philanthropic and social programs they may decide to engage.

The number of *migrant children in cities* is even more difficult to estimate than that of adult migrant workers, as many of them do not attend formal schools. Their number has probably reached *20 million* — over 1/15 of all Chinese children.[44] According to the Ministry of Education, in 2011, 12.6 million children within the compulsory education age moved with their parents who work away from their rural homes, representing 938,000 more than in 2010.[45] Most of migrant children live in big cities, especially in China's southern and eastern regions. Over 60 percent of migrant workers in Beijing, Shanghai and Guangzhou have their kids with them.[46] One third of migrant children are born in their current city of residence and one third have stayed there for at least five years.[47] However, they remain second-class citizens in cities, where they face both institutional barriers to school and healthcare, and social discrimination — especially from their urban peers at school.

Even larger is the group of children "left behind" in the countryside by parents who migrate for work. Their number was estimated by a 2008 report by the All-China Women's Federation to be 58 million, accounting for 21.72 percent of rural children aged 17 or less.[48,49] According to the

---

[44] Attané, I. (2011), *Au pays des enfants rares. La Chine vers une catastrophe démographique*, Paris: Fayard, p. 182. A similar estimate (19 million) is given by: Millions of Chinese Rural Migrants Denied Education for Their Children, *The Guardian*, March 15, 2010.

[45] China Has 12.6 Million Migrant Children, *China Daily*, September 4, 2012, http://www.chinadaily.com.cn/china/2012-09/04/content_15733495.htm, accessed June 10, 2013.

[46] *Global Times* (2012), *op. cit.*

[47] Attané (2011, p. 182), *op. cit.*

[48] Millions of Chinese Rural Migrants Denied Education for Their Children, *The Guardian*, March 15, 2010.

[49] China Advised to Set Up National Committee for Minors Left Behind by Migrant Parents, *Xinhua*, March 9, 2008.

Ministry of Education, in 2011, there were 22 million "left-behind" children of school age — 712 000 less than the year before.[50] Migrant children tend to have a higher dropout rate, a lower attendance rate and a lower graduation rate than their urban counterparts.[51] Many do not follow the compulsory nine years of schooling. About three quarters of migrant children in cities are in the primary school age group[52] and schooling rates strongly decrease among migrant children above 12 years.[53] Many teenagers either go back to their village or start working in a city.

Those who managed to attend high school face the impossibility of taking the *gaokao* (college entrance examination) outside their place of "permanent residence". This not only implies a costly trip, but also smaller chances to enter university, due to geographical quotas. In the last few years, several migrant "collective visits" to the Education Ministry aimed at reclaiming the lifting of those *hukou* restrictions for *gaokao* sitters. A new policy has been announced in August 2012 (the third one after 2001 and 2003) but a full suppression of restrictions looks unlikely in the short term, especially in large cities where there are more education resources, such as Beijing, Shanghai and the Pearl River Delta region.[54]

Private schools managed by migrants (sometimes with the support of NGOs) are viewed as an acceptable solution for many parents, because of their affordable fees and smaller relational problems between migrant and urban pupils, or with the schools' principal and teachers. However, most of these schools do not meet even basic safety standards (quality of construction, equipment, food, etc.) and are not able to attract and retain qualified teachers. Low qualifications of the teaching team and a high staff turnover strongly impact learning conditions. Pupils do acquire basic knowledge, but their academic results lag far behind those of their counterparts in public schools.[55]

---

[50] *China Daily* (2012), *op. cit.*

[51] The Children of Migrant Workers in China, *China Labour Bulletin*, May 8, 2009, http://www.clb.org.hk/en/content/children-migrant-workers-china-3#part2_heading06, accessed June 10, 2013.

[52] *China Daily* (2012), *op. cit.*

[53] Hu, B. & J. Szente (2010), Education of Young Chinese Migrant Children: Challenges and Prospects, *Early Childhood Education Journal*, 37(6), 477–482.

[54] *China Daily* (2012), *op. cit.*

[55] *China Labour Bulletin* (2009), *op. cit.*

Due to schooling difficulties, costs generated by bringing children to cities, and their long working hours, most migrants choose to leave their children in their hometown (especially very young children and teenagers), with grandparents or other relatives. According to the China Women Association, in 2009, 58 million migrants were "left behind" by one or both of their parents — accounting for over one out of five rural children aged 17 or less.[56] Less supported in their school life, they tend to have worse academic results and higher dropout rates than their classmates. Beyond academic problems, many of them face social and psychological problems due to the lack of a good relationship with their parents.[57] Girls seem to pay an even heavier cost than boys, being less often chosen to accompany parents to the city, and being given less educational opportunities and more housekeeping tasks in their hometown.[58,59,60]

As education is increasingly perceived as a major tool for improving migrants' children integration to cities, some foundations and companies have started to sponsor programs in this area. For example, in June 2011, the Amway Charity Foundation, the first non-public foundation established by a multinational company under the direct supervision of the Ministry of Civil Affairs, was launched, with a focus on programs (Project Sunshine, the Rainbow Project and the Spring Sprout Project) in favor of migrant workers' children (Box 8.3).[61]

---

[56] *Xinhua* (2008), *op. cit.*

[57] Chen, X. & X. Du (2011), *Liushou nütong jiaoyu wenti yanjiu zongshu* (Research on educational problems of left-behind girls), *Journal of Shandong Women's University*, 95(1), 73–76: 90. (陈晓晴,杜学元 《留守女童教育问题研究综述》, 山东女子学院院报 2011年95卷01期).

[58] Li, D. & M.C. Tsang (2003), Household Decisions and Gender Inequality in Education in Rural China, *China: An International Journal*, 1(2), 224–248.

[59] Tan, L. & Y. Song (2005), Does Gender Make a Difference Understanding Chinese Current Equality in Compulsory Education?, in I. Attané & J. Véron (eds.), *Gender Discriminations Among Young Children in Asia*, Pondicherry: All India Press, pp. 207–224.

[60] Monteil, A. (2012), Éducation: La longue marche des Chinoises", in M. Lieber et T. Angeloff (eds.), *Chinoises au XXIe siècle. Ruptures et continuités*, Paris: La Découverte, pp. 43–62.

[61] A Breakthrough for Corporate Citizenship in China, *Amway*, June 6, 2011, http://blogs.amway.com/onebyone/2011/06/06/a-breakthrough-for-corporate-citizenship-in-china/, accessed June 10, 2013.

Box 8.3. Amway Charity Foundation

Launched in 2011, Amway Charity Foundation (ACF) is the first non-public foundation with a multinational corporate background that is under the direct supervision of the Ministry of Civil Affairs. With a starting fund of RMB 100 million, it was established by Amway China in accordance with the Regulation on Foundation Administration.[62] ACF aims to help children of migrant workers and create a better environment for them to live, learn and achieve; foster a volunteer organization with high standards and dedication; and effectively promote the healthy and sustainable development of philanthropy in China through research, cooperation and exchanges.[63]

One such project under ACF, the *Spring Sprout Project*, acts to better the nutrition of rural boarding students in poverty-stricken areas by establishing Spring Sprout Kitchens and training kitchen administrations in boarding schools in mid- and western China with high concentrations of left-behind children.[64] Another project, the *Sunshine Project*, promotes social integration for migrant children in cities by building Sunshine Cultural Activity Rooms and sending outstanding teachers from top schools to teach after-school courses for them.[65]

The *Rainbow Project* provides educational aid to left-behind children in poor areas in western China by sponsoring postgraduate volunteers from famous Chinese universities to teach them, creating more opportunities for left-behind children by upgrading school facilities, assisting dropouts to return to school, as well as organizing recreational and sports activities.[66]

8.5. Social Coverage

When it comes to CSR-related issues within the corporation's internal working and management, social coverage constitutes another

---

[62] Amway Charity Foundation, http://www.amwayfoundation.org/en/cf_intro.html, accessed May 24, 2013.

[63] Amway Charity Foundation, http://www.amwayfoundation.org/en/cf_mission.html, accessed May 24, 2013.

[64] Amway Charity Foundation, http://www.amwayfoundation.org/en/cf_xiangmujieshao.html, accessed May 24, 2013.

[65] Amway Charity Foundation, http://www.amwayfoundation.org/en/cf_xiangmujieshao2.html, accessed May 24, 2013.

[66] Amway Charity Foundation, http://www.amwayfoundation.org/en/cf_xiangmujieshao1.html, accessed May 24, 2013.

field of discussion and discernment. For sure, companies have to first fulfill legal obligations, with seemingly little room left for specific corporate policies. However, as we have seen in other fields, some dispositions are left to the corporation's appreciation, implementation of the dispositions can be left open to interpretation, and more broadly, the texts recently enacted intend to make the corporation develop a social sensitivity that goes beyond the letter of the law. Additionally, assessing how social coverage issues determine the prospects and worries of its work force helps the company to better appreciate how to deal with its workers so as to ensure a win-win model of cooperation.

On July 1, 2011, China's first comprehensive social insurance law came into effect.[67] Until then, after the dismantling of the "iron rice bowl" in the late 1990s, the building of a new social insurance framework was highly fragmented, with variations from one locality to another and major discrepancies between urban and rural residents. The new law does not create a fully unified system, but consolidates and standardizes rules. China's social insurance system consists of five elements: (1) retirement; (2) medical; (3) unemployment; (4) work-related injury; and (5) maternity insurance. The Social Insurance Law is the first law to state explicitly the establishment of these five mechanisms at the state level. Until then, the social insurance framework was mainly made of administrative regulations (such as the *Provisional Regulations on Collection and Payment of Social Insurance Premiums* promulgated by the State Council in 1999 and the *Work-related Injury Insurance Regulations* adopted by the State Council in 2003).

Employers must contribute to all the five plans listed above, while mandatory contribution from employees only include pension, medical and unemployment insurance premiums. Employees' share is withheld and paid by employers. The law does not specify the contribution rates or the basis for calculating each kind of social insurance.

---

[67] *Shehui baoxian fa* (Social Insurance Law), promulgated on October 28, 2010. Chinese full text available at: http://www.china.com.cn/policy/txt/2010-10/29/content_21225907.htm, accessed May 24, 2013. English translation: http://www.bycpa.com/html/news/20116/1585.html, accessed May 24, 2013.

Local labor and social security bureaus (at the provincial and municipal levels) are responsible for such tasks, taking into account local economic conditions.

Besides reinforcing the governance of social insurance funds, the Social Insurance Law tightens supervision over the payment of social insurance premiums. Employers must register for their employees within 30 days of employment. They are responsible for transferring premiums (including those withheld on employees' salary) to relevant authorities in a timely manner. In case of failure, an initial warning is to be issued by the social insurance agency. If the overdue payment is not made within the stipulated period of time, the social insurance premium collection department is entitled to request employers' bank information and to obtain the transfer of the outstanding premiums directly from its bank account.[68] The same department is also entitled to submit applications to the People's Courts for seizing and auctioning the employer's property in order to recover the amount of social insurance premiums outstanding. Faulty employers may be subject to penalties ranging from 100 percent to 300 percent of the contributions due, in addition to a daily late payment interest surcharge of 0.05 percent on the unpaid or underpaid amount.[69]

The way Chinese workers understand social coverage issues and react to them is strongly colored by historical memories: from the 1950s to the 1990s — the period of the "iron rice bowl" system, urban employees benefited from a relatively good level of social protection, while rural residents accessed basic healthcare for free. The end of the "work unit" society and the privatization of the health system made the access to care unaffordable for a large part of the Chinese population, especially in the countryside. The building of a mandatory

[68] Jiang, J. & X. Li (2011), The Social Insurance Law: A Milestone in Chinese Legislation, *King and Wood's China Bulletin*, February, http://www.kingandwood.com/Bulletin/ChinaBulletinContent.aspx?id=965a52f0-f255-43a1-b79e-dd040a3e6329, accessed May 24, 2013.

[69] China's New Social Insurance Law, *KPMG Tax Alert*, n°17, September 2011, http://www.kpmg.com/cn/en/IssuesAndInsights/ArticlesPublications/Newsletters/Tax-alert/Documents/tax-alert-1109-17-2.pdf, accessed June 10, 2013.

nationwide social security system sponsored by government has become a top priority in the 2000s. In 2003, less than one third of China's population had a health insurance.[70] In 2008, as much as 90 percent of China's rural population still had no health insurance coverage. Three years later, 94 percent of the population was at least covered by a basic scheme.[71] The utilization rate of hospital services by rural Chinese has almost doubled over the past five years, and the out-of-pocket spending as a percentage of China's total health expenditure went down from 55.8 percent in 2003 to 35.5 percent in 2010. Progress has been less impressive for the pension system, which still covered only 55 percent of urban employees in 2010.[72]

Extension of the social security coverage has been gradual. Starting with urban employees of public companies in the 1990s, the health insurance system has progressively been extended to employees in other form of companies, to other urbanites (including self-employed workers and children), to rural residents and to migrant workers. But mechanisms, premium rates and benefits still vary from one group to another. The Social Insurance Law stipulates that individual private businesses, part-time employees and other "flexible" workers who do not participate in the basic pension insurance provided by their employer, may participate in the basic pension insurance and basic medical treatment insurance if they pay insurance premiums on their own. The transferability of social insurance (for both medical and pension insurance) across different districts has been advertised as a major innovation for migrant workers, as it would allow employees to work in different locales without concern

---

[70] Liu, Y. (2011), Great Progress, but More Is Needed, *The New York Times*, November 1, 2011, http://www.nytimes.com/roomfordebate/2011/11/01/is-china-facing-a-health-care-crisis/chinas-health-care-reform-far-from-sufficient, accessed May 24, 2013.

[71] Kiff, S. (2011), China's Health Reform Challenge, *The Washington Post*, February 11, 2011, http://www.washingtonpost.com/blogs/ezra-klein/post/chinas-health-reform-challenge/2011/11/02/gIQAxlRLgM_blog.html, accessed May 24, 2013.

[72] New Study Details China's Pension Reform Options, *IPA*, June 11, 2010, http://www.ipe.com/asia/new-study-details-chinas-pension-reform-options_35703.php#.UbWP2hYykbA, accessed June 10, 2013.

over whether they are able to retain the full value of payments made to their insurance funds. In fact, this measure was already provided for in the Labor Contract Law of 2007. The repetition of this principle should only increase pressure over local labor bureaus to attain an effective implementation. The main progress for rural residents and migrants lies in the possibility to participate in an urban social insurance scheme and, upon cessation of employment, to transfer back to their rural social insurance program.

Despite the impressive extension of the social security net, progress is still impeded by difficulties met by informal workers (including part-time workers) to get insured, and by the strong out-of-pocket fees still required from patients (the average reimbursement rate of inpatient expenses are only 48 percent for urban residents and 44 percent for rural residents, with significant inter-regional inequalities). The challenge is now to pass from "nominal coverage" to "effective coverage", by increasing reimbursement rates, by improving the primary care system, and by equalizing public health services across the nation.

Demographic trends make the building of a comprehensive social insurance system more urgent than elsewhere. Population ageing is progressing at the fastest pace in the world: the ratio of 65 year-olds to those aged 15–64 years, currently at 11 percent, is projected to increase to 38 percent by 2050. During the next 20 years, the Chinese ageing process will be equivalent to what France will experience in 120 years. New social and professional behaviors also tend to weaken intergenerational solidarity and reinforce the need for a stronger public pension system.

Not only social stability, but also economic equilibrium and sustainability of the Chinese growth are at stake: since 2008, the international crisis has highlighted the limits of an export-driven development model. It is now acknowledged that the domestic market needs to be strengthened. Reinforcing the social protection system is a strong lever to reduce precautionary savings and to guarantee the population a minimal consumption capacity even in case of crisis. At the international level, Chinese efforts to build a more effective social protection system also fit into the United Nations' Social Protection Floor initiative — a global social policy approach promoting integrated strategies for providing access to essential social services and income security for all.

8.5.1. *Minimum wage*

The Chinese legislation about minimum wage rates has been put in place progressively from the mid-1990s. Each province, autonomous region and municipality can set its own standards. Even if implementation is still far from satisfying (and if those standards only apply in the formal sector, thus excluding a major part of the working population), the existence of such standards is progressively becoming a real tool for workers' protection, for the limitation of revenue inequality, and for a wage elevation prone to domestic consumption increases.

According to Article 48 of the 1994 Labor Law, "The State shall implement a system of guaranteed minimum wages. The employer shall pay laborers wages no lower than the local standards on minimum wages."[73] Ten years later, in order to strengthen workers' protection, the Ministry of Labor and Social Security issued the Provisions on the Minimum Wage.[74] Minimum wage requirements apply to all forms of employing entities, including public and private enterprises and even the small "individual industrial and commercial households" (*getihu*) with employees (Article 2). Overtime payment cannot be taken in account to reach the minimum wage standard (Article 3). There are two sets of standards: a monthly one that applies to full-time employees and an hourly one for part-time workers (Article 5).

The Labor Contract Law that came into effect in January 2008 also makes several references to the minimum wage system:

- Wage during the probation period (Article 20);
- Level of compensation stipulated in a collective contract (Article 55);
- Workers' remuneration by staffing firms during periods where there is no work (Article 58);
- Hourly remuneration for part-time workers (Article 72);

---

[73] English translation of the law available at http://www.jus.uio.no/lm/china. labor.law.1994/doc.html, accessed May 24, 2013.

[74] *Zuidi gongzi guiding* (Provisions on Minimum Wages), Ministry of Labor and Social Security, 2004, http://www.molss.gov.cn/gb/ywzn/2006-02/15/ content_106799.htm (in Chinese), accessed May 24, 2013. English translation: http://www.asianlii.org/cn/legis/cen/laws/pomw308/, accessed May 24, 2013.

- Supervision and inspection of the labor administrative departments of the local people's governments about the minimum wage implementation by employers (Article 74); and
- Employers' punishment in case of violation of minimum wage requirements (Article 85).

The *Provisions on the Minimum Wage* recommended minimum wages to be set at 40–60 percent of average monthly wages. In practice, in major cities, such as Beijing and Shanghai, the minimum wage in 2010 was less than 20 percent of the average monthly wage.[75] Even after the recent series of raises of local minimum wage rates, this requirement is still far from being met (Box 8.4). The minimum wage is only at 30 percent of the average monthly salary in Beijing and Chongqing, and 33 percent in Shanghai. In February 2012, the Employment Promotion Plan (part of the 12th Five-Year Economic Plan) implicitly acknowledged this failure by setting the objective that minimum wages reach 40 percent of average local salaries by 2015.[76] Box 8.4 describes in detail the differences in minimum wage by province, district and municipality.

Box 8.4. Minimum Wage, Multiple Local Standards

Each province, autonomous region and municipality has to set its own minimum wage standards according to the local economic situation (i.e. cost of living, average wage, unemployment rate, social insurance premium, employees' contribution to the housing construction fund, etc.). In addition, most municipalities set separate standards for downtown districts and suburbs. For instance, in Nanchang (the capital of Jiangxi province), the minimum wage standard in 2012 was 870 yuan/month (or 8.7 yuan/hour) in the downtown districts, but only 800 yuan/month (or 8 yuan/hour) in other districts, or even 730 yuan/month (or 7.3 yuan/hour) in remote areas of the municipality.

---

[75] Wages in China, *China Labour Bulletin*, February 19, 2008, http://www.clb.org.hk/en/node/100206#part4, accessed May 24, 2013.

[76] State Council (2012), *Cujin jiuye guihua 2011–2015* (Plan for Employment Promotion 2011–2015), http://www.china.com.cn/policy/txt/2012-02/08/content_24584303.htm, accessed May 24, 2013.

The local administrative department for human resources and social protection determines minimal wage standards in consultation with the local branches of the China Labor Union and the China League of Enterprises. Its proposals have to be approved and registered at the national level. It is also responsible for the supervision and inspection over the employing entities' fulfillment of the minimum wage requirements. In case of suspected violation of the minimum wage standards, labor unions can report to this department. As for any other labor dispute, a mediation committee should examine the conflicts between employers and employees about the minimum wage. The conflict can also be brought to a labor dispute arbitration committee composed of representatives of the administrative department of labor, the trade union at the corresponding level and the employing units. In case of arbitration failure, parties can refer to the People's Court. In case of violation of minimum wage rate, employers may be condemned to pay the infringed employee compensation up to five times the amount of the owed wages.[77]

In practice, those enforcement mechanisms prove to be weak. In August 2010, a survey by the Hainan provincial trade union showed that one sixth of migrant workers in Hainan earned less than 500 yuan a month, far below the legal minimum wage of between 680 yuan a month and 830 yuan a month.[78] Many workers still receive less than the minimum wage. For instance, the Guangdong Labor and Social Security Bureau points out that many employers illegally deduct costs for accommodation and meals from employees' wages.[79]

During the 11th five-year plan, minimum wage standards grew at a 12.5 percent annual average rate.[80] It was frozen from November 2008 to February 2010 in response to the global economic crisis, but rose nationwide by 22 percent on average in 2010 and 2011. In 2012, the increase was not as strong because of the pressures on the export-reliant

---

[77] Chen, K. (2011), *Labour Law in China*, Alphen: Kluwer Law International, p. 80.
[78] *China Labour Bulletin* (2008), *op. cit.*
[79] *Ibid.*
[80] *Ibid.*

manufacturing sector.[81] The new five-year Employment Promotion Plan set the objective of an annual average increase of 13 percent until 2015. The minimum wage standards increases reflect a rising trend across the Chinese manufacturing industry. It can be seen as a response to increasing rights consciousness and mobilization among workers. In 2010, strikes at Honda, Foxconn and other neighboring factories resulted in substantial wage rises, and were quickly followed by the announcement of increases of minimum wage standards in Guangdong and in a number of other provinces and municipalities.

In the new Employment Promotion Plan, the progressive elevation of minimum wage standards is presented as a way to improve revenue repartition, thus maintaining a social stability that is threatened by the huge and worsening revenue gap. The apparently large scale of annual increases has to be studied in relation with the sharp surge in the cost of living. Benefits accrued by low-skilled workers after minimum wage raises have largely been wiped out by inflation. The objective is also to increase the revenues of the low and middle classes, so as to boost domestic consumption. Chinese provincial authorities are now adjusting wages competitively to attract migrant workers: as already noted, demographic data from China's statistics agency shows that the Chinese population is ageing quickly and the rural labor pool shrinking.[82] Such trends may have a strong impact on global social dumping practices. After having moved to poorer inland regions (but these provinces also strongly increased their legal minimum wage, for instance, Sichuan raised it by 23.4 percent in January 2012), some manufacturers now look to countries such as Vietnam, Bangladesh, Cambodia, and Indonesia, where wages are still low.[83] But the movement launched by China has already started to influence

---

[81] China Pushes Minimum Wage Rises, *Financial Times*, January 4, 2012, http://www.ft.com/intl/cms/s/0/847b0990-36a2-11e1-9ca3-00144feabdc0.html#axzz1qVdqSJ8c, accessed May 24, 2013.

[82] China Eyes 13% Rise in Minimum Wage by 2015, *Huffington Post*, February 8, 2012, http://www.huffingtonpost.com/2012/02/08/china-minimum-wage_n_1261752.html, accessed May 24, 2013.

[83] China Province Raises Minimum Wage by 23%, *BBC News*, December 23, 2011, http://www.bbc.co.uk/news/business-16311751, accessed May 24, 2013.

its neighbors: Thailand, Indonesia and Philippines all slightly increased their minimum wage standards in the last months.[84]

$$*\quad*\quad*$$

What can this survey teach corporations when it comes to CSR-related policies directed toward their workforce? The lessons to be drawn are very much in line with the ones taken from our examination of China's labor contract regulations, the shift in: (a) regulations; (b) demography; (c) generational expectations; and (d) China's economic comparative advantages all require companies to engage with their workers in strategies aiming at well-defined social policies and benefits packages, so as to attract and mould employees in such a way as to ensure both loyalty and excellence. Such a shift can only be gradual, but it makes CSR imperatives and business strategies become more and more interconnected. It links social issues with the bettering of the environment in which the supply chain operates, including factory improvements and capacity building initiatives. The evolving social context of China and its changing economic equation (in terms both of consumers' expectations and of its work force characteristics) call for the building up of strong corporate cultures, characterized both within the corporation and outside of it, by the emphasis on trust, communication abilities, creativity and attention to human factors when it comes to redefining social, production and business strategies.

---

[84] *Quand l'Asie devient fordiste* (When Asia Turns to Fordism), *Les Echos*, March 21, 2012.

CHAPTER NINE

Gender Equality/Training/Well-Being at Work

In the previous chapter, we discussed an array of issues that are largely framed by a body of regulations. While legal imperatives remain very much a factor in the issues we are now going to examine, this section focuses on cutting-edge questions, which are becoming part of CSR-related concerns and strategies. In other words, this section is more "experimental" in nature. At the same time, it is precisely on experimental and rapidly emerging issues that a company's corporate culture can deploy its inventiveness.

9.1. Gender Equality

Equality among men and women is a topic that was already of paramount importance for Chinese intellectuals of the first half of the 20th century, in reaction to the traditional mores of China. It became a central policy of new China, asserted in laws and policies. Compared to many other societies, China promotes women's rights and opportunities. This also applies to the workplace. However, observations in the field show that there still exists a gap between principles and realities.

Since the start of the economic reforms, women have suffered from growing insecurity in the field of employment. They are exposed to economic insecurity (unemployment and enforced early retirement) to a greater extent than men. Besides, men are advantaged in the new highly competitive labor market, accessing better paid jobs more easily, while women face a "glass ceiling". In 1990, the average income of female city-dwellers had reached 77.5 percent of their male counterparts, but 20 years later, it was only two-thirds of the average male income.[1] Li *et al.* (2011) remarked that the gender wage gap widened markedly between 1995 and 2007, especially in the period 2002–2007, and an increasing proportion of the gap could not be unexplained. As noted by Li *et al.* (2011), from 1995 to 2002, with an influx of young, poorly educated women in low-grade occupations and industries who were subjected to market discrimination as a result of market reform, the gender wage gap grew dramatically among low-income earners. In the period 2002 to 2007, the market showed a bias toward male employees through returns to education and selectivity on the part of enterprises with different forms of ownership. This resulted in the expansion of the gender wage gap among urban employees, especially among high wage earners.[2] Though it is true that, in absolute terms, high-income females encounter the least discrimination, the gender wage gap is a complex and multifaceted phenomenon that is not limited to one sector of society. It also does not automatically recede with time, which means that, sometimes, proactive policies are called for. Still, Li *et al.* (2011) argued that the main focus needs to remain on the fact that "young women with low educational levels and poor jobs" are subject to severe and increasing discrimination. As most of the female labor force is employed in low-end jobs, in competitive industries and in the private sector, some of the factors leading to labor market segregation also exert a marked influence on the expansion of the gender wage gap.[3]

Even in more progressive Hong Kong (where men still make for 70 percent of managers and administrators), women groups were reporting bias in the workplace as recent as in 2011: a survey led by the China Women's Commission showed that two-thirds of the 3,000 respondents believed that such bias and discriminations existed.[4] In China and Hong Kong, discrimination came in the form of differences in income

[1]Attane, I. (2012), Being a Woman in China Today: A Demography of Gender, *China Perspectives*, 2012/4, pp. 5–15, http://chinaperspectives.revues.org/6013, accessed July 17, 2013.

[2]Li, S., J. Song & X. Liu (2011), Evolution of the Gender Wage Gap among China's Urban Employees, *Social Sciences in China*, 32(3), p. 163.

[3]*Ibid.*, p. 177.

[4]Chui, T. (2011), Women's Group Sees Sex Bias in Workplace, *China Daily* (Hong Kong Edition), February 15, 2011, http://www.chinadaily.com.cn/hkedition/2011-02/15/content_12008593.htm, accessed August 8, 2013.

and promotion prospects, as well as chances for employment for pregnant women and those responsible for the care of family members. "Family responsibility" was a major reason why, in Hong Kong, some women did not seek employment, and why 25 percent of women surveyed "did not want themselves to be very successful" because they perceived "conflicts between commitment at work and family duties". This led the Commission to call, among other measures, for the extension of paternity leave rights, so as help reduce discrimination against working women who had to take leave after becoming pregnant. The Commission also noted that discriminations were affecting most part-time and low-income women, a finding which is solidly confirmed in the Mainland (see Box 9.1).

Box 9.1 Migrant Women Earn Less, Toil With Lower Skills and Lesser Education

"Shanghai's expanding population of migrant women earn 40 percent less than local employees on average due to their low occupational skills and educational background, according to the Shanghai Women's Federation. A report released by the federation yesterday said the average monthly income of migrant women in Shanghai was 2,334 yuan (US$370), compared with the city's overall average income of 3,896 yuan. The figure is 470 yuan less than the average wage for migrant men. 'The reason is that most migrant women took up low-skill or labor-intensive jobs with low occupational skill demand,' according to the report. Shanghai is home to more than 8.9 million migrants, in which 3.04 million are women. About 80 percent of the non-local women came from rural areas, according to the latest national census. The federation surveyed 1,000 employed migrant women aged between 20 and 39 about their jobs and living conditions in Shanghai. Most said they worked in manufacturing and low-end service jobs such as catering, cleaning and domestic help, or *ayi*. Over 60 percent said they had never received any occupational training... The survey showed that more than 80 percent of migrant women were unhappy with their lives, yet one-third of them said they want to settle down in Shanghai because the city has more job opportunities, better public security and educational resources, which should help their children."

Source: Zhao, W. (2012), Migrant Women Earn Less, Toil With Lower Skills, Education, *Shanghai Daily*, March 27, 2012, http://mobile.shanghaidaily.com/article/?id=497537, accessed July 17, 2013.

A number of cases have also shed light on discrimination in hiring practices. Boxes 9.2 and 9.3 provide some examples.

A 2002 survey commissioned by the All-China Women's Federation found that women were still in a "passive and disadvantageous" position in the workplace.[5] The employment rate of women aged between 18 and 49 had decreased by more than 16 percentage points around 2000 compared to 1990. More than half of all laid-off workers (mostly from state-owned enterprises) were women. Women working in the cities had an average income roughly 70 percent of their male counterparts, representing a disparity about 7 percentage points wider than the figures a decade ago. When it came to office atmosphere and politics, while most of the men surveyed said their suggestions had been

---

Box 9.2 Women Protest — Firm Accused of Discrimination

"A group of women calling for workplace equality demonstrated on Tuesday outside a Beijing company that has been accused of rejecting a job candidate because of her gender... An organizer of the event, who gave her name only as Li, said the demonstration's purpose was to raise awareness of the problems female job-seekers face. 'Discrimination ... takes place every recruitment season,' said Li, a college student who traveled 20 hours from the Guangxi Zhuang autonomous region. The protesters targeted Juren Education because it is being sued for alleged sex discrimination. A woman surnamed Cao, originally from Shanxi province, filed her case with Beijing's Haidian district court. Cao claims a human resources employee at the company told her she had been rejected for an office assistant's job because it was a 'man-only' position... Liu Xiaonan, an associate professor at China University of Political Science and Law, who specializes in labor discrimination, said the case could be the first lawsuit filed over job-recruitment sex discrimination since the Employment Promotion Law went into effect in China."

Source: Women Protest Firm Accused of Discrimination, *China Daily*, July 25, 2012, http://www.china.org.cn/china/2012-07/25/content_26004673.htm, accessed July 17, 2013.

---

[5]Women in Workplace on the Slide, *Xinhua News Agency*, December 16, 2002, http://www.china.org.cn/english/Life/51282.htm, accessed August 8, 2013.

Box 9.3 Far from a Harmonious Society: Employment Discrimination in China

"Women have experienced discrimination in age and appearance, especially from consumer-oriented companies who are seeking to increase their market shares. It is common to see job advertisements specifying that the applicant must be 'young, female and attractive'. 'Five facial organs in the right place', 'decent-looking', and 'with elegance' are common phrases used in requirements for attractive employees... Middle-aged women are regularly told that they are too old, too fat, too ugly and too short for service positions such as waitresses or salespersons... Sexual harassment is also extremely prevalent in Chinese employment. Working environments have become increasingly unsafe for women... Despite the laws in place, harassment continues in the workplace. In a national survey of 8,000 people, conducted by two major media organizations, 79 percent of women said they had experienced sexual harassment, compared to 22 percent of men."

Source: Roberts, C. (2012), Far from a Harmonious Society: Employment Discrimination in China, *Santa Clara Law Review*, 52(4), http://digitalcommons.law.scu.edu/lawreview/vol52/iss4/11, accessed July 17, 2013.

taken on board, most of the women said their suggestions had only brought "negative" results. Summing it up, it has to be recognized that traditions and social climate allow for a still subordinate female role in relation to the male role. The 2002 survey found that 20 percent of the men had promotion opportunities in the past three years, while a little more than 16 percent of their female counterparts did. There is no reason to think that these figures were significantly altered during the following decade.

Though pervasive, discrimination practices are often difficult to point out and remedy. They are rooted into the climate and culture of the workplace more than in any existing regulation. Proactive policies that can be enacted by a company include:

— An explicit stress must be put on implementing and checking an effective policy of non-discrimination in hiring and in opportunities for promotion in the course of one's career.

— An assessment of the workplace climate, culture and facilities often needs to be conducted, so as to radically eliminate sources of abuse and humiliating situations.

— Equality in social packages must be pursued. When possible, paternity leave should be considered, as they level the field between men and women candidates for a position. More generally, a balance between personal and professional lives, for women as for men, must be looked for, benefiting both the company and its employees in the long term.

— Special attention should be given to women who are migrant, part-time workers and/or in the lower range of the income scale, as they are the most likely to suffer from hardships and discriminations that often go unnoticed.

— Finally, philanthropic policies may choose to concentrate on women's promotion in areas of poverty (rural or urban), as much resources is still needed in this sector and the empowerment of this specific segment of the population have proven to be a lever for overall social development.

Box 9.4 illustrates how Mary Kay Cosmetics has been working with the China Women's Development Foundation to help women break out of poverty.

An additional remark is in order: gender equality constitutes a field of action heavily determined by China's demographic challenge — the unbalanced sex ratio might become a major concern in the next decades. The last population census showed that in 2010 there were 118 males born for every 100 females — a worse imbalance than that revealed by the 2000 census.[6] China has 34 million "extra" men. More than 24 million Chinese men of marrying age could find themselves without spouses in 2020. This issue of "missing" women, combined with the one-child policy, contributes to a population increase rate that may become too low to sustain China's economic needs. There will be fewer workers around to take care of a rapidly expanding elderly

---

[6]Census Data Demonstrates Positive Changes in China Over Past Decade, *People's Daily/Xinhua*, April 30, 2011, http://english.peopledaily.com.cn/90001/90776/90882/7366454.html, accessed July 17, 2013.

Box 9.4 Mary Kay Cosmetics and China Women's Development Foundation

— Assisted a total of 30,000 women in 20 provinces to shake off poverty and increase income;

— Company determines the screening criteria of the target person receiving the sponsorship, reviews projects proposed by the Women's Federation and holds inspections at an early stage, middle stage, and ending stage of the project;

— Offered funds to construct 10 Mary Kay Spring Bud primary schools across China, funded 60 Spring Bud classes and helped 3,000 impoverished children to return to school;

— 3 sources of financial funding:

- Company donations;
- Mobilize and guide the employees and the Sales Force to make contributions; and
- Mary Kay-sponsored donation matching for donations provided by employees.

Source: Excerpt from AmCham Shanghai CSR Awards Best Practices.

QUESTIONS

— In our company, what is the proportion of male and female employees at each level of the hierarchy? What is the average salary for male and female employees at each level, taking seniority into account?

— What conclusion can we draw from these data when it comes to: (a) the proportion of female employees and wage practices at the lower end of the hierarchy; and (b) the gender distribution for senior management posts?

— Does our company have policies explicitly taking into account gender issues, especially when it comes to the following areas: recruiting; promotion, wages, parenthood and office culture?

— Do these policies coalesce into a consistent whole, and have their practical effects been evaluated?

— Are supplementary policies considered? If yes, for what reasons? And has their potential impact been appraised?

population.[7] Pursuing improved gender equality is also a means for China to work against such a basic imbalance.

9.2. Training and Learning Opportunities

A corporation's training program depends first on its core business activities, and necessarily stresses technical skills and *ad hoc* training sessions. However, it also aims at developing its employees' capacity for discernment, decision-making, empathy and communication skills — all qualities that constitute the bedrock on which a sense of corporate responsibility can be fostered at the individual as well as the team level. In China especially, companies' training programs often need to compensate for the deficiencies in employee training and reflexive capacities that affect the curriculum offered by many educational educations, be it at the manager level or below. Training is the field *par excellence* where a company can inculcate and fine-tune its CSR values and policy (Box 9.5). In China, the task is facilitated by the willingness shown by most employees to engage in training programs, as the country as a whole still attaches utmost importance to educational opportunities. At all levels, Chinese employees generally prove to be very receptive to new methods and content, which they perceive as positively complementing the model that has governed their years of schooling.

9.3. Suffering at Work

Among psychologists, and throughout the corporate world, there is a growing realization that the nature and organization of work — including mechanisms of evaluation, communication and work sharing — have a lasting impact on employees' mental health. *Boredom, tiredness* and *anxiety* are the three overwhelming symptoms of the mental stress that affects workers. There is often a growing gap between the psychic aspirations of the worker and the way work is

---

[7]Burkitt, L. & J. Chin (2011), China's Race with the Gender Gap, *WSJA*, April 29, 2011, http://blogs.wsj.com/chinarealtime/2011/04/29/china%E2%80%99s-race-with-the-gender-gap/, accessed July 17, 2013.

Box 9.5 Case Study: Integrating CSR-related Behaviors and Values into the Training Program

Saint-Gobain's training program is based on a general code of "principles of conduct and actions" emphasizing professional commitment, respect for others, integrity, loyalty and solidarity. It develops into an online training based on case studies, with specific applications for managers: the "Managerial Core Competencies Frame of Reference" defines performance-related skills, leadership skills and cross-business skills expected from managers. They emphasize behaviors inspired by vision, innovation, teamwork, listening, openness and networking. An e-learning module is available on the corporate training website. It reviews the definition of a managerial competency and presents numerous workplace scenarios that the viewer needs to assess.

Source: Saint-Gobain Managerial Core Competencies Frame of Reference.

"More than 2,000 group employees have tested their knowledge thanks to the 'Sustainable Pursuit' board game developed in-house. Both fun and educational, the game enables employees to gain a better understanding of sustainable habitat and development and to discover what Saint-Gobain has already achieved in these areas and what remains to be done. It involves nine players, divided into three teams, answering questions in nine different categories. Distribution began in 2011 and will continue during 2012 to reach a greater number of employees in all our host countries."

Source: Saint-Gobain Sustainable Development Report 2011.

UESTIONS

— How does our corporation balance training in technical skills and employee training?
— What are the target groups of our training program? What percentage of our workforce receives training? What is the percentage of women

(Continued)

(Continued)

receiving training relative to their percentage in our workforce? What is the proportion of managers versus non-managers?
— Does our training program include assessment of behaviors and values? Are skills such as listening, teamwork and networking emphasized?
— Does it make our employees more able to share the CSR vision and sustainability model of our company?
— Have we invested enough in e-learning modules that provide our employees with opportunities for ongoing training in our managerial values and understanding of CSR issues?

distributed, evaluated and rewarded. The stress on individual, short-term performances rather than team performances and long-term goals is certainly the main reason for workers' frustration, which translates into stress, professional mistakes, lack of creativity and even a number of illnesses. Such a trend has a heavy cost, and many of us can relate to this in our lives.

It must also be noted that the way suffering at work is triggered and managed has strong cultural overtones, as the way work is lived, shared and rewarded differs from one culture to another. Still, some factors, such as overwork, seem to create the same results from one culture to another. Empirical study has confirmed the strong relationship between high overtime and low well-being in Chinese context: Chinese workers in the information and communication technology sector based in offices were found to put in many hours of overtime work, and high overtime was associated with low levels of psychological well-being.[8] Box 9.6 illustrates the severity of stress Chinese workers face, relative to the world.

At the same time, one should always note that working with others is a major factor of psychic integration and satisfaction for individuals, and that people excluded from the working community suffer

---

[8]Houdmont, J., J. Zhou & J. Hassard (2011), Overtime and Psychological Well-Being Among Chinese Office Workers, *Occupational Medicine*, 61(4), p. 273.

Box 9.6 Survey Shows Chinese Workers Stressed Out

"Nearly eight out of ten Chinese workers became more stressed in the past year, a new survey has found. The survey by Regus, a global workplace-solutions provider, recently polled more than 16,000 workers in 80 countries. Seventy-five percent of Chinese workers polled said that their stress levels had risen in the past year, according to the survey. It found that 48 percent of workers globally felt growing pressure in the past year. The smallest increases in stress worldwide were in Australia and the Netherlands, where just 38 percent and 40 percent of workers said they had experienced more stress. Chinese workers' stress mainly comes from work, individual financial status and clients, the survey found. In China, workers in Shanghai and Beijing felt the highest rise in stress in the past year, it said. In Shanghai, 80 percent of workers said their stress levels rose. In Beijing, the figure is 67 percent... A recent survey by Insight China, a state-run magazine that looks into Chinese people's welfare, showed that nearly 70 percent of Chinese are overworked and more than 40 percent spend less than 10 hours a week on leisure."

Source: Chen, X. & J. Shi (2012), Survey Shows Chinese Workers Stressed Out, *China Daily*, October 19, 2012, http://www.chinadaily.com.cn/china/2012-10/19/content_15829619.htm, accessed July 17, 2013.

not only material disadvantages but psychological deprivation as well. Work goes along with symbolic gratifications. In this respect, acknowledgment and appreciation of the value of one's work by the surrounding community, especially by one's supervisor, is something that the employees care about much more deeply than it is often recognized. Stress management within a corporation must start from the respect shown to the contribution made by each member of the team, from realistic demands made upon workers, and from mechanisms of evaluation that take into account the wisdom and know-how of the teamwork, taking care not to shatter the self-esteem of the persons under scrutiny.

Still, suffering related to work obviously depends first on the nature of the activity performed, the status of the individual within the corporation and the practicality of working conditions. The issues brought up in our chapter on social standards (Chapter 8) determine the basic sense of well-being or ill-being experienced by workers throughout the production process. The suicides at Foxconn illustrates this well (Box 9.7).

The issues differ with respect to white-collar workers. However, psychological pressure and gruelling working hours may take an extremely heavy toll on one's mental health. One practical point may require special attention: although corporations need flexibility to adapt quickly to changing market forces, deceiving employees by the manipulation of their "objectives, means and rewards" is a particular unacceptable way of managing people by pushing them to the limits in the hope they will deliver a superior performance and thus to extract better productivity. This ultimately generates distrust, bitterness and, sometimes, creates good excuses for delivering expedients to fulfil the contract — with possibly huge costs to the entire

---

Box 9.7 Suicide — Workers' Last Cry for Help

"In 2010, eighteen workers, all born after 1978, and between the ages of 17 and 25, attempted suicide at the then little-known Taiwanese company called Hon Hai Precision Industrial Company, now more commonly known as Foxconn; fourteen of these workers died. Within days of each suicide attempt — dubbed the "suicide express" in the Chinese media — images of these workers began to appear in the Chinese press and blogosphere, and soon in the Western press. Foxconn responded by putting up safety nets between factory and dormitory buildings on its factory complexes and by bringing in professional psychologists to counsel workers who, management believed, had serious, hidden psychological problems, which supposedly predated their arrival on the factory floor. It was as if suicide in a factory setting could not have anything to do with the conditions under which these young workers toiled — the long hours, the repetitious tasks on the factory floor, the lack of overtime pay, the crowded dormitory spaces, the alienation from home, and the empty modernity promised through a life of urban factory living."

Source: Litzinger, R. (2013), The Labor Question in China: Apple and Beyond, *The South Atlantic Quarterly*, 112(1), p. 173.

organization. The end result is likely to be the incubation of unethical practices for the satisfaction of short-sighted economic indicators, resulting in shattering the sense of social responsibility of the firm. In Box 9.8, the Michelin case study provides a positive exemplar of how companies should manage their employees.

Summing up, working is a social apprenticeship (Box 9.9): it is about learning to live together, forming consensual opinions and being proud of collectively achieving a goal. In this respect, in China

---

Box 9.8 Teamwork and Collective Responsibility

"We encourage our employees to progress in their duties, via a justified level of demands. We encourage them to work as teams, which is the best way to provide appropriate answers to complex questions demanding the sharing of different experiences, trades and cultures... We expect our management to delegate, in a spirit of trust, enabling the responsibility for each task to be assigned to the person best suited for the job, providing one and all with freedom of initiative and action."

Source: Excerpt from Michelin Performance and Responsibility Charter.

UESTIONS

— To what extent is teamwork encouraged within our organization?
— Does teamwork go with a collective evaluation of performance, or is evaluation solely focused on individuals, perhaps unduly increasing the level of stress put on each employee?
— Can work teams collectively determine performances they deem feasible, sharing rewards and responsibility when evaluating whether the objectives were achieved or not?
— Are we able to evaluate the degree and frequency of stress-related sickness and traumas affecting employees of our company, and can we relate them to specific features of our organizational model (including labor division, determination of objectives and evaluation methods)?

Box 9.9 The Centrality of Work

"Work involves not just the practical intelligence of an individual, but mostly also the intelligence of a collective. The analysis of intelligence involved in work is almost always in the plural form. No work without cooperation, we might say… Cooperation designates precisely the redevelopment of coordination through the collaborative elaboration of concrete rules by and between the workers, to perform the tasks for which the coordination of work was set up in the first place… In order to produce effective work rules and job rules, cooperation requires a minimum of consideration of others and of conviviality. Cooperation is based on a minimal form of communal life. To put it in a motto: "Work is not only production; it is also learning to live together." … When working deliberations function well, work can give individuals the chance to learn the essential civic virtues that are conditions of democratic practice: cooperation, collective life, and solidarity. On the other hand, when the communal underpinning of cooperation has been destroyed, work can lead to the worst… Well-functioning workplaces educate individuals into forming a consensual opinion by taking into account the different views, capacities and needs of all. Dysfunctional workplaces can be the birthplace of a radical disregard of the views and vulnerability of others… A form of collective education acquired through work-related social relationships has a major impact on the evolution of society itself. Under the influence of new forms of work organization, in particular the individualized evaluation of performances (which has a powerful effect on the breakdown of the collectives of work, communal living and solidarity), each worker is practically forced to fall back on a frenzied defensive individualism. If workers learn to be wary of everyone at work, including their own colleagues, they are hardly likely to show generosity or consideration towards others in the private sphere or in the wider society."

Source: Dejours, C. & J.P. Deranty (2010), The Centrality of Work, *Critical Horizon*, 11(2), pp. 175–177.

and in East Asia as in the global corporate culture, three major preoccupying trends require attention and debate:

— The stress on individual performance rather than on team building destroys solidarity within the workplace: anxious as we are about the way we will be personally evaluated, we forget that our performances depend also on our colleagues and on how we interact with them.

— The focus on short-term performance has perverted our sense of time, making us blind to the benefits of organic growth: pressed as we are to achieve results, sometimes on a weekly or monthly basis, we live in continuous anxiety, and, as a result, we lack the imagination necessary for devising new paths for growth and achievements, be it in our personal life or as a corporate actor. It seems that our work environment pressures us to forcefully "help our crops to grow", even though they are not yet ready for harvest (拔苗助长); as a story of the *Mencius* puts it: "There was a man from Song who was worried about the slow growth of his crops and so he went and yanked on them to accelerate their growth. Empty-headed, he returned home and announced to his people: 'I am so tired today. I have been out stretching the crops.' His son ran out to look, but the crops had already withered."[9]

— The continuous overflow of information prevents us from sitting down and listening, so as to better understand one another. More and more quantitative data monopolize our attention, digital information rivets us to screens, and our workplaces are starting to look like archipelagos of "digital islands" that exchange information with remote continents but are not any more aware of the fact that they belong to the same ecosystem.

Our work can give us a sense of achievement, and working with others should be a gratifying experience. So as to make members of the working force regain their inner drive and sense of personal dignity, our offices and factories must learn to foster in their midst a capacity for collective discernment and mutual support. However, it is true that schools and families are where we should first begin to nurture such attitudes. In this respect, the pandemic that "suffering at work" has become both reveals and aggravates social dysfunctions affecting the entirety of our lives. The workplace offers a setting where the symptoms and reason of this pandemic can be first addressed and, to some extent, remedied.

---

[9]Mencius, *Gongsun Chou* I (2A.2).

CHAPTER TEN

Conflict Management and Prevention

The way to manage tensions and conflicts within the organization, the measures taken for preventing their appearance, the style of dialogue and communication fostered in a given corporate culture, all of these are definitely part of CSR, insofar as we define it — as we have consistently done — as a regulation mechanism through which an organization monitors its conformity to laws and regulations and optimizes its behavior towards its stakeholders. There is, as everyone knows, a strong cultural dimension to conflict and bargaining, shaped by dominant values, styles of communication and historical memories that facilitate or impede the expression of disagreement. There are also different legal, social and political frameworks channeling these expressions. Conflict prevention and bargaining is certainly one area in which the knowledge of Chinese context and culture is of particular importance for any company that wants to both act ethically and work in accordance with local conditions and mores.

10.1. New Labor Challenges

During the years 2010–2012, well publicized labor conflicts (Box 10.1) affecting the supply chain of major international companies have highlighted: (a) the plight that remains one common to a very large number of workers; (b) the changing nature of China's working force; and (c) the communication challenges that such conflicts create.

The story related above would not be complete without recognizing the changes which have occurred both in firms' and workers' attitudes during the year 2012. The company at the center of the story, Foxconn, China's largest private employer (1.4 million employees in

195

Box 10.1 New Labor Attitudes Fed Into China Riot

"The pressures threatening China's status as the world's factory floor have been laid bare by a riot this week at a factory that makes parts for Apple Inc. and other electronics companies, a clash that workers said was sparked by onerous security and repressive living conditions... Dozens of workers questioned on Wednesday said the rioting on Sunday, which caused 40 injuries and led to the mobilization of some 5,000 police, was in part the result of growing tensions as guards severely enforced strict rules on the campus... [A worker] added that since the violence, workers haven't been directly informed about the issue at all, allowing rumors to spread across the campus. He said police and guards targeted workers who were attempting to photograph or record the incident with their mobile phones. Although little known in the West until a spate of factory suicides in 2009 brought the company notoriety, Foxconn makes components and parts, and assembles devices for many of the world's largest electronics companies... Workers described being yelled at or physically intimidated, and two workers said there had been previous attacks by guards on the campus. Foxconn has been ahead of most other factories with wage increases to make sure it doesn't face labor shortages as it ramps up production for products, like the iPhone 5, that are critical to the success of its customers. Several employees said they were thinking about leaving the plant, pointing to the 'ferocity' of the guards, and a number of other grievances that fostered an environment in which a small dispute became a 2,000-person riot. They said pressures from working long hours — shifts of 10 to 12 hours are common — on assembly lines, recent transfers of large groups of workers from other locations and discontent about a lack of overtime work during the approaching weeklong National Day holiday were all likely contributing factors to the violence."

Source: Mozur, P. (2012), New Labor Attitudes Fed Into China Riot, *The Wall Street Journal Asia*, September 26, 2012, http://online.wsj.com/article/SB10000872396390 444549204578020342979518814.html?mod=WSJASIA_hps_MIDDLESixthNews, accessed July 17, 2013.

China), has also pledged to sharply curtail workers' hours, significantly increase wages and improve working conditions. Still, it remains true that, after a wave of suicide attempts that occurred in the same company in 2010, the implementation of the pledges made at the time had been subject to questioning.[1] And a number of incidents have made Foxconn remain at the center of public attention: Large-scale confrontations among the company's workers have occurred in several instances and locations, renewing questions about the company's management style. However, such incidents are not limited to one company or industrial sector. Amid slower economic growth and intensified pressure for higher wages, the summer of 2013 has probably witnessed a doubling of strikes and protests compared with the ones having occurred during the same period of the preceding year.[2]

The shift is affecting not only subcontracting companies but also leading companies such as Apple, Hewlett-Packard and Intel, as they realized that the electronics industry's reputation was at risk. In 2012, Apple has tripled its CSR staff, and has "re-evaluated" how it works with manufacturers, has asked competitors to help "curb excessive overtime in China" and has "reached out to advocacy groups it once rebuffed"[3], joining the Fair Labor Association, one of the largest workplace monitoring groups.[4] Even with these reforms, chronic problems remain. Many laborers still work illegal overtime and some employees' safety remains at risk. Among other press reports, articles published in the *New York Times* in January 2012 had been detailing punishing and sometimes very hazardous working conditions on assembly lines of iconic products such as the iPhone and iPad.[5] This was one of the

---

[1]Students and Scholars Against Corporate Misbehavior (2011), *Foxconn and Apple Fail to Fulfill Promises: Predicaments of Workers after the Suicides*, http://sacom.hk/archives/837, accessed July 17, 2013.

[2]Mozur, P. (2013), Foxconn Says 11 Injured in Large-Scale Fight at Chinese Campus, WSJA, September 23, 2013, http://online.wsj.com/article/SB10001424052702303759604579092641376933788.html?mg=id-wsj, accessed September 26, 2013.

[3]Bradsher, K. & C. DuHigg (2012), Signs of Changes Taking Hold in Electronics Factories in China, *New York Times*, December 26, 2012, http://www.nytimes.com/2012/12/27/business/signs-of-changes-taking-hold-in-electronics-factories-in-china.html?pagewanted=1&_r=0&ref=global-home, accessed July 17, 2013.

[4]See Fair Labor Association (2012), *Independent Investigation of Apple Supplier, Foxconn*, http://www.fairlabor.org/report/foxconn-investigation-report, accessed July 17, 2013.

[5]See for instance: DuHigg, C. & D. Barboza (2012), In China, Human Costs Are Built Into an iPad, *New York Times*, January 25, 2012, http://www.nytimes.com/2012/01/26/business/ieconomy-apples-ipad-and-the-human-costs-for-workers-in-china.html?_r=0, accessed July 17, 2013.

reasons for the changes subsequently happening at Foxconn and other subsidiaries of Apple. Apple itself pledged to go from considering labor conditions as "engineering puzzles" to a more human approach, listening more carefully to workers' complaints and outside recommendations.[6] The company also allowed pollution audits by Ma Jun, a well-known Chinese environmental advocate.

These evolutions belatedly mirror what happened in footwear manufacturing (Nike), clothing retailing (Gap Inc.), and in apparels (Patagonia). However, shifting from secrecy to public leadership and transparency is required for changing an entire industry.[7] In its effort to develop an alternative social model, Quanta, a competitor of Foxconn and a supplier of Hewlett-Packard, has taken the initiative to dedicate employees solely to the task of listening to complaints by fellow workers — hoping also that, by listening to employees' woes and by improving living conditions, turnover and training costs will fall. This goes with slightly higher labor costs, though at the same time workers' salaries in Quanta are slightly inferior to the ones paid at Foxconn.[8] Taken together, these facts are indicative of the shifts currently occurring.

In the last decades, China has been facing the challenge of moving from the "interest-integrated labor-capital relations" of the command economy era — when the state was considered as standing for the entire society, to relations between employers and workers recognized as two interest groups with diverging interests.[9] In the first years of economic reforms, however, creating mechanisms for defending workers' rights and facilitating their collective representation was far from being a priority. In the 2000s, the situation changed as labor conflicts increased and more attention was being paid to workers' rights.

---

[6]Bradsher & DuHigg (2012).

[7]Apple (2012), Apple Supplier Responsibility 2012 Progress Report, http://images.apple.com/supplierresponsibility/pdf/Apple_SR_2012_Progress_Report.pdf, accessed July 17, 2013.

[8]Bradsher & DuHigg (2012).

[9]Qiao, J. (2012), Between the Party-state, Employers and Workers: Multiple Roles of the Chinese Trade Union During Market Transition — A Survey of 1.811 Enterprise Union Chairpersons, in M. Hishida, K. Kojima, T. Ishii and J. Qiao (eds.), China's Trade Unions — How Autonomous Are They?, London/New York: Routledge, p. 52.

But the main focus was on workers' individual rights rather than on collective bargaining mechanisms.[10] However, in the recent period unionization efforts increased significantly, targeting especially foreign invested enterprises and multinationals. Launched in 2008, the "Rainbow plan" set the objective of establishing collective bargaining practices in 80 percent of these enterprises by 2013 (and 100 percent of the Fortune 500 companies working in China).

10.2. Trade Unions, Bargaining and the Social Scene

Let us first recall the legal background in which labor conflict, conflict prevention and bargaining take place. Chinese workers do not have the right to strike, a right removed from the Constitution in 1982. In 1988, the All-China Federation of Trade Unions (ACFTU) attempted to get this right included in the revision of the Trade Union Law, but failed.[11] Nevertheless, no law explicitly prohibits strikes, and the right to strike is mentioned in the UN Covenant on Economic, Social and Cultural Rights, ratified by China in 2001. Despite the lack of legal framework, there has been in the last decade an increasing number of labor disputes, including strikes, sit-in and demonstrations within and outside factory compounds. The official number of collective labor disputes increased from less than 1,500 in 1994 to over 19,000 in 2004, and the number of workers involved in labor disputes grew from less than 78,000 to about 780,000 during the same decade.[12] Beyond this quantitative increase, there also has been a qualitative leap. Worker movements shifted focus from a reactive response to labor rights violations toward more proactive demands for higher wages and improved working conditions. Some of the recent labor conflicts have even included claims about reorganizing trade unions.

---

[10]Xin, S. (2011), *Xuezhe jianyan zhongguo zhubu shixian laozi zizhi* (学者建言中国逐步实现劳资自治), June 21, 2011, http://china.caixin.com/2011-06-21/100271691.html, accessed July 17, 2013.

[11]Pringle, T. (2011), *Trade Unions in China. The Challenge of Labor Unrest*, New York/London: Routledge, p. 5.

[12]Qiao (2012, p. 53).

In the late 1990s, most workers' movement gathered laid-off workers, who felt they were victims of public enterprise restructuring. In the second half of the 2000s, migrant workers started to get involved in collective actions. The migrants' increased propensity to fight for their rights happened as labor shortages emerged from 2004, and as a "second generation" of migrants entered factories. More educated and more aware of their rights, they became conscious that entering in a strike might help them improve their fate, whereas the "first generation" saw no choice apart from accepting existing working conditions or leaving their job. This growing sense of collective strength is also rooted in a cluster effect: successful strikes encourage other workers to consider action. Such a trend might be even stronger in case of strikes in hinterland regions, where workers might get support from the local community, while they were lacking such a support in distant coastal regions. The changing attitude of authorities, from repression to conciliation, with a focus on avoiding violence and defusing the protests, also played a role in the process. As an example, a regulation issued in 2003 in Anhui province called for disciplinary action and even criminal prosecution of enterprise managers and local officials whose actions resulted in repeated, large-scale collective petitions.

New information and communications technologies proved crucial in all recent mobilizations. Short messages sent by mobile phone, information diffused through instant messaging platforms, microblogs and other social media help workers to organize and allow them to attract public attention outside their enterprise. Most migrant workers have a mobile phone even if it represents a heavy burden on their budget. The development of alternative information channels put official media under a new pressure, resulting in better reporting on workers' movements. Therefore, the stereotype that describes the Chinese worker as submissive and passive no longer fits the reality of today's industrial relations in China (Box 10.2).[13]

The recent evolutions should not hide the fact that social bargaining in China is still far from becoming a mature way of managing

---

[13]See *China Labor Bulletin* (2012), A Decade of Change: The Worker's Movement in China 2000–2010, March 28, 2012, www.clb.org.hk/en/node/110024, accessed July 17, 2013.

Box 10.2 Workers' Voicing Out Grievances

"China's new generation of workers is increasingly educated and gives voice to a range of desires and perspectives about the state, its relationship with the global capital, and the ways of life, living, and labor along different points of the supply chain hierarchy. They have acquired unique organizing skills, some learned through histories of labor organizing during the socialist period, some acquired through social networking platforms and other transnational and transregional connections. They are also disrupting production. In late September 2012, for example, a 'riot' broke out at the Foxconn Taiyuan facility in Shanxi, shutting down production for three days. Workers used smartphones to distribute scenes of the protests on the internet, using the very tools they produce to circulate their grievances. As China becomes the epicenter of global labor struggles, workers are not acquiescing. They are fighting for higher wages and humane working conditions, increasingly through direct and, at times, violent confrontation."

Source: Litzinger, R. (2013), The Labor Question in China: Apple and Beyond, *The South Atlantic Quarterly*, 112(1), p. 177.

tensions. Struggling for interests is a proactive behavior that can best be achieved by collective bargaining, but the idea of collective bargaining has not yet penetrated the consciousness of the vast bulk of Chinese workers.[14] Due to institutional, legal, political and social constraints, it will be some time before China can develop an industrial relations system in which workers' interests can be voiced and genuinely represented by the ACFTU. Instead, China has been heading in a direction that is becoming increasingly litigious, interrupted sporadically by industrial violence.[15]

And indeed, although China ratified the International Labor Organization (ILO) Tripartite Consultation Convention n°144 in 1990, the development of tripartite social dialogue has been hampered by the nature of Chinese trade unions.[16] Unlike their counterparts in most

---

[14]Chan, A. (2011), Strikes in China's Export Industries in Comparative Perspective, *The China Journal*, 65, p. 49.

[15]*Ibid*.

[16]Clarke, S. & C.-H. Lee (2002), The Significance of Tripartite Consultation in China, *Asia Pacific Business Review*, 9(2), p. 62.

countries, they are unified into a single organizational system. In most companies, the vice enterprise CPC branch director serves as chairperson of the grassroots union.[17] Article 38 of the Trade Union Law prescribes that the trade union shall support the enterprise in exercising its power of operation and management in accordance with law. It is thus clear that Chinese trade unions not only represent workers' interests, but also need to respect and support the enterprise's executive power and strategy.[18] Unions generally act as mediators rather than as the workers' representative. On occasion, trade unions have even appeared in arbitration hearings on behalf of the employer.[19] In many enterprises, they also act as welfare institutions. Union-sponsored mediation organizations received some 406,000 labor dispute cases in 2010, a year-on-year rise of 12.1 percent.[20]

Some changes have been recently taking place in the management style of unions. This sometimes translates into the direct election of trade union chairpersons and committees at the enterprise level; some local trade unions now select union leaders through open recruitment; after a probation period, they may be officially installed through democratic election of the member assembly; some local trade unions decided to pay wages and other welfare services to union leaders in place of enterprise unions, so as to encourage their independence; in the same vein, some local tax bureaus have been entrusted to collect grassroots union dues from enterprises for ensuring that legal requirements are effectively met. According to the Trade Union Law, unions can apply for court enforcement order if the employer refuses to allocate union membership dues, i.e. 2 percent of the aggregate enterprise wage.

Breaking somehow with the past, ACFTU is now actively promoting the establishment of trade unions in all types of enterprises — especially foreign-invested ones, with the objective of achieving a 100 percent

---

[17]Qiao (2012, p. 60).
[18]Liang, L. (2011), Latest Development and Characteristics of Chinese Trade Unions, *King & Wood Mallesons*, August 5, 2011, http://www.kingandwood.com/Bulletin/ChinaBulletinContent.aspx?id=3aef5bc2-bd65-4198-a9de-531407510471, accessed July 17, 2013.
[19]Pringle (2011, p. 109).
[20]*China Daily*, Unions Push For Collective Wage Move, January 4, 2011.

enterprise unionization rate. Under Article 10 of the Trade Union Law, as amended in 2001, enterprises with more than 25 employees are indeed required to establish an enterprise union committee, while those with fewer than 25 employees may either establish their own union committee or set up a joint union committee with one or more companies similar in scope and activity. Many enterprises have not complied with this regulation yet. Some of them recently received notices from trade unions at higher levels requiring them to set up their own unions. Expanded union coverage may be a first step toward the reorganization of the union. In some localities with a high unionization rate, such as Shenzhen, the ACFTU is now considering innovations in the organizational forms of trade unions: in some large enterprises, it plans to form a united trade union by combining the trade union of the parent company with those of its affiliates and adopting a full-time trade union president. This would increase coordination among the trade unions in the same enterprise group, thus helping them to gain bargaining power.

As noted already, the social scene is rapidly changing. In several instances, workers have started to self-organize and defend their rights. In some factories, workers have already established an embryonic system of collective bargaining. Migrant workers who studied law by themselves or have already defended their own rights in front of a court establish organizations that are usually not registered — or registered as an enterprise, and several of them get funding from foreign organizations (NGOs, foundations, development agencies, etc.).[21] They help migrants to prepare their legal file in order to sue employers, in case of violation of labor rights (unpaid wages, work-related diseases, compensation of work-related injuries, etc.). Some have even represented migrants in court. They also organize workshops to increase migrants' legal awareness and give them advice on how to negotiate with employers or how to organize for a collective action. Ostensibly independent from the ACFTU, those grassroots workers' protection groups do meet with suspicion. But in a context where the authorities want to

---

[21]Froissart, C. (2012), Les 'ONG' de défense des droits des travailleurs migrants: L'émergence d'organisations proto-syndicales, Chronique internationale de l'IRES, 135 (March), p. 25.

avoid the saturation of courts and to favor conflict resolution within the workplace, some collaborative behaviors emerge. More and more employers and official trade unions are now recognizing informal worker organizations as a legitimate medium for solving conflicts.

10.3. Collective Contracts and Other Issues

The negotiation of collective contracts between trade unions (or worker representatives) and employers, under the supervision of the local labor bureau, allows workers of specific industries, in a specific zone, to improve their wages and working conditions. Collective contracts set standards (e.g. baseline wages for major jobs in a specific industry) above local statutory minimums. Clauses of the collective contract will be applied where an individual employment contract fails to provide for certain matters, or where it fails to meet the requirements of the collective contract. Collective contracts at the enterprise level were first authorized in 1992, in the Trade Union Law, and further formalized in the 1994 Labor Law. But they really became effective on a national level only in 2004, when the Ministry of Labor and Social Security issued the Provisions on Collective Contract. They seek to eliminate some of the obstacles observed under the earlier negotiated agreements in order to achieve more comprehensive contracts, and they authorize employees to initiate the process through more authentic representatives to prepare proposals on a wide scope of subjects clearly beyond the usual statutory labor standards and protections.[22]

The 2008 Labor Contract Law (article 51–56) reinforces this legal framework. It allows collective agreements not only by industry, but also by geographic zones, thus allowing enterprises in different industrial sectors to negotiate together with employees' representatives (usually trade unions). In case the enterprise has not yet established a labor union, it shall conclude the contract with a representative nominated by the employees under the guidance of the labor union at the next higher level. The draft of the collective agreement negotiated

---

[22]Brown, R. (2006), China's Collective Contract Provisions: Can Collective Negotiations Embody Collective Bargaining?, *Duke Journal of Comparative and International Law*, 15(35), pp. 36–37.

between employees' representatives and employers shall be presented to the Employee Representative Congress or all the employees for discussion and approval.

By the end of 2011, 1.74 million enterprises had carried out collective wage negotiations, covering over 100 million workers, and the government set the objective that collective wage negotiations were carried on in 80 percent of corporate units having set up labor unions by the end of 2013. To convince employers, the ACFTU points out that collective bargaining helps avoid shutdowns or strikes, and may help to attract new workers and reduce the turnover rate of employees.[23] In May 2011, a senior ACFTU official, Guo Chen, emphasized that unlike Western unions which always oppose the employer, Chinese unions are "obliged to boost the corporation's development and maintain sound labor relations"; he also pointed out that mid-level managers, not production-line workers, should represent employees in negotiations.[24]

Beyond national policies, progress sometimes originate from local experiments: in 2010, Shenzhen adopted a "Regulation on Employment Relationship and Collective Bargaining" which attempts to enhance the legal responsibility on employers to respond to workers' requests of collective bargaining, and to protect employee representatives undertaking the negotiations.[25] These initiatives meet with contrasted results: also in 2010, Guangdong government's attempt to adopt "Regulations on the Democratic Management of Enterprises" shed some light on the difficulty to develop better collective consultation structures.[26] The regulations stated that, when over a third of the workers demanded collective wage negotiations, the enterprise trade union should take the demand to the company. This clause provoked reactions from the Hong Kong business associations, their members'

---

[23] *China Daily*, The Sign of Collective Compromise, April 13, 2012.

[24] *The Guardian*, China's Main Union Is Yet to Earn Its Job, June 26, 2011.

[25] Ligorner, K.L. & T. Liao (2010), The Renewed Unionization Campaign in China Coupled with Collective Bargaining, *Paul Hastings*, p. 4, http://www.paulhastings.com/assets/publications/1718.pdf , accessed July 17, 2013.

[26] Cf. Zhu, Y., M. Warner & T. Feng (2011), Employment Relations 'with Chinese Characteristics': The Role of Trade Unions in China, *International Labour Review*, 150(1–2), pp. 127–143.

factories being mostly located in the province, and the government eventually backed down, putting the bill on indefinite hold.

10.3.1. *Foreign staff*

Foreign staff based in China has also expressed concern over the way they are dealt with by some local companies or subsidiaries of international firms, even sometimes on the advice of international law firms. When they are hired under local work contracts, foreign employees often have a precarious resident situation. From time to time, unscrupulous employers have been known to exert pressure not only on the employees but also on their families, to make them accept terms and conditions that are detrimental to the employee. Cases of human resources (HR) malpractices have been reported in China, including early termination of the working contract without cause, no respect of the notice period, pressure on the work and residence visa aiming at the whole family so as to force the employee into signing working contract amendments and even cases with default on the payment of the monthly salary, thus putting the employee under financial pressure. However, observations on the field indicate that, more and more often, Chinese Courts have ruled against such practices. At stake is China's capacity to attract talents from overseas and be a "safe haven" for business, especially when these practices are used by foreign companies that stress their commitment to CSR-based values at home while indulging in contradictory behaviour in China.

* * *

This panorama of both the legal framework and the changing social conditions governing conflicts and bargaining within the corporation bear several lessons for the implementation of CSR-based values and strategies in the field:

— Companies have to deal with an evolving landscape — there are now a diversity of actors intervening in the shaping of workers' standpoints and strategies: official trade-unions, informal workers' associations and affiliated NGOs; national and local governments;

and public opinion as mediated by social media. Social demands are more pressing and precise than was the case in the past; and finally employees have access to a greater variety of channels through which to press their demands. This evolving landscape requires corporations to pay special attention not only to the content of the demands they meet with but also to the style and the channels through which these demands are expressed. It requires them to progressively ascertain a style of communication and a bargaining method that responds to the expectations of a workforce, the diversity and volatility of which we have already noted.

— The communication and bargaining style developed within the corporation is an integral part of the CSR-based values that it intends to foster and implement: social bargaining is to be formative in nature, helping employees to internalize the vision and value system proper to the company they work for; trust, leadership and transparency are to be demonstrated in the way social demands are tackled; and the sense of stewardship as well as the ultimate vision of the company needs to strike an ultimate balance between the positions championed by the different actors. Said otherwise, social negotiations constitute a field of opportunities through which the company is also able to spell out and inculcate its vision and values at all levels of the organization. Consistency between words and deeds is the keystone through which social bargaining can eventually build up trust and cooperation among all the actors involved.

— Social bargaining in China will probably become more intricate in the near future. This is not only a result of the larger number of actors involved and the increase in the means of pressure and negotiations; it also has to do with the fact that a diversified workforce and greater social stratification and sophistication will result in more specific cases and demands. In other words, companies will need to deal with an array of requests, some of them involving target groups — women, migrants, handicapped workers, temporary workers, etc. Again, companies may find here an opportunity to specify their values and priorities, and to meet these demands according to a consistent CSR strategy, which employees can refer to in written documents provided by the company, and with which they can easily identify.

PART THREE

TRANSVERSAL ISSUES:

A BLUEPRINT

Part One has defined the scope and rationale of a company's CSR commitment, specified its implications in the Chinese context, and tried to identify resources specific to China that may help companies to implement CSR-based practices. Part Two has focused on areas of application, analyzing concerns and strategies linked to environmental issues, safety, social standards, gender equality, well-being and training in the workplace, and conflict management and prevention. Part Three turns the focus to transversal issues: it aims at helping companies and other stakeholders to appropriate the questions and resources gathered in the course of the preceding chapters by analyzing ways of proceeding and tools of discernment conducive to the efficacious implementation of a CSR strategy. It will thus discuss: (a) ways of engaging sound ethical assessments; (b) the relationship between CSR concerns and corporate governance; (c) the setting up of instruments such as codes, foundations, pilot projects and networks; (d) the opportunities offered by the development of social entrepreneurship; and it will conclude with (e) an overall vision of the role that corporations are called to play in tomorrow's China.

CHAPTER ELEVEN

Making Ethical Assessments: Finances, Engineering and Conflicts of Interests

We have seen that the expression "Corporate Social Responsibility" refers to an array of behaviors, choices and practices that goes beyond the field of "business ethics". Though the two largely overlap, it can be said that the reference to "CSR" leads one to preferentially examine the policies set up by a corporation for proactively making its operations consistent with a social vision inspired both by its own corporate culture and public expectations, while "business ethics" refers to a set of principles through which a company may be led to correct such policies or such aspects of its management practices. The use of one term rather than the other is determined by focus rather than by content. This chapter will try to offer a way of tackling corporate ethical concerns, firstly by suggesting an approach to the art of "discernment", secondly by centering on two fields of special importance, namely finance and engineering, and thirdly by devoting attention to "conflicts of interests" as they may be lived and solved at different levels of a corporation's operations.

11.1. Practicing Discernment

Examining CSR practices under the "business" ethics focus allows one to point out the importance of *discernment* in business operations. Lived ethics is about recognizing and qualifying the problem met by operatives (bribery, conflicts of interests, neglect of procedures, insider trading) — especially when veiled interests blur the issues at hand. People involved in a business situation sometimes experience what

211

has been called *moral blindness* (see Box 11.1 for an example). This may be the case because they are transfixed by what is at stake: be it maximizing profit, fear of losing one's job, or even — to put it bluntly — pride or hedonism.

Box 11.1 Compliance and Moral Blindness — A Business Case

Charles Smith, a member of the executive committee of an international services firm, greets his colleague Alan Wang. They haven't seen each other for some time and the conversation is friendly. As they are vividly discussing business, Smith tells Wang that he is contemplating to push business development to new limits for the firm in China. Wang enquires about it. Smith explains that he is chasing new "high profile clients" introduced by some of the firm's good customers. He benignly hands out a long wine list, of exceptional "Châteaux" and rare vintages, and tells his colleague that this unique wine selection will be tasted during a special event organized to honor him. Smith explains that this 16-guest event is supposed to set the mark for the most exclusive VIP dinners in China. Smith then asks Wang to flip the wine list card and have a look on the other side at the 12-course menu prepared by one of the most prominent "haute cuisine" chef. Smith explains that the chef will be flown by private jet from New York to China, together with fresh oysters. Smith looks at Alan Wang with a long gaze expecting him to be impressed. As the story sounds a bit incredible, Wang just manages to utter something like "Charles, good for you. I hope it will unlock great opportunities". Then Smith candidly asks Wang if he has any idea of the tag price for such dinner, and announces it is in the region of 99,000 RMB per guest. Wang makes him repeat the number, and Smith confirms with a smile. As Wang steps back, a reply does not come out easily. The awkward question in Wang's mind is: "Is this real, is the firm paying for this event?" Before Wang could formulate his question, a blitzing answer comes out from Smith mouth with a blink: "By the way, I got invited to this event by our client ..." This odd conversation leaves Wang quite puzzled based on what he knows of the firm's corporate standards, the code of conduct, and usual business dinner practices in China. Wang still wonders whether Smith is serious or not. Later on, he gets the confirmation that this is no joke at all.

Source: Fictional story based on real world situations.

Recognizing that we are indeed facing a moral issue, stating the exact terms of the issue at stake, clarifying the set of criteria that apply in the case, and setting in motion a decision process allowing for subsequent implementation — all of these steps are linked with the nurturing of a capacity that may be called moral reasoning (Box 11.2).

Once the issue has been clearly stated, the task is to identify the measures and procedures that apply in such cases. This rarely amounts to an automatism: in practice, the complexity of human and technical dealings makes decisions and responsibilities intricate, and decisions meant to remedy a morally loaded situation have to be weighted according to ethical and prudential criteria. In other words, decisions must show appreciation of both the nature of the situation and the suitability of the solutions required to engage into a discernment process. Laws and regulations, codes enacted by professional associations, case studies, peer groups' support and an educated moral judgment — all of these concur to the solving of the ethical challenges met in the course of business operations. These resources can hardly be mobilized by one single person, which implies that a corporation

---

Box 11.2 Moral Reasoning

"In order to make an ethical decision and act ethically, the first step is to identify that an ethical issue exists for you ... Once the ethical issues have been identified, the next step is to apply *moral judgment* to reason out what is the most ethical action to take. We should consider how our actions affect others using ethical reasoning methods such as harms and benefits (Utilitarianism) and not violate the rights (Rights Theory) of others. It would be wrong for an accountant or auditor to go along with materially misleading financial statements because it violates the rights of shareholders and creditors to receive accurate and reliable financial information. These stakeholders make decisions based on the information so it must be in accordance with generally accepted accounting principles and be transparent ... *Ethical intention* must follow ethical reasoning to turn decisions into action."

Source: Mintz, S. (2013), Moral Blindness. Why Good People Sometimes Do Bad Things, March 5, 2012, http://www.ethicssage.com/2012/05/moral-blindness.html, accessed March 9, 2013.

has to cultivate the capacity to engage in *corporate ethical discernment*, helped during this process by its own body of standards and jurisprudence and by people it appoints as referees, arbitrators or mediators (see Box 11.3 for elaborations on how the ethics mediator work). At the end of the chapter, we will spell out further the steps that corporate ethical discernment may include.

Box 11.3 Case Study: The Ethics Mediator

"The Chairman and Chief Executive Officer of Arkema appoints the Ethics Mediator for a term of four years. The Ethics Mediator is a Group employee who has broad experience of the Group's businesses and disciplines, and holds a position that guarantees the necessary independence and freedom of judgment ..."

The Ethics Mediator
— Recommends procedures, or at his discretion responds in the strictest confidence to any questions that the Group's employees may have on the application of or compliance with the Code of Conduct in specific circumstances...
— Is required, generally and at all times, to observe the strictest confidentiality toward third parties about the identity of the authors of the questions, and to keep secret any information that could lead to their identification; this obligation may, however, be amended with regard only to those individuals who need to be informed, as far as is strictly required to respond to or deal with the matter raised, these individuals being also subject to the same obligation of confidentiality.
— May himself take in hand any ethical matters concerning the Group; he makes recommendations on matters of ethics that he may deem necessary, and he puts forward to the Chairman and Chief Executive Officer any modification to the present Code of Conduct he may deem necessary or appropriate, based in particular on specific situations he may have encountered or on amendments to laws or regulations.
— Has the right to visit any Group facility or subsidiary.
— Is assisted by the Group Audit Department and the Legal Department, with whom he maintains regular contact.

(Continued)

Box 11.3 (*Continued*)

— Advises the Group's training department on including, where appropriate, a presentation of the Code of Conduct in training programs, in particular those for new recruits and for executive posts.
— Submits an annual report to the Executive Committee and to the Board of Directors.

Source: Excerpts of Arkema's Code of Conduct.

UESTIONS

— Is there a person or a group within our organization, the independence of which has been sufficiently guaranteed, responsible for reviewing our proceedings in such a way as to ensure that they conform to our inner regulations and to existing laws?
— Is this person or group also able to propose amendments to our existing procedures, and how are such proposals reviewed?
— Are ethical assessments regularly submitted to our governing structures?
— Are these assessments effective for enriching our training program, and are they integrated into the review of our audit and legal departments? Do we nurture a corporate ethical culture that makes our "ethics mediator" and our company's employees operate on a body of common assumptions?

Engaging in corporate ethical discernment requires a company to set up *ad hoc* bodies, mechanisms and procedures: "Institutionalizing ethics in organizations means that it is made clear that preventing, reporting and effectively and fairly correcting illegal or unethical actions, policies and procedures are the responsibilities of organizations and their employees."[1] This also requires the corporation to spell out practical rules that guide its employees when they meet with

---

[1]Sims, R.R. (2003), *Ethics and Corporate Social Responsibility: Why Giants Fail*, London: Praeger, p. 268.

moral dilemmas. In areas of special importance, rules need to be made as specific as possible (see Box 11.4). For instance, the compliance mechanism must address issues such as auditing and inspections of factories, factories cheating, auditors taking bribes and other sensitive issues. The tackling of such challenges is a prerequisite for engaging further in programs having to do with factory improvement and capacity building initiatives.

11.2. Financial Ethics

The principles of corporate financial ethics can be articulated only in relation to the way the financial sector operates within the overall economic system. Money, specifically *fiat* money, serves two purposes: a) settling transactions; and b) accumulating capital. When financial

---

Box 11.4 Making Anti-Bribery Policy Specific

Anti-bribery/Principles and Rules: Our Business Partners

Don't
— Accept any payment or advantage from suppliers in exchange for conclusion of a procurement contract.
— Appoint people or firms as intermediary that have been convicted for bribery or are known to be involved in bribery.

Do
— Apply strictly the provisions of Bureau Veritas Code of Ethics: Principles & Rules (Article 3.3.5).
— Make sure that payments are made to the real and final beneficiary.
— Make sure that the remuneration of an intermediary is proportionate to his efforts and skills.
— Refuse unusual financial arrangements with a customer or a supplier (such as over-invoicing or under-invoicing) for payments on their behalf to a party not related to the transaction.
— If you are in doubt about the legitimacy of a payment that you have been requested to make, seek the advice of your direct line manager or of a lawyer.

Source: Excerpt from Bureau Veritas's Code of Ethics.

institutions and markets are functioning properly and are regulated in an effective manner by governments, they make an irreplaceable contribution to the harmonious development of society.

The relationship between economic agents through markets is based on money being made available as a quasi free and trustable common good developed between economic agents acting purposefully together for the exchange of present goods against other present or future goods. In this context, under the guidance of the State Council, the People's Bank of China formulates and implements monetary policy, prevents and resolves financial risks, and safeguards financial stability.[2] In China, the objective of the monetary policy is therefore to maintain the stability of the currency value and thereby promote economic growth.

A significant change in money supply, related to accommodating policies and speed of circulation of money in the economy, tends to have a significant impact in the redistribution of wealth, as it primarily hits some groups in the population and tends to exclude others. How and when the state should inject money in the system is debated by economists, but the analysis of the 1929 crisis in light of the one that struck the Western world in summer 2007 made clear that: a) sufficient liquidity must be available to serve the needs of the economy; and b) money needs to keep its fiduciary status, especially in the context of shocks, such as a burst of asset bubbles putting the system to the test.

For the last decade and more, monetary policy worldwide has been unusually accommodative. Excessive liquidity, inflation, asset price bubbles, periodic non-performing loans and other risks have build up to a point where it undermines asset quality and the resilience of the financial sector.[3] A key lesson from the current crisis is that risk prevention should focus not only on a single financial institution or a single sector, but also on systemic risks and individual responsibility. Scandals and crises are not caused only by policy-making issues

---

[2] People's Bank of China (n.d.), Major Responsibilities, http://www.pbc.gov.cn/publish/english/967/index.html, accessed July 17, 2013.

[3] People's Bank of China (PBOC), Opening Remarks at the High Level Seminar of "Macro-prudential Policy: Asian Perspective".

but also — and more importantly so — by micro economic problems closely connected to financial ethics and sound business practices. The failure to set up reasonable performance objectives plays a particular role in this process. Furthermore, problems with credit rating agencies, accounting rules, lax lending standards and the frivolous development of derivative products, among other factors, have all played a role in what has become a systemic crisis of confidence. Corporate financial ethics and macroeconomics meet exactly at this level.

11.2.1. *Financial institutions must provide a fair assessment of risks*

Corporations and financial institutions in China often operate in a climate where the transparency of financial operations remains dubious. As of the end of 2011, total assets of banking institutions were over RMB 113 trillion, while total liabilities amounted to RMB 106 trillion. In terms of asset size, however, the five largest commercial banks accounted for 47.3 percent of the sector, and the total number of banks in China amounted to 765.

The first macroeconomic duty of policymakers is to ensure the safety of money deposited in the banks to keep the economic system working smoothly. A number of tasks and reforms are associated with the fulfillment of this duty:

— The supervision of financial institutions has been complicated in China by the rapid development of off-balance sheet instruments, and the risk monitoring technology that lags behind. At of the end of 2011, the off-balance sheet balance of banking institutions was RMB 39 trillion, 35 percent of the total assets on the balance sheet.[4] As the sophistication of derivative instruments increases, these non-transparent pools of potential liabilities in the area of wealth management, credit assets transfer and inter-bank payments represent a substantial management risk to the stability of China's financial system over the long run.

---

[4] PBOC (2012), China Financial Stability Report 2012, p. 34.

— At the border of the regulated banking system, 4,282 micro-credit companies, 5,237 pawn houses, and 8,402 credit guarantee institutions play an active role to serve rural areas and SMEs. In spite of their positive effect on social funding, these non-financial institutions need to enhance internal discipline and risk prevention capabilities. In certain regions, some non-financial institutions diverged from their main businesses to usurious interest financing and illegal fund-raising.

— It is expected that financial institutions make even more efforts to shield the banking system from risks originated in loan sharks and usury, underground banks, illegal fund raising, Ponzi scheme, private financing, etc. and that rigorous measures should be taken to address misconduct of the non-financial institutions. However, this can only come together with extra efforts to address directly the funding problems of the disadvantaged groups, industrial sectors and backward regions, which are the origins of such uncontrolled financial schemes.

— The 2008 crisis shows that the suppression of risk as a relevant pricing factor may ultimately result in a specific form of market blindness, endangering large cross sections of the financial system. The ample and very low-cost funding in global financial markets contributes to the build-up of financial system vulnerabilities in the form of leverage, regional imbalances and large mismatches across currencies and maturities. Easy money policy tends to delay structural adjustments by allowing the public and private sectors to postpone the necessary debt reduction. Some smoothing of the process can be beneficial, but indefinite postponement is not an option.[5]

11.2.2. Financial markets players are encouraged to comply with integrity framework

At the end of 2011, there were 109 securities firms in China, 161 futures firms, and 69 companies were authorized to engage in the fund

---

[5]Cajuana, J. (2012), Bank for International Settlements, 48th SEACEN Governors' Conference Ulaanbaatar, November 22–24, 2012.

management sector. The total assets of securities firms amounted to RMB 1.6 trillion, total assets of futures firms were reported to be RMB 40 billion, 915 funds were managed by the fund management companies in total, with a total net asset value of RMB 2.2 trillion. In the past years, the most shaky securities firms were closed down and some important ones received government capital injection and were restructured. Now, both the securities companies and securities industry have been asked to ensure a strong sense of social responsibility.[6]

However, the question of maximizing returns on investment puts the whole industry under permanent stress and, as a consequence, encourages the creation of high marked-up products capable to deliver the target performance, often at a never accounted for off-balance sheet cost. The growth of the Chinese economy, and the relative lack of sophistication of its financial instruments (in particular in derivative products) have temporarily helped contain the situation, but has not cured the roots, as the biggest problem in China's financial system is also its lack of innovation.[7]

Apart from the above, the recurrent problems in the Chinese financial market arena include:

— Insider trading, with well-identified consequences on asset management, trading and M&A operations. Strict respect of confidentiality between various departments of a same company ("Chinese wall") and strict prohibition of personal enrichment through the participation of dubious schemes should be strictly enforced. The proprietary trading of most of the market intermediaries is an area where transparency and respect of strict ethical guidelines should be improved.

— Market manipulation, spanning from Ponzi or "pyramid" schemes to "rat trading" in artificially distorting the supply and demand or

---

[6] 2012 Draft on Approach and Measures on Promoting the Opening-up and Innovative Development of Securities Companies.

[7] Guo, S. (2012), Carry Out Explorations and Creative Development in a Proactive and Prudent Manner, May 7, 2012, http://www.csrc.gov.cn/pub/csrc_en/news-facts/release/201207/t20120723_213014.htm, accessed July 17, 2013.

the liquidity of certain financial instruments to inflate or depress the market price of assets. This involves the deception of investors or the manipulation of financial markets. Scammers often try to make a new venture sound like a sure-fire money-maker, but investments always involve risk.

— Fraudulent listings encouraged by financial intermediaries (I-banks, brokers, underwriters), through the provision of erroneous financial documentation to get market listing approval, also resulted in audit scandals of CPA firms in China. The development of independent and strong sell-side research capabilities together with independent auditing of fair market values must be encouraged to deliver unbiased, clear and trustable information to all market participants.

— False disclosure of accounting information from listed issuers, including the use of "creative accounting" with the objective to inflate the corporate performance and deceive investors with overestimated revenues and earnings. Efforts will foster reliable information disclosure, improving the quality of financial reports and dampening any window dressing attempt by issuers.

As is the case in other countries, Chinese individual investors are easily drawn to "insider news" and "hot topics" and therefore, tend to trade on rumors and chase performance. As a result, small investors bear the major risks caused by high offering prices. This, together with investors' preference for new, small and poorly-performing stocks, has undermined the stock market's function of resource allocation and distorted the market structure at the most basic level.[8]

Financial scandals are eroding the confidence of investors and trust among all actors in the market. This is ultimately causing some in-depth damage to the financial framework, which may take years to repair, spreading the belief that the market is a place for manipulation and distrust. To rely only on the central authority while failing to act

---

[8] PRC Government (2012), CSRC Chairman Calls for "Rational Investment", March 2012, http://english.gov.cn/2012-03/02/content_2081378.htm, accessed July 17, 2013.

at the individual responsibility level is not sufficient, and increases the risks of wrong-doing. Industry practitioners and especially senior executives should honor their ethical codes, serve the interests of investors, and refrain from trespassing legal boundaries.[9]

Table 11.1 recalls some of the scandals having happened in recent years. Possibly, the lessons drawn from them may contribute to a progressive maturing of the Chinese financial market.

In July 2012, the China Securities Regulatory Commission has enacted a package of measures entitled "Interim Measures for the Supervision and Administration of Integrity in the Securities and Futures Markets" (see Box 11.5). The overall objective of these dispositions is to strengthen integrity constraints on market participants and their behavior by

---

Box 11.5 Ensuring Integrity in the Securities and Futures Markets

"*Article 4.* Citizens, corporate bodies and other organizations engaged in activities in the securities and futures markets shall be honest, abide by laws, administrative regulations and rules, as well as legally formulated self-disciplinary rules. Dishonest acts that damage the legal rights and interests of investors such as fraud, insider trading and market manipulation are prohibited.

Article 5. The China Securities Regulatory Commission (CSRC) encourages honest citizens, corporate bodies and other organizations to engage in activities in the securities and futures markets and carry out integrity constraints, incentives and guidance.

Article 33. Industry organizations for the securities and futures markets shall educate and encourage their members and employees to abide by laws and remain honest, and may commend or reward those who have done so."

Source: Extracted from CSRC (2012), Interim Measures for the Supervision and Administration of Integrity in the Securities and Futures Markets, July 25, 2012, http://www.csrc.gov.cn/pub/csrc_en/laws/rfdm/DepartmentRules/201212/t20121204_217612.htm, accessed July 17, 2013.

---

[9]Guo, S. (2012), We Need a Powerful Wealth Management Industry — Speech at the First Fund Industry Annual Conference and Founding Ceremony of Asset Management Association of China (AMAC), June 7, 2012, http://www.csrc.gov.cn/pub/csrc_en/newsfacts/release/201207/t20120703_212215.htm, accessed July 17, 2013.

Table 11.1   Selected examples of scandals involving listed companies.

Name of Company/Individual	Year	Insider trading	False disclosure	Fraud listing
Changfeng Communications (长丰通信)	2008		✓	
Lili Electronics (立立电子)	2008			✓
Jiugui Liquor (酒鬼酒)	2009		✓	
Beiya Industrial (北亚实业)	2009		✓	
Huang Guangyu (黄光裕)	2010	✓		
Green Land (绿大地)	2010		✓	✓
Hontex International Holdings Company (洪良国际)	2011		✓	✓
Real Gold Mining (内蒙古公司瑞金矿业)	2011		✓	
Zhongshan Public Utilities (中山公用)	2011	✓		
Xinjiang TianshanWoolTex (天山纺织)	2011	✓		
Metersbonwe (美特斯邦威)	2012		✓	
Shanghai Pharmaceutical (上海医药)	2012		✓	
Puda Coal (普大煤业)	2012			✓
China Sky One Medical Inc. (天一药业)	2012		✓	

Source: Compiled by the author.

launching several institutional arrangements, i.e. carrying out integrity information inquiries, building an integrity supervision cooperation mechanism, imposing administrative punishments on illegal and dishonest acts, and so forth. Article 7 specifies the categories of individual and institutional actors for which "integrity files" are to be created.[10] These measures are not only the first integrity rules for China's capital market but also an important step for market authorities to enhance public integrity information management and encourage integrity-based market behaviors in the course of developing a fully open and trustworthy public market system.

11.2.3. *An enhanced degree of financial ethics must be achieved*

In China as elsewhere, financial ethics needs to be understood and implemented in relationship with an array of operations that prove to be more and more complex: trading conditions, financial contracting, consultancy services, tax payments, audit practices and executive compensations, among other operations. Creative accounting, earnings management, misleading financial analysis, insider trading and bribery are among the practices that need to be clearly identified as malpractice and banned. Ethical discernment has first to do with plainly identifying such practices behind the garb under which they take place and are justified. A few trends and issues need to be recognized:

— China's rapid economic development and globalization goes along with a growing sophistication in financial practices, with the benefits attached to added expertise and dangers associated with fraudulent behaviors becoming potentially harder to identify. This requires business schools to morally qualify the financial know-how acquired by their students. This also requires financial

---

[10] CSRC (2012), Interim Measures for the Supervision and Administration of Integrity in the Securities and Futures Markets, July 25, 2012, http://www.csrc. gov.cn/pub/csrc_en/laws/rfdm/DepartmentRules/201212/t20121204_217612. htm, accessed July 17, 2013.

institutions, especially the leading ones, to properly train and monitor their operatives.

— A large proportion of fraudulent financial practices are of a transnational nature. Financial ethics is an area that calls less for acculturation than for strict international standards expressed in a language that translates easily from one language or culture to another.

— A partial antidote to fraudulent financial practices in China may be found in corporate strategies aimed at fostering positive financial behaviors: such behaviors are to be nurtured in a sense of time and wisdom centered around the notion of *sustainable investment* (Box 11.6). "Sustainable investment" is defined here as domestic and foreign investment in China's listed companies using strategies

Box 11.6 The Case for Sustainable Investment

"China has an opportunity to further leverage the role of sustainable investment to significantly benefit the country and its business community. With rising awareness and understanding of ESG (Environmental, Social and Governance) among mainstream investors, requirements for transparency would increase, which would lead to better corporate governance and ultimately, more successful companies. The market would reward the most innovative companies that address the country's most critical sustainability challenges, and financial resources would be more efficiently allocated. With the right incentives and commitments from government, and large mainstream investors on board, sustainable investment could flourish and lend support to yet another of China's transformations."

Source: BSR (2009), Sustainable Investment in China, p. 10 , September 2009, http:// www.bsr.org/reports/BSR_IFC_Report_SHORT_Updated_30_Oct.pdf, accessed August 9, 2013.

"China is determined to ensure the sustainability of its economic and social development as it enters the 21st century. To this end, sustainable investment has an important role to play, not only in mitigating risks for the economic and financial system, but also as a means of allocating resources to entities with better ESG (Environmental, Social and Governance) performance."

Source: BSR (2009), Sustainable Investment in China, p. 93 , September 2009, http:// www.bsr.org/reports/BSR_IFC_Report_SHORT_Updated_30_Oct.pdf, accessed August 9, 2013.

that take environmental, social and governance issues into consideration. These strategies include negative screening, positive screening, best-in-class, and shareholder activism, as well as "integrated" approaches such as engagement and non-financial risk auditing/analysis.[11]

This is not to say that nothing has happened in China in the field, far from it. The role played by the leading institutions remains certainly too limited, but is sending signals in the right direction: China Construction Bank, Shanghai Pudong Development Bank, China Merchant Bank and others thereafter have adopted sustainability reporting, although they still lack evaluation mechanisms.

Also worth noticing is the fact that in 2006 China's central bank (PBOC), in collaboration with the Ministry of the Environment, launched the "green lending campaign", which included pollution records in databases of corporate entities asking for credit (Box 11.7). In 2007, the CBRC (China Banking Regulatory Commission) proposed to link energetic performance to credit standing position. In the same

---

Box 11.7 PBOC Green Credit Guidelines (Excerpts)

"3. Banks shall promote green credit as a strategy, support economy to grow in a green, low-carbon and recycled model through business innovation, manage environmental and social (E&S) risks, improve banks' own E&S performances, and in doing so optimize credit structure, improve services and contribute to the transformation of the economic growth pattern.

4. Banks shall effectively identify, assess, monitor, control or mitigate E&S risks in business operations, develop E&S risk management systems, strengthen credit policies and processes that are related."

Source: Notice of the PBOC on issuing the green credit guidelines, February 24, 2012, http://www.pfbc-cbfp.org/docs/news/avril-mai-13/RDP12-Mars-2013/DCC-China%20Banking%20Regulation%20-%20Green%20Credit%20Guidelines.pdf, accessed August 9, 2013.

---

[11] BSR (2009), Sustainable Investment in China, p. 11, September 2009, http://www.bsr.org/reports/BSR_IFC_Report_SHORT_Updated_30_Oct.pdf, accessed August 9, 2013.

year, it issued the "Recommendations on Strengthening Large Commercial Banks' Social Responsibilities" that urge the major Chinese banks to take measures coherent with the ten principles of the UN Global Compact. The two major Chinese Stock Exchanges have also exhibited a willingness to work toward the advancement of socially responsible investing practices. Shenzhen Stock Exchange has launched in 2006, the "CSR guidelines for Listed Companies". In 2008, the Shanghai Stock Exchange had issued a "Notice on Strengthening Listed Companies' Assumption of Social Responsibility" and a "Guidelines on Listed Companies' Environmental Disclosure". The Exchange has introduced the concept of "social contribution" as a viable mechanism to assess the value the issuer is creating for its investors. CSR indices appeared in 2009 when, following the example of the FTSE4GOOD and Dow Jones Sustainability Index, both the Shanghai and Shenzhen Stock Exchanges launched the SSE Social Responsibility Index (000048) and the SZSE CSR TRN Index (399340). In September 2010, the CSI ECPI China ESG 40 Equity Index was launched as a joint venture between the Chinese Securities Index Company and ECPI, a European indices research company.[12] The index is composed by 40 domestic companies and responds to demands made by institutional investors for greater transparency.

The concept of sustainable investment has given rise to "Socially Responsible Investment" (SRI), based on the conviction that the social responsibilities of the financial sector go beyond "honest business practices": financial intermediaries can also influence the practices of their business partners by their investment policies.[13] SRI is also a developing concept in China: in February 2011 the SRI Fund of China Universal Management Co. Ltd. was approved, the first in its genre, by the Securities and Futures Commission. China Industrial Bank, China

---

[12] ATMonitor (2010), ECPI and CSP Launched 40 Highest ESG-rated companies Index in China, September 20, 2010, http://www.atmonitor.co.uk/news/newsview.aspx?title=ecpi-and-csp-launched-40-highest-esg-rated-companies-index-in-china, accessed July 17, 2013.

[13] Asslander, M.S. & M. Shenkel (2012), SRI as Driver for CSR? Ethical Funds, Institutional Investors and the Pursuit of the Common Good, in C. Bonanni, F. Lépineux & J. Roloff (eds.), Social Responsibility, Entrepreneurship and the Common Good: International and Interdisciplinary Perspectives, New York: Palgrave McMillan, p. 182.

Merchant Bank, Bank of Shanghai and Shenzhen Development Bank have signed the UNEP FI agreement — a partnership in between the UN and the financial world that aims at addressing the issue of sustainability from the perspective of its impact upon financial performance. However, the Global Principles for Responsible Investors (the result of a joint effort by the UNEP FI and the UN Global Compact Global Reporting Initiative) still elicits a poor response from Chinese investors.

SRI paves the way to "community investment", e.g. to investment consented in sectors or geographical areas traditionally deprived of financial support. Targeting poorer or marginalized communities, it aims at generating specific developmental dynamics while emphasizing the importance of both financial returns and community sustainability. A 2009 survey of 20 large-size corporations operating in China, 13 of them MNs and 7 Chinese, found that 55 percent of them had entered a wide range of partnerships, depending on the focus of their community investment projects. Companies overwhelmingly chose as partners Chinese NGOs with strong government background and relations, and international NGOs with a recognized capacity to work on the ground in China (and with the relevant experience to do so).[14] The survey was a sign among others that the concept of "community investment" was indeed developing fast, though the skills and modes of partnership for making it effective were still lacking. We will come back on community investment at the end of Chapter 14, centered on social entrepreneurship.

Fostering financial ethics in China requires all parties involved to go into two directions: (a) fully integrating China into the globalization of financial ethics and of the mechanisms that go with it: China will not reform its financial practices and culture quicker than its counterparts do, but there is no reason either that it does this later than them; (b) directing financial operations — starting with investment strategies — toward the social, human and environmental needs of China, making the notion of sustainable investment a key component for nurturing a Chinese corporate culture of financial ethics.

---

[14]See CSR Asia Beijing (2009), *CSR Asia: Survey on Community Investment of Companies Operating in China*, March 1, 2009, http://www.csr-asia.com/cdf/download/Report_pre_CIRT_Beijing.pdf, accessed July 17, 2013.

11.3. Engineering Ethics

We have already met with engineering issues, and have stressed the extent to which the topic of products and process safety is central in today's China. China is already graduating roughly twice as many engineers a year as the US. At the same time, as we have already noted, the training of Chinese engineers remains weak when it comes to ethical assessment and critical thinking.[15] There is a lot of pressure weighing on engineers to speed up timetables and sometimes bypass testing and other procedures. The support provided by peer groups, professional associations and reference to codes of conducts proves ordinarily to be weaker than it is the case in Europe or the US.

As noted earlier in this book, engineering ethics sets out and teaches engineers the obligations that go with their task — namely the design (and subsequent operations) of devices and systems for the benefit of society.[16] It develops into rules and codes of conduct aiming at ensuring the safety, health and welfare of the public, as well as sustainable development. The first section (or "canons") of the US National Society of Professional Engineers' Code of Ethics provides us with a good example of the basis on which such Codes are developed: engineers, in the fulfillment of their professional duties, shall:

— Hold paramount the safety, health and welfare of the public;
— Perform services only in the area(s) of their competence;
— Issue public statements only in an objective and truthful manner;
— Act for each employer or client as faithful agents or trustees;
— Avoid deceptive acts; and
— Conduct themselves honorably, responsibly, ethically, and lawfully so as to enhance the honor, reputation and usefulness of the profession.[17]

---

[15] On the relationship between engineering studies and ethical thought in Chinese history, see Zhu, Q. (2010), Engineering Ethics Studies in China: Dialogue between Traditionalism and Modernism, *Engineering Studies*, 2(2), pp. 85–107.

[16] For an overall presentation of the field and its methodology one can refer to Harris, C.E., M.S. Pritchard & M.J. Rabins (2009), *Engineering Ethics, Concepts and Cases (fourth edition)*, Belmont CA: Wadsworth Cengage Learning.

[17] Discussion of the "canons" can be found in: Vesilind, P.A. (2010), *Engineering Peace and Justice, The Responsibility of Engineers to Society*, London: Springer, pp. 85–94.

As in all areas of applied ethics, engineering ethics makes use of case analysis in order to examine all the issues arising with the production, material and immaterial handling of products and processes. It also provides guidelines that help engineers to assess risks and innovate. It should be noticed that engineers are traditionally organized into professional organizations, one of their tasks being the maintainence of the honor and integrity of the profession. These professional organizations are privileged partners of corporations, in the sense that they guarantee the quality of the services that engineers provide them with. Professional organizations also may work with corporations when problems that require elucidation of the procedures being followed arise. Practically, business ethics gradually evolves due to the fact that engineers and their organizations analyze accidents and other dysfunctions, so as to prevent future loss. At the same time, the evolving framing of codes and regulations now happens in a globalized world, which makes engineers work across cultural frontiers.

"Engineering ethics" provides other professions with the example of a realistic and sophisticated approach to the ethical challenges of our societies today. Its methods and concepts can be applied to the field of bioethics or financial ethics for instance. Its study offers a methodology for tackling other corporate challenges as well. In the Chinese context, the priority is to encourage engineers to enter into the prudential approach that has characterized the development of engineering ethics, with its stress on case analysis, critical and pragmatic thinking, and the peer-to-peer culture presiding to its elaboration.

Companies operating in China may consider the following initiatives:

— To facilitate the building up of engineering ethics resources (websites, textbooks, conferences and chairs) in Chinese engineering schools;

— To encourage the setting-up (when needed) or the reinforcement of professional associations monitoring the reputation of the branch they cover;

— To foster within their organization an engineering culture working on peer-to-peer assessment, collective review of cases, and transparency, encouraging engineers to come up with issues such as testing procedures, timetable, external pressures and conflicts of interests.

When it comes to the second proposal, a note of caution should be struck, which does not apply only to China: from observations made in the field, it appears that, if some professional associations fulfill the missions expected from them, other may sometimes foster illicit agreements among operators. Similar questions have been raised when it comes to standardization committees. In such a context, what is expected from responsible corporations is both to edict strict norms as to engineers' participation in these instances, and to work toward improved ethical standards in their midst, as professional associations remain central to the self-regulation of a profession.

11.4. Conflicts of Interests

Conflicts of interests affect virtually all branches of any organization, from engineering to marketing. That conflicts of interests may arise is probably inevitable. As is the case for financial ethics, the first correct response to the issue is to overcome moral blindness and to properly qualify the facts and the problem at stake (see Box 11.8 for a case study). The second step of any ethical assessment is to find out the rules and procedures that apply to the case. Here, a corporate culture of trust and transparency as well as the wording of the codes of conduct enacted in the company prove to be of crucial importance.

Box 11.8 Case Study — Conflicts of Interests

Examples of regulated situations:

— To hold any position with a competitor or a client or to acquire an interest in their share capital;
— To conduct any company business with any member of our family;
— To employ a member of our family without approval of our direct line manager;
— To have been directly involved in the design, manufacturing, supply, installation, use or maintenance of the objects to be inspected; and
— To be directly involved, for a shareholder or employee of Bureau Veritas, in the design, manufacturing, supply, installation, use or maintenance of the objects to be inspected by Bureau Veritas, and to be involved in the inspection of such objects.

Source: Excerpted from Bureau Veritas's Code of Ethics.

UESTIONS

— Are potential conflicts of interests clearly spelled out in our internal regulations?
— Do they cover the entirety of our lines of business and operations, and are they updated according to situations happening in the field?
— Are the procedures to be activated in case of regulated situations clearly stated?

Conflicts of interests are partly determined by cultural components, as they depend upon the way different societies experience and emphasize the strength of family links, the role of the state apparatus or loyalty to the company; hence the necessity to modulate codes and regulations according to national contexts, providing employees with examples that illustrate the corporate principles to be applied, not withstanding the cultural baggage that they may have to carry.

* * *

As we try to account for the diversity of fields and issues studied throughout this chapter, it is useful to observe that a discernment process follows a few steps that are common to finance, marketing, engineering or personnel management:

— Identify the conflict with as much degree of clarity as possible.
— Spell out the values promoted by the corporate and individual decision-makers that are relevant to the conflict.
— Determine various possible actions and their outcome.
— Name the "attachments" (i.e. the vested interests, automatic course of action, blind inclination) that the organization holds to each possible outcome. (An "attachment" may be the short-term maximization of profit at the cost of infringing on a value officially promoted by the organization. Another attachment would be to avoid troubles by hiding a technical or financial irregularity that has occurred.)

— Once the inclinations have been clarified, take time to creatively imagine and formulate the decisions that can be taken if these attachments are put aside.

— Reflect on the consequence of each possible course of action — and ask the question "What will bring more?" (more adherence to our core values, more fulfillment, greatest good for all).

— Engage in discussion with people affected by the decision that will be taken.

— Once the decision has been taken after the due process, have trust in it and live by it.

— When considering a specific decision the first criterion used for checking its adequacy will be to clearly differentiate between goals and means. Goals are objectives based on values expressly stated. Means are the way we move toward the goal.

— The second criterion will be: Which alternative could produce better results, i.e. more fruit?

— The third criterion will be: Which of the alternatives gives the organization an opportunity to grow in all dimensions (consent among actors, ethical fulfillment, rationality, sustainability)? Which brings a sense of "rightness" and lasting result?[18]

Finally, let us recall that, as argued in Chapter 3, Chinese cultural resources offer a corporation content and inspiration for conducting a discernment process that makes use of concepts and references intelligible in a certain context. Discernment is first and foremost a dynamic that nurtures an ongoing conversation, a conversation held within the consciousness of the decision-makers, within the corporation, and between the corporation and its stakeholders.

---

[18] This paragraph is freely adapted from Nettiffee, D. (n.d.), Ignatian Spirituality and the Three-Fold Model of Organizational Life, http://www.stthomas.edu/ cathstudies/cst/publications/seeingthingswhole/STW14_Nettifee.pdf, accessed July 17, 2013, and other resources available on the "Ignatian discernment process", http://www.documbase.com/Ignatian-Discernment-Process.pdf, accessed July 17, 2013.

CHAPTER TWELVE

CSR and Corporate Governance

The exercise of corporate ethical discernment is fostered by codes that anchor business ethics into a company's culture. If the corporate culture is subsequently permeated by the principles and mechanisms these codes define, CSR would have been infused into all aspects of a corporate culture: the understanding of the company's vision and ultimate objectives; its decision-making process; allocation of resources and strategic priorities. In practice, however, CSR often remains in *one sector* of the company's organizational chart, which does not allow for the creative feedbacks that a more synergic approach would foster. The question raised in this chapter is thus about the ways to make CSR an integral part of corporate governance.

12.1. Codes and Their Implementation

In recent years, corporations have been steadily developing a number of codes, which are sometimes called *codes of ethics* (the stress is then on the listing of general principles and values) or *codes of conduct* (setting out the procedures to be used in specific situations having ethical implications). These codes are distinct from the *codes of practice*, which are adopted by a profession in view of self-regulation. In all cases, the ethical standards as well as the rules of procedure and behavior provided by a given code are meant to preserve the reputation of the organization (corporation or profession), benefit to its stakeholders, and respect the rights of all people affected in one way or another by the operations of the organization. Box 12.1 elaborates on the functions for such codes.

The rise in the number of codes enacted by corporations can be explained by at least three phenomena: (a) the increasing complexity

Box 12.1 Case Study: What are Codes Useful for?

"The objectives of this Code of Ethics (herein after "the Code") are to set up common fundamental ethics principles and rules, to refer to the Group's corresponding internal procedures and to give some practical examples (the list being not exhaustive) in order to provide clear directions to employees in the areas of their daily business activities where questions could arise with respect to the Group's ethical standards. The Code is intended as a guide to making the 'right choice'."

Source: Excerpted from Bureau Veritas' Code of Ethics.

"The DSM Code of Business Conduct has an umbrella function for, among other things: Trade Control Compliance/Competition Law Compliance/ Code of Conduct for Information Security/DSM Health Safety and Environment Policy/DSM Supplier Code of Conduct/DSM Rules, on the holding of and executing transactions in DSM financial instruments and certain other financial instruments."

Source: Excerpted from the DSM Code of Business Conduct.

UESTIONS

— How many codes, charters or other sets of rules are there presently in our corporation?

— Did we choose to separate these codes or to integrate them in one document, and what were these reasons for the choice we made?

— Are the areas of application of these codes precise enough?

— Are these codes fully consistent among themselves?

— Do some of them need to be updated, and for what reasons?

— Are these codes illustrated with examples? Do these provide the reader both with intangible principles and with space for discernment and interpretation?

of the situations that the organization and the individuals working for it are meeting with; (b) the necessity to summarize the general principles inspiring international and national legislations regulating the activities of the corporation, and to spell out the congruence of the corporate culture with the said regulations; (c) the internationalization of the corporate activities, with a felt need to translate into another culture rules and values that may be more naturally understood in the country of origin of the corporation. This last reason is of particular importance in the Chinese context: foreign companies operating in China have been experiencing the necessity to make explicit a certain number of rules governing behaviors linked to the safety, honesty and transparency of their industrial and business operations. In a similar vein, the changing economic and cultural context has led a number of Chinese companies, especially the ones with international operations, to enact their own codes of ethics and conduct. Sinopec is a point in case (Box 12.2).

Some codes are rather elliptical in their formulations, while others contain detailed requirements and provide employees and other stakeholders with grids of questions and interpretations. An excellent example of the latter is provided by the code of conduct of The Insurance Corporation of British Columbia (ICBC), enacted in 2011. Its table of contents already makes the reader aware of the range of issues encompassed (Box 12.3).

Three major features of the code offered by this specific corporation, and by many others, are of particular interest if and when applied to the Chinese context:

(1) Rules must go with some *criteria of interpretation*, otherwise they become void of meaning and are quickly ignored; the code of ethics quoted here provides the reader with examples that may help him/her to exercise his/her personal judgment in similar circumstances. Box 12.4 shows some sample questions that may enhance an employee's capacity for personal discernment.

(2) The code is complemented by a set of *forms*, tailored according to the responsibilities of the different stakeholders, which makes it clear that contravention of the code is a serious matter resulting in

Box 12.2 Sinopec

"Sinopec bases its corporate governance on the Code of Corporate Governance for Listed Companies, as issued by the China Securities and Regulatory Commission (CSRC), under the State Economic and Trade Commission; Company Law of the PRC.

In line with the Basic Standard for Enterprise Internal Control issued by the central government, Sinopec comprehensively systemized all businesses and major events and finished its compilation of the 'Internal Control Instruction'. The Instruction includes several parts, such as internal environment, risk evaluation, control activity, information and communication, internal supervision and so forth.

Staff Code

The aim is to further regulate the behavior of Chinese and international staff, strengthen exchange and cooperation with foreign entities and build a coherent, capable and progressive working team in a safe, harmonious and orderly work environment. We aim to promote corporate culture development by enhancing the staff's sense of honor, loyalty and commitment.

1. Ethic Codes: five fundamental career ethics requirements toward staff including loyalty, honesty and integrity, diligence and devotion, complying with rules and regulations, and observing social ethics.
2. Codes of Conduct: requirements in the aspects of workplace discipline, workplace order, staff relations, education and training, company resources, business activities, conflicts of interests, and self-discipline.
3. Workplace Protocols: clear-cut business etiquette, dress code and language use at workplace.
4. HSE Requirements: demand staff to learn HSE policy, goals and obligations by heart.
5. Confidentiality: requests in intellectual property, information disclosure and security."

Source: Sinopec (n.d.), Health Safety & Environment, http://english.sinopec.com/investor_center/corporate_governance/health_safety_environment/, accessed July 17, 2013.

Box 12.3 ICBC Code of Conduct (Table of Contents)

Introduction: Our Values in Action
ICBC's Code of Ethics
Living Our Values
Application of the Code

Integrity
Conflicts of Interests
General Principles on Conflicts of Interests
Acceptance of Gifts and Entertainment
Personal Relationships in the Workplace
Interaction with Stakeholder Businesses
Offers of Bribes
Purchase of Salvage and Other Company Property
Political Participation
Personal Transactions with the Company
Use of Corporate Property

Dedication to Customers
Customer Privacy

Accountability
Employee Personal Conduct
Compliance with Laws
Protection of General Corporate Information
Alcohol and Illegal Drugs

Caring
Maintaining a Respectful Workplace

Appendix 1 — Anonymous and Confidential Reporting System
ICBC's Commitment to an Ethical Workplace
What Are My Options to Report a Concern?
How to Make an Anonymous and Confidential Report
Reports to the Chair of the Audit Committee
Frequently Asked Questions

(Continued)

Box 12.3 (*Continued*)

Appendix 2 — Conflicts of Interests Guidelines for Board Members
Disclosure
Outside Business Interests
Outside Employment or Association

Appendix 3 — Form of Declaration for Board Members
Appendix 4 — Form of Declaration for Bargaining Unit Employees
Appendix 5 — Form of Declaration for Management Group Employees
Appendix 6 — Form of Declaration for Contractors Doing Business with ICBC

Source: ICBC's Code of Ethics.

Box 12.4 Assessing Potential Conflicts of Interest

"You should always consider the following questions in relation to gifts or entertainment:

— Would the gift or entertainment be likely to or appear to influence my objectivity or the objectivity of the person to whom I am giving the gift or providing the entertainment?
— Is the invitation from someone who is, or could be involved in a planned competitive process to provide services to ICBC?
— Would my impartiality or the impartiality of the person to whom I am giving the gift or entertainment be compromised in any way or appear to others to be compromised?
— Is the entertainment for a private purpose as opposed to being for a business purpose? Is business going to be discussed as part of the event or only in a very limited way?
— Would the gift or entertainment be considered unique or extraordinary?
— Would it be a problem or would you be embarrassed if you were to disclose the gift or entertainment to other employees or third parties?

If the answer to any of the above questions is "yes" or "perhaps", or could be perceived by third parties to be "yes" or "perhaps", by accepting or offering such gifts or entertainment, you are creating the appearance of a conflict of interests."

Source: ICBC's Code of Ethics.

disciplinary action, possibly including dismissal. By signing the form, board members and employees acknowledge having received the code and agree to adhere to it as a condition of one's continued employment with the corporation.

(3) Going beyond the example offered here, let us also note that codes written for the Chinese context must include provisions referring explicitly to the local legislation on the issues at stake — labor conditions, gender equality, corruption, and consumer rights. This contributes both to the effectiveness of such regulations and to the rooting of the company into its social environment.[1]

The questions we just raised are typical of the issues met when trying to live in a world of *cross-cultural ethics*: "In an increasingly global business environment, one of the central challenges facing firms is how to balance the desire for standardized global policies, with appropriate consideration of the specific norms of various cultural contexts... The presumed effectiveness of a global code of ethics is built on the assumption that a code of conduct is equally meaningful as a guide to action in different cultures. The factors that individuals consider at different elements of the decision process, and their relative power of influence, may vary with culture. In other words, while agreement may be reached upon the content of a global code of conduct, the processes and mechanisms through which a corporation may effectively ensure global compliance with this code are not universal."[2] Furthermore, there are well-documented cases of forced acceptance by local employees or subsidiaries of codes imposed by parent companies, which only generates dislike and distrust.[3]

Codes constitute the expression that a company gives to itself of its specific commitments when it comes to the decisions, small and

---

[1]Cf. Hanson, K.O. & S. Rothlin (2010), Taking Your Code to China, *Journal of International Business Ethics*, 3(1), pp. 69–80.

[2]Thorne, L. & S.B. Saunders (2002), The Socio-Cultural Embeddedness of Individuals' Ethical Reasoning in Organizations (Cross-cultural Ethics), *Journal of Business Ethics*, 35(1), pp. 1 and 14.

[3]Helin, S. & J. Sandstrom (2010), Resisting a Corporate Code of Ethics and the Reinforcement of Management Control, *Organization Studies*, 31(5), pp. 583–604.

big, that it necessarily has to take. As they are tools for discernment, codes need to be carefully worded, and scrupulously taught to the ones who will have to put them into application. Even more important, they need to be devised, explained and revised in such a way as to foster the employees' participation and sense of belonging: they are written, improved and applied throughout a series of interactions: "An organization that desires a centrally controlled ethics will only stifle the possibility of a reflected and considered ethics."[4] Codes are not to be enshrined; rather, they are *living standards*, they need to be interpreted or revised according to the ethical and practical experience that the corporation gathers through the self-assessment of its results and practices.

12.2. Integrating CSR within Governance Mechanisms

To speak of "corporate governance" in the Chinese context may actually lead to misunderstandings (see Box 12.5 for more details): the undertones of the expression are colored by the historical process that has led to the entry of China into the market economy — a context much different from the one that has popularized the word "governance" in Western societies.

In its Western acceptation, "corporate governance" refers at least to three interconnected dimensions; (a) the set of processes through which a corporation is managed; (b) the rules, formal and informal, defining the relationships among the various stakeholders; and (c) the way the corporate goals are set up, implemented and assessed. The style of governance of a company will define for instance how whistle-blowing is perceived, encouraged and regulated — whether whistle-blowers may remain anonymous or not, for instance. There are no absolute solutions to this kind of problems: if any style of governance is deemed to encourage transparency, trust and integrity, it remains that the legal structure, business focus, social constraints and cultural

---

[4]Clegg, S.R., M. Kornberger & C. Rhodes (2007), Business Ethics as Practice, *British Journal of Management*, 18(2), p. 117.

Box 12.5 Ethical Issues in the Evolution of Corporate Governance in China

"The Chinese notion of corporate governance is closely linked to what is perceived by the authorities to be the "modern" corporate system... The notion of "modern" corporations in China is closely linked to a perception of superior corporate performance. A modern corporate system is generally understood among Chinese policy-makers and commentators to possess the following attributes: (a) clearly clarified property rights; (b) designated authorities and responsibilities; (c) separated functions between the government and enterprises; and (d) scientific management. The first three really reflect the transitional nature of China's reform from a centrally planned economic system to a market-oriented economy. In practice, the modern corporate system is often equated to the incorporated joint stock company form, particularly companies that are publicly listed. The joint stock company of course represents the most common form of business organization in the industrialized economies, and public companies dominate the key economic sectors there. Their corporate governance arrangements, primarily in the form of the stylized Anglo-American model, have accordingly been held up as the governance paradigm. China's Company Law has indeed enshrined many stylized features of the corporate governance arrangements of that model. As far as government policies are concerned, the development of corporate governance in China is guided by a desire to install the stylized features of that model, primarily through a prescriptive and legalistic approach... There have also been considerable confusions over what corporate governance is in the Chinese context. It is not uncommon to find that corporate governance is understood by many Chinese managers and officials as being just a modern way of organizational management, or a set of structures and procedures for regulators and owners of enterprise to supervise managers."

Source: Tam, O.K. (2002), Ethical Issues in the Evolution of Corporate Governance in China, *Journal of Business Ethics*, 37(3), pp. 308–309.

factors will definitely influence the mechanism of deliberation and decision.

The quality of corporate governance can be evaluated according to the capacity it shows to integrate new dimensions when redefining strategies and regulations for the organization. In this respect, in recent years, how well corporations have been able to integrate the sustainability imperative into their vision, policies and practices has been a good indicator of the overall quality of their governance model. In China, such a systemic approach to corporate governance remains to be popularized. The restrictive understanding of the concept certainly impedes the consideration of CSR values and practices within the corporate process of deliberation and decision. The example used in Box 12.6 shows both the limitations and the openings that characterize the current situation.

Box 12.6 CSR, Strategic Choices and Recruitment Policy

"It is still rare to find companies that fully integrate CSR initiatives in every part of their organization. A recent study by SynTao, a Chinese CSR consulting company, concludes that local companies are generally not aware of the value of CSR reporting and performance monitoring. The study found that only 121 Chinese companies published sustainability reports between January and November 2008. (As of October 2009, the Shanghai Stock Exchange alone has more than 800 companies listed on it.) What's more, some companies publishing CSR reports only offer the public abridged versions or grant only government authorities and supervisory organizations access to them. According to the study, companies in China decide to issue a CSR report for two main reasons: to enhance their corporate image as part of an increasing awareness and dedication of CSR among senior management, and to satisfy government requirements. For the most part, according to a consultant specializing in government relations in China, MNCs in particular view CSR as part of their "government relations package"... Employing more than 3,000 people in 12 offices and an R&D center, Cisco China has a dedicated CSR department with full-time employees, which reports directly to corporate affairs in Cisco's US headquarters. Although the parent company sets the global CSR strategy and allocates budgets, Cisco China's CSR department is responsible for implementing national activities within those parameters. To get country initiatives in motion, the Chinese CSR department devises its own action plan and is not limited by directives from headquarters.

(Continued)

Box 12.6 (*Continued*)

Another CSR pioneer in China is Caterpillar, a large manufacturer of earth-moving and construction equipment as well as diesel and natural gas engines and turbines. In 1996, the Peoria, Illinois-based company established Caterpillar (China) Investment Co. Ltd. in Beijing. Today, it has 18 facilities and offices in China, employing over 5,000 people in more than 60 business units. Caterpillar's program is handled by a local corporate affairs department, which helps with the approval and funding of local business units' CSR activities. The corporate affairs team works closely with the Caterpillar Foundation, an independent charity founded in 1952 with a worldwide presence, to determine which CSR initiatives to fund. In addition to relying on the foundation for financial support, Caterpillar China recently began allocating a portion of its budget to support local initiatives.

Both companies, as many others do, align their CSR initiatives with Chinese government programs. For instance, Caterpillar's current initiatives focus on education, healthcare and environmental protection. The company has based its initiatives in communities where it has factories, contributing to local human capital development, with the added benefits that the program can be a good way to source its future engineers. As for Cisco, it focuses on improving the livelihoods of its employees. Its initiatives include career advisory services, diversity initiatives and support for NGOs that employees are involved in. Outside the company, Cisco focuses on developing education and healthcare ... A recurring theme in CSR development in China is its undeveloped talent pool. But Chinese companies now know that CSR is at the forefront of the government's agenda. The government has begun promoting CSR as a social objective in China, helped by its recent mandate that state-owned enterprises set up independent CSR departments. This could help attract more people to the field... Enlightening the general public and employees is also necessary to develop CSR. For example, in 2009, Shanghai's municipal government sponsored a social venture competition, in part to raise awareness of CSR-related issues. The general public should also be reminded that they, in addition to the government and investors, represent an important group of stakeholders.

(Continued)

Box 12.6 (*Continued*)

Foreign and Chinese companies can strengthen the expertise in the field by recruiting and developing professional CSR staff. By acknowledging that finding specialized professionals to integrate CSR into an organization's business strategy is a major challenge, companies can create dedicated CSR posts and provide these employees with formal training. Companies can also enhance the autonomy and capability of their CSR departments, enabling intra-company specialization with regard to CSR. In addition, they can encourage the growth of a socially conscious public by providing incentives to their employees to participate in CSR activities, being creative in communicating these activities to customers, improving how they engage the media and developing products that feature their contributions to society."

Source: Huang, J., J. Lee, M. Lo, L. Navarro & A. Owa (2010), *Zhongguo de qiye shehuizeren* (China's CSR), April 29, 2010, http://www.knowledgeatwharton.com.cn/index.cfm?fa=viewArticle&articleID=2218, accessed July 17. 2013.

At the present stage, recruiting local staff specializing in CSR-related issues and awareness certainly constitutes an option to be considered. However, this makes sense only if the persons employed are not entrenched from the rest of the organization but rather work at an inter-departmental level, fostering awareness, training and cooperation, in such a way as to make CSR issues an essential component of any corporate deliberation and decision, for strategic choices as well as for everyday decisions.

12.3. Governance, Transparency and the Media

Companies in China need visibility so as to build up brands and reputation. At the same time, a policy of visibility and communication (including the public presentation of their results in terms of CSR) makes them even more exposed to criticisms, some of them possibly spread by competitors. The problems met by companies involved in food distribution have been very widely publicized.

As an example, in March 2012, the Chinese state television has accused McDonald's and Carrefour of selling expired chicken products amid public anxiety in China over food safety. The report said a McDonald's restaurant in Beijing sold chicken wings 90 minutes after they were cooked through the company's rules set a 30-minute limit. It said employees at a Carrefour store in the central city of Zhengzhou changed expiration dates on some chicken and sold regular chickens as more expensive free-range birds.[5] Officials from the State Food and Drug Administration asked McDonald's franchise restaurants in China to examine their food-processing procedures. Later on, McDonald's issued an apology for violating operational standards on its website. The CCTV program, "315 Evening Gala", has been aired on March 15 every year since 1991. Coming in conjunction with International Consumer Rights Day, the program is intended to reveal business misconduct and to help consumers protect their rights. The supermarket chain Carrefour has also been accused of deceiving consumers by selling expired meat and chicken stripped of feathers that it misidentifies as free-range chicken and then sells at a higher price. Those misdeeds are alleged to have taken place in one of the company's stores in Zhengzhou, capital of Henan province, according to the program.[6]

At the transition between 2012 and 2013, it was Yum Brands' turn to meet with trouble — the company operates more than 4,000 KFC outlets and more than 700 Pizza Huts in China. On 23 November 2012, the website of a state-run newspaper alleged that a KFC supplier had been raising chickens in unsanitary conditions, and was using hormones and antibiotics to grow "quick chickens" in 45 days. The

---

[5] Abrams, S. & China Hearsay (2012), China Celebrates Consumer Rights Day with a Trumped Up Investigation of McDonald's, March 16, 2012, http://articles. businessinsider.com/2012-03-16/home/31199233_1_chicken-wings-carrefour-china-central-television, accessed July 17, 2013.
[6] Zheng, X. & Z. Jin (2012), McDonald's Restaurant Closed in China for Rule Violations, *Yahoo! News Singapore*, March 17, 2012, http://Sg.News.Yahoo.Com/Mcdonalds-Restaurant-Closed-China-Rule-Violations-084004206.Html, accessed July 17, 2013.

allegations quickly spread online. While defending its record, Yum Brands had to come up with an apology: the company failed to address problems quickly and had poor internal communications, said the chairman and chief executive of its China operations, in a statement posted on Weibo. The criticisms and consumers' reactions were particularly harsh due to the fact that companies such as KFC have long been seen in China as the "benchmarks of safety and success", so customers feel "betrayed" when they fail to live up to expectations.[7] KFC earns a 39 percent market share in China's fast-food market, but the impact of local media coverage of the probe may have hurt that reputation. A *WSJA* article reported on how companies everywhere have had to adapt to the power and influence the internet wields over their companies' reputations.[8] Yet, it can be particularly hard to handle China's increasingly wired-in and quality-conscious consumers — and the growing influence they now possess. As the article elaborates, local sites and social media frequently carry allegations against companies, many of which are unfounded and peculiar — partially stemming from the skepticism toward the government's long-standing lack of transparency. In particular, foreign companies are under greater scrutiny, and it is difficult to predict which rumors might blow up into a crisis (see Box 12.7 for an example).

At the same time, the way to deal with transparency and visibility is a question that must be put into context: the Chinese market is still evolving, and consumers' demands are changing. Greater stress is being put on products' safety and reliability, environmental footsteps, workers' conditions, and — as it comes out very clearly from internet forums — on a company's transparency when it comes to pricing,

---

[7] Burkitt, L. (2013), Yum Brands Apologizes Amid Chicken Probe, *WSJA*, January 10, 2013, http://online.wsj.com/article/SB10001424127887324081704578232279133 6513864.html?mod=WSJAsia_hpp_LEFTTopStories, accessed July 17, 2013.

[8] Jargon, J. and L. Burkitt (2013), KFC's China Flap Holds Lessons for Investors, *WSJA*, January 11, 2013, http://online.wsj.com/article/SB10001424127887324 4423- 04578234261756463182.html?KEYWORDS=KFC%27s+China+Flap, accessed August 9, 2013.

Box 12.7 Public Opinion, Protests and Rumors

"A solar panel manufacturing plant in Zhejiang Province has been ordered to suspend production and deal with the pollution it caused after more than 500 protesters gathered outside the plant. The local government in Haining held New York-listed Jinko Solar Holding Co. Ltd. responsible for discharging toxic water that killed large numbers of fish. But it also said rumors that dozens of people in Hongxiao village had contracted cancers — including leukemia — because of the firm are false. A man has been detained for spreading the rumors on the internet. Haining officials said there were four cancer patients in the area last year and two this year. It was rumored that 31 villagers had contracted cancers and six of them had leukemia. Because of the rumors, more than 500 villagers went to the factory on Thursday night demanding an explanation, the Haining government said in a statement. Some protesters charged into the factory compound, over-turning eight company vehicles and destroying its offices, the government said. On Friday, four police vehicles were damaged... The factory's waste disposal system has been failing pollution tests since April and despite warning from authorities, the plant had not effectively controlled the pollution, Xinhua News Agency cited Chen Hongming, deputy head of Haining's environmental protection bureau, as saying. Toxic waste from the plant, which manufactures photovoltaic panels, cells and wafers, contained excessive fluorine... The incident was the latest major environmental protest in China. Last month, 12,000 residents in the northeastern city of Dalian protested after storm waves broke a dike at a chemical plant and raised fears that floodwaters could release toxic chemicals. Officials have pledged to relocate the plant."

Source: Wang, Y. (2011), Protest Shuts Solar Plant, *Shanghai Daily*, September 19, 2011, http://www.shanghaidaily.com/nsp/National/2011/09/19/Protest%2Bshuts%2Bsolar%2Bplant/, accessed July 17, 2013.

product specifications and general operations. It can be said that transparency is one of the social needs most widely expressed in today's China, and that this concern is directed toward company operations as well as toward public agencies.

Specifically, the devising of a CSR strategy takes place in a world in which conflicting information and symbols are exchanged on TV and computer screens. Sometimes, it will be a story about the rapid spread of a virus, a leakage or a natural disaster, sometimes the declaration of an official will start a polemic, and sometimes a story about the possible side effect of certain medications or industrial products will create public concern. From one country to another, the communication style on these topics will be somehow different: in some countries, elected officials will multiply declarations and will be easily engulfed into polemics; in other countries, administrators and experts will lead the show. Some communication policies will heavily rely on the impact of new media (social networks, songs circulating on the internet, etc.), while in other cultures more traditional channels still carry much weight. Communicating about risks is a risky process *per se*... When observing public reactions to widely exposed stories (such as the H1N1 pandemic), the good news is that new media play a role that is much more positive than expected. For sure, the internet can spread false rumors at an astounding speed. But it constitutes also the best tool for dispelling them and for quickly rectifying false information. New media can work as "knowledge networks", as systems that disseminate, rectify and enrich information, and can optimize collective behaviors when needed: peer groups prove to be excellent channels for encouraging responsible behaviors, especially for educating and mobilizing the younger generation. Box 12.8 sketches general principles for companies' dealings with media.

Box 12.8 Dealing with the Media

"The media play a vital role within society and we recognize the importance of fast, comprehensive and reliable information. In our relationships with the media (television, radio, written press, electronic media), we aim for honest debate, based on mutual respect and the constructive pursuit of relevant, objective information. Accordingly, we refuse all and any relationships contrary to the basic principles of integrity."

Source: Excerpted from Michelin Performance and Responsibility Charter.

QUESTIONS

— Does our media plan include provisions about the way we deal with CSR-related issues?
— Do we have a strategy ready in case of campaigns detrimental to our reputation as a reliable agent of sustainable development and social responsibility?
— Is such a strategy based on facts that are periodically re-checked?
— Do we deal with the media in a way consistent with our values of integrity, transparency and trust?

Today, communication on public matters, such as pandemics or environmental hazards, involves much more that the diffusion of information from top to bottom. It is a process of cross-fertilization between technical information, public debate, knowledge enrichment and evaluation of actions already taken. Through the collective appraisal of the crises we face together, contemporary societies are forging the tools that help them to grow in maturity and solidarity. Such a process of collective appraisal and networking is the one in which the devising of CSR policies takes place, and it gives new meaning to "transparency", "accountability" and "stewardship" — words that define the core values on which CSR relies.

CHAPTER **THIRTEEN**

Reports, Foundations, Projects and Networks

This chapter deals with the strategic tools that companies commonly utilize for enhancing their corporate image: reports, foundations, pilot projects and participation in networks. The stress here is on what companies may learn through a thoughtful use of such tools, going beyond mere image building, so as to incorporate the humane and financial investment consented into an organization's overall corporate self-understanding and strategy.

13.1. Reporting

Research shows that large companies, be they national or multinational, already dedicate a sizable part of their communication effort to their CSR practices, though they tend to do so less in China than in Western countries. Their efforts are often detailed through extensive CSR reports.[1] In 2011, 898 Chinese enterprises released their CSR reports, 18 percent more than the previous year. This number is estimated to be 1200 in 2012.[2] For sure, corporate reports on CSR suffer

---

[1] On CSR reporting by Chinese companies and its recent evolutions, see Xu, H. & J. Xu (2011), Analysis and Reflection on the Disclosure of Social Responsibility Information of Chinese Enterprises — Based on China's 95 Listed Companies' Evidence (*Zhongguo qiye shehuizeren xinxi pilou xianzhuang jiexi yu sikao — ji yu zhongguo 95 jia shangshi gongsi de jingyan zhengju*), *Accounting Forum*, 20(2), pp. 32–54. (许慧、许家林，《中国企业社会责任信息披露现状解析与思考 — 基于中国95家上市公司的经验证据》，会计论坛 2011 第2辑，第32–54页，http://www.docin.com/p-393724984.html, accessed July 31, 2013.)

[2] Jiang, X. (2012), The Development of Corporate Social Responsibility under China's Economic Transformation, http://www.csrmanagernetwork.it/wp-content/

from obvious limits. Analyzing a sample of six reports, three from Chinese companies and three from American companies, an author concludes: "The CSR reports analyzed thus reveal the use of three different 'interdiscourses': the discourse of promotion, which more overtly draws on the rhetorical strategies of 'establishing credentials' and building the importance to promote the company at a competitive, social, national, and international level; the discourse of goodwill, which emphasizes open communication channels and the company's caring for society to promote the engagement of a company with the wider society, while also reassuring stakeholders about the nature of the company; and the discourse of self-justification which emphasizes the economic and historical demands the company faces to illustrate its resourceful nature and excuse its practices by attributing its actions on external conditions."[3] However, when reading beyond the rhetoric, CSR reports often contain important information that needs to be critically but carefully assessed. They illuminate the self-understanding a corporation nurtures, and the way it maps its course of development; they highlight areas of concerns and scale priorities. Read over a number of years, they allow the observer to evaluate a company's consistency, capacity for adaptation and even its qualitative results, being therefore more telling than the company may suspect.

The yearly reports are now often available through the internet, and together with other information available on companies' websites, allow the analyst to get an overall understanding of corporate philanthropic efforts (Box 13.1).

13.2. Foundations and Charities

The number of corporate foundations operating in China has known a sharp increase in recent years (see Box 13.2). Their volume

---

uploads/2012/11/Outlines-of-Speeches-by-CFIE-Delegation-Members.pdf, accessed July 31, 2013.

[3] Bhatia, A. (2012), The Corporate Social Responsibility Report: The Hybridization of a "Confused" Genre (2007–2011), *IEEE Transactions on Professional Communication*, 55(3), p. 235.

Box 13.1 Corporate Philanthropy

"Companies engage in the following types of public philanthropy with descending frequencies: environmental conservation (78.8 percent), disaster relief (63.6 percent), financial assistance to primary and secondary education (59.1 percent), financial assistance to higher education (53 percent), development and poverty reduction (51.5 percent), other contributions to education (48.5 percent), arts and culture (39.4 percent), and sports (34.8 percent). 28.8 percent of companies mentioned responsibilities toward/of suppliers on their websites, while 36.4 percent mentioned responsibilities toward shareholders. In terms of responsibilities toward customers, 69.7 percent of companies mentioned product quality and 42.4 percent mentioned product safety. In terms of responsibilities toward employees, companies in the sample mentioned employee health and safety (40.9 percent), employee welfare (40.9 percent), employee development (40.9 percent), and equal opportunity for all employees (22.7 percent). Companies practice CSR in the following ways: donation (71.2 percent), company policy (68.2 percent), sponsorship (50 percent), volunteering (47 percent), establishing foundations (45.5 percent), building partnerships with NGOs (43.9 percent), universities (34.8 percent), and governments (31.8 percent), publishing CSR reports (27.3 percent), and establishing awards (21.2 percent)... In the Chinese context, companies engaged in *ad hoc* public philanthropy emphasize themes such as education, sports, art and cultural events, development, poverty reduction, disaster relief, and health. They contribute to these causes mainly through donation, sponsorship and volunteering. Companies practicing CSR as *ad hoc* philanthropy often acknowledge their responsibilities to society in general. However, their contributions to CSR through donations and sponsorship are often irregular, event-based, and thus lack a strategic goal and a long-term agenda."

Notes: Based on an analysis of the Chinese-language websites of the Fortune 100 Chinese companies and of the 44 Fortune 100 global companies having operations in China. The total of these companies having a section of their Chinese website dedicated to CSR amounts to 66.

Source: Tang, L. & H. Li (2009), Corporate Social Responsibility Communication of Chinese and Global Corporations in China, *Public Relations Review*, 35(3), pp. 204, 205, 208.

Box 13.2 Foundations and CSR in China

"The Regulation on Foundation Administration, which allows private firms to use assets donated by individuals or organizations to set up private foundations, was enacted in 2004. The number of private foundations has risen rapidly ever since, creating a new channel for corporations to participate in charitable activities. Although it is still a rather new phenomenon, the rise of private foundations is one of the most significant signals bearing witness to the development of CSR in the country. By the end of 2008, there were 1,597 foundations in China, with a total sum of assets reaching 30 billion yuan and an annual total of collected donations of 20 billion yuan. This emerging CSR movement is creating new possibilities for more dynamic corporate philanthropic practices and closer partnerships between companies and non-profits to achieve a win-win situation, serving both commercial imperatives and social needs. For companies pursuing long-term commercial success with a CSR agenda, cooperation with non-profits could improve their public image and reputation, and for non-profits, partnering with companies."

Source: Yu, X. (2011), Social Enterprise in China: Driving Forces, Development Patterns and Legal Framework, *Social Enterprise Journal*, 7(1), pp. 1 and 15.

and range of activities as well as the quality of the projects they initiate and support have been experiencing a parallel progression. Among other large-size corporate foundations, the China Mobile Charity Foundation was set up in 2009 with an initial investment of 100 million yuan in order to standardize the operations of the company's charitable resources. As is generally the case for state-owned companies' charitable activities, the Foundation works under the guidance of the Ministry of Civil Affairs. The projects have included selected actions in development aid for poverty-stricken districts in Heilongjiang, Tibet and Qinghai, for a total of 220 million.[4] Other actions centered on agriculture and herding have accompanied China Mobile's focus on rural districts. Mobile applications

---

[4]China Mobile (2012), *China Mobile Limited 2012 Sustainability Report*, p. 25, http://www.chinamobileltd.com/en/ir/reports/ar2012/sd2012.pdf?year=2012, accessed July 31, 2013.

centered on agricultural management, health, environment and education are part of the core business generated by China Mobile, and the charitable actions the company sponsors often further or illustrate these commercial services targeted at the poorer part of China's population.

Though legal provisions still strictly govern their status and actions, foundations are seen both by Chinese and foreign companies as a privileged channel through which to express and implement their sense of corporate responsibility. This does not go without ambiguities: as has been stressed since the beginning of this book, CSR cannot be reduced to philanthropy, though philanthropy may be indeed a key component of a company's corporate culture. It sometimes happens that the establishment of a foundation and the financing of a few philanthropic actions make a company complacent when it comes to the exercise of its other social responsibilities. In a few cases, important companies invest so little in the foundations they create that their social involvement may be put in doubt rather than asserted by their initiatives. For remedying such limitations, foundations must be part of the *self-regulating mechanism* that defines a sense of corporate responsibility embedded into the daily functioning of a company. This can be done through a number of ways:

— The scope of a corporate foundation's activities may be defined in accordance with the nature of the business of the parent company, valorizing its technical know-how and selecting specific areas related to its products: issues related to healthcare, education, consumers' awareness, road safety or the environment can be accordingly privileged.

— Companies may encourage their employees to become actively involved in the projects that the corporate foundation has chosen to support (see Box 13.3 for a case study on Intel), or even make the projects initiated by employees a core component of the foundation's operations. The foundation thus becomes the symbol and channel of the employees' own awareness of their company's CSR vision, which is in turn perpetually enriched by the employees' participation and range of actions.

Box 13.3 Case Study — Intel Foundation

Intel® Foundation Volunteer Matching Grant Program was launched in 2005 in China. The goal of this program is to improve school education facilities by encouraging Intel employees to earn money for schools through volunteer activities. This program promotes education in science and math, the use of technology, and safety in the school system. Under this program, Intel® Foundation has donated USD43,338.[a] The *Innovation Initiative for Non-profits*[b] was launched by Intel China in 2010 under the guidance of the Ministry of Civil Affairs of China. It aims to promote social innovation and discussion on how non-profits can help solve pressing social and environmental challenges in China. Intel Foundation made an initial grant of one million RMB to support this program.[a]

Sources: [a] Intel China, http://www.intel.com/cn/intel/csr/index.htm, accessed July 31, 2013.

[b] Song, J. (2012), Awards and Aid for Grassroots Innovators, *China Daily*, May 9, 2012, http://www.chinadaily.com.cn/bizchina/2012-05/09/content_15251990.htm, accessed July 31, 2013.

In all these cases, corporate foundations do not work in isolation from the activities of the company that had made them part of its corporate image and policy. And integrating foundations into the self-regulating mechanism through which companies are reminded of their social responsibilities makes them better express and symbolize the values and spirit that the corporation wishes to publicly associate with.

It is worth spending some time studying the range of activities in which corporate companies operating in China have been involved. This will help us to recognize and rank social priorities as discerned by companies themselves, while assessing what still can be done after the philanthropic flourishing we have been witnessing these last years.

UESTIONS

— Are our employees involved in the philanthropic projects we support? If yes, in which ways?

— Are we aware of the range of activities in which our employees are involved, and of their potential integration within the range of our initiatives?

— Do we provide employees with incentives for exercising their social responsibilities, and do we help them to network on this?

— Do we encourage them to come up with suggestions on the way we may express our CSR vision through philanthropic initiatives?

— A corporate foundation can also be used for fostering and implementing CSR imperatives in various contexts: it can support networks aimed at establishing specific professional codes, especially in China, where many professions still do not have such codes; it can endow chairs of business ethics and CSR in Chinese institutions of tertiary education; it may encourage research on CSR areas of special concern for the company: financial ethics, consumers' awareness, labor law or women issues, for instance.

Boxes 13.4 to 13.6 each describe a corporate foundation's operation in China.

13.3. Pilot Projects

Chinese culture traditionally gives precedence to *stories* over *concepts*. Many Chinese companies chose to focus on cases and actions that move the public mind, even if the thread between the projects supported by the company is not always obvious. However, this approach has a consistency of its own: (a) the company highlights its own creativeness and social flair; (b) concentrating on a given case, the company can treat the operation with care and acumen; (c) proceeding through trials and errors, it is also able to determine its CSR strategy in a pragmatic fashion, progressively assessing what actions best coincide with its corporate culture and strategy; and finally, (d) such an approach can better suit small and medium-size companies.

Box 13.4 GE Foundation

Education, environment protection and disaster relief are focus areas of GE Foundation in China. The *GE Foundation TECH Award*[c], launched in 2002, is designed to stimulate innovation in new technology, design, research methods and applications among university students in China. Areas covered include energy, water, electronics and electrical engineering, machinery and mechanical processing, chemistry and material science. About 250 students have already benefited from this award since 2002.[d] The *GE Foundation Scholarship* started in 1995 is another initiative to support talent development in university, mainly those famous in science and engineering fields.[e] It sponsored the *Teacher Training for Hope Project*[f] from 2005 to 2009 by donating 1.67 million dollars to the China Youth Development Foundation Teacher Training Center, eventually holding 42 training courses, benefiting 11,863 teachers and over 300,000 students. It sponsored training on *"environment protection"* for the teachers in middle and western regions in China — named the Green Seed Campaign by the project executive body, Beijing Normal University, from 2005 to 2008. The program covers building database and courses for environment protection education, environment protection training for teachers, and thematic environmental advocacy activities to arouse the environment protection awareness of students in primary, middle and high school.[g] After the Sichuan earthquake, GE foundation donated 10 million RMB to the Red Cross Society of China for disaster relief.[h]

Sources: [c]Institute of International Education (2013), GE Foundation Tech Award, http://www.iie.org/en/Programs/GE-Foundation-TECH-Award, accessed July 31, 2013.

[d]GE Global Research (2011), GE Foundation TECH Award Winners Announced, http://ge.geglobalresearch.com/blog/2011-ge-foundation-tech-award-winners-announced/, accessed July 31, 2013.

[e]*Shanghai Morning Post* (2003), *Chuangxin cong daxue peiyang qi* (Innovation Begins from University Education), http://old.jfdaily.com/gb/node2/node17/node33/node31545/node31569/userobject1ai469615.html, accessed July 31, 2013.

[f]China Youth Development Foundation Teacher Training Centre (2010), GE *jijinhui* (GE Foundation), December 21, 2010, http://www.cydf-jspx.com/Detail.aspx?ID=52362, accessed July 31, 2013.

[g]Li, H. (2005), *Tongyong dianqi jijinhui zizhu zhongguo huanbaojiaoyu shizipeixun* (GE Foundation Sponsors China's Environmental Training Activities), February 24, 2005, http://news.xinhuanet.com/newscenter/2005-02/24/content_2614745.htm, accessed July 31, 2013.

[h]People's Net (2008), GE *bingcheng chengxinjingshen zaofu yu shehui* (GE: Holding Up Integrity to Benefit Society), November 7, 2008, http://mnc.people.com.cn/GB/8301769.html, accessed July 31, 2013.

Box 13.5 Citi Foundation

Citi Foundation in China centers on microfinance, small and micro enterprise development, poverty alleviation and education. The China Banking Association's *Citi Microentrepreneurship Awards* is established in China in 2005 through the support of the Citi Foundation to recognize the contribution of China's most outstanding microentrepreneurs and to raise awareness of the power of microfinance to alleviate poverty and build prosperity.[i] *Citi-HPP Wanzhou Rural Small Enterprise Development Program* is made possible in 2012 by a Citi Foundation grant. The program aims to provide small and growing household enterprises in this district with technical and practical training on sustainable agricultural production and animal husbandry, with the objective of increasing farmers' income levels while generating the "triple bottom-line" — economic, environmental and social benefits.[j] Another program, *Citi-CFFPD Sustainable Rural Enterprise Train-the-Trainer* was launched in Hubei Province in 2011, aimed at helping 1,200 rural household enterprises increase income levels by at least 30 percent.[k] The *Citi-FDI Green Enterprise Incubator* is initiated in 2010 through a grant of USD100,000 from Citi Foundation in partnership with Fuping Development Institute, a leading non-profit organization dedicated to social innovation, poverty alleviation and sustainable development. This project aims to promote sustainable economic and social development by supporting the growth of green microenterprises and small enterprises.[l] The *Financial IT Education Program* launched in 2007 under a grant of USD1.24 million from Citi Foundation is the first program in China that specializes in encouraging and cultivating talent in the financial IT

Sources: [i]Citibank China (2011), 2011 China Banking Association — Citi Microentrepreneurship Awards Held in Beijing, October 18, 2011, http://www.citi.com.cn/html/en/news/11/2011101801.html, accessed July 31, 2013.
[j]Citibank China (2012), Citi Supports Development of Rural Small Enterprises in Chongqing, March 13, 2012, http://www.citi.com.cn/html/en/news/12/2012031301.html, accessed July 31, 2013.
[k]Citibank China (2011), Citi Supports New Initiative to Help Rural Enterprises in Hubei Province, May 11, 2011, http://www.citi.com.cn/html/en/news/11/2011051102.html, accessed July 31, 2013.
[l]Citibank China (2010), Citi Partners with Fuping Development Institute to Boost Green Economy in China, January 8, 2010, http://www.citi.com.cn/html/en/news/10/2010010801.html, accessed July 31, 2013.

(Continued)

Box 13.5 (*Continued*)

profession.[m] The *Better Finance Better Future Program*, a financial education program, is launched under the support of Citi Foundation in 2011 in Beijing to equip migrant youths with the ability to set financial goals, track expenses, make a budget and save for the future.[n] The *Citi-CPAFCC English Teachers' Training Program* and *Young Financial Leaders Summer Camp* are two other examples of what Citi Foundation finance in China.

Sources: [m] Citibank China (2007), Citi Announces Major New Grant of US$1.24 Million to Expand Support of Financial IT Education in China, November 30, 2007, http://www.citi.com.cn/html/en/news/07/2007113001.html, accessed July 31, 2013.
[n] Citibank China (2011), "Better Finance Better Future" Program Launched in Beijing, January 18, 2011, http://www.citi.com.cn/html/en/news/11/2011011801.html, accessed July 31, 2013.

Box 13.6 Shell Foundation

Sustainability/green is the main theme underlying the programs initiated by Shell Foundation in China, with a special focus on clean energy, sustainable transportation and microfinance.[o] Shell Foundation in 2003 supported the Energy Research Institute of the National Development and Reform Commission of China with a USD760,000 grant to strengthen the country's energy and environment planning capabilities, and produce a medium-term energy plan. The *Rice Straw Gasification Project* sponsors developing advanced biomass gasification technology in partnership with the Institute of Thermal Power Engineering of Zhejiang University. *Shanghai Sustainable Transport Program* aims to create a set of sustainable transport indicators and to design an innovative mass transit system in partnership with Shanghai Municipal People's Government Construction and Management Commission and EMBARQ. It is part of a global sustainable transportation

Source: [o] Shell (2003), Sustainable Development Report of Shell 2003, pp. 5 and 6, http://reports.shell.com/sustainability-report/2010/servicepages/previous/files/shell_report_2003.pdf, accessed July 31, 2013.

(*Continued*)

Box 13.6 (*Continued*)

initiative by the Shell Foundation.[p] *Sustainable Farming* is a three-year project started in 2002 with a grant of USD303,000 to develop sustainable farming techniques for farmers in erosion-prone areas of Gansu and Inner Mongolia.[p] *Economic Empowerment of Rural Women* supports microfinancing for poor rural women so they can create small, sustainable handicraft businesses in partnership with the China Foundation for Poverty Alleviation.[q]

Sources: [p] *Zhongguo lvse shibao, Kepai jijinhui 'lv' zai zhongguo* (Shell Foundation's Green Efforts in China), http://www.jiaoyitong.com/ibusiness/i_news_show.php?id=7755, accessed July 31, 2013.
[q] For more on the role of the China Foundation for Poverty Alleviation in the empowerment of rural women, see Wang S. & J. Richter (2008), Rural-Based Development and Potential for Enhanced Credit Access in Modern China, April 24, 2008, http://www.microfinancegateway.org/gm/document-1.9.55708/RURAL%20BASED%20DEVELOPMENT%20AND%20THE%20POTENTIAL%20FOR%20ENHANCED%20CREDIT%20ACCESS%20IN%20MODERN%20CHINA%20Wang_Richter.pdf, pp. 20–24, accessed August 9, 2013.

Boxes 13.7 to 13.9 illustrate how such pilot projects have been initiated in various companies.

Even for companies working on the basis of a more systematic approach, concentrating on pilot projects comes with specific rewards. Much can be learnt from the follow-up of a small-scale project such as training sessions on safety or accounting held in a village or at a school, an exhibit organized for helping a workshop started by local actors in a minority area, the cleaning-up of a neighborhood, or a local microcredit program. Practical difficulties as well as potential for managerial improvement can be explored at length, the lessons being then transposed on larger scale projects. Besides this, the stories collected throughout the duration of the experiment prove to be inspirational both within the company (which may decide on new directions for CSR implementation through this creative and pragmatic process) and for the public to whom such stories are relayed. The role of social media, the circulation of videos or the publication of illustrated books and brochures create long-term capital of sympathy and commitment. Nothing is more helpful to buildup a company's CSR image than a

Box 13.7 Legend Holdings Limited: "Lenovo Venture Philanthropic Capital"

Legend Holdings Limited (Lenovo hereinafter) was founded in 1984, by Liu Chuanzhi and ten other researchers, with funding of 200,000 yuan (USD 30,000) from the Computing Institute of the Chinese Academy of Sciences. In 2007, Lenovo decided to support innovative philanthropy projects focusing on employment and business startups. During the years 2007 and 2008, in total, 16 non-governmental organizations have benefited from these programs with nearly 3 million yuan of funds.

In 2009, Lenovo started a nationwide program named "Youth Social Entrepreneurship Program". 120 colleges across the country, gathering about 3.2 million students, were involved and 18,000 proposals handed in. 10 teams were finally selected and each of them received 100,000 RMB as venture capital from Lenovo, as well as professional support from Lenovo.

Sources: Legend Holdings (2013), Company Overview, http://www.legendholdings.com.cn/en/About/Overview.aspx, accessed July 31, 2013.
Legend Holdings (2013), Assisting Entrepreneurs, http://www.legendholdings.com.cn/en/About/CSR/Entrepreneur.aspx, accessed July 31, 2013.
Wang, R. (2010), *Lianxiang jituan: Qianghua gongyi chuangtoushengji CSR celve* (Legend Holdings: Strengthening the CSR Strategies), http://istock.jrj.com.cn/article,hk00992,1634603.html, accessed July 31, 2013.

well-narrated story coming from the field, provided such stories are consistent with the corporation's overall discourse and objectives.

13.4. Knowledge Networks, a Path for Reflection and Action

Attempting to sketch a transversal approach to CSR in China, we have examined its integration into corporate governance, the role played by foundations, and the importance to be accorded to pilot projects, pragmatically selected and assessed. In accordance with the lessons drawn from the preceding chapters, we have sensed how important it is to foster interactions among different stakeholders so as to share information, analyses and insights, in a way that helps all actors to perpetually adapt their strategies and projects in the ever-changing

Box 13.8 Shanghai Tang Initiatives

Shanghai Tang is a Chinese luxury brand, and a parent company of Richemont. In 2008, in partnership with *The Teacher of Ten Thousand Generations Foundation*, which assists underprivileged children and their families by providing them with educational opportunities, Shanghai Tang has sponsored an exhibition of drawings from children of the Lianshan Foshan Hope School and Lianshan Jitian School at its stores as a fundraising activity. In a similar vein, in 2011, during the breast cancer awareness month, Shanghai Tang offered 888 pieces of limited edition Pink Longevity Rabbit key ring, in honor of its seventh year of collaborating with the Hong Kong Cancer Fund Pink Revolution. Also, since 2008, Shanghai Tang has been collaborating with Save China's Tigers in its efforts to protect, conserve and raise awareness about the plight of the South China tigers.

Sources: Richemont (2013), Richemont's 2012 Corporate Social Responsibility Report, p. 26, http://www.richemont.com/investor-relations/reports.html, accessed July 31, 2013. Teacher of Ten Thousand Generations Foundation (2003–2012), Events, http://www.confuciusfoundation.org/events.php, accessed July 31, 2013.

Box 13.9 Alfred Dunhill World Community Project 2012, Shanghai

Alfred Dunhill, Ltd. is a British-based company, specializing in men's luxury leather goods, writing implements, lighters, timepieces, fragrances and clothing. The Alfred Dunhill World Community Project 2012 brought together 50 employees from across the world in May 2012 to deliver real and lasting change to a community in need. Anyone working for Alfred Dunhill could apply. For the 2012 project, Shanghai was chosen, being the location of Alfred Dunhill's China office and its Twin Villas "Home". Participants came together to build an adventure playground and to renovate all five classrooms within a poorly funded migrant workers' school for over 160 children. For two days, they sawed and hammered, painted and sanded, bolted and built. It was hot, hard work. On the last afternoon, when 80 of the children arrived to see the outcome of their work, the rewards were huge.

Source: Richement (2013), Richemont's 2012 Corporate Social Responsibility Report, p. 47, http://www.richemont.com/investor-relations/reports.html, accessed July 31, 2013.

environment in China. This leads us to formulate anew what it means to foster and implement CSR values and strategies in China today: *Companies create and disseminate CSR-based value when they share their experiences on the optimizing of social resources and welfare within the corporation itself and with other stakeholders, in such a way as to help all actors to perpetually adjust the balance between the interests and concerns that define their social environment* (see Boxes 13.10 and 13.11 for some case studies). In other words, we return to the lessons learnt in our first chapter: Companies, when they realize what it means to be *interdependent selves*, enter into **knowledge networks** that produce CSR-related values — trust, transparency and sense of responsibility.

"Network", it could be said, is a *loosely used word* that refers to *loosely structured ways* of exchanging information, supporting each other and/or leading common actions. It links people and groups at various levels, local or global, sometimes for their own mutual benefit, sometimes in the interest of a cause that transcends and unites the members of the network. The reach and efficiency of networks has

---

Box 13.10 Shanghai Fosun Pharmaceutical (Group) Co., Ltd: Anti-Malaria Initiatives

Shanghai Fosun Pharmaceutical (Group) Co., Ltd. ("Fosun Pharma"), was established in 1994 and listed on the Shanghai Stock Exchange in August 1998. Fosun Pharma has supported Professor Nicholas J. White's AQUAMAT project (Africa Quinine Artesunate Malaria Trial). Fosun has also offered artesunate injections for free in Africa, and has established a clinical database on the efficacy of anti-malaria drugs.

Through the "Malaria Control Seminar" organized since 2006, 29 officials representing the medical system of 16 countries suffering from malaria have been in dialogue with Focun Pharma. Another program, called the "Malaria Control Seminar for Officials", has trained 202 experts from 56 developing countries on anti-malaria policies.

Sources: Fosun Pharmaceutical (2012), Company Overview, http://www.fosunpharma.com/about, accessed July 31, 2013.
Fosun Pharmaceutical (2012), *Chixu chuangxin gongxiang jiankang* (Continued Innovation in Celebration of Health), http://www.fosunpharma.com/responsibility, accessed July 31, 2013.

Box 13.11 Chinese Youths: "We Impact"

"At We Impact, we place a great deal of importance on knowledge. As part of our digital knowledge library, we have been authoring Intelligence Reports on Sustainable Lifestyles to raise the profile of an individual's capacity to bring about a more sustainable future. In effect, they provide blueprints for positive action toward a sustainable lifestyle, with an emphasis on Chinese Youths but also in reflection of global trends. These reports are also thoroughly referenced to further resources available on the subject.

Change is the name of the game in China and you can see it clearest in Chinese youths. Making the most of growing cities and rising standards of living, they have become enthusiastic consumers of luxury products. Yes, they are still saving more than any consumer in the globe but they look for quality and rather spend smartly as a reward for their hard work. Chinese youths have become intelligent consumers in our new-age global economy, using review sites on the Internet to guide their choices."

Source: We Impact (2013), http://www.we-impact.com/, accessed July 31, 2013.

been greatly enhanced by the internet. This might be partly because the internet allows for horizontal relationships, and horizontal relationships are very much at the core of networking, distinguishing networks from other organizational structures.

Exchange of knowledge is another characteristic of networks. This is already true of "social networks", exemplified by the Old Boys associations. For sure, social networks primarily provide emotional and cultural support, but they constitute also the nest through which information that might help one to change one's career path or get valuable tips on the stock market are exchanged. Information becomes even more central when we come to what can be labeled as "knowledge networks": this kind of network is basically a space for discussion that helps to determine research directions (for an academic community) or action strategies (for an association of people and groups committed to a social or environmental cause for instance.) Otherwise said, *it is only within knowledge networks that "information" truly becomes "knowledge", i.e. crystallized into a body of consistent and mutually reinforcing assumptions.* It is also within knowledge networks that knowledge receives a meaning that leads a group to enact value judgments and maybe to decide on a course of action.

The spread of knowledge networks testifies to the way scientific assessments, policy-making and grass-roots activities are now mutually interacting. Also, the globalization of issues such as environment imbalance, financial transparency, consumers' or workers' rights, induces people to connect to groups that share similar concerns in various cultural and political contexts. International networks are partly a product of the eroding power of the nation-state, and partly a response to the increased influence of other players, such as multinational companies.

Verkoren (2006) has identified a few conditions under which knowledge networks can function correctly:[5]

— The network does not exist in isolation; exchanges going through the network and real life activities are linked in a sustainable way.
— The purpose of networking is clear, as are the possibilities offered by the network and the limits of what it can achieve.
— Capacity for learning, room for discussion, and openness in membership, discussion and sharing are requisites for the efficacy of the network.
— While being able to operate autonomously, the network must be linked to a wider environment, so as to be able to give and to receive.
— Results of the interaction have to be visible at some stage.
— To facilitate and moderate a network requires time and expertise.
— Finally, the flexibility of the network helps it to facilitate exchanges, action and empowerment without trespassing over its boundaries, rather than aiming to become an all-encompassing knowledge system.

---

[5] Verkoren, W. (2006), Knowledge Networks: Implications for Peacebuilding Activities, *International Journal of Peace Studies*, 11(2), pp. 27–62, http://www.gmu.edu/programs/icar/ijps/vol11_2/11n2VERKOREN.pdf

In the field of CSR, there might be no stronger incentive to the spreading of the knowledge network model than the concerns raised around sustainability and governance. The debate on environmental changes shows that scientific conclusions are themselves reached through the nurturing of a permanent network of information and debate. Interconnections between companies, experts, state agencies and citizens encourage all these groups to go from traditional lobbying to innovative networking. Technical expertise is not sufficient for tackling broadly-shaped issues, and groups of citizens will continue to debate on consumption models, the resurgence of values such as frugality and solidarity, hopefully advancing toward formulations and insights that will develop a cultural model in line with the technical imperatives linked to the issue at stake. The mobilization of corporate and cultural resources for nurturing sustainable development — a mobilization achieved through a dialogue on core values, sharing of success stories and exchange of strategic analyses — is exactly what a knowledge network might want to achieve.

UESTIONS

— Are there knowledge networks that I — or my company — are presently engaged in?
— Are these networks akin to my real interests and current concerns, or should I try to engage into new ones?
— May I possibly be active in a web of relationships that could develop into a real knowledge network, sharing information among its members and with other networks, provided that I encourage the group to take the necessary steps for becoming more reflexive and participatory?
— What kind of knowledge networks does my company need, and can I become instrumental in fostering such alliances?

CHAPTER FOURTEEN

Social Entrepreneurship

Still an emerging concept in China, social entrepreneurship may be defined as private *business ventures primarily aiming at solving some of societies' most pressing issues*; or — otherwise said — *business ventures organized around a social or collective purpose rather than the search for profit*. Although "social enterprise" (SE) came out as a specific concept as late as the 1970s, pioneering endeavors could be found in Europe at a much earlier date (Florence Nightingale and the first nurse schools in the UK). The movement has since become a global trend, which is now reaching China. SEs can be developed through the effort and investment of private entrepreneurs, through support from private sector financing (Danone social fund, Grameen Bank) or, in a few cases, through governmental support.

14.1. A Sector in the Making

"Social Enterprise" appeared in the Chinese lexicon around 2001, and the concept became popular after 2004. The year 2007 witnessed the establishment of several "social startups" and a series of thematic seminars. In June 2008, the British Council started to offer capacity building training sessions to China's social entrepreneurs, a program that has been taking place every year in different Chinese cities since then. International symposiums on SEs were organized in Beijing in 2009 and in Shanghai in 2012. The 1st China Social Investment Forum was held in Beijing in November 2012.[1] It is interesting to note that Chinese actors in the field now prefer to use the expression "social

---

[1] Yoopay (2011), 1st China Social Investment Forum, https://yoopay.cn/event/00540605, accessed July 31, 2013.

startup" (社会创业) or "startup for public good" (公益创业), with a dedicated publication, *Social Startup-er* (社会创业家) published since October 2009. [2]

The Canyou Group (残友集团), a Shenzhen-based software company started in 1997, is the largest SE in China with more than 3,700 staff, most of them people with disabilities. Chinese SEs are generally small and poorly founded, but some of them are starting to benefit from the help of large corporations: In 2007, Lenovo (联想) initiated the first venture philanthropy fund in mainland China, and has run an annual Social Enterprise Award ever since. In 2010, Intel followed suit. In 2012, DBS (星展银行) — a Singaporean bank with branches in Shanghai — has initiated banking services for Chinese SEs, sponsoring capacity building of four local SEs. Still, the sector is not mature yet: There are still misperceptions by the public at large; most startups are more "social" than "entrepreneurial" in spirit, lacking a viable business model; a good number of Chinese SEs depend heavily on grant or procurement from government; talented people still hesitate to engage in the sector; opportunities for training remain few; and the field of action remains limited, with more companies trying to "catch fishes" for the people they aspire to serve rather than "teaching them how to fish" or changing the fishing industry...[3] As a consequence, many of the experiences are short-lived; some companies are actually charities, the solvability of which is ensured by parent organizations; the label is often used in a rather indiscriminate fashion. Still, a progressive maturation of the market and the actors can be observed. Boxes 14.1 and 14.2 provide two case studies of successful SEs in China.

"Ventures in Development", started in 2006 by Marie Tze Kwan So and Carol Chyau, provides the analyst with another interesting case: It makes use of the resources provided by yaks, an abundant resource in Western China, for developing unique products for the high-end

---

[2] *Shehuiqiye zai zhongguo jueqi* (Social Enterprises on the Rise in China), May 24, 2012, 21 *shiji jingji baodao* (21 世纪经济报道), http://finance.ifeng.com/news/macro/20120524/6505062.shtml, accessed July 31, 2013.

[3] Cf. Gu, Y. (2012), Major Issues in Social Enterprises' Development in the Mainland China, *Social Entrepreneurs Newsletter*, 139, December 10, 2012, http://www.hksef.org/files/files/Social_Entrepreneurs_Newsletter_No__139.pdf, accessed July 31, 2013.

Box 14.1 Dialogue Social Enterprise (DSE)

DSE is a German-based SE that provides employment opportunities to vulnerable groups, through both exhibitions (*Dialogue in the Dark*) and executive workshops led by visually impaired trainers. It works toward eliminating prejudice and discrimination against disabled and disadvantaged groups, as well as strengthening interpersonal communication and trust. It entered China in 2011, and an overseas Chinese, Cai Shiyin, has become its global COO and its Chinese branch's CEO. There are at least 19 million visually impaired people in China. For many years, their options for work were limited to massage. DSE, through the workshop it organizes, provides them with new working opportunities, while confirming its reputation as a successful social business.

Source: Robards, K. (n.d.), Dialogue in the Dark, http://www.shanghai247.net/style/feature/dialogue-dark, accessed July 31, 2013.

Box 14.2 Shanghai Young Bakers: On the Road to Sustainability

Founded in 2008, Shanghai Young Bakers (SYB) provides a fully-sponsored French bakery training to disadvantaged Chinese youth (aged 17–23), enabling them to find qualified jobs and lead independent lives after graduation. During the one-year training, SYB students follow classes in a traditional Western bakery, learning lifeskills and English, combined with a practical internship at international hotels. Thanks to the help of corporate sponsors such as Carrefour Foundation and PSA Foundation, SYB has gradually developed its own resources. Through a long-standing partnership with the French bakery school EFBPA, SYB trained their best students in France so that they could take on the responsibility of the program's training and technical development independently. As a SE, SYB offers three main services: public baking classes for friends and companies, catering and sale of students' production at markets, and consulting for F&B professionals who need expertise in French bakeries and pastries. After a careful start in the second half of 2011, the SYB now raises enough to cover 10 percent of its charity training financial needs, and aims to increase this part to 15 percent in 2013 and 50 percent in 2015.

Source: Shanghai Young Bakery (2011), About Us, http://www.shanghaiyoungbakers.com, accessed July 31, 2013.

international market (luxury textile and gourmet yak cheese), having met with several challenges along the way when it comes to logistics and marketing: "Chasing yaks were never in our plans when we prepared for our education at Harvard, nor was it anticipated from our professors, who were training us to be practitioners for the World Bank, the UN or national policy makers."[4] The sense of adventure experienced by several social startup-ers certainly testifies both to the entrepreneurial spirit that inspires them and to the way a company's potential objectives are presently broadening, as a trend already noted in the course of our first chapter.

The setting up of SEs often fosters collaboration between various actors jointly interested in the creation of shared social value, as illustrated by Box 14.3.

Reflecting on the scope of operations covered by social entrepreneurship, Yu Xiaomin observes that China's SEs are currently operating throughout a wide range of sectors, notably work integration, social care, healthcare, poverty alleviation and education development. The recent rise of SEs in China was driven by forces that emerged during the market reforms — the state's efforts to privatize public services, the third sector's endeavors to play a greater role in solving social problems, the private sector's growing interest in CSR and venture philanthropy, and international players' activities to foster social entrepreneurship in China.[5] However, compared to Western countries, the institutional and financial context is less favorable to the development of SEs. Notably, the concept of "social ownership" or "multi-stakeholder ownership" is not enshrined into a specific legal status. Existing SEs in China are registered as for-profit companies, the ownership and control rights being legally retained by investors and not necessarily shared with other stakeholders, especially the beneficiaries.[6] Still, the development of a more

---

[4]So, M.T.K. & C. Chyau (2010), China Case Study, in R. Gunn & C. Durkin (eds.), *Social Entrepreneurship: A Skills Approach*, Bristol: The Policy Press, p. 151.

[5]Yu, X. (2011), Social Enterprise in China: Driving Forces, Development Patterns and Legal Framework, *Social Enterprise Journal*, 7(1), pp. 9–32.

[6]The legacy of Maoism has nurtured in China a strong disinclination toward cooperative business.

Box 14.3 Netspring Social Enterprise: A Pilot for Creation of Shared Value in China

Netspring is a SE that aims at mobilizing key industry players in the e-recycling economy whilst bringing digital education to underprivileged children in China. Netspring, with its *Green IT Classrooms* program, is committed to reduce environment and poverty issues by developing the recycling economy, creating shared value between developed and under-developed Chinese areas and helping vulnerable groups such as poverty-stricken students or people with disabilities. Through e-waste pollution reduction and the building of IT classrooms, the company aims at becoming a successful SE, a pioneer in China, and thrives to achieve a sustainable business model in order to help more poverty-stricken children and protect the environment in the long run. Nowadays, more and more computers and other electronic equipments become obsolete, as the replacement rate of electronic products increases. In China, at least five million computers are discarded and turned into e-waste every year. Over 70 percent of them are collected by illegal private recycling vendors are dismantled, and even burned. Such practice causes massive toxic chemical release, heavily polluting the air, the water and the soil, and is harmful to human health. However, a good number of these computers are still in good working conditions and could be reused after appropriate repair. At the same time, more than 50 million Chinese students in under-developed rural areas have no access to computers and other ways of digital communication. They are longing for opportunities to learn more and to widen their horizon and their opportunities. Netspring SE focuses on mobilizing companies and educational institutions to build IT classrooms for the underprivileged with their old IT equipment, whilst protecting the environment via certified environmentally friendly disposal of electronic waste.

autonomous third sector in China is a trend presently nurtured by a strong social drive (Box 14.4).

14.2. Fair Trade and Related Movements

Associated with the SE movement are the Fair Trade organizations. Fair trade labeling organizations most commonly refer to a definition

QUESTIONS

— Are there sub-products of our business that could be managed in such a way as to generate social value?
— Would these sub-products be better managed directly by our company, or could the creation of a SE be more appropriate?
— Under which conditions could this SE be able to creatively manage our sub-products or other aspects of our businesses which could help solve a given issue or answer special needs, if sufficient attention, good planning and creativity are brought to the task?
— How do we develop the management team's skills so as to ensure its sustainability?

developed by FINE, an informal association of four international fair trade networks (Fairtrade Labelling Organizations International, World Fair Trade Organization (WFTO), Network of European Worldshops and European Fair Trade Association (EFTA)): Fair trade is a trading partnership, based on dialogue, transparency, and respect, that seeks greater equity in international trade. It contributes to sustainable development by offering better trading conditions to, and securing the rights of, marginalized producers and workers — especially in the South. Fair trade organizations, backed by consumers, are engaged actively in supporting producers, raising awareness and in campaigning for changes in the rules and practice of conventional international trade. For coffee, the best-known Fair Trade product, producers sell to a primary cooperative, which sells to secondary or tertiary cooperatives in charge of the exporting. The importer must pay a minimum price for coffee at times when the world price collapses, and at all times must pay 10 percent per pound above the world price for any coffee it intends to sell as Fair Trade. The higher price goes to the exporter. The higher price is called the "social premium" and the exporting cooperatives and primary cooperatives use it on business expenses and on the costs of reaching Fair Trade standards and getting certification. The exporting cooperatives and primary

Box 14.4 China and the Global Social Entrepreneurship Trend

"In 2007, the Youth Business Development International initiative of the Oxford Saïd Business School introduced its experiences to China by establishing Youth Business Development China (YBDC). As a student-led organization, YBDC strives to empower young Chinese social entrepreneurs and promote social entrepreneurship in China by providing competition, training, networking opportunities and support to current and future social entrepreneurs. Similarly, since 2008, the CESBE in China has organized three sessions of 'Social Entrepreneur Skill Training'. Jointly sponsored by the China Social Entrepreneur Foundation and the Narada Foundation, the program has provided professional training to over 370 potential social entrepreneurs in China... In April 2010, the ECSEL 2010 Program brought Chinese students to the USA for a weeklong program designed to assist aspiring social entrepreneurs on their path to building businesses that create positive change. Leading microfinance institutions, such as the Grameen Bank, have made increased efforts to implement in China the innovative financial service model targeting impoverished people as a vehicle for reducing poverty and enhancing socio-economic development... The most concrete progress was achieved in October 2009, when the Grameen Trust of Bangladesh and the Alibaba Group decided to join hands to create Grameen China, an initiative aiming to provide microcredit financial services to China's poorest residents, with a view to creating income-generating opportunities for the latter and helping them achieve a higher standard of living... Venture philanthropy is another field where international investment institutions are playing an active role to support social entrepreneurship in China."

Source: Yu, X. (2011), Social Enterprise in China: Driving Forces, Development Patterns and Legal Framework, *Social Enterprise Journal*, 7(1), p. 17.

cooperatives also use it on social projects in education, health or recreation among others. Box 14.5 highlights some organizations in China that promote fair trade.

Such a trend needs to be closely watched by corporations, as it may help them to redirect their CSR and philanthropic efforts throughout inventive channels by initiating partnerships with employees, young

Box 14.5 Some Organizations Involved in Fair Trade in China

Fair Trade Guide — China (http://www.ifairguide.org/web/index.jsp): the first organization in China involved in fair-trade — specialized in handicrafts, with sales via the internet, and also in some stores and cafes.

Mannong Ancient Tea Association (http://www.fairtradenap.net/mannong-ancient-tea-association/): tea producers.

Fly-Out Products Limited (http://www.ecvv.com/company/chinacraftgift/profile.html).

Organic and Fairtrade Soybean (http://www.gongchang.com/Organic_and_Fairtrade_Soybean-dp10776825/).

Dongguan Hengjin Packaging Products Co., Ltd. (http://www.tradevv.com/chinasuppliers/cndghs): only t-shirt bags are fair-trade products.

Source: Compiled by the author.

entrepreneurs or advocacy groups so as to help to ensure the sustainability and professional management of specific social initiatives. SEs can be strategically planned as startups, initiated by corporations and achieving their independence early on, or they may remain on quasi-subsidiaries of the parent company, desirous to manage its social or philanthropic mission through the specific instruments they offer.

14.3. From Social Entrepreneurship to Community Investment

There is one remaining issue that deserves more detailed discussion: We have already noted that the social impact created by Chinese SEs remains very much limited in practice. Many promising initiatives still fail to foster a grassroots dynamic within the targeted local communities. Linking social entrepreneurship and community investing strategies may help all actors to engineer a more integrative approach. Community investment aims at financing or guaranteeing loans to individuals and organizations for housing, the creation of small business, public health, education or environmental preservation. It generally comes with training and other types of support and expertise so as to ensure success on the ground as well as financial returns. In a context reshaped by significant community investment, SEs may then develop specific skills and projects inserted within an overall local strategy. For instance, a minority district of, say, Southwest China — where youths come back to the land after an extended period in coastal cities as migrant workers — may benefit from an integrated developmental strategy centered on eco-tourism, niche productions and new educational opportunities, while dedicated SEs provide locals the skills and jobs that make the community strategy effective and sustainable.

In other words, when trying to devise relevant initiatives for community development, all actors will need to rely on potential partners and to assess the way various participants in the process may complement each other. When it comes to social startups, they should target precisely the sector or area of their operations and make sure that they are rooted into an integrated developmental strategy. Planners trying to devise an area's community project will need to attract active and capable social startup-ers, so as to combine loans or grants destined to the community as a whole, with investment aimed at commercial projects that are both social and profitable. And corporations participating in the process on the basis of their social responsibilities will need to cement *ad hoc* partnerships. However, studies show that, till now, while many corporations — both national and international — somehow invest in community development (especially in education and disaster relief), most companies have no system or measurement tool to measure the impact of the company's contributions to communities. Additionally, most of them had no fixed budgets for these actions, or were not clear on the exact amount of their spending. Though companies involved in community development feel generally extremely positive about it, they have to recognize their lack of know-how when it comes to selecting the best partners and communicating with them, finding projects related to their core business, and measuring the impact of projects.[7] A three-way partnership between: (a) local planners

---

[7] See CSR Asia Beijing (2009), *CSR Asia: Survey on Community Investment of Companies Operating in China*, http://www.csr-asia.com/cdf/download/Report_pre_CIRT_Beijing.pdf, accessed July 31, 2013.

and communities; (b) capable and focused SEs; and (c) corporations committed to their social responsibilities may be a privileged way to foster innovative community development in China, provided that adequate financial investment is allowed and carefully monitored. An example of the relationship established between community development and a company's core business is provided in Box 14.6.

Box 14.6 China Mobile: Integrative Approach to CSR and Community Investment

China Mobile, a state-owned telecommunication company, also listed on the NYSE and Hong Kong stock exchanges, is the world's largest mobile phone operator by number of subscribers and in 2012, is ranked 29th on business magazine Forbes' "Global 2000" 2013. It traditionally possesses a larger rural market share than its competitors. To these subscribers, it offers services such as sale and purchase of agricultural products, access to market prices, transfers, withdrawals, and payments.

China Mobile's Sustainability Report 2012 takes an integrative approach to CSR, primarily stressing anti-corruption measures, supply chain initiatives, protection of customer privacy and information security. Employees' occupational health and safety are described at the second axis of the company CSR's policy. Programs to help alleviate poverty, promote education development, as well as volunteering services, come in third place, while the focus on energy saving and emissions reduction measures throughout the entire life-cycle of the networks is described as the fourth priority.

"For China Mobile, targeted poverty alleviation does not simply mean the provision of funding support, but rather that poverty-stricken areas can only be truly helped through the adequate use of the company's resources, technology, and management expertise... In Gansu, we invested one million yuan to improve basic facilities and alleviate chronic water shortages. In addition, agricultural and herding specialists were invited to teach in many villages on topics such as animal breeding, crop horticulture, and to provide on-site guidance to farmers, in order to improve rural residents' technological abilities in cultivation and breeding. In Hebei, we raised 620,000 yuan to implement drinking water projects for people and livestock in Su Jia Ju village to resolve residential and industrial water

(Continued)

Box 14.6 (*Continued*)

problems suffered by the villagers for almost 30 years. In addition, projects encouraging the modernization of chicken, pig, and sheep breeding facilities and vegetable greenhouses successfully commenced. In Guangdong, we carried out over 150 person-times of training for junior level rural cadres in Qingyuan city. The trainings, conducted based on our experience in establishing strong performance management, aimed to improve agricultural management links and support the design and development of the Excellent Village Management Model."

Source: China Mobile (2012), *China Mobile Limited 2012 Sustainability Report*, p. 25, http://www.chinamobileltd.com/en/ir/reports/ar2012/sd2012.pdf?year=2012, accessed July 31, 2013.

CHAPTER FIFTEEN

The Role of the Corporation in Tomorrow's China

We now intend to mobilize resources that may help companies operating in China to enrich and further the corporate vision governing their CSR strategies and practices. These resources come mainly from task-forces or from international institutions working together with the Chinese government. Though the scope of vision of the reports and analyses we build upon may seem to go beyond the corporate field of action, the interconnectedness of the issues that China and the international community are dealing with makes it necessary for all actors to engage in a global assessment of their priorities and means of action.

15.1. The Corporation and Global Public Goods

In 2006, an international taskforce (The International Task Force on Global Public Goods, originally created through an agreement between France and Sweden) submitted a report called *International Cooperation in National Interest, Meeting Global Challenges*.[1] The approach it develops enriches the way we understand the scope and the ultimate goal of international cooperation and the horizon in which to situate a style of corporate governance wholly integrating sustainability and CSR imperatives.

Some of the goals that the international community taken as a whole strives to achieve can be understood in reference to the concept of "global public goods". Technically, public goods are those that share two rare qualities — non-excludability and non-rivalry, in economists' jargon. This means, respectively, that when provided to one party, the

---

[1]http://www.cic.nyu.edu/scarcity/docs/archive/2006/Global%20Challenges.pdf

public good is available to all, and consumption of the public good by one party does not reduce the amount available to the others. Traditional examples of national public goods include traffic control systems and national security — goods that benefit all citizens and national private actors but none of which could manage or supply on their own initiative. Public goods can be regional or global in character, as well as national. There are many cross-border challenges that are more effectively dealt with at the regional or global rather than the national level. Clear examples of regional public goods are the provision of tsunami early warning systems, the management of river basins and measures to deal with cross-border transmission of human and animal diseases. Global public goods are those whose benefits could in principle be consumed by the governments and peoples of all states. Examples include mechanisms for ensuring financial stability, the scientific knowledge involved in the discovery of a vaccine and international regulations for civil aviation and telecommunications. Once such global standards and systems are established, they are available to all states, and consumption of the good by one state or its people in no way reduces its availability to others.

The report focuses on six global public goods whose provision is critical: preventing the emergence and spread of infectious disease; tackling climate change; enhancing international financial stability; strengthening the international trading system; achieving peace and security — which underlies and is essential to all the others; and the cross-cutting issue of knowledge.

15.1.1. *Preventing the emergence and spread of infectious diseases*

Infectious diseases have the potential to threaten the health of every person and the prosperity of every nation. National health defenses are inadequate and will not work in isolation. The actions of other countries matter to any nation seeking to defend its population. Ideally, the risk of emergence and spread of infectious disease would be met by a fully functioning surveillance system and a fluid supply of vaccines for the most deadly diseases.

15.1.2. Tackling climate change

A growing body of evidence demonstrates that global warming is occurring and the pace of change is increasing. Its long-term consequences will likely be severe. The most efficient response is to broaden the use of carbon taxes, which would both reduce emissions of carbon dioxide, the most important greenhouse gas, and generate revenues to pay for global public goods.

15.1.3. Enhancing international financial stability

Policies and actions that promote financial stability and prevent instability are clearly in the international public interest, for financial turbulence tends to spill across borders and has substantial economic and social costs.

15.1.4. Strengthening the international trading system

Despite its remarkable evolution, the multilateral trading system is not quite as global, as public or as good as potentially it can be. Notwithstanding the ideal of universality and the principles of reciprocity and non-discrimination that have been present since its origins, as the system has grown, over time it has accommodated rules that, in contradiction to those principles, allow for discriminatory treatment of products and trading partners. The system has permitted greater protectionism in products of significant export interest for developing countries.

15.1.5. Achieving peace and security

In the absence of an effective collective security system, not only will the levels of war, terrorism and other forms of strife increase, but international prosperity will also be at risk or even reversed. There are many urgent and important policy challenges ahead in this area, but the report emphasizes three fronts in need of urgent action: combating international terrorism; nuclear non-proliferation and disarmament; and agreement on when the use of military force is legitimate.

15.1.6. *Generating knowledge*

Knowledge is perhaps the clearest example of a public good. Knowledge, once generated, can be shared at the same time by large numbers of people (at least in principle), and it is hard for creators of knowledge to maintain exclusive property of it. Hence, if left to market forces alone, there would always be a tendency to under-invest in the generation of knowledge. Knowledge is not only a national public good; it is a global public good as well, its diffusion not being stopped by borders. People in any nation could in principle benefit from scientific or technological knowledge produced in other nations. Knowledge is by itself critical for development, at the same time as it serves as an input to the provision of other global public goods. However, the spontaneous globalization of knowledge does not occur, largely because many countries, due to deficiencies in their educational systems, have limited capacity to assimilate existing and new knowledge. Another important barrier to spontaneous globalization is that knowledge has been made to some degree excludable by the adoption of intellectual property rights.

Private companies are not direct channels for the distribution of such public goods, as the growth of these goods and the access to them are driven by international cooperation and governed by the principle of gratuity. However, corporations are clearly among the actors that create the potential needed for increasing and sharing these goods, doing so through innovation, business practices, cooperation among themselves and sometimes philanthropy. Once a company identifies the relationship between its line of business and the public goods that a society strives to nurture and share among its citizens, it becomes able to reformulate its vision and social contribution in ways that resonate with a large coalition of actors. It also helps the company to better determine its policies regarding innovation, sharing of resources, cooperating with public and private actors, and its sustainability model. China is both a large consumer and producer of global public goods, and has a stakeholder's interest in their growth. The way public goods are perceived and pursued can be illustrated, in the Chinese context, by the work conducted together by the World Bank and the Development Research Center of China's State Council, summarized in the next section.

UESTIONS

— Can we describe and locate our operations and products in relation to global public goods such as the prevention of disease; the tackling of climate change; financial stability; the strengthening of the international trading system; peace and security, and the sharing of knowledge? Is there any direct or indirect relationship between our core activities and such goals?

— If these goals seem be too lofty or very far away from what we achieve and deliver, can we define in our own way the "public goods" that our activities contribute to produce, enrich and distribute?

— Can we further specify these goods in relation to the Chinese context, according to the priorities and concerns described in this book and our experience in the field?

15.2. China 2030

The report *China 2030: Building a Modern, Harmonious, and Creative High-Income Society*[2] has received widespread attention: stemming from a joint effort by the World Bank and China's State Council (see Box 15.1). Compliant with the directions set up by the 12th National Plan, the report aims at framing the course through which China may enter a new, more sustainable stage of development, and directly inspires the current process of structural reforms. The joint report pushes for six major shifts, the first three being of more direct interest for our topic:

— The government is to provide less tangible public goods and more intangible public goods and services like systems, rules, and policies, which increase production efficiency, promote competition, facilitate specialization, enhance the efficiency of resource allocation, protect the environment, and reduce risks and uncertainties.

---

[2]World Bank (2012), China 2030: Building a Modern, Harmonious, and Creative Society, February 27, 2012, http://www.worldbank.org/en/news/2012/02/27/china-2030-executive-summary, accessed July 31, 2013.

Box 15.1 China 2030: Moving Toward Green Development

"Concerned that past and current economic growth patterns are environmentally unsustainable and that the environmental base needed to sustain economic prosperity may be irreversibly altered, the Chinese authorities proposed a new approach toward green development in the 12th Five-Year Plan. The plan emphasizes continued rapid growth together with ambitious targets for energy efficiency, natural resource management, and environmental sustainability. This approach is consistent with the concept of green development used in this study, namely, a pattern of development that decouples growth from heavy dependence on resource use, carbon emissions, and environmental damage, and that promotes growth through the creation of new green product markets, technologies, investments, and changes in consumption and conservation behavior."

Source: World Bank (2012, p. 39).

In the enterprise sector, besides reforming further state enterprises, the focus is on private sector development and increased competition in all sectors and internationalization of China's financial sector. In the labor market, China needs to ensure that by 2030, Chinese workers can move in response to market signals, a move that must go along with measures to increase labor force participation rates, reform wage policy and social security instruments. Finally, rural land markets need to be overhauled to protect farmers' rights and increase efficiency of land use.

— The pace of innovation must be accelerated, with the creation of an open innovation system in which competitive pressures encourage Chinese firms to engage in product and process innovation not only through their own research and development but also by participating in global research and development networks. An additional focus should be on building a few world-class research universities with strong links to industry; fostering "innovative cities" that bring together high-quality talent, knowledge networks, dynamic firms, and learning institutions, and allow them to interact without restriction.

— The third new strategic direction is that China should "grow green". Instead of considering environmental protection and climate change mitigation as burdens that hurt competitiveness and slow growth, green development could potentially become a significant new growth opportunity. Government policies can motivate firms to innovate and seek technological breakthroughs. China could grow green by following a pattern of economic growth that boosts environmental protection and technological progress.

— Providing social security for all, strengthening the fiscal system, and engaging in mutually beneficial relationships with the rest of the world constitute respectively the fourth, fifth and sixth strategic priorities.[3]

The report intends to be a blueprint for the course of development to be followed during the next two decades, and provide an inspiration not only to policy-makers but also to all social actors bringing in their contribution to make China a greener, fairer and more affluent society. It explicitly stresses the role of social ethos at all levels of society (see Box 15.2).

Box 15.2 Grounding Economic Governance on Moral Awareness

"Social values and high moral standards will be important. There is widespread concern in China over many recent instances of 'moral failures' that were reported widely in the media. As China becomes a high-income society, its social values and moral standards should be reexamined and reinforced. From a social perspective, not only will this contribute to improving the quality of life, it will also provide a greater sense of community and enhance social cohesion. From an economic perspective, it will reduce transaction costs and improve the quality of economic governance. Promoting social values and high moral standards is not only the job of government; it is also the duty of social organizations and, indeed, every citizen. Moral awareness, not legal compulsion, should be the hallmark of a high-income, harmonious society."

Source: World Bank (2012, p. 20).

---

[3] Ibid., summary provided in pp. 21–23.

UESTIONS

— What does the expected shift of China toward a greener, fairer and more affluent society within the next two decades mean for our operations?
— Are we alert to what such evolutions imply when it comes to the structure of our workforce and the expectations of our consumers?
— Do we adapt our corporate strategy and image to the trends envisioned by the national leadership and international organizations?
— Do we participate in the drive toward more creativity and high-quality research in China, by partnering with Chinese universities for instance, or through our internal training programs?
— Is China seen by us only as a "market", or is it strategically included into the global vision defined by our company, insisting on the contribution it can make to our corporate model and our qualitative development?

The wording of the orientations sketched here proves to be most helpful for companies trying to map their vision and strategy in the changing economic, cultural and social landscape of China. At the very least, grasping their background and rationale averts the risk of making major mistakes on the developmental path to be followed by a corporation, making it alert to the challenges and directions identified at the highest level. It also enables a company to integrate these challenges and directions into its new corporate vision for China and to craft a localized, appropriate response grounded on its specific resources.

CHAPTER SIXTEEN

Conclusion and Prospects

Throughout this book we have tried to articulate as a whole a number of findings, the most important of which can be summarized as follows:

1. A sense of CSR is a regulating mechanism through which a company asserts the degree of consistency existing between its vision and values on the one hand, and its actual practices on the other, and tries accordingly to optimize the effect of its operations on all its stakeholders.

2. There is a strong cultural dimension to the rise and expression of corporate responsibility, and the concept evolves according to different times and countries. At the same time, many requirements and values defining the field of application of CSR are now globalized and are shared from country to country, this being linked to international regulations (UN Global Compact), the transnational character of business operations, the rise of an international public opinion, and the progressive formulation of what could be called world ethics.

3. China is fully part of such a trend, and CSR-related concerns have emerged here sooner than it is often realized. Even the complaints often heard in the Chinese social media about low ethical standards and the unsustainable character of many business operations testify to the interest raised by these issues and their integration within the ongoing social and entrepreneurial debate.

4. Chinese traditional cultural resources are often described as being difficult to conciliate with CSR-based values. Opposite opinions hold that the Chinese traditional culture is rooted deeply in values like integrity, loyalty and trust that are conducive to CSR-inspired

behaviors. Though both arguments have merits, they show a tendency to rigidify given expressions of the "Chinese culture", neglecting the fact that the content and style of the latter widely varies according to the times and schools of thought.

5. It is better to envision Chinese culture in its conversational and interpretative dimension: Cultural tenets are continuously reinterpreted, taking into account changes in situations, new interlocutors entering the dialogue, evolving cultural resources, and the diversity of wisdom traditions that have all contributed to define and to change China. Seen in this light, Chinese culture — including its most recent expressions — provides the country with precious and flexible resources with which to enter the global conversation on corporate responsibility and sustainable development.

6. The new focus on corporate responsibility and sustainability is supported by a growing corpus of laws and regulations. Even if some of these texts sometimes fall short on specifics, they map a way of proceeding that will determine more and more the expectations and principles on which companies are perceived and judged by the state and by the public.

7. It is thus not enough for companies to follow the letter of the law. Regulations, laws and other official documents call on them to adopt a proactive attitude through which to implement CSR in its broadest sense. We have detailed in this book the growing range of domains that CSR in China now covers.

8. Additionally, sustainability, social fairness and alignment on international standards now constitute the key dimensions through which the Chinese government — supported in this view by international institutions — hopes to reform its current course of development. This ensures that CSR imperatives are not an additional burden on companies as they were sometimes perceived, but rather the cornerstones of a new developmental model.

9. This must encourage corporations operating in China to further integrate CSR practices and policies within their overall business strategy, which may sometimes lead them to rephrase their vision and mission in a way that enlarges their scope and appeal.

10. To do so, they can mobilize a variety of traditional instruments and channels — communication policy, mechanisms of social dialogue, innovation centers, evaluation procedures, foundations, subsidiary companies organized as social enterprises — the stress being on the consistency of the approach being fostered and on the creative and synergic use of such instruments.

11. The framing of codes, the devising of examples and case studies, an ambitious policy of human and technical training based on attractive modules, and the implications of employees both in training programs directed toward other stakeholders and in CSR-inspired pilot projects, all of this progressively makes CSR and sustainability the core of a company's corporate culture.

12. Finally, when engaging in such actions, the company consistently considers itself as an *interdependent self*, and associates closely with an array of local and international knowledge networks, Chinese universities, research centers and constituencies, national and local governments, so as to learn from all these agents, share with them its goals and experiences, establish trust and reputation, and continuously adapt its policies according to evolving challenges and conditions.

It is on the basis of these findings that we have tried to connect facts, case analysis and proposals into a cogent argument, while keeping the narrative flexible enough to allow for varying interpretations and focuses according to the core business of the companies and decision-makers who wish to use this material for assessing, redefining and implementing their own CSR strategy. While this conclusion tries to develop the implications of our analysis, Chapter 17 gathers together the proposals sketched or detailed along these pages, so as to help decision-makers map a subsequent course of action.

16.1. Global Challenges and the Art of Interpretation

Rather than coming with ready-made solutions, we have tried to approach CSR as an exercise in creative and critical thinking. We have stressed the fact that Chinese culture (if the term is to receive a specific meaning) is based on the art of *interpreting* classics and traditions — and philosophizing in China amounted for a long time to the task of writing commentaries, one's thoughts being tested and developed through the interpretation of a previous body of writings. Interestingly enough, the same can be said of CSR assessment and implementation: Companies and decision-makers confronted to the task of making their operations more ethical and sustainable need first and foremost to interpret batteries of indicators, employees' expectations, public opinion and evolving state policies, so as to convert all these factors into a consistent, creative and sustainable policy. The lesson of this analogy can be further enlarged: *To be an "interpreter" is what a leader needs to be in Asia today, as Asia deals with an immense and disconcerting array of cultural, social and human resources.*

Making sense of diversity — an operation that grounds the interpretative process — can be equated with the task of developing *meaningful encounters* between people of different cultural, spiritual, linguistic and social backgrounds. To speak of a "meaningful" relationship is to spontaneously refer to an array of feelings and perceptions: First, there is some kind of a *taste* developing throughout the exchange, the pleasure that arises from conversation, mixing of languages, exoticism, discovery, and perhaps even friendship; second, there is the mutual acknowledgment that reciprocal displacements are taking place in the process — broadening of views, change in opinions and prejudices, and, to a certain extent, sharing of emotions and memories, be they collective or personal. A "meaningful" relationship transforms, creates, and carries forward *meanings*, seen as bits of perception, evaluation and interpretation of facts, people, places, texts or events. Eventually, a "meaningful" relationship develops from or evolves into shared projects and practical cooperation in order to fulfill common objectives.

The first glimpse of "meaning" that appears in a trans-cultural exchange — be it mediated through corporate interactions or in other contexts — has to do with the discovery of some *commonality*. However, ordinarily such a commonality is not of a positive nature but rather of a negative one: It is about the sharing of crises and challenges. *Globalization is first and foremost the globalization of crises and challenges.* This might mean discovering — not only through words but through shared experience — that deforestation, waste of natural resources, the spread of contagious diseases or the opacity of financial markets are indeed challenges for all of us. The feeling of commonality might also arise from shared feelings about the collapse of traditional ways to understand one's world, identity and culture. Or it might come from a reflection upon the spreading of a culture of violence at school or in society at large, a reflection upon the difficulty to implement mechanisms of harmony and reconciliation. What we share first is a feeling of urgency and disarray.

The second stage of the process is to realize anew the *variety of the resources we mobilize or could mobilize for answering such challenges.* If we do confront common problems and crises, it is true also that there remain tremendous differences among world views rooted in Taoism, Buddhism, Islam, Christianity or among the core values found in Confucian, African or European societies. On life itself, on authority structures, on relationships with nature or with the other, on processes of discussion and evaluation, our ground intuitions, logical approaches, canonical texts and ingrained norms of behavior are as varied, divergent or contradictory as one can possibly imagine. Furthermore, our cultural traditions are embedded into historical memories that conflagrate one with another. Discovering the wide array of our differences might be, at the same time, exhilarating and extremely puzzling.

This is where a strategic choice is to be made: "Meaning" continues to flow and to circulate *whenever leaders decide to make this tremendous variety of cultural resources the toolbox that enables them to interpret anew their own tradition and culture (their corporate culture included) and to devise creative solutions on this very basis. Our cultures, world views and strategies are being reformulated through the interpretative resources offered by the other cultures, world views and ways of proceeding — and this operation happens simultaneously for all participants in the exchange.*

In this light, we become sensitive to the fact that corporate cultures need indeed to be reshaped and reinterpreted through a process of intercultural exchange, a process that the internationalization of China has opened up for many companies, be they Chinese or foreign. The intensity of the exchanges that have already taken place allow us to say that the globalization process and China's rise — both accelerated during the course of the 1980s — have been two faces of the same coin. Specifically, the attention on CSR and sustainability exhibited in a given corporate culture is reshaped and reinterpreted through the resources and challenges met by the corporation in the Chinese context — and likewise the solutions the corporation progressively devises will be shaped by its Chinese experience.

16.2. Ethical Empowerment, Cultural Diversity and Sustainable Development

In the current Asian and Chinese context, a focus on the synergic dimension of CSR-based concerns helps corporate leaders to assert their vocation at being *interpreters*, people who make sense of the array of technical, cultural and human resources that surround them, so as to give meaning and focus to the endeavors they desire to promote. Ultimately, responsible leadership today might be based upon three pillars: *ethical empowerment; sense of cultural diversity, and commitment to sustainable development*. None of these pillars can support the whole edifice if the other two are lacking.

"Ethical empowerment" refers here to the conviction that the capacity for discernment is not reserved to an elite, be it managerial or otherwise. Discernment is democratic: Everyone is entitled and has the duty to assess the situations she/he is involved in, be it at the corporate or the personal level, so as to enact value judgments and to act accordingly. This focus on "ethical empowerment" also enlarges and enriches our approach to "leadership": Real leaders are the ones who empower their employees in such a way as to nurture their independence, critical thinking and sense of humaneness. Again, this is to be the cornerstone of any corporate CSR policy, otherwise at the grassroots level implementation might never follow. Furthermore, the sense of "empowerment" that education and corporate-based training provides us with is not meant for our sole benefit, it is akin to an accrued capacity for discernment. A person who is ethically awakened will be more conscious of the challenges that threaten the environment at large. "Ethics" is a set of resources for improving and maturing not only as an individual but also as a corporation and as a community.

At the same time, a focus on cultural diversity means that we mobilize the whole array of resources available in our corporation and our larger environment for devising solutions to the challenges that we are meeting. Culture, as we have previously said, is to be seen as a set of resources to be creatively interpreted and reinterpreted according to the challenges we face. Being able to "interpret" our own cultural resources also makes us able to communicate across language, mindset or culture. The act of communication that takes place through our differences is the cornerstone on which trust and solidarity within our organization (and beyond it) can be built. Harmony and cooperation are to be understood as a dynamic; they arise from an awakened desire, and are not to be identified to an immutable state of things.

Finally, "sustainable development" is not to be defined in primarily technical terms; rather, it has to do with our capacity to devise an "integral development" model, linking an array of concerns and resources into a coherent whole throughout an unfolding conversation. By focusing on the durability of any developmental process, the expression "sustainable development" opens up questions linked to the "Why" of our collective action (thus relating to the realm of self-examination and self-awareness) while borrowing from the diversity of our cultural resources for inventing new answers to the various challenges that our value systems and our corporate experience help us to assess and to order into a scale of concrete priorities. The three dimensions mentioned above do reinforce each other, and the goals they are pointing to will be achieved only as an organic whole.

16.3. Corporate Cultural Resources and China's New Developmental Model

The approach we have been sketching is meant to help us: (a) to assess the way our cultural resources (corporate culture, educational models, spiritualities and traditional wisdoms, and the civil society's modes of action) can be mobilized to shape the new model of development that China is striving to invent; (b) to see whether the Chinese experience in this field could bring in lessons for Asia and the world; and (c) to stress the fact that the very diversity of these resources constitutes by itself a factor of sustainability. Let us summarize in a few statements some of the principles, analyses and insights developed throughout this book.

1. China can successfully tackle its developmental challenges insofar as it relies on its regional, cultural, and intellectual diversity, while interpreting anew these resources and contributing their riches to the global community. This sense of diversity is nurtured by an international outlook that is largely developed through the conversation and cooperation undergone between the state, civil society and the corporations operating in China.

2. Sustainable development can be fostered only through the nurturing of a critical and creative mode of thinking itself grounded into humanistic culture and education; "humanism" takes different shapes across time and space — and Confucian culture was and remains an humanism — but it always induces individuals and societies to develop ethical and productive relationships, among peoples, among nations, cultures and regions, and also between humankind and nature. Sustainability is the new name given to a truly integral, humanistic developmental process, a process to which China is called to contribute.

3. Local development is always based on characteristics that make it impossible to simply repeat a developmental model from one area to another. In China's developmental "new frontiers", notably in the West, retrieving traditional lifestyle and cultures, restoring biodiversity and inventing a new "pastoral" developmental model could become an integral and systemic endeavor.

4. Nurturing networks of solidarity is not equivalent to creating sustainability *per se*. However, the development of such networks is a prerequisite to further reflection and action toward sustainability insofar as it makes all sectors of society (including the marginal ones) contribute in the endeavor; it also progressively fosters a new social consciousness about issues larger than the ones defined by one's immediate environment, and, through the power of

internet, allows new resources to be mobilized where they are lacking most (rural education and hygiene, ecotourism in regions struck by deforestation, etc.).

5. In the same vein, anti-pollution efforts, the development of bio-agriculture and eco-tourism, and the mitigation of the consequence of the rural exodus can succeed only if they are rooted into "community sustainability", i.e. the shared consciousness and sense of mission that local communities are able to discern, debate and act together, thanks to a knowledge of their past and a vision of their future.

6. Progress and investment in education are a prerequisite to any shift in developmental models, but educational efforts are prone to fail when local communities lack confidence in their own capacity to build up their future, and when their culture is challenged or denied in a way that destructs their capacity to come together as stakeholders of a given territory. Deforestation and erosion, exodus toward cities and the disappearance of traditional cultural resources and knowledge are symptoms of the same phenomenon. Sustainability can be achieved only when existing local resources are nurtured and enhanced. Conversely, local communities that have achieved a reasonable level of economic success and self-organization show a tendency to naturally shift their concerns toward environmental protection and the collective decision-making process.

7. "Safety" is intrinsically linked to sustainability, and it is often through safety concerns that companies enter into a global vision of what their social responsibility is about. "Safety in the work-place" and "food safety", to cite two examples, are not only about the shaping of technical regulations, they are eventually ensured thanks to: (a) the education of workers and consumers; (b) the way companies envision and enrich their own mission; and (c) the progressive mobilization of resources, images, symbols and values through some form of storytelling.

8. "Ethical empowerment" at the personal and collective levels (the way individuals and groups are able to discern and decide in a reflexive and prejudice-free way) as well as the "knowledge

network" (the mutual enrichment of one's experience through sharing, feedbacks, debate and support) allows all of us to make "ripples": Provided proper follow-up is ensured, collective assessment, networking and pilot projects do possess an impressive multiplying effect.

Ultimately, a corporate strategy that focuses more and more on CSR values and practices sees its creative potential greatly enhanced. The change in focus, the enlargement of one's field of vision and the connection with a whole new field of ideas and partners open up executives to hitherto unsuspected possibilities. This is even truer in China: The scope of the country, the intricate character of the challenges met by companies and the richness of the cultural and social fabric provide entrepreneurs with an abundance of new resources and viewpoints through which to rethink their mission and methods. Implementing CSR in China amounts to make sustainability and creativity one and the same endeavor, while anchoring solidly one's ethos and practices into the Chinese soil.

CHAPTER SEVENTEEN

Recommendations

CSR should be understood and implemented not only as a specific dimension of the corporate strategy but also — and more importantly — as an internal driving force nurtured by the contribution of the individual team members of the corporation. The objective of these recommendations is to foster, in the Chinese context, the emergence of a self-adapting CSR engine capable of delivering better insights for tackling corporate and developmental challenges.

17.1. Structures and Processes

1. Assessing, formulating and exercising CSR in China starts with assigning responsibility and defining structure, so as to clarify the sometimes confusing levels of decision existing within a given corporation. For foreign-owned companies, it also means that the company's China division or subsidiary will play a major role not only in the implementation but also in the assessment and formulation process.

2. The contribution of the China division or subsidiary to a company's global CSR strategy is not limited to China but should potentially enrich and focus the overall CSR strategy of the corporation.

3. The CSR assessment usually starts with a review of the record of the company in this domain and the production of a gap analysis when compared to the values and mission statement of the company.

4. Conceiving itself as an interdependent self, the corporation reviews not only its practices but its stakeholders' performances

and expectations as well. It pays special attention to the dialogue with and auditing of all partners involved into its supply chain.

5. The taskforce in charge of the CSR strategy is expected to develop a dialogue and consultation with all parties concerned, to write a policy statement, to develop corporate objectives and an action plan, to establish quantitative and qualitative targets and indicators, and to make sure that the formulation of the CSR policy it makes is embedded into the core business strategy.

6. Once the policy is established, performances must be communicated, and progress or failures need to be periodically monitored and reported, starting with the scrupulous observance of the legal framework for compliance.

7. Values and principles asserted in the chart or in the codes enacted by the company can be expressed and translated through a large array of concepts and expressions. However, they always need to stress the importance of accountability, transparency, sense of ethics and networking with all stakeholders. Such principles can be inculcated only if the functioning of the company and the behavior of its leadership rely on the same principles as the ones its discourse extols.

8. The formulation of a company's core business is to be conducted against the background of sustainability and CSR issues, with a special focus on China's main concerns and priorities; it needs to clearly express the contribution that the company can make to the solving of these challenges through the carrying out of its normal business operations.

9. It is also the duty and interest of the company to foster large coalitions, including actors from Chinese corporations, state and local organizations, university or research center, NGOs and social enterprises, concerned with the sustainability issues specifically linked to the exercise of its core business.

10. Within the corporation, it is recommended to appoint a person or a group — the independence of which has been sufficiently guaranteed — responsible for reviewing corporate procedures in such a way as to ensure that they conform to inner regulations and to existing laws. This person or group must also able to propose

amendments to the existing procedures and to forward ethical assessments regularly submitted to the governing structures. These assessments should also be used for enriching the training program, and they should be integrated into the review of the audit and legal departments.

11. A company should recruit local staff specializing in CSR-related issues and awareness. The persons employed must not be entrenched from the rest of the organization, rather they should work at an inter-departmental level, fostering awareness, training and cooperation, so as to make CSR issues an essential component of any corporate deliberation and decision, for strategic choices as well as for everyday decisions.

17.2. Policy Areas

12. The management and empowerment of personnel, well-being in the workplace, environmental issues, safety in process and products through the fostering of sound engineering ethics, and the establishment of strict financial ethics standards are requisite areas of concentration for any CSR strategy in China.

13. The understanding and internalization of the growing corpus of Chinese laws and regulations related to CSR cannot be restricted to the application of their specific regulations. The law itself calls for a dynamic, proactive and evolving enforcement of the standards it details or sometimes merely suggests. What is now asked from companies is to build, inculcate and implement their corporate culture in such a way as to make it fulfill not only the letter but also the spirit of the law.

14. Companies do not limit their CSR strategy to a revision of their own standards: They expect responsible behaviors from their business partners as well, especially from their suppliers, and they must frame their requirements in such a way as to allow for periodic reporting.

15. The use of natural resources is to be monitored through clear and reliable indicators. The search for technical decisions that reduce resource consumptions and drastically limit the risks associated

with them is at the core of all environmentally responsible corporate practices. This is especially true in China where natural resources are depleted and environmental risks are pervasive, throughout the entire chain of production and distribution.

16. The practical experience acquired in the process of reducing both consumption and risks must be clearly formulated and communicated. The corporate policy of waste and risk reduction must engage subsidiaries, providers, local communities and other stakeholders.

17. In their industrial practice as well as in their social and philanthropic initiatives, corporations should also pay attention to the maintenance and nurturing of biodiversity.

18. Corporate practices must go beyond the respect of legal and internal safety standards within the premises of the company: They should bring technical and cultural resources to their social environment, contributing to a progressive rise of safety standards. To that effect, employees should receive training empowering them to become disseminators and educators. Some pilot projects should focus on safety issues, and be implemented at the level of a village where a plant is located or in other local settings.

19. Corporate social policy should take into account the changing nature of the Chinese working force, focusing, on the one hand, on quality issues, and paying special attention, on the other, to the demands of marginalized constituencies, such as the much discriminated-against women migrant workers or other groups to be determined by the company according to the nature of its working force.

20. Labor standards need to be audited and implemented throughout the entire supply chain. The recurrence of issues, such as underage labor, grueling working conditions and bonded labor at some factories, calls for the building up of coalition among the stakeholders bearing shared responsibility for the social standards effectively applied. The danger of diluted responsibility and its corrosive effect on issues as sensitive as child labor make a corporation especially sensitive to what happens all along its supply chain. This implies that corporations should:

verify product supply chains so as to evaluate and address risks of abuses and maltreatments; obtain relevant certifications from direct suppliers; maintain internal accountability standards and procedures; and provide training to employees with direct responsibility for supply chain management. Besides, companies should be alert to global trends that tend to extent CSR practices to the monitoring of the entire supply chain, and to the international implications of laws and regulations passed in one given country.

21. The attention paid to the situation of migrant workers should be of a holistic nature, including training, attention to local development and to children's education. It would be hypocritical for corporations to strictly prohibit child labor within their factories without reflecting on its causes and integrating the issue into their proactive CSR policies. Lack of alternatives, such as affordable schooling, is a powerful factor driving child labor. Besides, as education is more and more perceived as a major tool for improving migrants' children integration to cities, corporate philanthropic programs may consider support programs conducted in this area.

22. Companies that are operating in China are now expected to focus on working contracts, wages and workplace environment as part of their overall strategy and image. The continuous improvement of employees' morale, training and living standards should be approached as both an ethical and a managerial imperative. The social dimension of CSR-related strategies accompanies a shift in China's global economic model and prospects, a shift that modifies the way the comparative advantages of conducting production and business in China must be evaluated.

23. When it comes to gender equality, the stress must be put on implementing and checking an effective policy of non-discrimination in hiring and in opportunities for promotion in the course of one's career. Furthermore, an assessment of the workplace climate, culture and facilities often needs to be conducted, so as to radically eliminate sources of abuse and humiliating situations. Whenever possible, paternity leaves should be considered, as

they level the field between male and female candidates for a position. And philanthropic policies may chose to concentrate on women's promotion in areas of poverty (rural or urban), since much resources is still needed in this sector and the empowerment of this specific segment of the population have proven to be a lever of overall social development.

24. A corporation's training policy must strike a balance between providing training in technical skills and programs aimed at personal development. Indicators on the target groups of the training programs, the percentage of the work force receiving training, the percentage of women receiving training relative to their percentage in the work force, and the balance between managers and non-managers in such trainings all need to be closely monitored.

25. Training programs must include the teaching of skills such as listening, teamwork and networking, encouraging employees to share the CSR vision and sustainability model of the company. This is often achieved through e-learning modules that provide employees with opportunities for ongoing training in managerial values and understanding of CSR issues. Brainstorming sessions should be held in order to solve complex CSR issues. The leadership should encourages authentic, honest and thorough exchanges on such matters so as to avoid CSR topics being equated to "ready-to-deliver" on the shelf assessments.

26. Suffering at work obviously depends first on the nature of the activity performed, the status of the individual within the corporation and practical working conditions. Its alleviation must start by ensuring that humane working conditions be provided to all, starting with the respect of minimal legal standards enhanced by specific proactive policies. Likewise, it requires respect shown to the contribution made by each member of the team, realistic demands made upon workers, and mechanisms of evaluation that take into account the wisdom and know-how of the teamwork and do not shatter the sense of self-esteem of the persons under scrutiny. The stress on teamwork must go with collective evaluation of performance rather than with a system of evaluation solely focused on individuals that unduly increases the level

of stress put on each employee. Ideally, work teams collectively determine performances they deem feasible, sharing rewards and responsibility when evaluating whether the objectives were achieved or not.

27. The evolving social landscape requires from corporations to pay special attention not only to the content of the demands coming from their employees but also to the style and the channels through which these demands are expressed. It requires them to progressively ascertain a style of communication and a bargaining method that responds to the expectations of their work force. The communication and bargaining style developed within the corporation is an integral part of the CSR-based values that it intends to foster and implement: Social bargaining is to be formative in nature, helping employees to internalize the vision and value system proper to the company they work for; trust, leadership and transparency are to be demonstrated in the way social demands are tackled.

28. Corporations can learn from the development of social entrepreneurship in China and elsewhere, identifying sub-products of their business that could be produced and distributed in such a way as to generate social value. Such sub-products can be managed directly by the company proper, or the setting up of a subsidiary social enterprise could be considered. The setting up of SEs often fosters collaboration between various actors jointly interested in the creation of shared social value.

17.3. Ethical Issues

29. Compliance mechanisms set up within a corporation must directly address auditing and inspections of factories, factories cheating, auditors taking bribes and other sensitive issues. The tackling of such challenges is a prerequisite for further engaging programs having to do with factory improvement and capacity building initiatives.

30. Anti-corruption regulations originating from within the company proper should generally be stricter than the ones enacted by the

national legal framework, especially when it comes to gift practices. In China, an international corporation should be aware of the fact that, should an official be investigated for corruption, his contacts with foreign-owned companies will be under particular scrutiny. It also happens that competing companies accuse each other of illegal practices, and strict internal regulations will help a firm to protect itself against such allegations if they are unfounded.

31. China's rapid development and globalization goes along with a growing sophistication in financial practices, with the benefits attached to added expertise and dangers associated with fraudulent behaviors potentially harder to identify. A large proportion of fraudulent financial practices are of a transnational nature. Financial ethics calls first for strict international standards expressed in a discourse that translates easily from one language or culture to another.

32. A partial antidote to fraudulent financial practices in China may be found in corporate strategies aimed at fostering "sustainable investment" or "socially responsible investment" (SRI), defined here as domestic and foreign investment in China's listed companies using strategies that take environmental, social and governance issues into consideration. These strategies include negative screening, positive screening, and shareholder activism, as well as approaches such as non-financial risk auditing/analysis. SRI also encourages "community investment", e.g. investments consented in sectors or geographical areas traditionally deprived of financial support.

33. Companies operating in China may consider facilitating the building up of engineering ethics resources (websites, textbooks, conferences and chairs) in Chinese engineering and business schools; encouraging the setting up (when needed) or the reinforcement of professional associations, provided these associations effectively monitor the reputation of the branch they cover; fostering within their organization an engineering culture working on peer-to-peer assessment, collective review of cases, and transparency, encouraging engineers to come up with issues such

as testing procedures, timetable, external pressures and conflicts of interests. However, some ethical issues have been raised when it comes to the behavior of certain professional associations and standardization committees. Therefore, corporations are both to edict strict norms as to engineers' participation in these instances, and to work toward improved ethical standards in their midst, as professional associations remain central to the self-regulation of a profession.

34. Potential conflicts of interest must be clearly spelled out in a company's internal regulations, cover the entirety of its line of business and operations, and be updated according to situations happening in the field. Additionally, the procedures to be activated in case of regulated situations must be clearly stated.

35. The areas of application of the codes, charters and sets of rules that a company chooses to enact must be precise enough, and it must be checked whether these codes are fully consistent among themselves or not. These codes must also be regularly updated and be illustrated with examples and case analyses, providing the reader both with intangible principles and — once the principles are settled — with space for discernment and interpretation. They must also be easily consulted and be introduced to all employees during training sessions.

36. Codes written for the Chinese context must include provisions referring explicitly to the growing local legislation on the issues at stake — labor conditions, social security, gender equality, corruption, consumer rights, and environmental standards. This contributes both to the effectiveness of such regulations and to the rooting of the company into its social environment.

37. CSR Reports must be written in such a way as to highlight areas of concerns and to effectively scale priorities. They must illuminate the self-understanding a corporation nurtures, and the way it maps its course of development. They must allow the reader to evaluate a company's consistency, capacity for adaptation and qualitative results.

38. A corporation's media plan must include provisions about the way it deals with CSR-related issues, and comprise a ready

strategy, in case of a campaign detrimental to its reputation, as a reliable agent of sustainable development and social responsibility. This strategy must be based on facts that are periodically rechecked. The media must be dealt with in a way consistent with the values of integrity, transparency and trust that are part of the company's core vision.

17.4. Channels of Action

39. The scope of a corporate foundation's activities may be defined in accordance with the nature of the business of the parent company, valorizing its technical know-how and selecting specific areas related to its products: healthcare, education, consumers' awareness, sharing of information technology, road safety or the environment can be accordingly privileged.

40. A corporate foundation can also be used for fostering and implementing CSR awareness and education in various contexts: It can support networks aimed at establishing specific professional codes, especially in China, where many professions still do not have such codes; it can endow chairs in business ethics and CSR in Chinese institutions of tertiary education; it may encourage research on CSR areas of special concern for the company: financial ethics, consumers' awareness, labor law or women issues, among others.

41. Companies may encourage their employees to become actively involved in the projects that the corporate foundation has chosen to support, or even make the projects initiated by employees a core component of the foundation's operations. The foundation thus becomes the symbol and channel of the employees' own awareness of their company's CSR vision, which is in turn perpetually enriched by the employees' participation and range of actions.

42. Stories collected throughout the duration of a successful local pilot project prove to be inspirational both within the company and for the public to whom such stories are relayed. The role of social media, the circulation of videos or the publication

of illustrated books and brochures create long-term capital of sympathy and commitment. Nothing is more helpful to build up a company's CSR image than a well-narrated story coming from the field, provided such stories are consistent with the practices of the corporation on the field.

43. Companies and employees must engage in knowledge networks related to their activities and concerns, sharing information among peers and with other networks, and helping the participants to take the necessary steps to become more reflexive and participatory. In some cases, corporations may encourage their employees or other stakeholders to start independent initiatives so as to creatively manage their sub-products or other aspects of their businesses that could help solve a given issue or answer special needs, if sufficient attention, good planning and creativity are brought to the task.

44. When trying to devise relevant initiatives for community development, all actors will need to rely on potential partners and assess the way various participants in the process may complement each other. Corporations participating in a process of community development as part of their social license to operate will need to cement alliances with local actors and, sometimes, active and skilled startup-ers. At the same time, they will need to set up a system to measure the impact of the company's contributions to communities. A three-way partnership between: (a) local planners and communities; (b) capable and focused SEs; and (c) corporations committed to their social responsibilities may be a privileged way to foster innovative community development in China, provided that adequate financial investment is allowed and carefully monitored.

17.5 Long-Term Vision

45. A corporation operating in China must be able to describe and locate its operations and products in relation to global public goods such as the prevention of disease; the tackling of climate change; financial stability; the strengthening of the international

trading system; peace and security, and the sharing of knowledge. If these goals seem be too lofty or very far away from what the company achieves and delivers, it then must take time to define in its own way the "public goods" that its activities may contribute to enrich and distribute, and to do so in the Chinese context.

46. The company must assess what the expected shift of China toward a greener, fairer and more affluent society within the next two decades means for its operations, and to be alert to the implications of these evolutions when it comes to the structure of its work force and the expectations of its consumers' base. It must strive to adapt its corporate strategy and image to the trends envisioned by the Chinese leadership and international organizations.

47. China must be strategically included into the global vision outlined by a company, which needs to clearly define the contributions that China makes to its corporate model, its CSR culture and its qualitative development.

Bibliography

I. A Selection of Reference Websites

BSR, The Business of a Better World, http://www.bsr.org/.

CASS-CSR.org (in Chinese), China's top theoretical research platform in the field of corporate social responsibility, http://www.cass-csr.org.

China Business Council for Sustainable Development, a platform in Chinese and in English for companies operating in China — both Chinese and foreign ones — to exchange views on CSR, sustainability and climate change issues, http://www.cbcsd.org.cn.

China CSR.com (in Chinese and English), providing news and information for corporate social responsibility professionals, http://www.chinacsr.com.

China CSR Map.org (in Chinese and English), an online comprehensive English-Chinese directory of major organizations and practitioners with CSR-relevant projects in China, http://www.chinacsrmap.org.

China Daily, http://www.chinadaily.com.cn.

Center for International Business Ethics (CIBE), international English edition that discusses business ethics, http://www.cibe.org.cn/en/.

CSR-China.net (in Chinese and English), CSR news and initiatives sharing platform with over a thousand domestic and international enterprises' CSR reports, http://www.csr-china.net.

CSR.infzm.com (in Chinese), an institute founded by the *Southern Weekly*, devoted to promoting CSR, http://csr.infzm.com.

Guangdong International Social Responsibility (广东省企业社会责任研究会), a research center funded by Guangdong Academy of Social Sciences and supported by universities and more than 600 companies, www.gdcsr.org.cn.

European Strategy on Corporate Social Responsibility (CSR) for 2011–2014, http://ec.europa.eu/enterprise/policies/sustainable-business/files/csr/new-csr/act_en.pdf.

Markulla Center for Applied Ethics, Santa Clara University, a forum and resources on business ethics, with some contributions on China, http://www.scu.edu/ethics/practicing/focusareas/business/.

Shanghai Daily, http://www.shanghaidaily.com.

Securities Times CSR Research Center, http://csr.stcn.com/.

United Nations Global Compact, http://www.unglobalcompact.org/AboutTheGC/index.html.

United Nations Development Programme, Human Development Report Office (2012), *Human Development Report*, http://hdrstats.undp.org/en/countries/profiles/CHN.html.

Wall Street Journal, China Real Time Report, http://blogs.wsj.com/chinarealtime/.

II. English Bibliography

Aglietta, M. & G. Bai (2013), *China's Development: Capitalism and Empire*, New York, Routledge.

Asslander, M.S. & M. Shenkel (2012), SRI as Driver for CSR? Ethical Funds, Institutional Investors and the Pursuit of the Common Good, in C. Bonanni, F. Lépineux and J. Roloff (eds.), *Social Responsibility, Entrepreneurship and the Common Good, International and Interdisciplinary Perspectives*, New York: Palgrave McMillan, pp. 181–207.

Attané, I. & J. Veron (eds.) (2005), *Gender Discriminations Among Young Children in Asia*, Pondicherry: All India Press.

Attané, I. (2012), Being a Woman in China Today: A Demography of Gender, *China Perspectives*, 2012/4, pp. 5–15, http://chinaperspectives.revues.org/6013, accessed July 17, 2013.

Bai, T. (2012), *China: The Political Philosophy of the Middle Kingdom*, London and New York: Zed Books.

Becker, J. & M. Elfstrom (2010), The Impact of China's Labor Contract Law on Workers, *International Labor Rights Forum*, May 12, 2010, http://www.laborrights.org/sites/default/files/publications-and-resources/ChinaLaborContractLaw2010_0.pdf, accessed May 24, 2013.

Bhatia, A. (2012), The Corporate Social Responsibility Report: The Hybridization of a "Confused" Genre (2007–2011), *IEEE Transactions on Professional Communication*, 55(3), pp. 221–237.

Boatright, J.R. (1999), *Ethics in Finance*, Malden, MA: Blackwell.

Broadhurst, R. (2012), Chinese 'Black Societies' and Triad-like Organised Crime in China, in F. Allum and S. Gilmour (eds.), *Handbook of Transnational Organised Crime*, London: Routledge, pp. 157–171.

Broadhurst, R., B. Bouhours, J. Bacon-Shone, L.Y. Zhong & K.W. Lee (2010), *Hong Kong, The United Nations International Crime Victim Survey: Final Report of the 2006 Hong Kong UNICVS*, Hong Kong and Canberra: The University of Hong Kong and The Australian National University.

Brown, R. (2006), China's Collective Contract Provisions: Can Collective Negotiations Embody Collective Bargaining?, *Duke Journal of Comparative and International Law*, 15(35), pp. 35–77.

BSR (2007), Corporate Social Responsibility in China's Information and Communications Technology (ICT) Sector, July 12, 2007, http://www-wds.worldbank.org/external/default/WDSContentServer/WDSP/IB/2007/09/07/000310607_20070907130905/Rendered/PDF/407790ENGLISH010social0ICT01PUBLIC1.pdf, accessed May 24, 2013.

BSR (2009), Sustainable Investment in China 2009, September 2009, http://www.bsr.org/reports/IFC%20Report%20LONG%20Updated%2016%20oct%20(2).pdf, accessed May 24, 2013.

Buhmann, K. (2005), Corporate Social Responsibility in China: Current Issues and Their Relevance for Implementation of Law, *The Copenhagen Journal of Asian Studies*, 22, pp. 62–91, http://ej.lib.cbs.dk/index.php/cjas/article/view/521/551, accessed September 24, 2013.

Cai, F., Y. Du & M. Wang (2009), *Employment and Inequality Outcomes in China*, Paris, OECD Seminar on Informal Employment, April 2009.

Cai, H., H. Fang & L. Xu (2011). Eat, Drink, Firms and Governments: An Investigation of Corruption from Entertainment Expenditures in Chinese Firms, *Journal of Law and Economics*, 54(1), pp. 55–78.

Cao, N. (2008), Boss Christians: The Business of Religion in the 'Wenzhou Model' of Christian Revival, *The China Journal*, 59, pp. 63–87.

Carroll, A.B., K. Davenport & D. Grisaffe (2000), Appraising the Business Value of Corporate Citizenship: What Does the Literature Say?, *Proceedings of the International Association for Business and Society*, Essex Junction Vt.

Chaibong, H. (2000), The Cultural Challenge to Individualism, *Journal of Democracy*, 11(1), pp. 127–134.

Chan, A. (2011), Strikes in China's Export Industries in Comparative Perspective, *The China Journal*, 65, pp. 27–51.

Chan, E.Y. & S.M. Griffiths (2010), The Epidemiology of Mine Accidents in China, *The Lancet*, 376(9741), pp. 575–577.

Chan, K.W. & W. Buckingham (2008), Is China Abolishing the Hukou System?, *The China Quarterly*, 195, pp. 582–606.

Chen, K. (2011), *Labour Law in China*, Alphen: Kluwer Law International.

China Labour Bulletin (2012), A Decade of Change: The Worker's Movement in China 2000–2010, March 28, www.clb.org.hk/en/node/110024, accessed September 24, 2013.

Ching, J. & H. Kung (1989), *Christianity and Chinese Religions*, New York: Doubleday.

Clarke, S. & C.-H. Lee (2002), The Significance of Tripartite Consultation in China, *Asia Pacific Business Review*, 9(2), pp. 61–80.

Clegg, S.R., M. Kornberger and C. Rhodes (2007), Business Ethics as Practice, *British Journal of Management*, 18(2), pp. 107–122.

Cooke, J.L. (ed.) (1993), *Cities of Jiangnan in Late Imperial China*, New York: Suny Press.

CSR Asia Beijing (2009), *CSR Asia: Survey on Community Investment of Companies Operating in China*, March 1, 2009, http://www.csr-asia.com/cdf/download/Report_pre_CIRT_Beijing.pdf, accessed July 17, 2013.

Dai, C. (2010), Corruption and Anti-Corruption in China: Challenges and Countermeasures, *Journal of International Business Ethics*, 3(2), pp. 58–70, http://www.americanscholarspress.com/content/BusEth_Abstract/v3n210-art6.pdf, accessed July 17, 2013.

Daubler, W. & Q. Wang (2009), The New Chinese Employment Law, *Comparative Labor Law and Policy Journal*, 30(2), 395–408, http://www.law.illinois.edu/publications/cllpj/archive/vol_30/issue_2/daubler&wangarticle30-2.pdf, accessed July 17, 2013.

Dejours, C. & J. P. Deranty (2010), The Centrality of Work, *Critical Horizon*, 11(2), pp. 167–180.

DeJoy, D.M. (2005), Behavior Change Versus Culture Change: Divergent Approaches to Managing Workplace Safety, *Safety Science*, 43(2), pp. 105–129.

DePasquale, J.P. & E.S. Geller (1999), Critical Success Factors for Behavior-Based Safety: A Study of Twenty Industry-wide Applications, *Journal of Safety Research*, 30(4), pp. 237–249.

Dong, B. & B. Torgler (2010), The Causes of Corruption: Evidences from China, BASEL, CREMA, *Working Paper No. 2010–07*.

Doucin, M. (2011), Corporate Social Responsibility: Private Self-Regulation Is Not Enough, *Global Corporate Governance Forum*, 24, http://www-wds.worldbank.org/external/default/WDSContentServer/WDSP/IB/2011/12/22/000386194_20111222042002/Rendered/PDF/661030BRI0Box365730B00PUBLIC00PSO0240CSR.pdf, accessed July 17, 2013.

Elvin, M. (1973), *The Pattern of the Chinese Past*, Stanford: Stanford University Press.

Elvin, M. (2004), *The Retreat of the Elephant, An Environmental History of China*. New Haven: Yale University Press.

Fair Labor Association (2012), *Independent Investigation of Apple Supplier, Foxconn*, www.fairlabor.org/report/foxconn-investigation-report, accessed July 17, 2013.

Froissart, C. (2012), Les 'ONG' de défense des droits des travailleurs migrants : l'émergence d'organisations proto-syndicales, *Chronique internationale de l'IRES*, 135(MARCH), http://www.ires-fr.org/images/files/Chronique/Cronique135/c135-3.pdf, accessed September 24, 2013.

Fu, H. (2011), The Upward and Downward Spirals in China's Anti-Corruption Enforcement, University of Hong Kong Faculty of Law Research Paper No. 2011/014, available at SSRN: http://ssrn.com/abstract=1883348 or http://dx.doi.org/10.2139/ssrn.1883348, accessed July 17, 2013.

Gao, Y. (2009), Corporate Social Performance in China: Evidence from Large Companies, *Journal of Business Ethics*, 89(1), pp. 23–35.

Gu, Y. (2012), Major Issues in Social Enterprises' Development in Mainland China, *Social Entrepreneurs Newsletter*, 139, December 10, 2012, http://www.hksef.org/files/files/Social_Entrepreneurs_Newsletter_No__139.pdf, accessed July 31, 2013.

Hanson, K.O. & S. Rothlin (2010), Taking Your Code to China, *Journal of International Business Ethics*, 3(1), pp. 69–80.

Harris, C.E., M.S. Pritchard & M.J. Rabins (2009), *Engineering Ethics, Concepts and Cases (Fourth Edition)*, Belmont CA: Wadsworth CENGAGE Learning.

He, Z. (2000), Corruption and Anti-corruption in Reform China, *Communist and Post-Communist Studies*, 33(2), pp. 243–270.

Heidenheimer, A.J. & M. Johnston (2002). *Political Corruption: Concepts and Contexts (Third Edition)*, New Brunswick, N.J.: Transaction Publishers.

Helin, S. & J. Sandstrom (2010), Resisting a Corporate Code of Ethics and the Reinforcement of Management Control, *Organization Studies*, 31(5), pp. 583–604.

Hinton, D. (transl.) (1998), *Mencius*, Washington DC: Counterpoint.

Hofman, I. & P. Ho (2012), China's 'Developmental Outsourcing: A Critical Examination of Chinese Global 'Land Grabs' Discourse, *Journal of Peasant Studies*, 39(1), pp. 1–48, http://dx.doi.org/10.1080/03066150.2011.653109, accessed July 17, 2013.

Holzman, D. (1956), The Conversational Tradition in Chinese Philosophy, *Philosophy East and West*, 6(3), pp. 223–230.

Houdmont, J., J. Zhou & J. Hassard (2011), Overtime and Psychological Well-Being among Chinese Office Workers, *Occupational Medicine*, 61(4), pp. 271–273.

Hsing, Y.-T. & C.-K. Lee (2009), *Reclaiming Chinese Society. The New Social Activism*, New York and London: Routledge.

Hu, B. & J. Szente (2010), Education of Young Chinese Migrant Children: Challenges and Prospects, *Early Childhood Education Journal*, 37(6), pp. 477–482.

Hutton, E. (2006), Character, Situationism, and Early Confucian Thought, *Philosophical Studies*, 127(1), pp. 37–58.

Idowu, S.O. & C. Lelouche (eds.) (2011), *Theory and Practice of Corporate Social Responsibility*, Berlin: Springer.

ILO (International Labour Organisation Office for China and Mongolia) (2009), *Fact Sheet: Domestic Workers in China*, September 1, 2009, http://www.ilo.org/asia/whatwedo/publications/WCMS_114256/lang--en/index.htm, accessed September 24, 2013.

International Task Force on Global Public Goods (2006), *International Cooperation in National Interest, Meeting Global Challenges*, http://www.cic.nyu.edu/scarcity/docs/archive/2006/Global%20Challenges.pdf, accessed July 31, 2013.

Jia, Z., L. Shi, Y. Cao, J. Delancey & W. Tian (2010), Health-related Quality of Life of "Left-Behind Children": A Cross-Sectional Survey in Rural China, *Quality of Life Research*, 19(6), pp. 775–780.

Jiang, X. (2012), The Development of Corporate Social Responsibility under China's Economic Transformation, November 19, 2012, http://www.docstoc.com/docs/157186141/The-Development-Of-Corporate-Social-Responsibility-In-China, accessed July 31, 2013.

Jin, Y., H. Wang & D. Wheeler (2010), Environmental Performance Rating and Disclosure: An Empirical Investigation of China's Green Watch Program, *The World Bank Policy Research Working Paper Series*, 5420.

Johnstone, C.L. (2009), *Listening to the Logos: Speech and the Coming of Wisdom in Ancient Greece*, Columbia: University of South Carolina Press.

Kang, X. & H. Han (2007), Administrative Absorption of Society: A Further Probe into the State-Society Relationship in Chinese Mainland, *Social Sciences in China*, 28(2), pp. 116–128.

Kang, X. & H. Han (2008), Graduated Controls: The State-Society Relationship in Contemporary China, *Modern China*, 34(1), pp. 36–55.

Karms, G.L. (2011), Stewardship: A New Vision for the Purpose of Business, *Corporate Governance*, 11(4), pp. 337–347.

Kolk, A., P. Hong & W. Van Dolen (2010), Corporate Social Responsibility in China: An Analysis of Domestic and Foreign Retailers' Sustainability Dimensions, *Business Strategy and the Environment*, 19(5), pp. 289–303.

Kotter, J. & T. Heskett (1992), *Corporate Culture and Performance*, New York: Free Press.

Kraisornsuthasinee, S. (2012), CSR Through the Heart of the Bodhi Tree, *Social Responsibility Journal*, 8(2), pp. 186–198.

Lagerwey, J. (2010), *China, A Religious State*, Hong Kong: Hong Kong University Press.

Laliberte, A., K. Wu & D. Palmer (2011), Social Services, Philanthropy and Religion in Chinese Society, in D. Palmer, G. Shive and P. Wickeri (eds.), *Chinese Religious Life*, Oxford: Oxford University Press, pp. 139–154.

Laliberte, A. (2009), Entre désécularisation et resacralisation: Bouddhistes laïcs, temples et organisations philanthropiques en Chine, *Social Compass*, 56(3), pp. 345–361.

Lam, M.L.-L. (2009), Beyond Credibility of Doing Business in China: Strategies for Improving Corporate Citizenship of Foreign Multinational Enterprises in China, *Journal of Business Ethics*, 87(S1), pp. 137–146.

Lan, T. & J. Pickles (2011), China's New Labour Contract Law: State Regulation and Worker Rights in Global Production Networks, *Capturing the Gains Working Paper No. 5*, October, http://www.capturingthegains.org/pdf/ctg-wp-2011-05.pdf, accessed May 24, 2013.

Li, D. & M.C. Tsang (2003), Household Decisions and Gender Inequality in Education in Rural China, *China: An International Journal*, 1(2), pp. 224–248.

Li, L. (2011), The 'Production' of Corruption in China's Courts, USALI Working Papers Series.

Li, S., J. Song & X. Liu (2011), Evolution of the Gender Wage Gap among China's Urban Employees, *Social Sciences in China*, 32(3), pp. 161–180.

Ligorner, K.L. & T. Liao (2010), The Renewed Unionization Campaign in China Coupled with Collective Bargaining, *Paul Hastings*, p. 4, http://www.paulhastings.com/assets/publications/1718.pdf, accessed July 17, 2013.

Lin, L.-W. (2010), Corporate Social Responsibility in China: Window Dressing or Structural Change?, *Berkeley Journal of International Law*, 28(1), pp. 64–100.

Litzinger, R. (2013), The Labor Question in China: Apple and Beyond, *The South Atlantic Quarterly*, 112(1), pp. 172–178.

Liu, J. *et al.* (2010), Urinary Tract Abnormalities in Chinese Rural Children who Consumed Melamine-Contaminated Dairy Products: A Population-Based Screening and Follow-Up Study, *Canadian Medical Association Journal*, 82(5), pp. 439–443, http://www.cmaj.ca/content/182/5/439.full.pdf+html, accessed July 17, 2013.

Lo, T.W. (2010), Beyond Social Capital: Triad Organized Crime in Hong Kong and China, *British Journal of Criminology*, 50(5), pp. 851–872.

Lu, J. (2007), Commercial Bribery: What Are the Boundaries, *China Law & Practice*, March, http://www.chinalawandpractice.com/Article/1690356/Channel/7576/Commercial-Bribery-What-are-the-Boundaries.html, accessed July 17, 2013.

McNeill, J.R. (1998), China's Environmental History in World Perspective, in M. Elvin & T.J. Liu (eds.), *Sediments of Time*, Cambridge: Cambridge University Press, pp. 31–49.

Mauro, P. (1997), *Why Worry About Corruption?*, Washington DC, MF, Economic Series 6, http://www.imf.org/EXTERNAL/PUBS/FT/ISSUES6/, accessed July 31, 2013.

Mele, D. (2008), Corporate Social Responsibility Theories, in A. Crane, A. McWilliams, D. Matten, J. Moon & D.S. Siegel (eds.), *The Oxford Handbook of Corporate Social Responsibility*, Oxford: Oxford University Press, pp. 46–82.

Miles, S. (2012), Stakeholders: Essentially Contested or Just Confused, *Journal of Business Ethics*, 108(3), pp. 285–298.

Mo, P.H. (2001), Corruption and Economic Growth, *Journal of Comparative Economics*, 29(1), pp. 66–79.

Monteil, A. (2012), Éducation: La longue marche des Chinoises, in M. Lieber & T. Angeloff (eds.), *Chinoises au XXIe siècle. Ruptures et Continuités*, Paris: La Découverte, pp. 43–62.

Monteil, A. & B. Vermander (2011), Un géant vert sans 'pieds d'argile', *Projet*, 326, pp. 18–25.

Moon, J. & X. Shen (2010), CSR in China Research: Salience, Focus and Nature. *Journal of Business Ethics*, 94(4), pp. 613–629.

Mostovicz, E.I., A.K. Kakabadse & N.K. Kakabadse (2011), The Four Pillars of Corporate Responsibility: Ethics, Leadership, Personal Responsibility and Trust, *Corporate Governance*, 11(4), pp. 489–500.

Muhle, U. (2010), *The Politics of Corporate Social Responsibility, The Rise of a Global Business Norm*, Frankfurt and New York: Campus Verlag.

Mullerat, R. (2010), *International Corporate Social Responsibility: The Role of Corporations in the Economic Order of the 21st Century*, Alphen: Kluwer Law International.

Nettiffee, D. (n.d.), Ignatian Spirituality and the Three-Fold Model of Organizational Life, http://www.stthomas.edu/cathstudies/cst/publications/seeingthingswhole/STW14_Nettifee.pdf, accessed July 17, 2013.

Nonaka, I. & R. Toyama (2007), Strategic Management as Distributed Practical Wisdom, *Industrial and Corporate Change*, 16(3), pp. 371–394.

NORMAPME (2011), *NORMAPME User Guide for European SMEs on ISO 26000 Guidance on Social Responsibility*, http://www.normapme.eu/public/uploads/files/csr%20user%20guide/User%20guide%20ISO26000_version%20EN_final_18072011.pdf, accessed July 31, 2013.

Ostrau, M.S, & A.C. Waler (2012), Corporate Social Responsibility and the Supply Chain, *Practical Law.com*, November, pp. 10–15. http://www.techlaw.org/wp-content/uploads/2010/07/Fenwick-Corporate-Social-Responsibility-and-the-Supply-Chain-August-2012.pdf, accessed June 10, 2013.

Porter, M.E. & M.R. Kramer (2011), Creating Shared Value. *Harvard Business Review*, 89(1/2), pp. 62–77.

Pringle, T. (2011), *Trade Unions in China, the Challenge of Labor Unrest*, New York and London: Routledge.

Qiao, J. (2012), Between the Party-State, Employers and Workers: Multiple Roles of the Chinese Trade Union During Market Transition — A Survey of 1.811 Enterprise Union Chairpersons, in H. Masahary, K. Kazuko, I. Tomoaki and Q. Jian (eds.), *China's Trade Unions — How Autonomous Are They?*, London and New York: Routledge, pp. 52–75.

Ramirez, C.D. (2012), Is Corruption in China "Out of Control"? A Comparison with the U.S. in Historical Perspective, Georges Madison University, Department of Economics, *Working Paper* 12–60, http://papers.ssrn.com/sol3/papers.cfm?abstract_id=2185166##, accessed September 24, 2013.

Reinhardt, F.L., R.N. Stavins and R.H.K. Vietor (2008), Corporate Social Responsibility Through an Economic Lens, *Review of Environmental Economics and Policy*, 1, pp. 1–22.

Roberts, C. (2012), Far from a Harmonious Society: Employment Discrimination in China, *Santa Clara Law Review*, 52(4), http://digitalcommons.law.scu.edu/lawreview/vol52/iss4/11, accessed July 17, 2013.

Rose-Ackerman, S. (1999), *Corruption and Government: Causes, Consequences, and Reform*, Cambridge: Cambridge University Press.

See, G.K.H. (2009), Harmonious Society and Chinese CSR: Is There Really a Link?, *Journal of Business Ethics*, 89(1), pp. 1–22.

Schwartz, B. (1964), *In Search of Wealth and Power: Yen Fu and the West*, Taipei: Rainbow-Bridge Book Co.

Sen, A.K. (1977), Rational Fools: A Critique of the Behavioral Foundations of Economic Theory, *Philosophy & Public Affairs*, 6(4), pp. 317–344.

Shafer, W.E., K. Fukukawa & G.M. Lee (2007), Values and the Perceived Importance of Ethics and Social Responsibility: The U.S. versus China, *Journal of Business Ethics*, 70(3), pp. 265–284.

Shen, X. (2005), China's Forests: Their Quality and Sustainable Management, *Chinese Cross Currents*, 2(4), pp. 100–129.

Shieh, S. & G. Deng (2011), Emerging Civil Society: The Impact of the 2008 Sichuan Earthquake on Grass-roots Associations in China, *The China Journal*, 65(January), pp. 181–194.

Sims, R.R. (2003), *Ethics and Corporate Social Responsibility, Why Giants Fail*, London: Praeger.

Skinner, G.W. (ed.) (1977), *The City in Late Imperial China*, Stanford: Stanford University Press.

So, M.T.K. & C. Chyau (2010), China Case Study, in R. Gunn and C. Durkin (eds.), *Social Entrepreneurship, A Skills Approach*, Bristol: The Policy Press, pp. 139–152.

Spires, A.J. (2012), Lessons from Abroad: Foreign Influences on China's Emerging Civil Society, *The China Journal*, 68, pp. 125–146.

Students and Scholars against Corporate Misbehavior (2011), *Foxconn and Apple Fail to Fulfill Promises: Predicaments of Workers after the Suicides*, http://sacom.hk/archives/837, accessed July 17, 2013.

Su, D. (2008), *Selected Poems and Prose*, Lin Yutang Chinese-English Bilingual Edition, Taipei: Cheng Chung.

Tam, O.K. (2002), Ethical Issues in the Evolution of Corporate Governance in China, *Journal of Business Ethics*, 37(3), pp. 303–320.

Tan, L. & Y. Song (2005), Does Gender Make a Difference Understanding Chinese Current Equality in Compulsory Education?, in I. Attané and J. Véron (eds.), *Gender Discriminations Among Young Children in Asia*, Pondicherry: All India Press, pp. 207–224.

Tang, L. & H. Li (2009), Corporate Social Responsibility Communication of Chinese and Global Corporations in China, *Public Relations Review*, 35(3), pp. 199–212.

Teets, J.C. (2009), Post-Earthquake Relief and Reconstruction Efforts: The Emergence of Civil Society in China?, *The China Quarterly*, 198(June), pp. 330–347.

Thorne, L. & S.B. Saunders (2002), The Socio-Cultural Embeddedness of Individuals' Ethical Reasoning in Organizations (Cross-cultural Ethics), *Journal of Business Ethics*, 35(1), pp. 1–14.

Tsoi, J. (2010), Stakeholders' Perceptions and Future Scenarios to Improve Corporate Social Responsibility in Hong Kong and Mainland China, *Journal of Business Ethics*, 91(3), pp. 391–404.

Verkoren, W. (2006), Knowledge Networks: Implications for Peacebuilding Activities, *International Journal of Peace Studies*, 11(2), pp. 27–61, http://www.gmu.edu/programs/icar/ijps/vol11_2/11n2VERKOREN.pdf, accessed September 24, 2013.

Vermander, B. (2007), *Chine brune ou Chine verte*, Paris: Presses de Sciences Po.

Vermander, B. (2010), Spiritual Empowerment and the Ignatian Tradition: Lessons for Today's Asia, in H.C. de Bettignies & M. Thompson (eds.), *Leadership, Spirituality and the Common Good, East and West Approaches*, Antwerp: Garant, pp. 71–82.

Vermander, B. (2011), Chinese Wisdom, Management Practices and the Humanities, *Journal of Management Development*, 30(7/8), pp. 697–708.

Vesilind, P.A. (2010), *Engineering Peace and Justice, The Responsibility of Engineers to Society*, London: Springer.

Waldmann, D.A. *et al.* (2006), Cultural and Leadership Predictors of Corporate Social Responsibility Values of Top Management: A GLOBE Study of 15 Countries, *Journal of International Business Studies*, 37(6), pp. 823–837.

Wang, H. (2013), Do Informal Institutions Tie the Autocrats' Hands? A Mixed-Method Study of Factional Politics and Anticorruption in China, University of Notre Dame, Department of Political Science, *Working Paper Series*, available at SSRN: http://ssrn.com/abstract=2206321, accessed September 24, 2013.

Wang, Y. & J. You (2012), Corruption and Firm Growth: Evidence from China, *China Economic Review*, 23(2), pp. 415–433.

Warner, M. & Y. Zhu (2002), Human Resource Management 'with Chinese Characteristics': A Comparative Study of the People's Republic of China and Taiwan, *Asia Pacific Business Review*, 9(2), pp. 21–43.

Wedeman, A. (2012), *Double Paradox: Rapid Growth and Rising Corruption in China*, Ithaca: Cornell University Press.

World Bank (2000), *Anticorruption in Transition: A Contribution to the Policy Debate*, Washington D.C.: World Bank Publication.

World Bank (2006), *Anticorruption in Transition 3: Who Is Succeeding… and Why?*, Washington D.C.: World Bank Publication.

World Bank (2007), *Governance, Investment Climate and Harmonious Society*, Washington D.C.: World Bank Publication.

World Bank (2009a), *Developing a Circular Economy in China: Highlights and Recommendations*, World Bank Technical Assistance Program, 48917, http://siteresources.worldbank.org/INTEAPREGT-OPENVIRONMENT/Resources/circularreport.pdf, accessed September 24, 2013.

Word Bank (2009b), Reconciling Urban Planning Capacity Building and Rapid Urban Growth in China, *China Urban Development Quarterly*, 6, pp. 1–2.

World Bank (2012), *China 2030. Building a Modern, Harmonious, and Creative High-Income Society*, http://www.worldbank.org/en/news/2012/02/27/china-2030-executive-summary, accessed September 24, 2013.

World Bank's Sustainable Development Unit for China and Mongolia (2008), *China Road Traffic Safety: The Achievements, the Challenges, and the Way Ahead*, http://documents.worldbank.org/curated/en/2008/08/10868536/china-road-traffic-safety-achievements-challenges-way-ahead, accessed September 24, 2013.

Wu, X. (1999), Business Ethical Perceptions of Business People in East China: An Empirical Study, in G. Enderle (ed.), *International Business Ethics, Challenges and Approaches*, Notre Dame and London: University of Notre Dame Press, pp. 323–342.

Xu, G. (2011), Global Governance: the Rise of Global Civil Society and China, *Fudan Journal of the Humanities and Social Sciences*, 4(1), pp. 1–21.

Xu, S. & X. Yang (2010), Indigenous Characteristics of Chinese Corporate Social Responsibility Conceptual Paradigm, *Journal of Business Ethics*, 93(2), pp. 321–333.

Yang, G. (2009), *The Power of the Internet in China: Citizen Activism Online*, New York: Columbia University Press.

Yu, K. (1999), The Rise of Chinese Civil Society and Its Significance to Governance, http://www. asienhaus.org/public/archiv/China-CS_YK.pdf, accessed September 24, 2013.

Yu, X. (2008), Impacts of Corporate Code of Conduct on Labor Standards: A Case Study of Reebok's Athletic Footwear Supplier Factory in China, *Journal of Business Ethics*, 81(3), pp. 513–529.

Yu, X. (2011), Social Enterprise in China: Driving Forces, Development Patterns and Legal Framework, *Social Enterprise Journal*, 7(1), pp. 9–32.

Yu, J. & S. Wang (2011), The Applicability of Governance Theory in China, *Fudan Journal of the Humanities and Social Sciences*, 4(1), pp. 22–36.

Yusuf, S. & T. Saichs (eds.) (2008), *China Urbanizes: Consequences, Strategies, and Policies*, Washington D.C.: World Bank Publications.

Yusuf, S. & K. Nabeshima (2010), *Two Dragon Heads: Contrasting Development Paths for Beijing and Shanghai*, Washington D.C.: World Bank Publication.

Zamagni, S. (2012), The Ethical Anchoring of Corporate Social Responsibility and the Critique of CSR, in M. Schlag and J.A. Mercao (eds.), *Free Markets and the Culture of Common Good*, Dordrecht: Springer, pp. 191–207.

Zhao, L. & J. Roper (2011), A Confucian Approach to Well-Being and Social Capital Development, *Journal of Management Development*, 30(7–8), pp. 740–752.

Zhou, Z., C. Nakano & B.N. Luo (2011), Business Ethics as Field of Training, Teaching, and Research in East Asia, *Journal of Business Ethics*, 104(1), pp. 19–27.

Zhu, Q. (2010), Engineering Ethics Studies in China: Dialogue between Traditionalism and Modernism, *Engineering Studies*, 2(2), pp. 85–107.

Zhu, Y., M. Warner & T. Feng (2011), Employment Relations 'with Chinese Characteristics': The Role of Trade Unions in China, *International Labour Review*, 150(1–2), pp. 127–143.

III. Chinese Bibliography

A. *Books*

Chen, J., Q. Huang & H. Peng (2011), *Research Report on CSR in China (Zhongguo qiye shehuizeren yanjiu baogao)*, Beijing: Social Sciences Literature Press. (陈佳贵、黄群慧、彭华岗等共同主编，《中国企业社会责任研究报告（2011）》，北京社会科学文献出版社，2011 年。)

Jiang, Q. & Q. Gu (2008), *CSR and Corporate Strategy (Qiye shehuizeren he qiye zhanlue xuanze)*, Shanghai: Shanghai People's Press. (姜启军、顾庆良，《企业社会责任和企业战略选择》，上海人民出版社，2008 年。)

Li, Y. *et al.* (2010), *Series of Publications on CSR Research (Qiye shehuizeren yanjiu xilie congshu)*, Guangzhou: South China Technology University Press. (黎友焕等，企业社会责任研究系列丛书，《企业社会责任》，《企业社会责任理论》，《企业社会责任实证研究》，华南理工大学出版社，2010年。)

Liu, J. (1999), *The Firm's Social Responsibility (Gongsi de shehui zeren)*, Beijing: Law Press. (刘俊海，《公司的社会责任》，法律出版社1999年。)

Liu, L. & K. Liu (2007), *Guidelines for the implementation of CSR standards in China (Zhongguo qiye shehuizeren biaozhun shishi zhinan)*, Beijing: Chemical Industry Press. (卢岚，刘开明，《中国企业社会责任标准实施指南》，化学工业出版社2007年。)

Lu, H. (2002), *Report on Corporate Donations and Charities in Shanghai (Shanghai qiye juanzeng shehui gongyi yanjiu baogao)*, Shanghai: Huaxia Press. (卢汉龙，《上海企业捐赠社会公益研究报告》，上海：华夏出版社，2002年。)

Shen, Y. (2007), *The Origin and Evolution of Corporate Social Responsibility (Gongsi shehui zeren sixiang qiyuan yu yanbian)*, Shanghai: Shanghai People's Press. (沈艺峰，《公司社会责任思想起源与演变》，上海人民出版社2007年。)

Tang, G. (2008), *Research on CSR's mechanisms (Qiye shehuizeren fasheng jili yanjiu)*, Changsha: Hunan People's Press. (唐更华，《企业社会责任发生机理研究》，湖南人民出版社2008年。)

Tian, H. (2011), *The Effects of CSR (Qiye shehuizeren xiaoying)*, Beijing: Economics Science Press. (田虹，《企业社会责任效应》，经济科学出版社2011年。)

Wang, L. (2008), *Research on CSR in the Context of Economic Law (Jingjifa yujing xia de qiye shehuizeren yanjiu)*, Beijing: Press of China's Procuratorate. (王玲，《经济法语境下的企业社会责任研究》，中国检察出版社，2008年。)

Wang, Z. (2012), *Compliance : First Responsibility of Enterprises (Hegui: qiye de shouyao qiye zeren)*, Beijing: Chinese Economic Press. (王志乐，《合规：企业的首要责任》，中国经济出版社2012年。)

Yin, G. & Z. Yu (eds.) (2009), *CSR in China (Qiye shehuizeren zai zhongguo)*, Beijing: Management Publishing House. (殷格非、于志宏共同主编，《企业社会责任在中国》，北京：企业管理出版社，2009年。)

Yin, G., H. Yu & S. Cui (eds.) (2008), *Corporate Competitiveness — Case Studies on the Best Practice of CSR (Qiye jingzhengli — Qiye shehuizeren zuijiashijian anli ji)*, Beijing: People's University Press. (殷格非，于志宏，崔生祥主编，《企业竞争力 — 企业社会责任最佳实践案例集》，中国人民大学出版社2008年10月。)

Yu, J., H. Jiang & J. Zhou (2008), *Chinese Civil Society Growing Through Participation: Research on the Chamber of Commerce of Wenzhou (Zai canyu zhong chengzhang de zhongguo gongmin shehui: ji yu zhejiang wenzhou shanghui de yanjiu)*, Hangzhou: Zhejiang University Press. (郁建兴，江华，周俊，《在参与中成长的中国公民社会：基于浙江温州商会的研究》，浙江大学出版社2008年。)

B. *Reports*

Chinese Securities Association (2012), Report on the CSR Performance of Securities Companies in 2011 (2011 *niandu zhengquan gongsi lvxing shehuizeren qingkuang baogao*), September 2012 . (中国证券业协会，《2011年度证券公司履行社会责任情况报告》，2012年9月。)

Chinese Listed Companies Association, Securities Journal (2012), Research on CSR of Chinese Listed Companies of Category A in 2012 (*Zhongguo A gu shangshi gongsi shehuizeren baogao yanjiu* 2012). (中国上市公司协会、证券时报社，《中国A股上市公司社会责任报告研究2012》，2012年。)

China International Council for the Promotion of Multinational Corporations (2011), Report on CSR issues of Multinational Corporations in 2011 (2011 *kuaguo gongsi shehuizeren wenti baogao*) November 2011. (中国国际跨国公司促进会，《2011·跨国公司社会责任问题报告》，2011 年 12 月 31 日。)

Eaton (2010), An Eaton White Paper : State of Green Products in China (*yidun zhongguo lvse chanpin hangye diaocha baogao*), June 2010. (《伊顿中国绿色产品行业调查报告》，北京：伊顿中国可持续发展研讨会，2010 年 2 月 26 日。http://www.csr-china.net/templates/node/index.aspx?nodeid=0ed932b0-db43-45a9-ad3a-ddb6ac82007f&page=contentpage&contentid=d8a96375-7eb2-4354-9637-8ef-326bf9282, accessed September 24, 2013.)

Jiao, J., L. Liu & P. Zheng (2010), Survey on the Best Practices of Green, Low-Carbon and Energy Saving Companies for the Hotelier Industry (*jiudian hangye ditan shijian — zhongguo jiuidan hangye lvse, ditan, jieneng xingdong zuijia anli diaocha*). (焦健、刘蕾、郑平，《酒店行业低碳实践 — 中国酒店行业绿色、低碳、节能行动最佳案例调查报告》，世界自然基金会，2010年 12 月。http://www.wwfchina.org/content/press/publication/LowCarbonPracticesinHotels-cn.pdf, accessed September 24, 2013.)

National People's Congress (2010), Twelfth Five-Year Plan Guideline (*Zhongguo di shi'er ge wunian jihua gangyao*). (中国第十二个五年计划纲要，中国人民代表大会，2011年3月16日。http://www.gov.cn/2011lh/content_1825838.htm, accessed September 24, 2013.)

National Bureau of Statistics of China (2011), Survey on the Migrant Workers in 2011 (2011 *nian wo guo nongmingong jiance diaocha baogao*), April 2011. (中国人民共和国国家统计局，《2011 年我国农民工检测调查报告》，2011年4月27日。http://www.stats.gov.cn/tjfx/fxbg/t20120427_402801903.htm, accessed September 24, 2013.)

Protiviti, Corporate Governance Research Center of Institute of World Economics and Politics of CASS (2012), Assessment of the Corporate Governance of the 100 Largest Chinese Listed Companies in 2012. (2012 *nian zhongguo shangshi gongsi 100 qiang gongsi zhili pingjia*). (甫瀚咨询、中国社会科学院世界经济与政治所公司治理研究中心，《2012 年中国上市公司 100 强公司治理评价》，http://www.protiviti.cn/zh-CN/Documents/CN-Headline/CN-2012-Corporate-Governance-Survey-Report.pdf, accessed September 24, 2013.)

Research Bureau of SASAIC (2012), Report on the Analysis of CSR Reporting of Central State-owned Enterprises in 2011 (2011 *nian zhongyang qiye shehuizeren baogao zhuanti fenxi baogao*), May 2012. (国务院国有资产监督管理委员会研究局，《2011 年中央企业社会责任报告专题分析报告》，2012 年 5 月，http://www.sasac.gov.cn/n1180/n13307665/n13307681/n13307825/14452102.html, accessed September 24, 2013.)

Research Center for CSR of Chinese Academy of Social Sciences (2012a), Blue Book on CSR in China (*Zhongguo qiye shehuizeren lanpishu*). (中国社会科学院经济学部企业社会责任研究中心，《中国企业社会责任蓝皮书 2012》，http://www.cass-csr.org/, accessed September 24, 2013.)

Research Center for CSR of Chinese Academy of Social Sciences (2012b), White Book on CSR Report of Chinese Companies (*Qiye shehuizeren baogao baipishu*). (中国社会科学院经济学部企业社会责任研究中心，《企业社会责任报告白皮书 2012》，http://www.cass-csr.org/, accessed September 24, 2013.)

Southern Weekly (2012), Blue Book on CSR in China of the Annual Conference in 2012 (2012 *zhongguo qiye shehuizeren nianhui lanpisu*), August 2012. (南方周末，《2012 中国企业社会责任年会蓝皮书》，北京：第四届中国企业社会责任年会，2012年8 月 31 日。)

Syntao (2011), Assessment of CSR Reporting of the 100 Largest Listed Companies (*Zhongzheng 100 CSR baogao pinggu*), March 2011. (商道纵横、北京中征，《中证 100 CSR 报告评估》，2011 年 3 月，http://www.syntao.com/Uploads/%7BA5B4319C-DAD3-484F-8313-81D63E2023AB%

7D_%E4%B8%AD%E8%AF%81100CSR%E6%8A%A5%E5%91%8A%E8%AF%84%E4%BC%B0%E6%8A%A5%E5%91%8A.pdf, accessed September 24, 2013.)

Transition Social and Economic Institute (2007), Supply Chain Responsibility Matrix (*Gongyinglian zeren juzhen*), September 2007. (传知行社会经济研究所,《供应链责任矩阵》2007 年 9 月, http://www.csrglobal.cn/upload/image/300223.pdf.)

WWF (2010), Chinese Enterprises of the 21st Century: Report of the Research on CSR and Sustainable Development (*Ershiyi shiji de zhongguo qiye shehuizeren ji kechixu fazhan yanjiu baogao*), April 2010. (世界自然基金会,《21 世纪的中国企业（II）企业社会责任及可持续发展研究报告》, 2010 年 4 月, http://www.wwfchina.org/content/press/publication/CSRRR_cn.pdf, accessed September 24, 2013.)

WWF China Programme Office, Financial Research Institute of Central Bank of China (2008), Towards a Sustainable Banking Strategy: Research on China's Banking Industry and Development Trends (*Maixiang kechixu fazhan de yinhangye zhanlue: zhongguo yinhangye gaige jincheng he fazhan qushi yanjiu*), July 2008. (世界自然基金会、中国人民银行金融研究所,《迈向可持续发展的银行业战略:中国银行业改革进程和发展趋势研究》, 2008 年 7 月, http://www.wwfchina.org/content/press/publication/08bankreport_cn.pdf, accessed September 24, 2013.)

Youcheng Foundation (2009), Research on Charity Indices of Chinese Companies in 2008 (*Zhongguo qiye gongyi zhishu yanjiu baogao 2008 nian*), December 2009. (友成企业家扶贫基金会、北京零点市场调查与分析公司,《中国企业公益指数研究报告 2008 年》, 2009 年 12 月, http://www.youcheng.org/uploads/pdf/20130609/20130609142905813.pdf, accessed September 24, 2013.)

WTO Tribune, International Research Center on CSR and Sustainable Development of Beijing University (2011), Research on CSR Reporting of Chines Companies in 2011 (*Zhongguo qiye shehuizeren baogao yanjiu* 2011), December 1, 2011.《WTO 经济导刊》杂志社、北京大学社会责任与可持续发展国际研究中心,《中国企业社会责任报告研究 2011》, 北京: 第四届中国企业社会责任报告国际研讨会, 2011 年 12 月 1 日, http://www.csr-china.net/templates/node/index.aspx?nodeid=0ed932b0-db43-45a9-ad3a-ddb6ac82007f&page=contentpage&contentid=99d38b37-fb5a-44ff-b822-9b42a8bb1371, accessed September 24, 2013.)

WTO Tribune, Golden Bees CSR Development Center (2011), Report of the Baseline of the CSR Practice of Chinese Companies in 2010 (2010 *Zhongguo qiye shehuizeren shijian jizhun baogao*), June 2011. (《WTO 经济导刊》金蜜蜂企业社会责任发展中心, 《2010 中国企业社会责任实践基准报告》, 2011 年 6 月 15 日, http://www.csr-china.net/templates/node/index.aspx?nodeid=0ed932b0-db43-45a9-ad3a-ddb6ac82007f&page=contentpage&contentid=2024739f-bd57-43b3-b025-c65e1e941dee, accessed September 24, 2013.)

C. *Articles*

Chen, X. & X. Du (2011), Education of the Little Girls Staying at Hometown (*Liushou nütong jiaoyu wenti yanjiu zongshu*), Journal of Shandong Women's University, 1/95, pp. 73–76. (陈晓晴、杜学元, 《留守女童教育问题研究综述》, 山东女子学院学报 2011 年 2 月, 第一期（共 95 期）, 73–76 页。)

Chen, X. et al. (2012), Special Issue on Innovation CSR in China's Top 100 Club (*Zhongguo qiye shehuizeren chuangxin* 100 *julebu tebie cehua*), Society and Charity (*Shehui yu gongyi*), 4, pp. 14–55. (陈雪娇等, 《中国企业社会责任创新 100 俱乐部特别策划》, 社会与公益 2012 年 04 期, 14–55 页, http://view.online.zcom.com/full/25221/9.htm?next, accessed September 24, 2013.)

Chen, Y., Z. Yang & L. Zhao (2009), CSR and CPA Practice (*Qiye shehuizeren yu zhuce kuaijishi de shijian*), *Audit Research (Shenji yanjiu)*, 1, pp. 55–57. (陈毓圭、杨志国、赵兰芳，《企业社会责任与注册会计师的实践》，审计研究2009 年第 1 期，55–57 页，http://mall.cnki.net/magazine/Article/SJYZ200901014.htm, accessed September 24, 2013.)

Cui, Y., J. Wang & T. Lu (2011), Research on CSR of Listed Companies in China — Based on the Survey of the Listed Companies of Shanghai Stock Market (*Woguo shangshi gongsi shehuizeren xianzhuang diaocha — jiyu hushi shangshigongsi diaocha wenjuan de shizheng yanjiu*), *Journal of Southwest Jiaotong University Social Sciences (Xinan jiaotong daxue xuebao shehuikexue ban)*, 2, pp. 92–97. (崔媛媛、王建琼、卢涛，《我国上市公司社会责任现状调查 — 基于沪市上市公司调查问卷的实证研究》，西南交通大学学报（社会科学版）2011 年 02 期，92–97 页。)

Feng, T. (2006), The Trend of CSR Development in China from the Angle of Labor Rights (*Cong laogong quanyi jiaodu kan qiye shehuizeren zai woguo de fazhan qushi*), *Contemporary World and Socialism (Dangdai shijie yu shehui zhuyi)*, 3, pp. 141–145. (冯同庆，《从劳工权益角度看企业社会责任在我国的发展趋势》，当代世界与社会主义 2006 年 03 期，141–145 页。)

Gan, M. (2011), Traditional Religious Culture and Charitable Activities of Chinese Entrepreneurs (*Chuantong zongjiao wenhua yu zhongguo qiye cishan shiye*), *World Religious Cultures (Shijie zongjiao wenhua)*, 2, pp. 1–5. (干满堂，《传统宗教化与中国企业慈善事业》，世界宗教文化 2011 年第二期，1–5 页。)

Ge, D. (2007), Current Situation and Policy Suggestion on Corporate Donation in China (*Woguo qiye juanzeng de xianzhuang he zhengcejianyi*), *Learning and Practice*, 3, pp. 120–123. (葛道顺，《我国企业捐赠的现状和政策建议》，《学习与实践》2007 年第 3 期，120–123 页。)

Guo, W. (2012), Introduction of the Development of Petroleum Engineering Ethics (*Zhongguo shiyou gongye gongchenglunli jianshe jinzhan shulue*), *Petroleum Education (Shiyou jiaoyu)*, 2, pp. 73–76. (郭文，《中国石油工业工程伦理建设进展述略》，石油教育 2012 第 2 期，73–76 页，http://www.cpes.com.cn/testpage/viewcontent.php?colindex=127&id=1293, accessed September 24, 2013.)

He, X. & H. Liu (2011), Research on Consumers' Awareness of CSR (*Xiaofeizhe de qiye shehuizeren renzhi yanjiu*), *Research on Financial and Economic Issues (Caijing wenti yanjiu)*, 8, pp. 11–16. (何小洲、刘晖，《消费者的企业社会责任认知研究》，财经问题研究 2011 年第 8 期，11–16 页，http://www.cqvip.com/Read/Read.aspx?id=38713822, accessed September 24, 2013.)

Ju, L. (2012), How Does the Trade Union in China Implement CSR — From the Angle of Labor Rights Protection (*Woguo gonghui ruhe guanche qiye shehuizeren — cong weihu laodongzhe hefa quanli de jiaodu*), *Journal of Ningxia University Social Science (Ningxia daxue xuebao renwen shehui kexue ban)*, 34(2). (鞠龙克，《我国工会如何贯彻企业社会责任 — 从维护劳动者合法权益的角度》，宁夏大学学报（人文社会科学版）2012 年 34 卷 02 期。)

Li, Y. & C. Gong (2009), Research on Development of CSR Theory in China (*Guonei qiye shehuizeren lilun yanjiu xinjinzhan*), *Journal of Xi'andianzi kexue University (Social Sciences Edition)*, 19(1). (黎友焕，龚成威《国内企业社会责任理论研究新进展》，西安电子科学大学报（社会科学版），2009 年 1 月，第 19 卷第一期。http://www.gdcsr.org.cn/Article/1354.html, accessed September 24, 2013.)

Liu, J. (2009), Research on Controversial Issues of CSR (*Gongsi shehuizeren zhengdian yanjiu*), *Tribune of Front Research of Civil and Commercial Law (minshangfa qianyan yanjiu luntan)*, 337. (刘俊海，《公司社会责任争点研究》，民商法前沿论坛第 337 期，2009 年 9 月。)

Qiu, J. *et al.* (2011), A Better Environment — Survey of CSR of Large Companies in 2009 (*Genghao de huanbaoxiu — 2009 nian dagongsi qiye shehuizeren diaocha*), *CBN Weekly (Diyi caijing zhoukan)*, April 2011. (邱珈等，《更好的环保秀 — 2009 年大公司企业社会责任调查》，第一财经周刊 2011 年 4 月。)

Qiu, X. & Y. Li (2007), Analysis on the Safety of Chinese Food Exportation from the CSR Perspective (*Jiyu qiye shehuizeren shijiao de zhongguo chukou shipinanquan wenti tantao*), *World Standardization and Quality Management* (*Shijiebiaozhunhua yu zhiliang guanli*), 12, pp. 51–53. (丘新强、黎友焕，《基于企业社会责任视角的中国出口食品安全问题探讨》，世界标准化与质量管理 2007 年第 12 期，51–53 页，http://uniondownpaper.cqvip.com/onlineread/onlineread.asp?id=26084109, accessed September 24, 2013.)

Research team on companies' donations for social benefit (*Qiye juanzeng shehuigongyi yanjiu ketizu*) (2001), Companies' Donation for Social Benefit Report — Research and Comments on Shanghai Companies' Donations for Social Benefit (*Gongsi juanzeng shehuigongyi yanjiu baogao — shanghai qiye juanzeng shehuigongyi qingkuang de diaocha pinlun*), *Sociology* (*Shehuixue*), 1, pp. 1–12. (企业捐赠社会公益研究课题组，《公司捐赠社会公益研究报告—上海企业捐赠社会公益情况的调查评论》，社会学 2001 年第1期，1–12页，http://2010.cqvip.com/onlineread/onlineread.asp?id=10512241, accessed September 24, 2013.)

Shu, L. (2010), Empirical Research on Awareness and Practice of CSR of Chinese Private Enterprises (*Minying qiye shehuizeren renzhi yu shijian de diaocha yanjiu*), *Soft Science* (*Ruankexue*), 24(10), pp. 97–102. (疏礼兵，《民营企业社会责任认知与实践的调查研究》，软科学 2010 年 24 卷 10 期，97–102 页，http://www.cqvip.com/Read/Read.aspx?id=3563835accessed September 24, 2013.)

Sun, J. (2010), Current Situation and Opportunities for Chinese CSR development (*Zhongguo shehuizeren fazhan de xianzhuang yu jiyun*), *WTO Tribune* (*WTO jingji daokan*), 6, pp. 1–5. (孙继荣，《中国社会责任发展的现状和机遇》，WTO 经济导刊 2010 年第 06 期，1–5页。)

Tian, K., J. Kang & D. Song (2007), General Considerations on Accounting Issues for CSR in China (*Zhongguo shehuizeren kuaiji wenti yanjiu zongshu*), *Friends of Accounting* (*Kuaiji zhi you*), 12, pp. 4–7. (田昆儒、康剑青、宋东亮，《中国社会责任会计问题研究综述》，会计之友（上旬刊）2007 年 12期，4–7 页，http://www.cqvip.com/Read/Read.aspx?id=26064161, accessed September 24, 2013.)

Wang, R. (2012), CSR and Chinese Enterprises' Overseas Acquisitions (*Qiye shehuizeren he zhongguo qiye haiwai binggou*), *Shanghai Economy* (*Shanghai jingji*), 2012, 2(1), pp. 38–43. (王仁荣，《企业社会责任和中国企业海外并购》，上海经济 2012 年底 2 卷 1 期，38–43 页。)

Xin, Y. (2011), Research on the Relation between CSR and Corporate Value (*Qiye shehuizeren yu qiye jiazhi de xiangguan yanjiu*), *Economic Angle*, 5. (辛悦，《企业社会责任与企业价值的相关性探究》，经济视角 2011 年 05 期。)

Xu, H. & J. Xu (2011), Analysis and Reflection on the Disclosure of Social Responsibility Information of Chinese Enterprises — Based on China's 95 Listed Companies' Evidence (*Zhongguo qiye shehuizeren xinxi pilou xianzhuang jiexi yu sikao — ji yu zhongguo 95 jia shangshi gongsi de jingyan zhengju*), *Accounting Forum*, 20(2), pp. 32–54. (许慧、许家林，《中国企业社会责任信息披露现状解析与思考—基于中国 95 家上市公司的经验证据》，会计论坛 2011 第 20 卷 2 辑，32–54 页。http://www.docin.com/p-393724984.html, accessed September 24, 2013.)

Yang, C., Y. Shi & B. Yu (2007), Analysis on the CSR Dilemma in China (*Zhongguo qiye shehuizeren kunjing jiexi*), *Science and Management* (*Keji yu guanli*), 2007, 41(1), pp. 54–56. (杨春方、石永东、于本海，《中国企业社会责任困境解析》，科技与管理 2007 年 41 卷 1 期，54–56 页，http://www.cqvip.com/Read/Read.aspx?id=23914078, accessed September 24, 2013.)

Yin, G. & Z. Cui (2008), CSR Reporting in China (*Qiye shehuizeren baogao zai zhongguo*), *WTO Tribune* (*WTO jingji daokan*), 8, pp. 3–5. (殷格非、崔征，《企业社会责任报告在中国》，WTO 经济导刊 2008 年第 8 期，3–5 页，http://www.cqvip.com/Read/Read.aspx?id=1000280514, accessed September 24, 2013.)

Zhang, L. & P. Qin (2007), The Creation of the CSR System of China's Construction Industry from the Viewpoint of CSR International Standards (*Cong shehuizeren guoji biaozhun kan woguo jianzhu qiye shehuizeren guanli tixi de goujian*), *Journal of Social Sciences of Tianjin University (Tianjin daxue xuebao, shehuikexue ban)*, 9(5), pp. 415–419. (张连营、秦沛，《从社会责任国际标准看我国建筑企业社会责任管理体系的构建》，天津大学学报社会科学版 2007 年第 9 卷第 5 期，416–419 页，http://2010.cqvip.com/onlineread/onlineread.asp?id=25758694 , accessed September 24, 2013.)

Zhang, Y. (2009), Analysis on Food Safety in China (*Woguo shipin anquan wenti tanxi*), *North Economy and Trade (Beifang jingmao)*, 10, pp. 113–116. 张佑林，《我国食品安全问题探析》，北方经贸 2009 年第 10 期，113–116 页，http://www.cqvip.com/Read/Read.aspx?id=32711831, accessed September 24, 2013.)

Zhou, Z., X. Wang & J. Wei (2007), Disclosure of CSR Information in China: Analysis and Suggestions (*Zhongguo qiye shehuizeren xinxi pilou de xianzhuangfenxi yu duicesikao*), *Soft Science*, 4, pp. 83–86. (周祖城、王旭、韦佳园，《中国企业社会责任信息披露的现状分析与对策思考》，《软科学》2007 年 04 期，83–86 页。)

Zhu, A. (2007), Response of China's Trade Union and CSR Implementation (*Qiye shehuizeren de luoshi yu zhongguo gonghui de yingdui*), *Trade Union Tribune (Gonghui luntan)*, 13(2), pp. 6–8. (朱爱武，《企业社会责任的落实与中国工会的应对》，工会论坛第 13 卷第 2 期，6–8 页，http://uniondownpaper.cqvip.com/onlineread/onlineread.asp?id=26782852, accessed September 24, 2013.)

Index

accountability   10, 11, 14, 18, 45, 47, 58, 69, 73, 163, 302, 305
accounting   213, 218, 221, 224
Africa   117
All-China Federation of Trade Unions (ACFTU)   148, 199, 201–203, 205
All-China Women's Federation   165
Anhui   200
anti-corruption (*see also* corruption)   4, 86, 87, 91, 93, 97
apparels   197
Australia   189

Bangladesh   150, 176, 277
banking   218, 219, 226, 227
bargaining   195, 198–200, 203, 205–207, 307
Beijing   40, 88, 105, 111, 112, 134, 136, 165, 166, 174, 182, 189, 245, 247, 262, 271
bioethics   230
bonded labor   162, 304
Brazil   79
bribery   79–85, 88, 91–96, 211, 216, 224, 307
Buddhism   42, 48, 52–55, 57, 63, 211, 216, 224, 295
business model   67, 69, 272, 275

Cambodia   150, 176
case analyses   230, 309
Central Committee   89
charities   43, 44, 256, 272
child labor   161–164, 304, 305
China Banking Regulatory Commission (CBRC)   226
China Securities Regulatory Commission (CSRC)   222
Chinese Communist Party   29, 31
Chongqing   85
Christianity   42, 295
circular economy   24, 25
civil society   41–43, 45, 297, 298
climate change   284, 287, 289, 311
coal   110, 118
codes   3, 235–242, 259, 293, 302, 309, 310
community investment   73, 228, 278–280, 308
community values   63
comparative advantages   67, 144, 153, 177, 305
compliance   29, 39
confidentiality   238
conflicts of interests   211, 230–232, 238–240, 309
Confucianism   48, 49, 51–53, 57, 62, 295, 298

corporate citizenship 5
corporate culture 12, 14, 23, 25, 55,
    66, 95, 99, 132, 133, 145, 177, 179,
    192, 195, 211, 228, 231, 235, 237,
    238, 257, 259, 293, 295–297, 303
corporate governance (*see*
    governance)
corruption (*see also* anti-corruption)
    1, 11, 18, 22, 40, 82–91, 93–97, 241,
    280, 307–309
create shared value 69, 73
criminal laws 91, 96
cultural communication 47
cultural diversity 22, 23, 296, 297
cultural resources 22, 23, 39, 47, 48,
    52, 55, 56, 99, 269, 291, 292, 295,
    297, 299, 304

Dalian 129, 130, 249
discernment 186, 193, 209, 211,
    213–215, 224, 232, 233, 235–237,
    242, 296, 309
discrimination 66, 143, 156, 165,
    180–184, 273, 285, 304, 305
Dongguan 149

East Asia 192
education 4, 22
electronics 196, 197, 275
employment contract 146–148, 158
engineering 36, 211, 229–232, 260,
    308
engineering ethics 129, 132, 303,
    308
environment 4, 5, 9, 10, 15, 16, 18,
    19, 21, 22, 24, 25
environmental health 33, 37, 101
environmental pollution 107, 112
environmental protests 249

equality 179, 182, 184, 186, 305, 309
ethics 12, 20
European Commission 8, 18
externalities 25–27

Fair Trade 275–278
farmland 113
fatalities (road traffic) 126, 134
filial piety 50, 51, 55
financial ethics 216, 218, 224, 225,
    228, 230, 231, 259, 303, 308, 310
financial institutions 217–219
financial markets 219–222
food safety 4
footwear 197
forests 104, 105, 114, 116, 118
foundations 42, 44, 253–262, 264,
    265, 293, 310
France 283

Gansu 263, 280
gender 179, 180, 182, 184–186, 241,
    305, 309
gifts 89, 93, 308
Gini coefficients 87
Global Compact 4, 5, 8, 227, 228, 291
global public goods 283–287, 311
global warming 115, 117
globalization 4, 5, 8, 268, 286, 295,
    296, 308
governance 235, 238, 242–244, 246,
    264, 269, 283, 289, 308
green development 288, 289
Green Watch 102, 106
Guangdong 44, 281
Guangxi 182
Guangzhou 111, 149, 165

H1N1 pandemic 250

Hainan 175
Haining 249
Han Fei Zi 63
Hangzhou 49
harassment 66
Harbin 106
harmony 59, 61, 62, 69, 295, 297
healthcare 155, 165, 170, 245, 257,
    274, 310
Hebei 280
Heilongjiang 131, 256
Henan 247
Hohhot 102
Hong Kong 11, 41, 81, 82, 180, 181,
    205, 265, 280
hukou 144, 154–156, 158, 160, 166
human rights 4, 8, 9, 18
Hunan 133

India 79
Indonesia 176, 177
injuries 121, 127, 135, 147, 151,
    158, 169
Inner Mongolia 263
integral development 297
interdependent self 266, 293, 301
International Labor Organization
    (ILO) 8, 161
Islam 295
ISO 26000 5–8, 10

Japan 74, 75
Jiangsu 50, 102
judiciary 90, 91
justice 48, 58, 62

knowledge networks 250, 264,
    266–269, 293, 311
Korea 75, 149

Labor Contract Law (LCL) 29, 32,
    143, 145–153, 155, 172, 173, 204
labor rights 199, 203
labor standards 4
Laozi 51, 52
leadership 12, 14, 19, 307
Lewis turning point 144, 157

Macao 81
mediators 214, 215
Mencius 51, 52, 193
microblogs 200, 248
migrant 32, 40, 41, 143, 144, 146,
    153–160, 164–168, 171, 172, 175,
    176, 181, 184, 262, 265, 279, 304, 305
migration 151, 154, 156, 158, 159
minimum wage 147, 158, 173–177
Ministry of Civil Affairs
    (MCA) 43, 44, 167, 168, 256, 258
Ministry of Environmental
    Protection 105, 106, 117
moral judgment 213

National People's Congress 145
Netherlands 189
non-governmental organizations
    (NGOs) 302
non-profit organizations (NPOs)
    42, 43

Organisation for Economic
    Co-operation and Development
    (OECD) 8, 9
overtime 188, 190

People's Bank of China 217, 226
pharmaceutical industry 92, 266
philanthropy 38, 40, 42, 50, 53,
    60, 72, 73, 154, 160, 165, 168, 184,

254–259, 264, 272, 274, 277, 278, 286, 304–306
phrônesis (practical wisdom)   56
pilot projects   253, 259, 263, 264, 310
pollution   33
professional associations   213, 229–231
profits   5
public goods (*see* global public goods)

Qinghai   256

Red Cross   44
reports   253–255, 267
retailing   197
Russia   79

SA8000   7
safety   29, 30, 32, 35, 37, 59, 60, 85, 92, 121–141, 166, 209, 218, 229, 236, 237, 247, 248, 255, 257, 258, 263, 280, 299, 303, 304, 310
schooling   155, 164, 166, 167
self-regulation   10, 35, 67, 138, 231, 257, 258, 309
Shanghai   34–36, 41, 50, 64, 82, 111
Shanxi   201
shareholders   5, 14, 15, 18, 20, 30, 59, 213, 226, 231, 255, 308
Shenyang   93
Shenzhen   35, 82, 149, 203, 205, 272
Sichuan   45, 176, 260
slave labor   145
social enterprises (SEs)   271–276, 278–280, 293, 302, 307, 311
social entrepreneurship   271, 274, 277, 278
social insurance   32, 33, 147, 152, 169–172, 174

Social Insurance Law   169–171
social license   72, 75, 311
social standards   143, 158, 304
'Socially Responsible Investment' (SRI)   227, 228, 271, 308
Songhua River   106
South Korea   79
Southeast Asia   117
stakeholders   5, 10, 14, 15, 17, 18, 59, 60, 64, 69, 72, 97, 99, 102, 109, 110, 133, 135, 143, 145, 195, 209, 213, 233, 235, 237, 242, 245, 254, 264, 266, 274, 291, 301, 302, 304, 311
startups   271, 272, 274, 278, 279, 311
State Council   36, 44, 137, 138, 144, 160, 169, 286, 287
state-owned enterprises   31, 38, 81, 87
stewardship   13, 14, 251
stock market   34, 35, 221
stockholders   60, 64
strikes   199, 200, 205
Su Dongpo   53
subcontracting   197
suffering   186, 188, 189, 193, 306
suppliers   68, 70, 303
supply chain   8, 15, 17, 18, 161–164, 177, 280, 302, 304, 305
sustainability   69, 75, 96, 104, 159, 172, 188, 225–228, 233, 244, 262, 269, 273, 276, 278, 280, 283, 286, 288, 292, 293, 296, 298–300, 302, 306
sustainable development   21, 22, 29–32
sustainable investment   225, 227, 228, 308
Suzhou   49
Sweden   283

Taiyuan   201
Taoism   48, 52, 57, 60, 62, 295
team building   192
teamwork   187–189, 191, 306
textile   7, 8, 34–36, 39
Tianjin   130
Tibet   256
Trade Union Law   199, 201, 202, 204
training   11, 18, 19, 27, 32, 39, 123,
    125, 127, 128, 134, 136, 137, 148,
    149, 153, 154, 160, 161, 163, 164,
    260–263, 271–273, 277, 278, 281,
    290, 293, 296, 303–306, 309
transparency   10, 11, 20, 37, 45, 237,
    242, 246, 248, 249, 251, 266, 268,
    276, 302, 307, 308, 310
trust   9, 11–14, 20, 45, 47, 65, 68, 71,
    85, 94, 177, 191, 207, 221, 231, 233,
    242, 251, 266, 273, 291, 293, 297,
    307, 310

United Front   81
US   64, 79, 83, 85, 107, 110, 118,
    163, 229

Vietnam   75, 150, 161, 176
volunteering   255, 258

wages   144, 146–148, 153, 154,
    157–159, 162, 174–176, 288, 305
weibo (*see* microblogs)
Wenchuan   38
Wenzhou   49, 121
Whistle-blowing Act   92
World Bank   24, 25, 78, 79, 86, 101,
    102, 106, 108, 134, 135, 144, 157,
    274, 286, 287
World Health Organization (WHO)
    101, 111, 112

Xiamen   93
Xi'an   82, 111

Yangzi   50
youths   262, 267

Zhejiang   50, 249, 262
Zhengzhou   247
Zhenjiang   102